CONSTITUTIONAL REFORMS IN CHINA

This book offers the reformist perspective of one of the most persistent and outspoken constitutional reformers in China. Through the analysis of landmark constitutional events in China since the late nineteenth century, it reveals the fatal dilemma faced by constitutional reform and the deadly dangers of any violent revolution that arises out of the frustration with the repeated failures of reform. Although there is no easy way out of such a predicament, the book analyzes available resources in the existing system and suggests possible strategies that might bring success to future constitutional reforms.

Qianfan Zhang is the leading constitutional scholar and public intellectual in China. He obtained his Ph.D. in Government from University of Texas at Austin (1999), and taught comparative constitutional law and administrative law at School of Law, Nanjing University, where he served as the Chief Editor of the faculty law journal, Nanjing University Law Review. He joined the law faculty in Peking University in 2003, where he is now the director of the Center for the People's Congress and Parliamentary Studies. He has published widely in the areas of Chinese and comparative constitutional law, moral and political philosophy.

COMPARATIVE CONSTITUTIONAL LAW AND POLICY

Series Editors

Tom Ginsburg *University of Chicago*
Zachary Elkins *University of Texas at Austin*
Ran Hirschl *University of Toronto*

Comparative constitutional law is an intellectually vibrant field that encompasses an increasingly broad array of approaches and methodologies. This series collects analytically innovative and empirically grounded work from scholars of comparative constitutionalism across academic disciplines. Books in the series include theoretically informed studies of single constitutional jurisdictions, comparative studies of constitutional law and institutions, and edited collections of original essays that respond to challenging theoretical and empirical questions in the field.

Books in the Series

Constitutional Reforms in China: Past, Present, Future Qianfan Zhang

The Entrenchment of Democracy: The Comparative Constitutional Design of Elections, Parties and Voting Tom Ginsburg, Aziz Z. Huq and Tarun Khaitan

Deciphering the Genome of Constitutionalism: The Foundations and Future of Constitutional Identity Ran Hirschl and Yaniv Roznai

Courts that Matter: Activists, Judges, and the Politics of Rights Enforcement Sandra Botero

The Story of Constitutions: Discovering the We in Us Wim Voermans

Democracy Under God: Constitutions, Islam and Human Rights in the Muslim World Dawood Ahmed and Muhammad Zubair Abbasi

Buddhism and Comparative Constitutional Law Edited by Tom Ginsburg and Ben Schonthal

Amending America's Unwritten Constitution Edited by Richard Albert, Ryan C. Williams, and Yaniv Roznai

Constitutionalism and a Right to Effective Government? Edited by Vicki C. Jackson and Yasmin Dawood

The Fall of the Arab Spring: Democracy's Challenges and Efforts to Reconstitute the Middle East Tofigh Maboudi

Filtering Populist Claims to Fight Populism: The Italian Case in a Comparative Perspective Giuseppe Martinico

Constitutionalism in Context David S. Law

The New Fourth Branch: Institutions for Protecting Constitutional Democracy Mark Tushnet

The Veil of Participation: Citizens and Political Parties in Constitution-Making Processes Alexander Hudson

Towering Judges: A Comparative Study of Constitutional Judges Edited by Rehan Abeyratne and Iddo Porat

The Constitution of Arbitration Victor Ferreres Comella

Redrafting Constitutions in Democratic Orders: Theoretical and Comparative Perspectives Edited by Gabriel L. Negretto

From Parchment to Practice: Implementing New Constitutions Edited by Tom Ginsburg and Aziz Z. Huq

The Failure of Popular Constitution Making in Turkey: Regressing Towards Constitutional Autocracy Edited by Felix Petersen and Zeynep Yanaşmayan

A Qualified Hope: The Indian Supreme Court and Progressive Social Change Edited by Gerald N. Rosenberg, Sudhir Krishnaswamy, and Shishir Bail

Reconstructing Rights: Courts, Parties, and Equality Rights in India, South Africa, and the United States Stephan Stohler

Constitutions in Times of Financial Crisis Edited by Tom Ginsburg, Mark D. Rosen, and Georg Vanberg

Hybrid Constitutionalism: The Politics of Constitutional Review in the Chinese Special Administrative Regions Eric C. Ip

Constitution-Making and Transnational Legal Order Edited by Tom Ginsburg, Terence C. Halliday, and Gregory Shaffer

The Invisible Constitution in Comparative Perspective Edited by Rosalind Dixon and Adrienne Stone

The Politico-Legal Dynamics of Judicial Review: A Comparative Analysis Theunis Roux

Constitutional Courts in Asia: A Comparative Perspective Edited by Albert H. Y. Chen and Andrew Harding

Judicial Review in Norway: A Bicentennial Debate Anine Kierulf

Constituent Assemblies Edited by Jon Elster, Roberto Gargarella, Vatsal Naresh, and Bjorn Erik Rasch

The DNA of Constitutional Justice in Latin America: Politics, Governance, and Judicial Design Daniel M. Brinks and Abby Blass

The Adventures of the Constituent Power: Beyond Revolutions? Andrew Arato

Canada in the World: Comparative Perspectives on the Canadian Constitution Edited by Richard Albert and David R. Cameron

Constitutions, Religion and Politics in Asia: Indonesia, Malaysia and Sri Lanka Dian A. H. Shah

Courts and Democracies in Asia Po Jen Yap

Proportionality: New Frontiers, New Challenges Edited by Vicki C. Jackson and Mark Tushnet

Constituents before Assembly: Participation, Deliberation, and Representation in the Crafting of New Constitutions Todd A. Eisenstadt, A. Carl LeVan, and Tofigh Maboudi

Assessing Constitutional Performance Edited by Tom Ginsburg and Aziz Huq

Buddhism, Politics and the Limits of Law: The Pyrrhic Constitutionalism of Sri Lanka Benjamin Schonthal

Engaging with Social Rights: Procedure, Participation and Democracy in South Africa's Second Wave Brian Ray

Constitutional Courts as Mediators: Armed Conflict, Civil-Military Relations, and the Rule of Law in Latin America Julio Ríos-Figueroa

Perils of Judicial Self-Government in Transitional Societies David Kosař

Making We the People: Democratic Constitutional Founding in Postwar Japan and South Korea Chaihark Hahm and Sung Ho Kim

Radical Deprivation on Trial: The Impact of Judicial Activism on Socioeconomic Rights in the Global South César Rodríguez-Garavito and Diana Rodríguez-Franco

Unstable Constitutionalism: Law and Politics in South Asia Edited by Mark Tushnet and Madhav Khosla

Magna Carta and Its Modern Legacy Edited by Robert Hazell and James Melton

Constitutions and Religious Freedom Frank B. Cross

International Courts and the Performance of International Agreements: A General Theory with Evidence from the European Union Clifford J. Carrubba and Matthew J. Gabel

Reputation and Judicial Tactics: A Theory of National and International Courts Shai Dothan

Social Difference and Constitutionalism in Pan-Asia Edited by Susan H. Williams

Constitutionalism in Asia in the Early Twenty-First Century Edited by Albert H. Y. Chen

Constitutions in Authoritarian Regimes Edited by Tom Ginsburg and Alberto Simpser

Presidential Legislation in India: The Law and Practice of Ordinances Shubhankar Dam

Social and Political Foundations of Constitutions Edited by Denis J. Galligan and Mila Versteeg

Consequential Courts: Judicial Roles in Global Perspective Edited by Diana Kapiszewski, Gordon Silverstein, and Robert A. Kagan

Comparative Constitutional Design Edited by Tom Ginsburg

Constitutional Reforms in China

PAST, PRESENT, FUTURE

QIANFAN ZHANG
Peking University, Beijing

CAMBRIDGE
UNIVERSITY PRESS

CAMBRIDGE
UNIVERSITY PRESS

Shaftesbury Road, Cambridge CB2 8EA, United Kingdom

One Liberty Plaza, 20th Floor, New York, NY 10006, USA

477 Williamstown Road, Port Melbourne, VIC 3207, Australia

314–321, 3rd Floor, Plot 3, Splendor Forum, Jasola District Centre, New Delhi – 110025, India

103 Penang Road, #05–06/07, Visioncrest Commercial, Singapore 238467

Cambridge University Press is part of Cambridge University Press & Assessment, a department of the University of Cambridge.

We share the University's mission to contribute to society through the pursuit of education, learning and research at the highest international levels of excellence.

www.cambridge.org
Information on this title:www.cambridge.org/9781009504119

DOI:10.1017/9781009504126

When citing this work, please include a reference to the DOI 10.1017/9781009504126

First published 2024

A catalogue record for this publication is available from the British Library.

Library of Congress Cataloging-in-Publication Data
NAMES: Zhang, Qianfan, 1964– author.
TITLE: Constitutional reforms in China : past, present, future / Qianfan Zhang, Peking University, Beijing.
DESCRIPTION: Cambridge, United Kingdom ; New York, NY : Cambridge University Press, 2024. | Series: Comparative constitutional law and policy | Includes bibliographical references and index.
IDENTIFIERS: LCCN 2024022106 (print) | LCCN 2024022107 (ebook) | ISBN 9781009504119 (hardback) | ISBN 9781009504133 (paperback) | ISBN 9781009504126 (epub)
SUBJECTS: LCSH: Constitutional history–China. | Constitutional law–China. | Law reform–China.
CLASSIFICATION: LCC KNQ2101 .Z447 2024 (print) | LCC KNQ2101 (ebook) | DDC 342.5103–dc23/eng/20240528
LC record available at https://lccn.loc.gov/2024022106
LC ebook record available at https://lccn.loc.gov/2024022107

ISBN 978-1-009-50411-9 Hardback

This book is dedicated to my parents, Zhang Chunyi and Li Suohua, who have experienced both successes and failures of Chinese revolution and reform.

谨以本书敬献我的父亲张纯益、母亲李锁华,

他们共同经历了中国革命与改革的成败。

Contents

Figures and Tables

FIGURES

TABLES

Preface

As I said in 2012,

> China's constitutional misfortune is not merely limited to itself, but may be sown, incubated, and exported beyond its borders. If a regime is irresponsible to its own people, so much the less can it be held accountable to the rest of the world.[1]

The point was attested in less than a decade, when the Covid-19 virus spread virulently in Wuhan, where the local police harshly suppressed the whistle-blowing of Doctor Li Wenliang (李文亮) and his colleagues in early 2020. The virus quickly spread all over the world and, in the next three years, caused at least 700 million infections and 7 million deaths.[2] The actual death toll is expected to be much higher than that figure since, when China suddenly decided to reverse its zero-Covid (清零) policy in December 2022, the instant spread of the virus caused the death of millions, primarily among the Chinese elderly.[3] The suppression of free speech in China, as the cumulative result of the repeated failures of its past and present constitutional reforms, has cost the world dearly. The future of its constitutional reform not only decides the fate of China, but also has much to do with the rest of the world.

This book collects six non-technical essays written over the past fifteen years or so, most of which are commemorations and reflections on China's constitutional history of the past century. I am not a historian by profession and have not conducted a systematic study of Chinese constitutional history.

1 Qianfan Zhang, *The Constitution of China: A Contextual Analysis* (Oxford: Hart Publishing, 2012), p. 261.

2 https://ourworldindata.org/explorers/coronavirus-data-explorer.

3 Bernard Orr, "Nearly 2 million excess deaths followed China's sudden end of COVID curbs, study says," Reuters (August 25, 2023), www.reuters.com/world/china/nearly-2-million-excess-deaths-followed-chinas-sudden-end-covid-curbs-study-2023-08-25/.

My writings have been largely "a hammer to the east, a stick to the west"; a centennial review on one event, a sexagenary (甲子) reflection on another. Looking back, however, I have found that these scattered events do connect themselves to form a line of more or less complete narrative. From the Outline of the Imperial Constitution (1908) to the Xinhai Revolution (1911) and the May Fourth Movement (1919), from the Cultural Revolution (1966–76) to Deng Xiaoping's Southern Tour (1992) and the death of Sun Zhigang (2003), these events were the major constitutional turning points in modern Chinese history. I have decided that I will *not* be writing any more commemorative essays of such kind in the near future, until things turn favorably for China's constitutionalism – in the past 120 years, it has never fared well, and we cannot keep living in the tragedies of the past. After learning painful lessons, we need to look and move forward. Having experienced setbacks, failures, difficulties, and regressions, China's constitutionalism needs new, positive milestones, which I believe *will* arrive before long.

The six pieces included in this book cover China's constitutionalism in its past and present as well as its prospects for the future. For the reader's convenience, the major signposts of China's modern constitutional history are summarized in Table P.1.

The first chapter, completed in March 2008, is a political commentary written to commemorate the 100th anniversary of China's first written constitution as a symbol of its constitutional reform. It was partly inspired by Ma Ying-jeou's election as the President of the Republic of China (Taiwan), which temporarily eased the tension across the Strait. Over the past century, there have been two founding events in Chinese constitutionalism: the promulgation of the Outline of the Imperial Constitution in 1908 and the Xinhai (辛亥) Revolution in 1911. In between there was also the hastily enacted and short-lived Nineteen Articles. If the Outline launched the Qing government's half-hearted constitutional reform when it was still confident about its control over China, the Nineteen Articles was the product of the forced reform of its political system when its confidence was fatally diminished by the Wuchang Uprising. Had the revolutionary party and Yuan Shikai (袁世凱) had enough wisdom to learn from the British Glorious Revolution or the Japanese Meiji Restoration, and followed the trend to maintain the imperial throne by surrendering the imperial power as stipulated in the Nineteen Articles, China would have long embarked on the path of a constitutional monarchy, and avoided a century of civil wars and the calamities of the ensuing totalitarian regime, such as the Great Leap Forward and the Cultural Revolution. Unfortunately, the Qing government, dominated by the small Manchu minority, repeatedly obstructed the constitutional reforms and squandered

TABLE P.1 *Major signposts of China's modern constitutional history*

Year	Events
1840–60	The Opium Wars. China's first defeat by the Western powers in its history compelled it to initiate the Westernization movement (洋务运动) aimed at developing modern industry, commerce, and military.
1894	The Sino-Japanese War (甲午战争). Shockingly defeated by the Japanese fleet, China began its constitutional reform.
1898	The Hundred Days' Reform (百日维新). Intellectual reformers persuaded Emperor Guangxu (光绪) to undertake massive institutional reforms, which were quickly suppressed by the conservative force under the leadership of Empress Dowager Cixi (慈禧).
1900	The Boxers' Rebellion. The Qing government secretly encouraged the civilian militia to attack and kill foreign missionaries, leading to the intervention of Allied Forces (八国联军) of eight major powers, which forced the imperial court to flee from Beijing.
1908	The Outline of the Imperial Constitution. Under international and domestic pressures, the conservative imperial government was forced to continue constitutional reform and promulgated the first written constitution highlighting imperial supremacy.
1911	(1) The Wuchang Uprising (武昌起义). A mutiny threatened the Qing government, which was challenged not only by increasing social discontent, but also by armed rebellion. (2) The Nineteen Articles (十九信条). The Luanzhou mutiny (滦州兵变) forced the Qing government to promulgate another constitution, reducing the imperial court to a constitutional monarchy with nominal powers. (3) The Xinhai Revolution (辛亥革命). The "uprising" was turned into what is much more widely known as a "revolution" after the imperial Prime Minister Yuan Shikai failed to negotiate a deal with the revolutionary force led by Sun Yat-sen, the founder of the Nationalist Party (KMT), who firmly demanded the establishment of a republic.
1912	The Republic of China (中华民国). The First Republic ended the millennia of Chinese dynastic cycles, while incorporating some elements from the old regime. Sun Yat-sen quickly yielded interim presidency to Yuan Shikai.
1913	The Assassination of Song Jiaoren. As a major Nationalist leader advocating parliamentary democracy, Song's untimely death ended the cooperation between the KMT and Yuan

(*continued*)

TABLE P.1 (*continued*)

Year	Events
	Shikai, prompting Sun Yat-sen to initiate the "second revolution" (二次革命).
1915–17	*The New Culture Movement* (新文化运动). A group of liberal intellectuals, represented by Hu Shih and Chen Duxiu at Peking University, initiated an overall liberal movement that aimed to modernize Chinese language and culture.
1919	*The May Fourth Movement* (五四运动). Furious about the Treaty of Versailles, which allowed Japan to take over Shandong province formerly unde German control, students initiated mass protests against the Western powers. In the meantime, the new Soviet regime in Russia, established in 1917, actively propagated communism in China.
1921	*The Founding of the Chinese Communist Party (CCP).* With the split of Chinese liberals, the leftist faction founded the CCP. Chen Duxiu served as its first General Secretary.
1924	*The First Nationalist–Communist Cooperation* (第一次国共合作). Sun Yat-sen decided to reorganize the KMT along Soviet lines and ally with the CCP in order to more effectively fight against warlords and grab national power.
1927	*The Northern Expedition* (北伐). After Sun's death in 1925, Chiang Kai-shek initiated war against warlords and achieved quick success. The KMT ended the First Cooperation, purged its Communist ally and established strict one-party rule over China.
1937	*The Xi'an Incident* (西安事变) *and the Second Nationalist–Communist Cooperation* (第二次国共合作). With Japan's comprehensive invasion of China, Chiang Kai-shek was under intensifying pressure to stop fighting with the CCP. He was kidnapped by his own officers, forcing him to agree to the Second Cooperation.
1946	*The Constitution of the Republic of China* (中华民国宪法) *and the Civil War* (国共内战). After Japan surrendered in 1945, the Republic of China finally passed a formal constitution. While the KMT briefly negotiated with the CCP to establish a coalition government, it never materialized as the two parties soon engaged in a bloody civil war.
1949	*The People's Republic of China* (中华人民共和国). Following the KMT's quick defeat and retreat to Taiwan, Mao Zedong led the CCP to take over the mainland, establishing a thorough totalitarian regime.

Year	Events
1958	*The Great Leap Forward* (大跃进). Among the numerous political movements launched by the new Communist regime, the Great Leap Forward was the most devastating, leading to the Great Famine in the next three years, with a death toll of at least 30 million.
1966	*The Cultural Revolution* (文化大革命). Mao's refusal to admit political failure despite the grave mistakes in his radical industrialization policies led him to mobilize students and the masses, leveraging the mass worship for him as a charismatic leader. He launched the Cultural Revolution to forcibly overthrow his political rivals within the party.
1976	*The Downfall of the Gang of Four* (四人帮). After Mao's death in 1976, the CCP veterans arrested Mao's widow and her political allies, marking the end of the Cultural Revolution.
1978	*The Reform and Opening* (改革开放). Learning from the lessons of the Cultural Revolution, the CCP mainstream initiated economic reforms to allow limited freedoms.
1982	*The Promulgation of the Current Constitution.* The Constitution symbolizes the consolidation of the reformist forces within the CCP led by Deng Xiaoping and others.
1989	*The Tiananmen Protests and Crackdown.* The untimely death of the widely respected former General Secretary Hu Yaobang sparked massive student protests. The CCP conservative mainstream, determined to suppress the peaceful protests, ousted the liberal General Secretary Zhao Ziyang.
1992	*The Southern Tour* (南巡). After the suspension of all reforms due to the crackdown, Deng Xiaoping decided to restart economic reforms, embarking on a tour of southern cities, where he delivered a speech advocating reform while intensifying political control, particularly over education and university campuses.
1999	*Judicial Reform.* The Supreme People's Court (SPC) launched a belated judicial reform to modernize the Chinese judicial process. Together with the Qi Yuling case in 2001, when the SPC referenced the Constitution for the first time in its legal interpretation, these events indicated the potential for an official path towards constitutional reform in China.
2003	*The Sun Zhigang* (孙志刚) *Incident.* The tragedy occurred amid the SARS pandemic, coinciding with the ascension of General Secretary Hu Jintao and Premier Wen Jiabao. Facing both international and domestic pressures, the new regime swiftly

(*continued*)

TABLE P.1 (*continued*)

Year	Events
	abolished the long-standing Detention and Repatriation (收容遣送) system, signaling the growth of China's civil society and the emergence of its popular path towards constitutional reform in the internet era.
2004	*Constitutional Amendment.* This significant amendment added liberal principles to the current Constitution, such as the respect and protection of human rights, governing the state according to law (依法治国), establishing a socialist state based on the rule of law (法治国家), the inviolability of private property, and compensation for taking.
2013	*The Neo-Totalitarian Revival.* China entered a new era as the reforms were systematically reversed with the ascendance of General Secretary Xi Jinping. Terms such as "constitutionalism" and "civil society," designated as "sensitive," have become untouchable in public discourse.
2022	*The White Paper Movement* (白纸运动). Having suffered severe restrictions on individual freedoms since the outbreak of the pandemic in early 2020, students and civilians in various cities took to the streets to protest the strict zero-Covid policy in late 2022. Within ten days, the policy was reversed, demonstrating the strength and viability of popular constitutionalism despite stringent state control.

its own opportunities of self-renovation by forfeiting the faith of the Chinese public. When it began to repent and reform, it was too late, and the Nineteen Articles was quickly reduced to a waste of paper. While the arrogant and myopic rulers of the Qing Dynasty (清朝) dug their own graves and deserved their fate, the success of the republican revolution meant the very end of constitutional reform. Although the First and Second Republics came one after another, China has decidedly drifted away from the path of constitutional reform over the past century.

The second chapter commemorates the centennial of the May Fourth Movement (1919), the turning point between the republican revolution and the Communist success, which verified the prophecy of Chinese historian Wang Guowei (王国维): "that which starts from republicanism is destined to end with communism." Prior to the publication of this relatively late article, I visited the Berlin Institute of Advanced Studies for nearly a year, where I developed the basic framework of reconstructing a social contract theory centered on the notion of "political natural law." The century-long predicament of Chinese constitutionalism lies not in its written constitutions, but in the complete absence of social contracts as the legitimizing foundation of any constitution. A violent revolution is necessarily against constitutionalism because it is opposed to the very idea of social contract. Whether revolutionary or counter-revolutionary, the political powers throughout Chinese history violated every single one of the political natural laws. Although the Xinhai Revolution did not shed much blood, it was carried out very much in a way opposed to the spirit of social contract. The imperial court and the royalist faction were an important social force at the time, but were completely swept out in the revolutionary process. Without the mediation of a third party, the temporary compromise reached by the Nationalists and Yuan Shikai would sooner or later collapse. Sure enough, in less than two years, the assassination of Song Jiaoren in 1913 put an end to the ill-fated political cooperation. Thereafter, the restoration of the monarchy and warlords took turns to grab power, making the people thoroughly frustrated with the republican trial with democracy. It happened to be the time when Western democracy was in a low ebb, with Europe devastated by World War I. The Chinese seemed to have lost patience with the practice of learning from the West that had gradually formed since the Opium War of 1840. The Treaty of Versailles, portrayed as harming China's territorial sovereignty, ignited the patriotic fire overnight, and set the stage for Communist ascendance. The frequency analysis of keywords from the Xinhai Revolution to the May Fourth Movement showed that anti-contractual concepts such as revolution, Leninism, and socialism had been soaring in popularity, and had become an intellectual trend by 1919. In a short span of three decades, the Communist revolution would ultimately achieve a comprehensive victory.

Once the totalitarian regime is established, various disasters are bound to recur. Constant movements arrived one after another, epitomized in the Anti-Rightist Movement (反右运动) in 1957. The Great Leap Forward (大跃进) launched by Mao Zedong in 1958 quickly led to the Great Famine. When Chairman Mao's authority was challenged, he launched an unprecedented catastrophe to maintain his power that he believed was dwindling. To commemorate the outbreak of the Cultural Revolution half a century ago, the third chapter analyzes the characteristics of a totalitarian regime and the path of transformation after its decline. A totalitarian state is diagonally opposite to liberal democracy, which is characterized by prevalence of horizontal connections, the sum total of which constitute a social contract. On the contrary, an ideal totalitarian structure is like a zero-impedance conductor: orders flow from the top of the power pyramid to the lowest level, and information from the grassroots to the very top, all without any obstacle. It was this totalitarian system that enabled Mao, the charismatic leader, to use his overwhelming social support to overthrow his political rivals within the system when his authority was challenged. Like a courtly struggle, the Cultural Revolution was for the sake of Mao's personal power, but the cost of social destruction was incomparably greater. Indeed, its legacy is lasting today, as the "seven dwarves"[4] of the top power circle in China at the moment, all educated during the Cultural Revolution, are truly "sons of the revolution."

The word for "crisis" (危机) in Chinese implies opportunities, however. Reform arrived after the Cultural Revolution was over. The fourth article commemorates – more accurately, mourns (祭奠) – the twentieth anniversary of Deng Xiaoping's Southern Tour, intended to restart reform after the suppression of the Tiananmen protests in 1989. In contrast to the deteriorating political environment today, Deng Xiaoping's pragmatic strategy of biding his time and keeping a low profile, even Jiang Zemin's "Three Represents" (三个代表) slogan and Hu Jintao's "No Stumbling" (不折腾) pledge, have become cherishable nostalgia of contemporary Chinese. Yet, once the constitutional reform is abandoned, opportunist pragmatism cannot last long, inevitably leading to today's predicament. Needless to say, China has been unfortunate throughout its history replete with calamities. All constitutional movements have so far ended in failures: the 1898 Hundred Days' Reform, the 1908 constitutional reform, the Xinhai Revolution that put an end to China's dynastic cycles, the 1927–28 Northern Expedition that established the Nationalist one-party dictatorship, the establishment of the Second Republic in 1949 after the Nationalist-Communist Civil War, followed by frequent political movements thereafter. Eventually, after the downfall of the Gang of Four in 1976, China was blessed with the "Golden Age" of reform, which ended tragically within a decade in 1989. To an extent, the failure of reforms is also attributed to the misfortune of reforming too early. As attested in Chinese history, genuine reform inevitably leads to a direct confrontation between the old and the new interests. The "second-generation leaders," such as Deng Xiaoping and Chen Yun, were still revolutionary vanguards, and would never allow a change of their regime. This is fundamentally different from the Soviet Union, established more than three decades earlier. China's failure served as a bloody lesson for the socialist Eastern Bloc, which had succeeded in the democratic transition since the fall of the Berlin Wall in November 1989. Reciprocally, adding to China's misfortune, the success of the Third Wave transition served as a lesson for the CCP to maintain its power in China, which strengthened the political control of the post-89 society.

4 The term refers to seven members of the Standing Committee of the CCP's Politburo, headed by the General Secretary Xi Jinping.

Deng's Southern Tour launched economic reforms without its political counterpart, and created huge interest groups that have benefited from – indeed, lived on – the post-totalitarian system, further hindering political reforms. Without political reform that makes the rulers accountable to the ruled, no matter how much freedom, wealth, or half-baked rule of law temporarily enjoyed by the ruled, all can be taken away overnight, as the zero-Covid policy has shown during 2020–22.

So what needs to be done? When the current General Secretary came to power in late 2012, partly due to his special family background, many Chinese liberals had high expectations for political reform, among whom I was one. I drafted an Initiative for Building Consensus on Reform. With the courageous support of Wu Si (吴思) and Hong Zhenkuai (洪振快), both being outstanding scholars in their own fields and the chief editors of *Yanhuang Chunqiu* (炎黄春秋), an influential liberal journal now taken over by an appointed leadership, we jointly held a seminar and collected joint signatures for the petition. Many liberal scholars, lawyers, and journalists, such as Professors Guo Daohui (郭道晖), Jiang Ping (江平), and Zi Zhongyun (资中筠), participated. Mr. Li Rui (李锐), who served as Mao's secretary and was then in his nineties, came in a wheelchair. Not surprisingly, the event had been interfered with and the venue had to be changed before it took place. I was required by my university not to participate and to cease to organize. In order to ensure the smooth progress of the conference, I could only make an opening speech, and left the rest to the co-organizers from the magazine. Although the magazine itself could not carry the Initiative, it was translated into various languages and widely circulated overseas. The first batch of joint signatures included more than seventy influential intellectuals, and two more batches were collected before the collection efforts were totally banned. This was the first large-scale joint activity of public intellectuals in China since the severe suppression of the Charter 08 movement. Consistent with my reformist strategy, the Initiative was moderate in tone and was not intended to directly challenge the authority. As a result, it did not bring any adversity to or deterrence on any participants. Yet, its moderate outlook was criticized by some radical liberals, who claimed among other things that we were "kneeling down" to the authority. I will leave the readers to judge for themselves whether such an accusation is fair after reading the content of the Initiative reproduced in this book.

In fact, I used the name "Initiative" instead of "Proposal," or "Advice," precisely because it was meant not merely as a "petition" to the authority, but also as a call directed towards the Chinese society at large, hoping to form a social consensus on the focus and direction of the reform through public discourse. Even at that time, which was characterized by a good deal more optimism than it is today, I was reminded by senior scholars not to pin too much hope on the current leadership. In retrospect, such a warning was prescient, but that advice would still characterize the Initiative as a sort of petition to leaders rather than the general public. In fact, even if it is no more than a petition, I still believe it is necessary in the sense that, when a new leader takes office, it is the obligation of the intellectual community to express its expectations on his leadership. True, later experience shows that he has taken the opposite direction, but that is his business. It is *our* business to speak out. Indeed, this is the attitude that any responsible citizen should have towards his or her own country. And I hereby reassert my unchanging reformist aspiration: if there is any turning point in the future, I will organize the joint signature event again, with the original text of the Initiative. Like China's constitutional reform itself, the Initiative is an ongoing process. While the so-called reform in the recent decade has taken the very opposite direction to our proposal, it is the duty of the liberal community to uphold the unfulfilled ideals of constitutional reform and publicly advocate these ideals.

The fifth chapter serves as a summary of the tortuous path of China's constitutional reform in the past century, analyzing the cultural causes of failures and exploring the possibilities of continuing reform in the current desperate situation. It was originally published on Christmas Day of 2011 as the centennial commemoration of the Xinhai Revolution in 1911. Since the hosting of the Olympic Games in 2008, in the short span of three years, as a result of the continuous fermentation of social events and the general disappointment near the end of the Hu Jintao–Wen Jiabao administration, China's social emotions in general and the liberal sentiment in particular have grown more pessimistic. This change in mood is reflected in the contrasting tones between this and the first chapter. As the title suggests, the "Manifesto" is filled with much more firepower. To be sure, pessimism is *not* necessarily a bad thing for what Max Weber saw as a "hopelessly optimistic" culture. China's failures in the past century are precisely attributed to the naïve optimism, believing that the world would be better no matter what the revolutionary vanguards do and how they do it, so long as they do for a benign purpose. A century of revolutionary turmoil has led China away from constitutionalism to the point beyond redemption, while "revolution" (革命) is still eulogized by the ruling party as well as the general public as a great cause for nation-building. A centennial judgment has to be made by an impartial observer for the interest of China's constitutional cause. Drawing on the American Declaration of Independence, the French Declaration of the Rights of Man and of the Citizen, and the Communist Manifesto, the Constitutional Manifesto is the most widely circulated document I have published in China to date. Despite its sharp language, its main theme is to explore the conditions and mechanisms of constitutional transformation, as well as the way out of the seemingly hopeless cycle of reforms and revolutions. The manuscript was delivered at a lecture under the title of "The Xinhai Revolution and Chinese Constitutionalism (辛亥革命与中国宪政)," invited by a Peking University student organization for the centennial commemoration of the republican revolution. Although the school administration for some reason moved the lecture to a smaller classroom right before it took place, the two-and-a-half-hour lecture attracted a large crowd and received a thunderous applause at the end. The publication of the essay on the internet soon stirred the Standing Committee of the Politburo, the top organ of the CCP, and I have been blacklisted since. The relatively free speech environment did last for a few more years, however. A censored version of the manuscript was published under different titles in the *Leadership* (领导者) magazine hosted by Mr. Zhou Zhixing and the *Lawyer Digest* (律师文摘) edited by Sun Guodong. Both magazines have been discontinued for many years by now, showing serious deterioration in China's political environment since 2013. Despite severe blocking, the video of the Manifesto lecture is still intermittently viral on the internet today.

At the beginning of 2020, the Covid outbreak showed many Chinese the importance of constitutional democracy for a healthy homeland. To explore the future framework of China's constitutional system, Guo Feixiong, a liberal activist later arrested for his harsh criticism of the totalitarian regime, drafted a Questionnaire on Constitutional Democracy for Chinese Liberal Intellectuals, which covers the basic concepts and institutional designs of constitutional democracy. I revised and finalized the Questionnaire, and provided my detailed answer to each of the thirty-six questions therein. On the occasion of the 101st anniversary of the May Fourth Movement in 2020, French sociologist Zhang Lun launched an academic website – "China: History and Future," which published my Answers as the first article.[5] It provides me with an occasion to summarize my thinking on constitutionalism over the past two decades. My general conclusion, as implied in the title, consistently reflects my reformist position: China's most

5 For Zhang Lun's editorial announcement "Thinking Future, Renovating Civilization" and Guo Feixiong's opening introduction and comment on my answer, see www.chinese-future.org,www.chinese-future.org/articles/l2ssnll7h7hte5sgcbh8tzyt8fbpnd, and www.chinese-future.org/articles/enr4pywjh3htjwajtmkdp7bac7s8zx.

pressing task is not making a new and better constitution, but rather formulating social contract through implementing the existing constitution, which does pay lip services to many political natural law precepts. Unlike many admirers of the American presidential system, I advocate for a Westminster-type parliamentary system, which has largely been borrowed by China's current Constitution, to be embedded in a federal framework through future constitutional reform. As the closing chapter of the book, the Answers can be taken as my intellectual preparation for future reforms in China, while actions are presently handicapped in an era of neo-totalitarian resurgence.

Chinese tradition often views the past as a guide to the present and future, likening it to a reflective "mirror" of history. To be sure, history itself never replays its exact course. Time never simply flows back to offer a chance to revisit past junctures and make alternate choices. The people, institutions, material, and cultural conditions, and motivating forces that shape critical decisions are all irreversibly different. Nevertheless, certain patterns do sometimes reemerge, especially in a society where the political system has remained largely unchanged. The recent zero-Covid policy bore resemblance to the lockdown during the Great Famine six decades ago, when fleeing peasants were forcibly detained by local militia to suffer starvation at their homes. Like that man-made tragedy, this one also persisted for three years until it was put to an abrupt end by the White Paper Movement – a seemingly insignificant but vital difference sixty years later. Should history indeed weave its patterns anew, we had better get ready for the next turn of events, which is swiftly approaching, in order to grasp the missed opportunities when they reemerge.

Acknowledgments

The collection of essays in this book grew out of my academic activities in mainland China during the last quarter-century, during which so many colleagues and friends have contributed to shaping my thinkings and writings. I am indebted to them all for their kind support and exchange of ideas, particularly Guo Daohui, Jiang Ping, Mao Yushi, Zhang Sizhi, Zhang Yihe, Zhou Xiaozheng, Zi Zhongyun, Chung-ying Cheng, Jerome Cohen, Donald Clarke, Paul Gewirtz, Tom Kellogg, Eva Pils, Ewan Smith, Jeremy Webber, Chen Min (Xiaoshu), Gao Quanxi, Guo Yuhua, He Weifang, Su Xiaoling, Xu Zhangrun, Yang Maodong (Guo Feixiong), and Zhang Lun, among others. I also thank Joe Ng for excellent editorial assistance and two peer reviewers for helpful comments. Last but not least, I express my gratitude to my wife, Wei Xiaoyang, and son, Zhang Yichi, for their understanding and patience throughout all these years.

Abbreviations

CCP	Chinese Communist Party
CCPCC	Chinese Communist Party Central Committee
CPG	Central People's Government
GDP	gross domestic product
KMT	Kuomintang (Nationalist Party)
PNL	political natural law
NGO	nongovernmental organization
NPC	National People's Congress
NPCSC	National People's Congress Standing Committee
SARS	severe acute respiratory syndrome
SPC	Supreme People's Court
SS	Schutzstaffel (Protection Squadron)

1

From the Third Cooperation to the Third Republic

A Centennial Anticipation

In late March 2023, Ma Ying-jeou (马英九) visited his hometown in mainland China and Sun Yat-sen's Mausoleum in Nanjing, the former capital of the Republic of China, for the first time as its former president. The visit rekindled hope for another cooperation between the Nationalist Party (国民党, KMT) and the Communist Party (共产党, CCP) after the previous two failed cooperations in 1924–27 and 1937–46. In fact, such expectations surfaced as early as 2008, when Ma was elected as the President of the Republic of China – essentially meaning Taiwan since the KMT retreated there following its defeat in 1949. The hope reignited as Chiang Wan-an (蒋万安), the great-grandson of Chiang Kai-shek (蒋介石) and the current mayor of Taipei, visited Shanghai in late August 2023, when he delivered a passionate speech on peaceful unification and actively engaged with the local people, fostering lively interactions on the streets.

1.1 INTRODUCTION: ANTICIPATING A THIRD COOPERATION

In 1908, China enacted its first written constitution, the Outline of the Imperial Constitution. Over the past century, China has experienced many ups and downs, undergoing numerous changes and facing various challenges. However, it is evident that the Outline was by no means a good constitution as it was filled with the traditional arrogance and tyranny of the imperial power. Hopelessly hindered by the vested interests of the Manchu minority, the Qing government failed to make significant progress in its promised reforms, particularly the reform of official system, leading to growing resentment among the Han majority. The Outline lasted for only three years, and the entire reform movement, spanning seven decades, was ultimately deemed a complete failure with the Xinhai Revolution in 1911. The root cause of the failure was the inability of the old regime to resolve the conflict of interest between the small circle of officials dominated by the Manchu minority and the population at large. While the Outline did incorporate some Western elements, such as "parliament," "free speech," "freedom," and "property," which were unfamiliar to the Chinese at that time, it took Chinese several generations to understand and even longer to practice these imported norms. Despite undergoing two revolutions and enacting a dozen constitutions, China has not effectively implemented any of them. Even today, although most of the political natural law precepts are included in the current constitution, they remain largely superficial. Having been plagued by warlord struggles, foreign invasions, totalitarian rule, and the subsequent human catastrophes of colossal scale, China seems to be forever mired in the trap of "having a constitution without constitutionalism" (有宪法无宪政).

A century later, in March 2008, the Nationalist candidate Ma Ying-jeou won the presidential election in Taiwan. Taiwan's success in the "second rotation" of the ruling party not only signified the maturation of its democracy but also helped to reduce – at least temporarily – the tension across the Taiwan Strait that had built up during the presidency of the Democratic Progressive Party. The call for the "Third Cooperation" (第三次合作) between the Nationalist and Communist parties has reemerged in China's public sphere and has even been put on the official agenda for discussion.[1] For peace across the Taiwan Strait, of course, this was good news. However, mere negotiations on policies, economic and cultural cooperation, and even the reconciliation of cross-strait relations would fall far short of making sustainable progress. For decades, the two totalitarian parties had been fighting and killing each other, which had not only devastated China, but also ruined critical opportunities for its constitutional reforms. It was not until the lifting of martial law in 1987 that constitutionalism began to take root in Taiwan. On the other hand, having failed the 1989 democratic movement, the mainland remains in a state of "having a constitution without constitutionalism" to this day. The social problems, unable to be solved through regular institutional channels, are bound to pile up to the point of social collapse. If we

[1] In fact, the concept of the "third cooperation" was proposed by the Communists as early as 1955, but was rejected by the Nationalists. See Wang Lefei, "The third cooperation before the stage and behind the scene," 人民网 (April 17, 2019), http://zhouenlai.people.cn/n1/2019/0417/c409117-31035474.html. With the mainland initiating Reform and Opening in 1978 and Taiwan undergoing democratic transition in 1987, the two governments frequently engaged in negotiations, culminating in the 1992 Consensus, which confirms the one-China principle. However, there has been no consensus on the interpretation of this principle across the Strait.

expect the one who tied the knot to untie it, the resolution of China's constitutional deadlock may indeed require a third cooperation between the Nationalists and Communists. But this time, it cannot stop with cooperation between two previously totalitarian brothers, as was the case for the first two cooperations, which were merely temporary alliances for dealing with internal turmoil (warlord separatism) or external enemies (the Japanese invasion), with each secretly plotting to grab total power and extinguish the other. The third cooperation, if it is ever to occur, is charged with a fundamentally different historical mission: bringing to China a true republic – the Third Republic (第三共和), if there is no better name for now.

In the past century, China has experienced two "republics": The first one overthrew the monarchy, while the second ended the Civil War. In both republics, the Nationalist and Communist parties were allies at times and enemies at others, but they shared several common characteristics. First, since both parties were revolutionary in nature, the republics they established were the result of revolutionary violence. The Xinhai Revolution, with the support of the Nationalist Party, overthrew the Qing dynasty, while the Communist Party overthrew the Nationalist rule in the 1949 revolution. Second, as a result of the two revolutions that were essentially the same in nature, both revolutionary parties implemented strict one-party rule, which inevitably failed to achieve a balance of power. Consequently, the revolutions created the third common problem: Neither republic achieved constitutionalism. Although the First Republic aimed for constitutionalism as its ultimate goal, it was not achieved until the Nationalists implemented one-party rule for thirty-eight years under martial law after retreating to Taiwan in 1949, when the Communists took over mainland China. The Second Republic has pursued "dictatorship" (专政) instead of constitutionalism from the very beginning to this day, even though strict totalitarian rule has been relaxed since 1978 until its recent resurgence. The prospect of a true republic seems to be nowhere in sight.

The first two republics have spanned over a century, during which hundreds of millions of Chinese killed each other for purposes they thought they knew without understanding the underlying reasons. Witnessing the revolutionary chaos of a century, China should learn at least one lesson: Revolution and constitutionalism are incompatible. Revolution is *not* constitutionalism, nor can it achieve it. The Nationalists and Communists have led two revolutions, which not only overturned the ancient political system and swept away traditional culture, but also permanently shelved constitutional reform. Since constitutionalism is the historical debt that both revolutionary parties owe to China, the Chinese have reason to demand that they cooperate once again to establish a Third Republic, one with genuine constitutionalism. However, this time it should be built not through revolutionary violence,[2] but based on peaceful competition between the two (or multiple) parties.

1.2 FAREWELL TO REVOLUTION

The tortuous road of a century of constitutional reform need not be elaborated on here. The shock of the defeat in the Sino-Japanese War (1894), the shame of the Treaty of Shimonoseki (which ceded Taiwan to Japan in 1895),[3] the passion of the scholars' Petitioning on the Royal Carriage (公车上书), the excitement of the Hundred Days' Reform (1898), the tragedy of the Six Gentlemen (the execution of whom quickly put an end to the reform), the hope and disappointment that came with the trial of constitutional government (仿行宪政) in 1908, the good fortune of the Xinhai Revolution in 1911, the travesty of the "Great President" (i.e., Yuan Shikai), the embarrassment of the "Bribed Constitution" (贿选宪法),[4] the helpless failure of the "Provincial Self-Government" (联省自治), the delight of the Nationalist success in the Northern Expedition followed by its bloody crackdown on the Communist ally (1927–28), the ultimate fruition and hasty defeat of the Republican Constitution (1946–49), and so on. The bewildering series of past events seem to have long vanished into thin air, and yet their legacies remain.

After 1949, mainland China finally regained its unity, but unrest and repression intensified. The 1954 Constitution was soon obliterated by the tumultuous waves of the Anti-Rightist Movement and the Great Leap Forward, and the maladies of the Cultural Revolution infected the constitutions of 1975 and 1978. It was not until after the Reform and Opening (改革开放) starting in 1978 that the people were able to live a peaceful life, while constitutional reform once again became a possibility – but only a possibility. While economic reform has achieved mixed success, the constitutional reform failed within a decade in 1989. For mainland China, constitutionalism is not a reality, but remains a remote goal for a hopeless pursuit.

[2] "Farewell to Revolution" was made a theme among Chinese intellectuals during the 1990s after Li Zehou (李泽厚) and Liu Zaifu (刘再复) coauthored a book with that title: *Farewell to Revolution* [in Chinese] (Hong Kong: Cosmos Books, 1995).

[3] For a gist, see Ma Yong, *Convoluted Changes: Opium, Guns and Canons, and China in the Progress of Civilization (1840–1915)* [in Chinese] (Beijing: Encyclopedia of China Publishing House, 2022).

[4] It was enacted by the "bribery president" Cao Kun (曹锟) in 1923, which has ironically been the best constitution being closest to a federal constitution.

Why is China's road to constitutionalism so long and difficult? The explanation starts with the original meaning of "constitutionalism," against which the CCP issued its latest warning in February 2023. Originally, constitutionalism was a rebellious proposition advocated only by political dissidents. After a long period of silence, however, the sixteenth CCP National Congress in 2002 valued the term positively, giving much hope to many people. With the rise of public awareness of constitutional rights, "constitutionalism" has become an increasingly popular term. Once the rights are violated, the victims instinctively turn to the current constitution, which provides for these rights. Constitutionalism has become inseparable from the concepts of rights, freedom, and rule of law. Even in the eyes of the lowest rank of Chinese society, constitutionalism has become a synonym for the better future. It is something everyone can understand since it closely relates to one's basic rights and interest.

In formal terms, constitutionalism is nothing more than governing according to the constitution – any constitution, in the same sense as the rule of law is nothing more than governing according to the law, even if the laws are not so good. However, achieving the rule of bad laws is not easy because general laws, particularly the constitution, are usually presented in an appealing manner. Nakedly bad laws are rare. Unless the ruler is hopelessly ignorant or arrogant, the constitution generally will not stipulate that the ruling family is to be "eternally revered for all generations," as in the Outline of Imperial Constitution, nor will it explicitly grant the "great leader" a demigod status or simply write his name into the constitution. The 1975 Constitution was established amid the tumult of the Cultural Revolution, but even such a revolutionary "constitution" reads quite innocently – perhaps laughably today. It contains passions, ignorance, and naivety, but not overtly positive evil if one is unaware of what actually happened during the Cultural Revolution. Even the terror of "dictatorship" was carried out under the sacred name of the "people." Indeed, everything is supposedly for the "people." All written constitutions, particularly the socialist constitutions, from the 1924 Constitution of Soviet Union to the 1972 Constitution of the "Democratic People's Republic of Korea," are written in this manner. Paradoxically, the louder the slogan of "people" is proclaimed, the poorer and humbler the people actually are.

Here is the difficulty, however. The more beautifully a law is written, the more difficult it is to put it into practice. Who exactly are the "people"? Can they speak for themselves? When the interests of the "people" are infringed upon, can they stand up to protect themselves? Modern autocrats know that the "people" is merely a fictitious construct that they can manipulate at will to help maintain the legitimacy of their rule. Even if the "people" are seen as concrete individuals, they are no more than a group of voiceless, disorganized, and unconnected strangers, who form a motley crowd, "much as potatoes in a sack form a sack of potatoes."[5] Without a political mechanism that unites them and enables them to express their preferences through elections, and obliges elected rulers to be accountable, they are no more than silent lambs awaiting slaughter by their owners. At the very bottom, in any given society and at any given time, since resources such as power and property are always limited, the way in which they are allocated depends on the nature of the state. While a constitution does regulate how rights and interests are distributed, and declares unequivocally that the interests of the "people" are supreme, how these interests are actually distributed hinges on the mechanism through which that the state is governed.

In an authoritarian regime, the rule makers and enforcers are not held accountable to the people, at least not to the majority of society. As a result, the actual rules are operated in their favor, while the rules supposedly "for the people" remain on paper. As Marx asserted, the law is merely an instrument of the ruling class, and a tool is always used for the benefit of its maker and user. Such is the basic requirement of instrumental rationality. Unless one is willing to believe that leaders are selfless "living Lei Feng" (活雷锋),[6] it is only logical that they will implement their rule in their own interests. After all, if the "people" sanctified in the constitutional text cannot speak or defend themselves in real life, why not prioritize "getting rich first" by exploiting their labor?[7] To be sure, the people's interests are also relevant in the long run. As the great Confucian scholar Xunzi (荀子) famously said, "water can carry a boat, just as it can capsize it."[8] It is certainly unwise for the exploitation of the people to reach a point of open rebellion. However, for any specific leader, the force of such rational persuasion is feeble for several reasons.

5 Karl Marx, "Eighteenth Brumaire of Louis Bonaparte," in Robert Tucker, ed., *The Marx–Engels Reader*, 2nd ed. (New York: W. W. Norton & Co., 1978), p. 608.

6 Lei Feng was a soldier who died on duty at the young age of twenty-one. After his passing in 1962, Mao Zedong advocated "to learn from Comrade Lei Feng," initiating an idol worship movement that continues to this day. Lei Feng has since been portrayed as a model by official propaganda, symbolizing those who selflessly sacrifice themselves for the well-being of others. However, in reality, he was a rather ordinary individual with human flaws and vanity. Tao Ke, "Insider recovers a true Lei Feng," 新华网 (March 6, 2014), https://gongyi.ifeng.com/news/detail_2014_03/05/34441619_0.shtml.

7 Deviating from the egalitarian Communist ideal, Deng Xiaoping's pragmatic slogan in the early stage of reform was "to allow some people to get rich first."

8 *Xunzi*, Ch. 31. The "boat" is a metaphor often referring to the regime (not a particular government).

First, since the term of any particular leader is limited, self-interested leaders will maximize their rent so long as the "boat" does not capsize during their own term. Such a mentality has turned the art of ruling into a game of "passing the buck." After seventy years of Marxist education, which thoroughly secularized Communist China, and four decades of market reform, effectively rationalizing every member of the ruling group, ordinary leaders are neither deterred by moral principles nor motivated by the aspiration to leave a good name in history. It would be naive to expect that a ruling group with the mentality of "Après moi, le déluge" will truly prioritize the public interest of ordinary people based on its long-term calculations. In fact, compared to hereditary rulers, whose estate is supposed to last indefinitely as long as they keep the "boat" steady, a supposedly "elected" leader with a limited term is much less motivated to avoid the consequences of "Après moi, le déluge."

Second, it is true that the ruling group in a large country like China is far from a single solid bloc. It is a composite group comprising various interests and personalities. Even after several decades of applying the reverse selection rule in the official circle since the crackdown in 1989, there are still reformers intending to make progress and even critics who are radically dissatisfied with the current state of affairs. However, they remain a small minority in the ruling group, whose overall behavioral pattern is determined by the dominant vested interest. In fact, in the face of such a dominant interest, even a reform-minded leader is rendered powerless. Emperor Guangxu's fate at the end of the Hundred Days' Reform was telling enough. Unless an enlightened monarch possesses the power and prestige of Mao Zedong during the heyday of personal worship, leaders who challenge the system will quickly find themselves fighting a losing battle.

Finally, everyone in the ruling group finds themselves caught in a Prisoner's Dilemma. While the corruption of one individual is not enough to cause a riot, individual integrity alone is insufficient to save a corrupt system. Therefore, maintaining a clean image would simply forfeit profit in vain. Once corruption and abuse of power become the "winning strategy," a constitution, no matter how well-written, proves to be a negligible obstacle. In fact, the constitution was *intended* to be a facade to begin with. This is why there has been a millennia-long divergence between the apparent rules and the "latent rules" (潜规则), which essentially means today "having a constitution without constitutionalism."[9] Ultimately, the mystery that has puzzled scholars since the Han dynasty (202 BC to AD 220) boils down to a simple

[9] Qianfan Zhang, "A constitution without constitutionalism? The paths of constitutional developments in China," *International Journal of Constitutional Law* 8 (2010): 950.

fact: The lawbook serves as little more than a cover-up for the naked exploitation of the ruling group, which operates the state according to the latent rules to maintain its vested interest.

It is thus plain that a despotic regime will not implement its constitution and laws except naked bad laws, which are rarely seen. While a "good law" safeguards the interest of all – at least that of the vast majority, a bad law is a law that protects the interest of a few at the expense of the vast majority. Since a rule made by a small minority of the ruling circle necessarily serves the interest of such a minority against the vast majority, to whom it is not held accountable, the typical practice of a despotic regime is to implement bad laws under the ruse of good laws. To be sure, there *are* exceptions. Someone may point to Singapore, a state that is deficient in democracy but does practice rule of law. Due to fortuitous factors such as the colonial experience of self-government and the rule of law, the presence of an educated and enlightened ruling circle, the wisdom and lasting influence of the founding fathers, certain countries may be fortunate exceptions. However, such exceptions are likely to be rare. Advocates of "authoritarian legality" can provide only a handful of examples, such as Singapore and Hong Kong.[10] In any case, whether authoritarian legality is considered valid or not, China's rugged journey towards constitutionalism over the past century has proved that, like most countries in the world, China is *not* a fortunate star specially favored by destiny.

This presents a conundrum that has vexed China's modernization for over a century. No sooner does a society become enlightened than its people demand reform, but such reform, however necessary, is impeded by the political and social structure of the old regime. Surrounding the ruling circle, the intellectual elites, political activists, and the populace expect to gain more interest and power, but this simply starts a zero-sum game since the first consequence of such reform is inevitably the diminution of the vested interests of the ruling group, for whom all rules have hitherto been designed and maintained. Indeed, the entire purpose of the state machinery has been to maintain and implement such latent rules under its control. When reform attempts to redistribute social interests without abolishing the existing power structure, its fate is doomed.

In this sense, absolute despotism is a ruling mechanism capable of self-healing. It not only violates every constitutional principle, but also creates the most natural anathema to constitutional reform. The formidable impediment

[10] See, e.g., Tom Ginsburg and Tamir Moustafa ed., *Rule by Law: The Politics of Courts in Authoritarian Regimes* (Cambridge: Cambridge University Press, 2008); Mark Tushnet, "Authoritarian constitutionalism," *Cornell Law Review* 100 (2015): 391.

is not only due to the cultural apathy long cultivated by the absolute tradition that is at odds with constitutional democracy, but also because it fosters a vested interest group naturally opposed to any constitutional reform meant to diminish its power. In a despotic regime, leaders of all sizes are beneficiaries of the regime, each taking a share of their own authority from the authoritarian power structure. Since they control critical political, economic, and social resources, as long as they are in power, they are the major obstacle that every reform must overcome in order to succeed. To carry out any reform within the existing system, they have to be benefited, at least not harmed or threatened. Once the reform threatens to change the power structure that sustains the vested interest, it is safe to expect that they will fight back to suffocate the reform. Following the promulgation of the Outline of the Imperial Constitution, the series of retrogressive actions taken by the Qing government during its institutional reform sufficed to illustrate this point. The success of a limited reform, which keeps the existing power distribution pattern essentially unaltered, depends on whether cooperation can be obtained from the vested interest groups.

Admittedly, cooperation with the ruling regime is not always impossible. Under exceptional situations, the ruling elite may also benefit from reform and even actively promote it. The four decades of Reform and Opening in mainland China witnessed such a fortunate process, despite major defeat of political reform in 1989. The regime gave up some of its power, thereby leaving society a degree of freedom with which it is able to develop vigorously. During this process, while the people's livelihood improved, officials still maintained considerable residual power that enabled them to seek rent and become the greatest beneficiaries of economic reform. This is why economic reform has been able to proceed, despite constant obstructions from the extreme leftist factions. The "China miracle" that the world has witnessed in the past four decades is little more than an appearance that seems all the more phenomenal in contrast to the pre-reform poverty. As the rigid planned economy had made the mainland so poor, and the political movements had made the people suffer so much, almost any deregulation would release social vitality, any development would increase GDP figures, and any reform would be beneficial as long as the reformers maintained basic sanity. The result is a Pareto optimum for almost everyone, from officials and entrepreneurs to intellectuals, workers, and peasants. All walks of life benefited to various extents. Since the cake is constantly growing, everyone keeps getting a bigger piece, despite dramatic differences in the size of pieces under the existing power structure – the leaders who control the power and resources naturally get the lion's share.

The simple logic also determines the fate of political reform, which is almost bound to fail because it threatens to take away the very means by which the ruling group protects its vested interest. Just as a fisherman may be willing to give up a few fishes, but will fight with all his strength to keep his fishing gear, a despotic leader may be willing to give up certain concrete benefits, but will do everything within his power to maintain the power by which all his privileges are derived and kept. For a ruling regime without vision and confidence, political reform is nothing short of a revolution. In order to avoid agitating the vested interest, a reform must be carried out timidly, as if walking on thin ice. Without touching on the political dimension, a reform can continue along the economic axis with the least resistance, but it is uncertain how far it can proceed along this path.

The experience of Chinese reform shows that economic growth cannot constrain political power. On the contrary, it further expands the power of the party-state by contributing revenues and legitimacy to the ruling regime. Sooner or later, the ruling elites at all levels would get carried away, and unscrupulously violate the basic interests of ordinary people, causing heaps of social conflicts, from forced demolition and eviction in cities to unfair compensation for land-taking in the countryside. As recurring social conflicts and protests are inevitable, political reform is increasingly urgent. If the leaders remain stubborn to resist political reforms, as the Qing government did before 1911, social crisis will only accumulate until the last straw breaks the regime's capacity to endure social pressure. At that time, the repeatedly frustrated reform will turn into a revolution, just as repeated failures of reforms during the late Qing dynasty eventually led to the Xinhai Revolution.

The repeated failures in political reform would make it appear that only a revolution can break the existing power structure together with the vested interest groups that obstruct necessary changes. However, China's lessons in the past century, written with blood and fire, have demonstrated that revolution is *not* the solution to cure the failures of reform. First, although revolution often aims for constitutionalism at the beginning, as Sun Yat-sen's republican revolution did around 1911, it usually fails to promote constitutionalism in the end because the success of the revolution itself will quickly produce new vested interest. Not only did the KMT refuse to negotiate with the Qing government to establish a constitutional monarchy, but also persecuted its CCP ally as soon as the Northern Expedition succeeded, establishing a strict one-party rule against constitutional principles.

In fact, compared to the old vested interest, the revolutionaries, who used to be marginalized and poor, will be all the more rapacious in enriching themselves and therefore equally if not more resistant to any constitutional reform that tends to take away their power. Moreover, in the violent process of overthrowing the old regime, the revolutionary party will inevitably pay a heavy price in terms of lives and blood, and will do everything to compensate itself, as it were, by reaping the hard-earned spoil when it comes to power. Indeed, one primary rationale that the CCP uses to justify its political monopoly is that "the blood of the revolutionary martyrs should not flow in vain," which is another way of saying that "anyone who wants us to step down should expect to pay the same price." Once the monopoly of power is considered as a reward or compensation for the blood sacrifice of the revolutionaries, the so-called revolution is no more than thug violence, except that it is now equipped with an attractive ideology, which will only carry its political dictatorship to an even higher level.

Second, since the success of a violent revolution typically relies on a highly centralized organizational structure, the ruling party is unlikely to relinquish its centralized power after achieving success. Instead, its governing principle necessarily opposes the constitutional separation of powers. Following the Xinhai Revolution, for instance, the KMT remained organizationally dispersed and militarily weak, relying on shifting alliances with various warlords to maintain itself. It was only after 1924, when the party reformed its organizational structure according to the Soviet model that it became a highly centralized and effective party, shortly leading to the Northern Expedition (北伐) and the reunification of China. However, this success marked the KMT's turn towards comprehensive dictatorship. Soon after reunification, the party purged its former leftist allies, particularly the Communists, and practiced monopolistic rule both within and outside the party. The Communist victory over the KMT in 1949 was similarly achieved through massive violence. In essence, a revolution replaces the old tyranny with an even more fearsome tyranny and conquers the old violence with greater violence. To confront the vested interest controlling the state machinery, a revolutionary party must be highly centralized, organized, and militarized to survive within the political environment of the old regime before it ultimately defeats it.

Consequently, a successful revolution aligns itself diametrically against the principles and organizational structure of a liberal democracy. After the revolution, the ruling party naturally continues its accustomed style of governance from the revolutionary period. Not surprisingly, revolution as a radical form of change only results in the violent replacement of rulers, echoing the Chinese saying "change the soup but not the medicine" (换汤不换药). The constitutional predicament persists – indeed, often worsens – as the new ruling group often becomes even more tyrannical.

Indeed, a revolution presents significant risks for a society undergoing change. In a despotic system where revolutions typically occur, it is difficult if not impossible for the public to clearly understand the arguments for or against the revolution and to test its promises through normal deliberations. Revolutionary slogans are often misleading or deceitful. After a successful revolution, when the new despotic order is consolidated, the new regime will not be held accountable to the people through regular elections. As a result, it is not obligated to fulfill the promises it made during the revolution in order to gain popular support. A notable example of a revolutionary party failing to fulfill its promises is the nearly four decades of "tutelage" (训政) exercised by the KMT, during which it failed to fulfill its constitutional promise to "return power to the people" (还政于民). Similarly, the CCP gained power largely through the support of the peasants by making appealing promises such as land ownership. However, soon after seizing power, it reclaimed peasant land and implemented the People's Commune system, which led to the devastating Great Famine of 1959–62, primarily affecting peasants. The peasants have also been deeply harmed by the discriminatory urban-rural policies implemented since the early 1950s. If the Chinese peasants had known the consequences, would they still support the Communist revolution at the beginning?

Furthermore, both the Nationalist and Communist parties once advocated federalism as part of their political promises, but abandoned those promises and practiced a centralized unitary system as soon as they gained power. The CCP, for instance, proposed federalism as early as its Second Congress in 1922. As late as October 1947, the Declaration of the Chinese People's Liberation Army promised ethnic minorities "equal autonomy and free partnership within the Chinese territory."[11] As soon as it seized power in 1949, however, it abandoned its ethnic policies. Today, "federalism" even became a forbidden topic. Revolutionary ideals can be enticing, but a society where revolution becomes necessary for change often lacks the very mechanisms to hold the revolutionary party to its promises after it achieves success.

Therefore, while constitutional reforms face various dilemmas, a simple revolution is not a solution for achieving constitutionalism. Fundamentally, as constitutionalism pertains to the interests of everyone, constitutional politics should be democratic in nature, ensuring everyone's right to participate. The outcome of practicing constitutionalism is an equitable distribution of powers, which ensures a relatively fair distribution of interests and resources. An inequitable power structure inevitably leads to an inequitable distribution

[11] Mao Zedong, Chinese People's Liberation Declaration (October 10, 1947), www.marxists.org/chinese/maozedong/marxist.org-chinese-mao-19471010.htm.

of interests. In a highly centralized system, the ruling group concentrates a disproportionate amount of social resources, creating a vested interest group that opposes any constitutional reform that threatens to diminish their power. The convoluted process of Chinese constitutionalism is attributed not so much to a misunderstanding of constitutionalism or outdated political ideologies incompatible with constitutional principles, but rather to the power structure and interest distributions under the old regime that have hindered every reform effort. Revolution may overthrow an old regime, but it cannot break the dynastic cycle and fundamentally change the nature of the regime, let alone establish and sustain a new constitutional order. Once a state becomes entrenched in absolute despotism, achieving constitutionalism becomes nearly impossible. From this perspective, the repeated failures of Chinese constitutionalism over the past century are a predictable outcome.

1.3 RECONSTRUCTING THE REPUBLIC

If constitutional reform seems hopeless and revolution is a dead end, then where is the way out? Nobody has the exact answer. Anyone claiming to have found the solution is either deceiving oneself or others, or both. Since revolution is not a viable option, reform becomes the only choice. How to reform a despotic regime depends on a series of unpredictable factors, such as the vision and courage of reformers, the level of enlightenment among the general public, the divided interests within the ruling group, the amount of tension created by social conflicts, and the impact of international political pressure. These uncertain factors make reform more of an art than a predictable science, akin to "crossing the river by feeling the stones" (摸着石头过河).[12]

Fortunately, an increasing number of Chinese people have come to realize the destination they are striving for, even though they may not yet know the precise paths to get there. While the liberals debated with the leftists whether the Chinese economy should be labeled as "socialist" or "capitalist," and intellectuals were perplexed about the future of the nation in the early stage of Chinese reform, those capable of independent thinking today recognize constitutional democracy, rule of law, and respect for human rights as their own aspirations. The occasional resurgence of leftist ideologies is merely a

[12] The oft-quoted phrase stands for a cautious, pragmatic strategy of development dating back to the 1950s, and was reintroduced by the conservative leader Chen Yun at the CCPCC work conference in December 1980. See Xu Qingquan, "Crossing the river by feeling the stones," *DW Chinese* (August 19, 2020), www.dw.com/zh/摸着石头过河漫话中共党史术语系列之三/a-54594439.

fading trend, as even the leftists are beginning to realize that their own future, like that of the liberals, lies in effective constitutional protection of basic freedoms.[13] Those utopian leftists who romanticize Chairman Mao are engaging in wishful thinking born out of total ignorance of modern Chinese history due to brainwashing. Just like the small minority of radical rightists seeking violent revolution, the utopian leftists will remain mere memories of history. They may persist for some time, but they cannot dominate the mainstream because idealistic visions or radical revolution cannot solve China's practical problems. Nor is maintaining the status quo a feasible solution because the current political system, unable to address the social problems it continually creates, will eventually collapse without reform, pushing China back to the forefront of revolution. After a century of constitutional failures, China today has no way out but to continue moving forward until it finds the true path to constitutionalism. With the exception of a small and short-sighted vested interest group, people from all walks of life in China, regardless of their positions, interests, classes, identities, or social status, have no reason or interest to oppose constitutional reform that will do them good. Since neither republican nor Communist revolution brought true constitutionalism to China, nor did they create a genuine republic, what China needs today is a new republican movement. Only through this third republican movement can constitutionalism find its destiny in China.

What does "republic" mean to China? "Republic" is not a legal concept with a precise definition. Various regimes can be labeled as "republics." Strictly speaking, for example, the United Kingdom is a monarchy, but it is also called a "commonwealth," something close to a republic. Unlike the Chinese emperor, the British monarch is not the sole supreme ruler; instead, the King in the Parliament, an association of the King and the two Houses, shares supreme governing power. Since the Glorious Revolution in 1688–89, the King's powers have gradually shifted to the Parliament and its elected Cabinet. Regardless of its name or form, the primary characteristic of a true republic is popular sovereignty.

To be sure, a republic is not simply a majoritarian democracy. It is commonly understood to be more moderate than a simple democracy because

[13] A prominent example was the labor movement in the summer of 2018, supported by the leftist students from major universities in Beijing and elsewhere. In fact, one of the student leaders, Yue Xin, was once a frequent attendee of my freshman constitutional law classes when she was an undergraduate at Peking University. The movement was quickly and harshly suppressed by the government. Ran Ran, "The rise of Chinese leftist youth and the official suppression," BBC Chinese News (December 28, 2018), www.bbc.com/zhongwen/simp/chinese-news-46616052.

pure majority rule may lead to the "tyranny of the majority," allowing a parliament representing the interests of the bare majority to deprive minorities of their basic rights through legislation. Instead, a republic in its Chinese expression, *gonghe* (共和), means "common peace (or harmony)," advocating for the respect of every person's basic rights, freedom, and dignity. This difference does not negate the fact that republicanism and democracy share the same foundation. To deserve the title of a "republic," the rulers of the state must be somehow held accountable to the people, and such accountability should be more than nominal. Almost all constitutions today refer to their own statehood as "republics," but the nature of the state ultimately depends on the actual conditions of democratic governance and human rights protection within that state. If the constitution provides for elections, yet the actual electoral process is so manipulated that officials at all levels are not held meaningfully accountable to the voters, then such a "republic" is merely a misnomer for dictatorship.

As shown above, a despotic state is trapped in the cycle of reform-revolution-tyranny. This is the very reason why such a state is prone to triggering revolutions or riots because a ruling group that is not held accountable to its people has no need to take their life and death into due consideration, and its callousness alone can create enough stupidity, misery, and anger to bring about its own downfall. The lack of democratic accountability has made it impossible to replace corrupt or inept officials through peaceful means and these officials, unrestrained by law or votes, are bound to act recklessly. Moreover, in a top-down system where the dictator has the final say, in order to maintain the facade of prosperity, stability, and harmony, the handicapped media can only report "good news" while concealing the bad. Most instances of corruption and social suffering are swept under the carpet of censorship. As a result, both leaders and ordinary people are kept in the dark about the true predicament in which they are situated. They may well be sitting on top of an imminent erupting volcano without knowing it. As social tensions build up faster than they are removed, there comes a point where massive conflicts erupt.

Worse still, a despotic regime not only hampers its own governing ability, but also hinders society from assisting and providing for itself. It exacerbates social disparities, creating a nation of strangers where the government and the governed, the rich and the poor, the elites and the grassroots, the leftists and the rightists mingle together without a common language and mutual understanding. Living with conflicting mindsets but sharing the same confined space, they inevitably generate friction, contempt, jealousy, and even hatred towards each other. While the owner of a luxury car may stigmatize bus riders as "scums," wage earners see their employers as "exploiters." In a society where people are not empowered to govern themselves through free communications, divisions, hatred and, ultimately, revolution become an inevitable outcome. As Tocqueville keenly observed, despotism and the resulting social ills are the very sparks of revolution.[14]

In comparison, the greatest advantage of a democratic republic lies in its capacity to maintain social stability and harmony. Since the people have the right to elect representatives of their choice every few years, unqualified officials will be eliminated in due course. In such a regime, the parliament will pass laws favored by the majority and empower an accountable administration to implement those laws. To be sure, occasionally a dishonest candidate may deceive a naïve electorate and fail to fulfill extravagant promises after assuming office, but their luck will quickly run out as the electorate will not be fooled once again in the next election. Before long, like a tarnished brand, they will have to pay the heavy cost of losing their political career. The 2008 presidential election in Taiwan served as another testimony to the fact that people are not idiots, nor are they mere puppets of politicians. Elections are more than a word game or a result of money politics. After several rounds, voters have become more mature, politicians better behaved, elections more genuine, and the fate of the common people is now in their own hands.

Once the government is made accountable, social problems can be readily solved. First, officials, now under the pressure of accountability, are motivated to address social issues promptly; otherwise, they run the risk of being removed from office. Second, even if current laws fail to align with the majority's preferences, social policies can be adjusted through an elected parliament, constantly alleviating social tensions. Last and most important, liberal democracy is based on freedom of speech and the press. How else would voters know who to vote for? Unrestrained expressions constantly bring emerging social concerns to public attention, and the natural empathy towards misfortune compels the common people to urge the government to take adequate actions, thereby preventing social issues from developing into major crises. In fact, even before the government intervenes, many problems can be resolved through face-to-face debates and negotiations among the people themselves. While there may be intense clashes of interests and opinions, even raucous mutual accusations, they are far better than forced silence and indifference. And even if argumentations fail to produce a viable

[14] Alexis de Tocqueville, *The Old Regime and the French Revolution*, trans. Stuart Gilbert (New York: Doubleday, 1955), pp. 107, 136.

solution, they at least provide all parties with the opportunity to air their views and vent frustration.

Therefore, in a mature republic, revolutions are rarely found. Since officials dare not act lawlessly, and effectively enforced laws continue to adapt to new realities, clearing away social problems like daily waste, most people live in a reasonably comfortable and pleasant environment, and the unfortunate few are hopefully cared for by a sympathetic majority. Even if a handful of radicals lose their minds and incite riots, they remain isolated crimes rather than a sweeping revolution that is dangerous enough to threaten the regime. While democracy achieves stability through shared harmony, despotism imposes coerced stability at the expense of true peace. A despotic regime is like a dam, with troubled water constantly rising. Once the dammed water reaches the limit, it will simply collapse under the unbearable weight. On the other hand, democracy is like a floodway, continuously adjusting its direction and relieving pressure by facilitating exchanges between the government and the governed. It may sound paradoxical, but the truth is that a despotic regime is the natural ally of revolution, while a democratic republic is its nemesis, preserving social peace through continuous legislative reforms. If a nation genuinely desires political stability, then a true republic is its only choice.

Of course, the hope of constitutional reform ultimately lies not in the leaders but in the people themselves, who alone have the most direct and durable interest in rational governance and social harmony. We bid farewell to revolution today in order to move away from tyranny and towards a true republic, and jointly found a constitutional government which the previous revolutions had failed to achieve. The Third Republic will no longer follow the old path of revolutionary violence, nor does it need a revolutionary vanguard, which will only lead China towards even harsher tyranny and farther away from constitutionalism. As a shared cause for common people, constitutionalism can only succeed through the joint efforts of all. If the people have been subjected to slavery for so long and, as a result, have become accustomed to the slavish way of life, then sadly they are only suitable for tyranny and cannot adapt to a republic, where citizens are the masters of their own destiny.

To break free from slavery, the people must first learn how to govern themselves, beginning with self-associations and the lowest level of governance. Direct face-to-face negotiations and mutual understanding will solve many problems without government intervention. Even though some employers are unconscientious, if workers have the rights to organize themselves, elect their own union leaders, use collective bargaining power, or appeal to the support of public opinion, then they do not have to beg the government to demand the wages for them, as the former Premier Wen Jiabao once did during his term for migrant workers.[15] While he was conscientious enough to help the unpaid workers, how many of them could a single man approaching his seventies possibly help? Nor is it necessary for any workers to commit suicide for that purpose, even if that is no more than a show to attract public attention.[16] In a republic, no one will be reduced to a totally helpless "vulnerable group" (弱势群体) due to factors beyond one's control, such as status, gender, age, or wealth. Even the smallest minority can still count on the protection of the judiciary or the sympathy of the majority. In a self-governing community, everyone has social resources on which one can rely. The greater the number of these self-governing individuals, the stronger is the community.

To be sure, the people still need the state to serve their interests, but citizens in a republic differ fundamentally from subjects in a despotic regime, who are weak and vulnerable before the government. While the constitution may provide for a long list of rights, none on the list has been substantially enforced. In fact, the government itself is reduced to moral vulnerability due to its lack of democratic legitimacy. As the legitimacy of the regime derives entirely from economic growth, it will lose the last vestige of its authority as soon as the economy stagnates. Officials at all levels are trembling about unexpected natural and human disasters within their jurisdiction, fearing that they will become the scapegoat of the "veto by single vote" (一票否决) mechanism in a "merit system" (政绩体制).[17] In contrast, in a true republic, a government will win votes, respect, and self-confidence as long as it does its own job without constantly trembling over unexpected emergencies beyond its control. Since "the eyes of the people are bright," as often quoted in official propaganda, ordinary people can judge the local officials' performance and responsibilities more accurately and fairly than their superiors. Without the pressure to achieve superficial "merits," local officials have no need to act as entrepreneurs, pulling in investments and running construction projects everywhere, by hook or crook, disregarding the social consequences of recklessly boosting local GDP. As long as they can ensure the basic common good

[15] Cai Chongguo, "The failure of Wen Jiabao," *BBC Chinese* (November 9, 2005), http://news.bbc.co.uk/chinese/simp/hi/newsid_4420000/newsid_4420900/4420946.stm.

[16] To be sure, some suicides were real. See "Seven peasant workers committed suicide after failing to get paid," 新京报 (October 27, 2004), http://news.sina.com.cn/c/2004-10-27/04164046097s.shtml.

[17] The veto system assesses an official's qualifications based on several key criteria. Failure to meet any single criterion results in disqualification. For instance, a major security incident occurring within a mayor's jurisdiction may lead to his disqualification. See Chapter 4 for more on the merit system.

in their jurisdiction – that eligible children have equal opportunity to go to school, the elderly have social security, and patients have medical insurance – in short, that the local people live a decent life commensurate with their dignity as humans, then they can safely expect to win at the ballot box. They will find that votes are more reliable than relationships in the official circle and that rational voters are more reasonable than unpredictable superiors.

The benefits of a republic to the ordinary people, as implied in the very nature of the polity, are self-evident. They no longer have to worry about losing their homes or land without just compensation, nor do they have to suffer from air, water, and food pollution caused by irresponsible "development." They no longer have to pay for the rampant corruption and all sorts of public waste, from luxury government buildings and cars to exotic medical care of officials at all levels, who will enjoy the full benefits even after their retirement, all out of their pockets as taxpayers. Nor do they have to silently endure endless stories of public power abuses. All of these abuses are a high-stakes gamble made by a few with the public interest as their wager. The republic merely returns it to its rightful owners from the hands of the gamblers. In a true republic, the interests and resources will no longer be plundered by these gamblers, since their distribution and utilization will be determined by representatives held accountable to their voters. As a result, the distribution of interests will be more balanced and the utilization of resources more efficient.

The hope of constitutionalism ultimately lies in the transformation of the people themselves – from subjects of a despotic regime to citizens of a democratic republic – because the precondition to a balanced distribution of interests is a balanced distribution of powers, which are effectively supervised only by competent citizens who put them in office. True citizens not only possess republican virtues such as reason, tolerance, love of freedom, and obedience to the law, but also hold certain expectations for the state institutions. They obey legitimate authority while maintaining their own dignity, tolerate the difference in opinions among their fellow citizens while retaining the freedom to criticize the government, maintain personal independence while insisting on the right to association and assembly, never evade taxes but always demand to know how their tax money is spent. They oblige themselves to participate in elections, but insist that the election must be meaningful, implying that their vote must be an informed and free choice. To be a choice, candidates must be freely generated rather than selected behind the scenes. The choice must be free, so it cannot be subjected to coercion or instructions of the party-state, and informed, so the communication between candidates and voters must be unimpeded: Candidates must be free to fully display their platforms, and voters have every right to obtain political information from free media. Put together, votes representing various choices must also be equally counted, ensuring "one-person, one-vote," regardless of voter's status as man or woman, rich or poor, urban or rural.

Representing the interests of the vast majority, the representative body thus elected will naturally be "oriented to the people," an ideal consistently expressed in the Chinese tradition, from Mencius (孟子) two millennia ago to Hu Jintao who proposed humanistic CCP slogans in 2003. The laws an elected parliament passes will no longer serve the interests of the few in power. The officials will no longer dare to build luxurious government buildings or use public funds to indulge in lavish dining and travel because all budgets must be approved by a parliament that is responsible to the voters. The air and water qualities will be improved by regulations made according to the law, which will be effectively enforced under public supervision; officers who fail to enforce the law will be arraigned and replaced by the parliament. Buying and selling official positions, so commonplace today, will become obsolete because the superior will no longer be able to usurp the people's power to appoint and dismiss the subordinates, thus having no position for sale, in an electoral democracy where the officials are ultimately responsible to the public rather than their superior. A citizen of a republic can thus stay far from the embarrassment of systematic scandals, corruption, pollution, and waste, and lead a peaceful life in proportion to his dignity common to all humans because the republican institutions operate for the benefit of all. Even if some social groups become minorities on particular issues, they can still uphold their constitutional rights through independent and impartial justice to counter the tyranny of the majority.

This is the type of life that a citizen can legitimately expect from a republic. It is nothing luxurious, but it is possible only in a true republic. If China is still far from achieving such a moderated condition despite two revolutions under the name of "republic," that simply means that it needs a new civil movement to found a true republic through which the Chinese become true citizens. Citizens and republic are an inseparable symbiont: The republic is based on citizens, and citizens need the republican institutions for the recognition and preservation of their political identity. "Citizen" in Chinese signifies a "public person" (公民) – "public" because citizens expect a public life, in which the republican institutions allow them to effectively control public power. As soon as the public power is out of control, the republic ceases to exist. To maintain a republic, then, it is necessary to cultivate the new generations with the public spirit. Once the people aspire to become citizens, the state is already a republic, even if not by name.

1.4 PATHS OF CONSTITUTIONAL REFORMS

Although a moderate republic outlined above is not an infeasible utopia, nor is it a free lunch that comes without effort. Particularly, the road on which a despotic regime transitions into a republic is full of blunders, constantly encountering the obstructions of vested interest, frustrations with reforms, and passions for revolution. The keen observation of a late Qing official, Zai Ze (载泽), accurately summed up China's century-long constitutional dilemma: "The implementation of constitutionalism is beneficial to the country and the people, but most detrimental to the officials."[18] The ruling elites have been the greatest obstacle to China's century-long trial of constitutionalism, which threatens to diminish their power and vested interest. To be sure, from a more enlightened view, constitutionalism is *not* disadvantageous even to officials; at least it would add much to the prestige, public trust, and thus the longevity of the party-state as a whole. However, constitutional reform cannot exclusively rely on the leaders' vision or goodwill. After all, mortals are self-interested, often myopically. Especially when the future is uncertain, they are most likely narrowly self-centered. There is no reason to expect that leaders possess exceptional qualities, enabling them to transcend ordinary human limitations. Constitutionalism is apparently disadvantageous to each incumbent, at least in the short term: Once free elections are allowed, incumbents face the serious risk of defeat. Even if re-elected, a genuine election itself will create unprecedented pressures on all officials, as in the reform experiments in some localities during the 1990s, since the election results are no longer guaranteed by near "unanimous approval."

As an example of a genuine election, Ma Ying-jeou's victory over Hsieh Chang-ting in Taiwan's presidential contest in 2008 was clear enough to make his win "secure," but a candidate accustomed to nominations within the party-state must have seen it as a frightening process full of suspense. Even if successfully elected, constitutional democracy will greatly constrain the official's power to control resources. While officials may still receive a decent salary, they will lose a variety of rent-seeking opportunities and sources of illicit income. Wealth and resources, previously controlled by the officials, now flow to society; a limited government, one which "stores wealth among the people" (藏富于民), is necessarily reduced to an "office of clear water" (清水衙门), offering little opportunity for profiteering. In such a government, official positions are no longer hot trade items since the limited benefit to be gained

[18] Jing Zhiren, *Constitutional History of China* [in Chinese] (Taipei: Taiwan Lianjing Press, 1984), p. 101.

from holding these positions will not compensate the cost. Candidates for villagers' committee elections in resource rich areas used to spend millions to buy votes – certainly not out of their altruistic desire to serve villagers. As soon as the power to control resources such as coal mines is regulated for the common benefit of villagers, they will immediately cease their seemingly foolish activities.[19] Indeed, many resource-stricken areas can hardly find a candidate to run for the village election.

As China's ruling group is still the greatest beneficiary of the current power structure, it is certainly unwilling to abandon or change such a system. Therefore, China's constitutional reform will not happen unless the ruling group becomes exceptionally enlightened. The chance for this to happen is slight, however, given the tortuous path of constitutional reforms in the past century. Only when it faces increasing social pressure, to the point where it can hardly survive without necessary reform, can reformers like Gorbachev or Chiang Ching-kuo appear in mainland China. Even then, the condition for a successful reform is demanding since it requires the reformers to maintain the ruling power after reform, so that they can dodge attacks of the vested interest, while sustaining political credibility and popular support among the grassroots.

Ultimately, the pressure or impetus for reform comes from the people themselves. Since constitutionalism is a cause in everyone's interest, it is evident that this cause shall be promoted by all. China's road to constitutionalism will not be guided by any philosopher, nor will it be pioneered by any wise ruling party or leader, but is to be gradually built at the first place by the people themselves in the process of making a new republic together. To paraphrase Lu Xun (鲁迅), perhaps the most influential left-wing writer in modern China, having experienced the long despotic tradition, particularly the totalitarian devastation in the past century, China had no path to constitutionalism to begin with; the path is opening up only in recent decades, when more people have started to "walk" it. In the four decades since the Reform and Opening in 1978, the Chinese people have become increasingly free. They not only broke the shackles of the "People's Communes" (人民公社) and the planned economy, and succeeded in meeting the basic needs of

[19] The best example was the Wukan village in Guangdong province, where the villagers voted out the villagers' committee that sold their land behind their back. Martin Patience, "China's Wukan village stands up for land rights," *BBC News* (December 15, 2011), www.bbc.co.uk/news/world-asia-china-16205654. In less than five years, however, the salutary democratic experiment was violently put to an end by the local government. Stephen McDonell, "China's protest village of Wukan crushed," *BBC News* (September 13, 2016), www.bbc.com/news/blogs-china-blog-37351737.

subsistence, even approaching the stage of "primitive prosperity" (小康), but also came into contact with new ideas, information, and institutions. At the same time as the opportunities for government corruption, power abuses, and rights violations increase, the people become more conscious of their rights and dignity. These two opposite trends inevitably clash. Although the current constitutional framework cannot effectively resolve the conflicts of interest between the government and the governed, and the news media cannot freely report "bad news," collisions between rights and power have still achieved some hard-won progress.

The landmark case was the Sun Zhigang (孙志刚) incident, which occurred during the SARS outbreak in 2003. The abnormal death of a university graduate in a detention center aroused national indignation, leading the State Council to abolish within a few months the Detention and Repatriation (收容遣送) system that had seriously violated personal freedom for decades.[20] The tragedy not only triggered massive protests, especially on the internet, but also drew the attention of the national leadership through a joint letter from three young legal scholars. Although the petition to the Standing Committee of the National People's Congress – the highest body authorized to interpret the Constitution – failed to receive a direct response that would have broken the zero record of constitutional interpretation maintained for three decades since the Constitution was promulgated in 1982, the Detention and Repatriation system was quickly reformed through administrative intervention. Despite its limitations, the Sun Zhigang incident demonstrated the driving force of social pressure towards constitutionalism.

More important, it opened up an era of constitutional movements. From then on, successful events of rights defense (维权) have largely followed the pattern of the Sun Zhigang incident, which can be properly categorized as "Sun Zhigang model." It starts with a local tragedy caused by a bad institution – one which has been encouraging serious abuses of public power. The report of such tragedy sparks a national protest, which ultimately succeeds in attracting the attention of the national authority. In order to maintain its public image, the ruling party directly intervenes, not only correcting certain local violations but, in some circumstances, also reforming the very institution that results in the tragedy. Both the She Xianglin (佘祥林) case (2005), which involved an eleven-year wrongful conviction caused by forced confession, and the Shanxi Brick Kiln (山西黑砖窑) case (2007), a long-standing slave labor factory allowed by the local governments, achieved limited success under

20 Zhang, "A constitution without constitutionalism? The paths of constitutional developments in China," 950–76.

limited media supervision, national pressure, and intervention from the central government.[21]

To be sure, more enlightened local governments will not wait for national instructions before correcting errors under popular pressure. For example, in June 2007, Xiamen citizens used text messages to gather in front of the city hall to "take a walk," knowing that a normal application for a parade would always be rejected by the police. They were protesting against the local plan for a PX chemical project, which was perceived as a threat to the local environment and health. After a few rounds of confrontations, the Xiamen government was forced to "suspend" the project.

Overall, however, incidents of successful rights defense are rare, and even when they are ultimately successful, they are extremely difficult to achieve. The Xiamen incident was achieved through the bravery, deliberate strategy, and persistent struggle of local residents despite many setbacks. Shortly after the incident, the national media was forbidden from reporting. The ultimate success seemed to rely not only on bottom-up popular pressure but also on unpredictable fortuitous factors. One year after the Xiamen incident, hundreds of Chengdu citizens took to the streets for a similar "walk" to protest against a very similar petrochemical project. The protest not only failed to change the government's plan, but also led to the arrest of six activists on various charges, such as illegal assembly, spreading rumors online, inciting riots, and even "subverting the state power."

In a situation where the existing power structure remains unchanged, all elections are heavily manipulated. As a result, the people's congresses at all levels essentially serve as "rubber stamps," and officials are accountable only to their superiors. Since China's rights movement is anti-establishment in nature, it is necessarily an uphill battle, experiencing many more failures than successes. The basic dilemma of China's rights movement is that it is superficially "within the system" (体制内), seeking to protect constitutional and legal rights through existing institutional arrangements. In substance, however, it threatens to take away spoils of the vested interest, an effort almost doomed to failure. Although the Constitution and laws provide for many rights, the nature of the party-state inherently opposes the effectuation of any right. The entire institutional setup, from its nominal election system to the unlimited, absolute party power and the absence of judicial independence, aims to protect the vested interest. If top-down proactive reform lacks sufficient momentum, bottom-up rights movements also face the basic dilemma of reforming the system from within itself: The state machinery is controlled

21 Ibid.

by the very vested interest that the reform might undermine. While the chance of success in such rights movements is indeed slim, it seems to be the only safe option available for China's constitutionalism.

To succeed in constitutional reform, organizational resources are critical. How can people from outside the system (体制外) exert pressures on those within the system to make decisions that are unfavorable to the vested interest? The way in which the question is posed makes it hard to answer, but it is not entirely hopeless because the Chinese rights movements are *not* completely without resources. First, social justice is on their side simply because they are fighting for the legitimate interests of the vast majority. The rights and interests of the people are not only morally just, but also explicitly stipulated in the Constitution and laws. To be sure, the Constitution is currently a useless facade, but if Chinese society has not completely degenerated into a jungle of brute force and if Confucius was right to an extent when he said that "if the cause is not upright, the speech will not be convincing; if the speech is not convincing, the thing will not get done,"[22] then even a facade is not completely insignificant.

For instance, when a sixty-year-old man stood in front of a developer's bulldozer holding the Constitution, he was undoubtedly physically weak. Even the compensation clause amended to the Constitution (in 2004) cannot add any weight to his property right.[23] However, without the seemingly "useless" Constitution he was holding in his hand, he would have been no more than one of thousands of feeble men and women whose property was taken away by their governments. Nevertheless, he could still cause a great emotional stir across the nation simply because the Constitution endowed him with moral power. In fact, the current Constitution is more than a mere collection of political slogans that have never been taken seriously; it also contains many provisions that can be activated in daily life. Since the ruling party itself emphasizes governing the state according to the Constitution and laws, at least constitutional arguments can be made from time to time. Although an effective implementation mechanism is conspicuously lacking despite recent efforts at establishing the filing and review (备案审查) procedure, the government has bowed to the rise of citizens' rights consciousness, as evidenced by constitutional amendments such as "the state respects and protects human rights," "private property is inviolable" and "compensation shall be given for expropriation" (all enacted in 2004). Despite the lack of constitutional implementation, the textual progress itself is the result of the

[22] *Analects*, 13: 3.
[23] "The strongest holdout sticks to the isolated house," 《新京报》 (23 March 2007).

citizens' rights movement. At the very least, the party-state is obliged to pay lip service to these clauses. Even though "constitutionalism" has become a sensitive word in recent years, the government has never been daring enough to openly assail the Constitution itself. The sentiment of the majority carries moral strength, which incites public opinion and exerts public pressure. Once the abuse of power exceeds the extent that the public is willing to tolerate, nationwide anger will generate mounting pressure on the government.

Second, the media in diverse forms contributes to the citizen's right to know despite tight state control. In a constitutional democracy where press freedom is protected, major events can never escape media coverage and public scrutiny. Although press freedom in China is severely restricted, more often than not, "paper cannot hold burning fire" (纸包不住火) after all. Incidents such as the Sun Zhigang tragedy, She Xianglin case, the Shanxi Brick Kiln scandal, the Xiamen chemical project and the chained woman in Xuzhou were all exposed one after another. As a vast nation, China has not only many local governments but also numerous media outlets with different positions, aspirations, and courage. Despite strict government regulations, it is difficult to keep all media outlets silent at every moment. In order to maximize news value, public attraction, and private profit, the Chinese media was becoming increasingly more diverse. Many media outlets hired "pseudo reporters," who claimed and acted as reporters without formal qualifications. In a regime where media is tightly regulated, however, the news they uncovered often turned out to be even more accurate than that of true reporters. With the increasingly developed internet and the growing number of netizens, controlling information exchange became an even more formidable task. Despite constant attempts of government control, online speech proved to be more elusive than traditional media. As the cost of media control rises with the increase of media diversity, the role of media in expressing public opinion and exerting public pressure is expected to become more significant. As a result, even though press freedom was extremely limited, greatly diminishing the power of public opinion, public opinion is something that the government cannot simply ignore once expressed.

A related consideration is the voices of Chinese intellectuals from various camps. As Liang Qichao observed in the late Qing dynasty, a despotic regime is characterized by a considerable gap between the government and the governed, resulting in mutual mistrust and a lack of affection.[24] The role of

[24] Liang Qichao, *On New People* [in Chinese] (Beijing: Chinese Literature and History Press, 2013), ch. 2.

constitutional democracy is precisely to bridge such a gap, in which intellectuals, situated somewhere between the government and the governed, are expected to play a unique role. Depending on their distance from the regime, some are "court-hired literati" (御用文人) who thrive within the system by defending the government, while others are reformers within the system, and still others are public intellectuals who survive on the fringes of the system, acting as advocates for the public interest and critics of governments. In an ideal situation, both reformers and public intellectuals can contribute to constitutional reform in their own ways: While public intellectuals can mobilize the people, reformers can advise the government. It should be noted that several progressive constitutional amendments, including liberal concepts such as the "rule of law," "human rights" and "private property," were passed with the advocacy of reformers within the system.

In fact, the ideological distribution among China's active intellectuals today, whether within academia or not, is astonishingly uniform with respect to constitutional reform despite apparent disparities in other issues. Unlike ordinary people who may have been thoroughly brainwashed, intellectuals with experience and knowledge of Western civilization hardly believe in the official propaganda. The "official literati" sound anti-Western not because they genuinely believe in what they say, but because they say it to please the government and promote their own interests. In fact, it is often said that their legs move more sincerely than their lips since they, along with the officials they flatter, are eager to send their money and families, particularly their offspring, to advanced Western countries. Hardly any intellectuals born from the 1950s to the 1970s are oblivious to past tragedies such as the Anti-Rightist Campaign, the Great Famine, or the Cultural Revolution. Nor does anyone seriously dispute today's rampant corruption, abuse of power, and human rights violations. Almost everyone agrees that these abuses and violations are illegitimate, and change is necessary.

Although camps with different ideological orientations may advocate different strategies, the debates primarily revolve around prioritization rather than overall goals. Both political and economic systems are in need of reform, but which should take precedence at present? Similarly, both democracy and the rule of law are deemed necessary, but which should be implemented first? The debates over values between liberals and the so-called New Left are natural in an increasingly pluralistic society, so long as the latter refrains from aligning with the totalitarian regime. The people themselves will decide the future winner of these debates based on the utility of particular schools of thought for China's social and political development, just as they did in the 1978 debate over the standards of truth (真理标准), which paved the way for market reform in the subsequent decades.[25] Overall, as mediators between the government and the people, Chinese intellectuals will contribute to China's constitutional reform in their own ways.

Finally, unlike a revolution, constitutional reform is impossible without the support of the government. A consistent reformer can be highly critical of the government without intending to demolish it, let alone criminalize the vast majority of ordinary civil servants or public employees who possess limited decision-making power and therefore limited opportunities for corruption. Despite decades of reverse selection since 1989, there still *are* "good people" (好人) within the system. Particularly in situations where personal interests are not involved, these people may actively promote institutional reform. Regions such as Shenzhen and provinces like Sichuan, Yunnan and Shanxi had previously broken through the constitutional framework by implementing direct elections of township and county chiefs.[26] Cities or districts like Wenling in Zhejiang, Minhang in Shanghai, and Wuxi in Jiangsu had taken the lead in carrying out administrative democratization experiments under the active promotion of enlightened local leaders.[27] In fact, in a residential self-governance experiment in Hebei, in which I am personally involved, many senior Communist members and cadres actively participated in elections and volunteer works. It is important to recognize the potential for reform within the ruling group while avoiding reliance solely on a few enlightened leaders to single-handedly drive reform forward.

The key question then is how to effectively integrate all available resources for constitutional reform. For instance, how can local experiments be promoted in the right direction, staying away from the superficial "merit system" and a perfunctory bureaucratic culture? Moreover, how can China end the historical cycles of "thriving when good people are there and dying when they pass away" (人存政举、人亡政息)? In essence, what kind of support can China's constitutional reform expect to find within the system? While the space for internal reform is diminishing in the absence of effective external pressure, there may still be some room for progress.

[25] The article, drafted by a philosophy lecturer at Nanjing University, was published and propagated by the major party newspaper. It featured a prelude to cleansing the leftist ideology and leader worship, paving the road to pragmatic reform. For the official description of the event, see "Practice is the sole standard for testing truth," www.12371.cn/2021/05/11/VIDE1620688440356938.shtml.

[26] For a constitutional analysis, see Zhang Qianfan, "Constitutional flexibility and local experimentation," 《法学研究》, no. 1 (2007), 63–73.

[27] For a book-length treatment of the "Wenling model," see Li Fan, *The Wenling Experiment and the Public Budgetary Reform of Chinese Local Government* [in Chinese] (Beijing: Intellectual Property Publishing House, 2009).

To begin with, the ruling group is not a homogeneous entity. Officials have varying personalities, interests and aspirations, and institutional reforms hold different implications for officials at different levels. For lower-level officials, promoting grassroots elections is tantamount to a revolution taking away their own power, leading to staunch resistance. However, higher-level officials may hear complaints and feel pressured, but are not directly affected by grassroots reforms, and thus may not necessarily oppose these reforms. In fact, direct elections of township leaders in provinces like Yunnan and Sichuan had been promoted by higher-level governments or party committees. Therefore, it is not impossible to gradually implement democratic elections at lower-level governments, where the deputies of people's congresses are constitutionally required to be directly elected by voters.

Of course, the bottom-up political process will inevitably clash with the top-down control of the party-state, just as village committee elections quickly encountered interference from township authorities. However, the differentiation of interests among officials at various levels has made it possible to promote grassroots reform. Particularly during the decade when Hu Jintao served as the CCP General Secretary, the central government introduced policies that were favorable to grassroots populations, such as peasants. However, these good policies, similar to the Constitution itself, were often hindered by local vested interest groups. As a result, the central government's orders were mocked for their inability to move beyond the confines of the Central South Sea (中南海), the highest power center of China's party-state. If the central government genuinely desires to adopt certain beneficial policies but is limited by its implementation capacity, it should support institutional reforms that make local governments more accountable to the local people, since the supervisory capacity of the central government is necessarily limited in a vast state like China. Therefore, a limited political reform can emulate the pattern of economic reform, which started from more liberal and daring jurisdictions like Guangdong, where brave local experiments were sustained by the central government and eventually spread nationwide under its auspices.

Indeed, grassroots elections can also be implemented within the ruling party itself. In the 1990s, some local party organizations in China conducted trials of "intra-party democracy" (党内民主), which reportedly yielded salutary results.[28] Competitive intra-party elections can promote the transformation of the ruling party's governing functions, rationalize its relationship with the

[28] Deng Ke, "The Yangji experiment: Electing candidates for town chief and party secretary," 《南方周末》(September 19, 2002).

government, strengthen its legislative leadership capacity, and help it gradually withdraw from its administrative and judicial functions that undermine the rule of law, a constitutional principle it purports to respect as expressed in the 2004 amendment.

Undeniably, in the absence of sufficient external and internal social pressure, these speculations may sound optimistic. If a ruling group lacks foresight and confidence, like the late Qing rulers, obstinate resistance to constitutional reform is a natural reaction. Such a trend had already appeared near Hu Jintao's second term when grassroots elections witnessed the worst central–local collusion: In order to maintain stability (维稳), the central government severely restricted press freedom, thereby granting local governments unlimited power to suppress campaign activities of independent candidates, the very soul of competitive elections. In the absence of rival competitors, the ruling party lacks sufficient pressure or motivation to initiate progressive institutional reform on its own. Since constitutional reform, qua reform, cannot be achieved without the cooperation of the ruling party, it is still necessary to tap into the potential for reform within the regime and promote the transformation of the ruling mechanism.

1.5 THE PROSPECT OF CHINESE CONSTITUTIONALISM THROUGH REUNIFICATION

The future of constitutionalism in contemporary China is just as uncertain as it was a century ago. It is neither doomed to fail nor destined to succeed. Every successful fight for rights requires enormous effort and optimal utilization of resources both inside and outside the system. Ultimately, the outcome still depends on the delicate balance of various factors. The success of individual local experiments relies on the vision and courage of a small minority of enlightened local leaders, and cannot solely depend on the sporadic support and instructions of the central government. While social awareness of rights is growing stronger, it is not yet powerful enough to compel officials at all levels to moderate their behavior and respect constitutional rights. It remains an uncharted territory as to whether the government and the governed, the central and local governments, the state, and the party, as well as different factions within the ruling party, will reconcile and establish stable institutional arrangements favorable to constitutional reform, such as term limits for the General Secretary and the separation of the Party and government.

This brings us to the issue of future political development across the Taiwan Strait. While civil society in mainland China remains weak and international support is undermined by nationalist rhetoric such as "patriotism" and "supremacy of sovereignty," it is important to remember that China still has three "satellites" – Hong Kong, Macao, and Taiwan – each enjoying varying degrees of autonomy. The future of China lies not in assimilating these institutional and cultural "exceptions" into the mainland's "mainstream," but in allowing the institutions of these "satellites" to develop and eventually influence the mainland. Obviously, China would benefit much more from having Hong Kong assimilate the mainland, rather than the other way around. However, the autonomy of Hong Kong and Macao was limited during their colonial periods, and their political democratization since their return to Chinese sovereignty is constrained by the shackles of the Basic Law, which was enacted *for* them by the National People's Congress, making them inappropriate to serve as a political model for the mainland. The prospect of the Hong Kong's influence is further diminished by the crackdown of the 2019 civilian protests and the amendment of its Basic Law incorporating the National Security Law enacted by the mainland's NPC Standing Committee, seriously undermining the "one country, two system" principle.

In contrast, Taiwan has been an independent jurisdiction and an equal competitor vis-à-vis the mainland to the claim of China's sovereignty since 1949. Despite the KMT governance under martial law for thirty-eight years, Taiwan ultimately broke free from one-party rule and achieved political transition in 1987. Judging from the presidential election in the following decades, Taiwan has emerged as a mature democracy. The electoral victory of the Nationalist candidate Ma Ying-jeou in 2008 marked the success of the second party rotation in Taiwan, not only signifying its democratic consolidation, but also alleviating concerns about the peace across the Taiwan Strait. The election convincingly demonstrated to people on both sides of the Strait that electoral democracy can be rational and trustworthy. With time and experience, people will acquire the wisdom and ability to discern extralegal factors such as disinformation, defamation and deception, and choose leaders who best represent their true interests. It is democracy that defends peace; it is the despotic regime that poses the greatest threat to the peace across the Taiwan Strait. The democratic success in Taiwan effectively shatters the myth that Chinese people are "unsuited" for democracy. It not only provides a viable constitutional framework for the peaceful reunification of China, but also exerts pressure on the mainland to undertake constitutional reform.

China's constitutional reform would receive a significant boost if, one day, the KMT in Taiwan and the CCP in the mainland could join hands for the third time and move beyond past "cooperation" to jointly establish a Third Republic. The two revolutionary parties would need to set aside past grievances, bid farewell to revolution and engage in peaceful competition with each other. Despite Taiwan's much smaller size and population compared to the mainland, its influence on the mainland is disproportionate. The mainland needs cooperation from Taiwan not only in areas such as cross-strait relations, international diplomacy, and economic and trade cooperation but, most importantly, in the prospect of sovereign reunification. These aspects can be leveraged by Taiwan to propose political cooperation for mutual benefits. Political cooperation is not only beneficial for constitutional reform in the mainland but also for Taiwan's crucial interests. Taiwan's future development, whether domestic or international, hinges critically on its relationship with the mainland. If the people of Taiwan desire peaceful coexistence with the mainland, the safest path is to help the mainland establish a government accountable to its people. Therefore, making a positive contribution to the mainland's constitutionalism is not an excessive demand on Taiwan, but aligns with Taiwan's basic interests as well as the basic interests of the world. Only through the third cooperation between the Nationalist and the Communist parties, leading to the establishment of the Third Republic, can lasting peace be achieved across the Strait.

Of course, such thinking is currently nothing more than wishful, especially in an era marked by rapid retrogression on the mainland's own reform. The political future across the Taiwan Strait will be the result of joint efforts by the people on both sides under favorable conditions, which cannot be predicted at the moment. To be sure, the third cooperation between the two parties is just one possible path, albeit perhaps the least costly one, for China's constitutional reform. If the two parties have the opportunity to "exchange swords for treasures" (化干戈为玉帛), confronting and competing with each other through the ballot box rather than on the battlefield, they can truly repay the past debts owed to China's constitutionalism. However, this is certainly not the only way. Just as Taiwan's constitutional reform succeeded without assistance from the mainland, constitutional reform in mainland China will ultimately rely on its own strength. Whether the KMT returns to the mainland in future, China's constitutional reform will continue to move forward, and the new republican movement will unfold with an irresistible momentum.

To paraphrase Sun Yat-sen, since constitutionalism has not yet succeeded, comrades still need to make efforts. Although Sun sincerely pursued a republican government, his relentless insistence on revolution and the seizure of absolute power, particularly through the adoption of the Soviet model, destroyed the seed of republican constitutionalism in China. Political developments after his death quickly proved that revolution could not bring about true constitutionalism. China today seems to have returned to the starting point of a century ago, facing the challenge of founding a republic once again. This time, however, it should not repeat the past mistakes as it did in 1911 or 1949. The new republican movement abandons gunpowder, bloodshed, and assassinations, but it requires no less wisdom, foresight, courage, and bravery than a war does. It has defendants but not enemies. It recognizes that talents, diligence, and opportunities are distributed unevenly across the population and encourages free competition. However, it does not recognize inherent superiority of any individuals, classes, or political parties, nor does it allow any faction to monopolize political power based on self-proclaimed legitimacy. It may never have its own name, but it is taking place and will continue. Unlike its predecessors, the Third Republic is to be created by the people themselves and thus truly belongs to them. It is not merely a dream cherished in their hearts, but a lasting, down-to-earth movement, through which China's constitutionalism will finally complete its unfinished journey of the past century.

The key to a true republic is the successful establishment of a social contract as its underlying constitutional foundation. As explained in this and the next chapters, however, China's First Republic had failed this mission, leading to a Second Republic that strayed to the very opposite end of constitutionalism.

2

From the Xinhai Revolution to the May Fourth Movement

Fatal Failures

2.1 INTRODUCTION

To paraphrase Tolstoy's famous opening in *Anna Karenina*: All happy nations are alike, every unhappy nation is unhappy in its own way. However, whether a nation is happy or not is neither a predetermined fate nor a result of selectively favorable "heavenly mandate" (天命).[1] While an individual may suddenly encounter good or bad luck, the fortune or misfortune of a nation has its own reasons. When examining world history, it is not difficult to find that only nations in which a substantial majority of people consciously accept the social contract are peaceful and prosperous. In such nations, the people not only live in harmony with each other, but are also capable of organizing collective actions to effectively constrain the abuse of state power. Conversely, if the vast majority of people are indifferent to or consciously reject the key elements of the social contract, peace and prosperity will remain for them an illusory dream.

As the first Chinese revolutionary leader advocated, "the trend of the world is mighty and unstoppable. Going with the flow will bring prosperity, while resisting it will lead to destruction."[2] Nations today are abandoning despotic

[1] This has been the dominant view in traditional China since at least the early Zhou (周) dynasty (ca. 1100–771 BC), when its first rulers rebelled against and defeated the Last Emperor of the Shang (商) dynasty, allegedly a tyrant who had lost the "mandate of Heaven" (天命). See Fung Yu-lan, "An outline of the historical development of Chinese philosophy," in Fung Yu-lan (ed.), *A Collection of Papers on the History of Chinese Philosophy* (Macao: Xinfeng Books, 1962), pp. 70–83.

[2] Wang Jia'an, "An examination of Sun Yat-sen's inscription on 'Global Trend,'"《团结报》(October 14, 2021), www.tuanjiewang.cn/2021-10/14/content_8918448.htm.

regimes one after another because they obstruct the free formation of their social contract. Without the social contract as the ultimate basis of political legitimacy, the state constitution will either make hollow promises or degenerate into straight bad law.[3] Such a system may maintain temporary peace, but it is destined to be a fragile peace, susceptible to major upheavals. As the inevitable result of centralized absolute despotism without a social contract, China's cyclical changes of dynasties were always accompanied by immense violence and loss of life.[4] Unfortunately, millennia of top-down vertical domination seem to have deprived its people of the ability to form horizontal agreements on a national scale. As a result, when opportunities to construct a political contract approached modern China, they were invariably squandered. Indeed, misguided by revolutionary ideologies, China not only failed to rid itself of traditional authoritarian tyranny, but also veered towards totalitarian dictatorship.

In 1911, the year of Xinhai (辛亥), the Wuchang Uprising (武昌起义) brought an abrupt end to the millennia-old imperial system in China and established the first republic in Asia. Unfortunately, revolution itself is the mortal enemy of social contract. The prerequisite for contract-based politics is that parties with conflicting interests and positions are willing to reach agreements through negotiation, leading to peaceful reforms. On the other hand, once revolutionary violence erupts, the opposing parties plunge into a life-and-death rivalry, making it impossible to form an agreement acceptable to all parties. In this sense, although the Xinhai Revolution is often eulogized as "China's Glorious Revolution," it differed fundamentally from the Glorious Revolution. From the Chinese perspective, indeed, the British Glorious Revolution of 1688–89 cannot be considered a typical "revolution" (革命), not only because it was essentially bloodless, but more importantly, the abdication of James II merely changed the monarch without altering the British monarchy.[5]

In contrast, although the Xinhai Revolution resulted in relatively little bloodshed, it was a genuine revolution because it not only ousted an emperor, but also abolished the monarchy. Revolutionary leader Sun Yat-sen was determined to "carry the revolution through to the end" until his Nationalist Party (国民党) succeeded in monopolizing state power. To be sure, compared with the Civil War between the Nationalists and the Communists in 1946–49,

[3] Qianfan Zhang, "A constitution without constitutionalism? The paths of constitutional developments in China," *International Journal of Constitutional Law* 8 (2010): 950–76.

[4] Qin Hui, *Out of the Monarchy* [in Chinese] (Beijing: Qunyan Press, 2015), pp. 47–55.

[5] John Miller, "The Glorious Revolution: 'Contract' and 'Abdication' Reconsidered," *The Historical Journal* 25 (1982): 544–55.

the almost bloodless Xinhai Revolution implied possibilities for contract-based politics after the Republic was established. Unfortunately, since both the idea and practice of social contract had been entirely foreign to traditional China, social reform had always depended on the top-down approach. If the supreme ruler refused to change, the only option was to remove the vested interest through revolutionary violence, which inevitably resulted in the winner-takes-all scenario and one-party rule. As a result, not only did the reforms towards the end of the Qing dynasty fail, but the cooperation between the new and old forces quickly disintegrated after the Xinhai Revolution. By 1919, the Chinese public and intellectuals had already grown disillusioned with republican politics, which was repeatedly hijacked by various warlords. Coupled with the decline of democracy in postwar Europe and the rise of the Soviet Union, China's mainstream ideology rapidly shifted towards totalitarianism and decisively departed from contract-based politics.

There have been many accounts of the Chinese reforms, revolutions, and the causes of their failure. Here is mine, a reformist perspective that relates to my theory of social contract and its critical role in constitutional reforms. This chapter begins by briefly summarizing the basic structure and formation of social contract, while highlighting its absence in traditional China and the resulting consequences. A comparison is drawn between Chinese and British political traditions to underscore the disparity. It then delves into the examination of the contract-based politics during the late Qing dynasty and early Republic, analyzing the reasons behind its failure. Finally, this chapter illustrates the systematic suppression of press freedom and the decisive shift in mainstream opinion before and after the May Fourth Movement, supported by the statistical data on the number of newspaper articles during that period featuring keywords such as "social contract" (民约), "reform," and "revolution" (革命). A free press is crucial for fostering a minimally sophisticated public opinion, which in turn is a necessary prerequisite for forming an informed, rational society capable of supporting gradual reforms and resisting irrational revolutionary ideologies. The complete ignorance and disregard for contract-based politics among China's ruling circle and society at large led to a rapid descent into an entangled trap of totalitarian politics in the post–May Fourth China.

2.2 THE STRUCTURE AND FORMATION OF SOCIAL CONTRACT

Before elaborating on the trial and failure of China's contract-based politics in the republican era, a brief conceptual explanation of social contract and its building mechanism is in order. Although social contract is an old topic, it is commonly misunderstood, making it necessary to clarify the concept before it can be taken seriously in political practice.

2.2.1 *The Basic Structure of Social Contract*

Since Hobbes published his *Leviathan* in 1651, various versions of social contract theory have presented the social contract as a normative fiction that provides justification for the establishment of the state. The social contract is depicted as either an agreement among the people to establish a sovereign (Hobbes), or a delegation of authority from the people to the sovereign based on trust (Locke), or a combination of both (Rousseau).[6] As a social contract agreed upon by all individuals has never actually existed, the classical theories treat it as a hypothetical thought experiment used to assess the legitimacy of the state. Given the theoretical fallacies and practical injuries resulting from those "thought experiments" based on wrong methodologies,[7] however, a genuine social contract theory must strictly adhere to methodological individualism and empiricism. The social contract is not merely a fictional construct; rather, it is a genuine agreement reached among real, concrete, and living individuals in the actual world. Ideally, it is a foundational agreement that all rational individuals, concerned with their long-term interests, would reach. In practice, however, not everyone is rational enough to actually reach such an agreement.

To be sure, it is impossible to achieve an ideal scenario where all members of society unanimously agree upon the social contract, regardless of how basic and indispensable it may be. In fact, this is precisely the challenge faced by every real society, where only a portion of the population can reach a basic agreement required for constructing a legitimate state. Such an agreement can either be explicitly expressed as laws or implicitly understood as unwritten norms. The crucial factor that determines the fate of a nation is the size and strength of the group of citizens constituting the "contract community." A "happy" or "lucky" nation is one where the contract community comprises a significant majority of society, capable of transforming the basic elements of the social contract into constitutional practices, from which the remaining individuals can simply benefit as free riders. Conversely, if the contract

6 J. W. Gough, *The Social Contract* (Oxford: Clarendon Press, 1957), pp. 142–73; Michel Rosenfeld, "Contract and justice: The relation between classical contract law and social contract theory," *Iowa Law Review* 70 (1985): 769, 865–73; Miller, "The Glorious Revolution," 543–4.

7 Qianfan Zhang, "Against the holistic temptations: A critique of three related fictions in constitutional theory," *Peking University Law Journal* 6, no. 2 (2018): 371–91.

community consists of only a few citizens, while the vast majority remain indifferent to or repulsed by the elements of the social contract, then that nation is destined for misfortune. Therefore, the practical impossibility of reaching unanimous consent on the empirical social contract does not imply its nonexistence or insignificance. On the contrary, the degree to which it exists in a society is pivotal to the destiny of that society.

In essence, the social contract represents an agreement to abide by a set of political natural laws (PNLs) that are essential for achieving and sustaining social peace and harmony. Analysis of nearly 400 civil wars worldwide since 1800 reveals that civil wars arise when at least one PNL is violated.[8] Drawing lessons from such historical events, rational individuals of various classes, identities, and interests should come to a basic agreement to uphold all PNLs. The resulting social contract empowers the contract community to formulate a constitution that embodies and elaborates on the PNLs, serving as the foundation for state power.

In summary, the social contract comprises three institutional components: (1) fundamental rights and freedoms, especially freedom of thought and belief, freedom of speech and press, and equal protection against discrimination; (2) a form of majoritarian decision-making mechanism based on universal suffrage; and (3) an administrative and judicial system that operates independently and free from political interference.[9] In other words, at the core of the social contract lies the "bounded majoritarianism," which entails democratic majoritarianism while respecting basic freedoms and the rule of law. Even a decision that is supported by a near 100 percent majority should not infringe upon individual basic rights and freedoms, nor the principles of administrative neutrality and judicial independence.

The social contract begins by acknowledging three fundamental rights and freedoms: freedom of religion and belief, freedom of speech, and equal protection against discrimination. To be sure, these rights are not necessarily the only ones to be included in the social contract. Obviously, other rights such as personal freedom, privacy, and private property are also important, and should be specified in the constitution. Therefore, the list of "contract rights" remains open. For the purpose of maintaining national peace, however, the significance of the aforementioned three rights is unparalleled. No nation can violate any of them without facing the consequences of oppression, internal conflicts, and even civil wars.

8 Qianfan Zhang and Xiaoyang Wei, "Political natural law and human dignity: An empiricist perspective," *Journal of Chinese Philosophy* 50 (2023): 196–208.

9 Ibid.

The Constitution of the United States has widely been considered as a successful model of contract-based politics, even though democracy at the time was limited to a minority of white, propertied males. Regrettably, less than eighty years after its founding, the issue of slavery divided the North and South, plunging the nation into a brutal civil war that nearly caused its disintegration, with a death toll of more than half a million. Even today, the United States remains deeply divided by racial discrimination and the resulting animosity.

Moreover, the theocratic states that intertwine religion with the state face grave consequences such as serious religious oppression, armed conflict, and turmoil. Last but not least, if freedom of speech is not respected and protected, the absence of free exchange of political information and ideas not only renders electoral democracy impossible, but also prevents the people from forming a social contract in the first place. This chapter will describe how the suppression of a free press hindered the Republic of China from embracing the conception of social contract during its early years of establishment.

The three contract rights, along with electoral democracy and the rule of law, form the core of PNLs, the "iron laws" that establish the necessary conditions for a nation to achieve social peace and maintain legitimate and stable political power. Only by upholding every PNL can a nation maintain a balanced distribution of social power and prevent private interests from growing disproportionally with the support of the state. Mature liberal democracies can sustain long-term peace and harmony precisely because the vast majority of their citizens agree to abide by the PNLs upon which the social contract is based.

In contrast, authoritarian and totalitarian states suffer from periodic crises of serious social and political unrest due to the absence of electoral democracy, making it impossible to address abuses and achieve the peaceful transition of political power. Additionally, democracy cannot be sustained without the rule of law. If daily governance is marred by extralegal interference driven by power, money, or personal connections, even an electoral democracy will fail to save the country from falling into lawless chaos. In short, if the majority of a society fails to reach a social contract on the delineated PNLs and take action against the contract violations, or disregards the PNLs for short-term gains, their pursuit of peace and happiness is destined to be futile, akin to seeking fish in a tree (缘木求鱼).

2.2.2 *The Institutional Conditions of Social Contract*

Liberal democracy and authoritarian regimes thus represent two contrasting situations. In a liberal democracy, the PNLs are widely respected and effectively upheld. Due to the robust protection of the basic rights and the shared understanding among the majority regarding the limits of state power, the cost of violating these rights by either the state or individuals is high, while the cost for individuals to defend their rights is relatively low. If the general public demands that the power games among the political elites adhere to certain basic rules, any political behavior that violates those basic rules will face social punishment, whether through public condemnation, periodic elections, or recall mechanisms. As a result, the constitutional rules are effectively enforced. People living in a liberal democracy may not necessarily be aware of concepts such as "political natural law" or "social contract" in the same way that a healthy person may not be preoccupied with the meaning of "health" in medicine, yet fulfilling the social contract has become an integral part of their daily lives.

During the Watergate scandal in the early 1970s, for example, President Nixon's subordinates engaged in illegal wiretapping of political rivals within the National Convention of the Democratic Party. When President Nixon refused to release the tapes that potentially contained criminal activity to the court, the American people responded with widespread demonstrations, protesting the president's defiance of the court order. Telegrams poured into Congress like snowflakes every day, urging the immediate impeachment of the president. Since members of Congress are directly elected by voters, consideration of personal political interest was enough to prevent them from aligning with a disgraced president, even if they belonged to the same party. Three PNLs – freedom of speech and assembly, electoral democracy, and judicial independence – worked together to swiftly remove a president suspected of serious legal violations. While the House of Representatives quickly initiated impeachment, the Supreme Court ruled that the president was obligated to hand over the tapes.[10] The entire episode came to a quick conclusion with Nixon's resignation.

In contrast, none of the conditions necessary for reaching a social contract is fulfilled in authoritarian regimes. The people do not feel that their rights are respected and protected, nor do they share broad consensus on the limits of state power. Activists who consciously defend their rights constantly face the danger of repression and persecution. Nor are political elites held accountable for violating the people's rights, leading to frequent disregard of the basic rules of the political game. An authoritarian order cannot coexist with a social contract because the people would never have agreed to such a system had they been given free choice. The establishment of a social contract requires

[10] *United States* v. *Nixon*, 418 US 683 (1974).

that the people have the right to determine the political institutions through which they are governed by engaging in free discussions and debates. If the people are not even given the right to elect their own representatives, how can they be expected to have a say in the mechanisms by which the representatives are chosen?

Of course, such an oppressive order cannot be sustained indefinitely. If the authoritarian mode operates in a closed circle, shielded from external challenges and comparison with alternative modes of governance, it may cycle forever, as seen in the Chinese dynasties over the past two millennia. Once alternative forms of governance are presented to the old regime, however, the cycle can be broken when comparisons are made and judgments are passed. Nations that refuse to endure voluntary degradation will yearn for a transition from the authoritarian tyranny that deprives the majority of their freedom to a liberal democracy that respects the dignity and right of every individual.

The transition from the authoritarian order to a liberal democratic order is, in essence, a process of establishing a social contract based on the general observance of PNLs. Authoritarian order tends to be "resilient," however.[11] Since a nation that has long been under authoritarianism lacks the political and cultural foundations supporting the establishment of a social contract, its transition process is bound to encounter twists and turns. While adopting a liberal democratic constitution may be an easy task, the actual establishment of a liberal democratic order through practical implementation is considerably harder. Many countries, including both the Republic and People's Republic of China, had stumbled in the transition process. The ultimate failure of these transitions is, of course, the failure to establish a social contract. In societies undergoing transition, the general population is typically lacking in power and knowledge, making it practically impossible to rely on them alone to establish a social contract. In most cases, the initiation of transitions rests with political and social elites.[12] A successful transition implies that these elites, with varying interests and positions, have reached a sustainable power-sharing agreement.

[11] Andrew J. Nathan, "China's changing of the guard: Authoritarian resilience," *Journal of Democracy* 14 (2003): 6–17.

[12] For the role of the English elites in the development of the Magna Carta and the Glorious Revolution, see Wm. S. McKechnie, "Magna Carta (1215–1915)," in Henry Elliot Malden (ed.), *Magna Carta: Commemoration Essays* (London: Royal Historical Society, 1917), pp. 11–22; William Sharp McKechnie, *Magna Carta: A Commentary on the Great Charter of King John*, 2nd ed. (New York: Burt Franklin, 1960), pp. 4–5; Barry Weingast, "The political foundations of democracy and the rule of law," *American Political Science Review* 91 (1997): 245–63, 261.

Conversely, a transition fails when the elite agreement is either broken or was never reached in the first place.

On the other hand, the elite agreement represents only a temporary stage characterized by a fragile balance between competing powers. If the general public fails to transform themselves and accept the social contract based on the PNLs, the elite pact is destined to be short-lived. In fact, the elite behaviors cannot be effectively constrained precisely because the majority of the population has not embraced a social contract that enables collective actions aimed at enforcing the elite pact. Within the power dynamics, political elites with opposing interests and positions compete for power. While some elites willingly follow the established rules of the game, others will pursue their objectives through any means necessary, even if it means flagrant disregarding the rules of the game, such as engaging in persecution and assassination, or staging a coup d'état. If such behaviors go unchecked without consequences, they will inevitably proliferate and ultimately destroy the very rules that are meant to govern elite behavior.

Regrettably, the people living under authoritarian regimes are deprived of the freedom necessary to develop the habit of engaging in voluntary agreements through free exchanges. When the authoritarian regime loosens its grip, there is a window of opportunity for the people to establish a social contract through practices and negotiations, but the opportunity is often missed due to lack of experience and time. Moreover, they are susceptible to the allure of the residual authoritarian power, which tends to undermine their efforts by employing a "divide and conquer" strategy, fragmenting their horizontal coalitions before a solid social contract can be formed. The defining character of an authoritarian order is the vertical relationship between the state and the people, which remains strong even as the old order begins to crumble. Not only do the common people, still living under the remnants of authoritarian legacies, find it difficult to form a self-governing coalition, but even the elites struggle to reach compromises among themselves due to a lack of sufficient trust. As a result, instead of reaching a mutual compromise and producing a pact by which all parties are willing to uphold, the elite groups often engage in endless infighting among themselves, until a winner emerges victorious and takes all power.

2.2.3 *The Absence of Contract-Based Political Tradition in China*

Unfortunately, China is one of those countries with long authoritarian tradition. Over the course of two millennia under the centralized imperial governance, the vertical political structure overshadowed any horizontal cooperation. Ancient China was characterized by a despotic order where the ruling elites governed an uneducated populace. While ancient China did possess a degree of local autonomy for the gentry, and individuals of common birth had opportunities to enter the ruling circle through the imperial examination system, the social mobility and local autonomy remained severely limited, unable to alter the nature of China's political system. The vast majority of ordinary people had minimal opportunities to participate in self-governance. The imperial examination provided negligible chance to change one's destiny, considering the low literacy rate during the late Qing dynasty, which was below 1 percent.[13] The educated gentry elites numbered little more than 1 million, accounting for less than 0.3 percent of the total population of 400 million. In other words, over 99 percent of the population were excluded from political participation. While the small gentry class did experience a degree of political engagement, the overwhelming majority of the masses were mere "bystanders" to the power struggles within the imperial court.

As the common people were unable to exert a positive influence on the elite power struggles and compromises, the elites had no incentive to seek support from the people themselves, but rather focused on gaining favor from those "above" – ultimately from the emperor. The lack of popular participation also exacerbated polarization among the masses at the bottom of society, resulting in two extremes – obedient subjects or violent rebels. The former served as stepping stones for imperial despotism, while the latter became fuel for revolutionary violence. Conspicuously missing was the centerpiece of self-governing citizens, who were capable of forming mutual alliances to defend their rights.

As a result, imperial China had complicated rules of propriety akin to an ancient constitution.[14] While private contracts were prevalent in practice, the concept of social contract was entirely foreign to its political culture and practices. To be sure, familiarity with private contracts is the prerequisite for envisioning a social contract. It is difficult to imagine a society that lacks the practice of making private contracts, which safeguard their immediate personal interests, while capable of establishing a social contract that pertains to their personal interests indirectly. Engaging in private contracts is only a necessary condition for making the social contract, as the private contracts

[13] Jing Zhiren, *Constitutional History of China* [in Chinese] (Taipei: Taiwan Lianjing Press, 1984), pp. 134–5.

[14] Hu Shih, "The natural law in the Chinese tradition," in E. F. Barrett (ed), *Natural Law Institute Proceeding* 5 (1953): 142–4.

solely address direct personal interests, with the state acting as a neutral arbiter rather than a political decision-maker. On the other hand, a social contract is an agreement among mutually committed individuals regarding the fundamental principles that the state is obliged to uphold.

For example, freedom of speech in a social contract encompasses not only the mutual respect for each other's freedom of speech, but also a shared commitment to refrain from invoking the state power to oppress one another's speech, relying instead on trustworthiness of our horizontal commitments. Only through such means can freedom of speech as stipulated in the constitution be firmly established. Otherwise, regardless of whether you or I align with the state, its suppression of speech can always find social support. Right-wing factions may endorse the suppression of left-wing perspectives, just as left-wing factions may celebrate the suppression of right-wing viewpoints. In either case, the state faces minimal societal sanctions for violating freedom of speech, rendering it an empty provision within the constitution. In this sense, a social contract, as described, has never existed in China.

As a consequence, neither the ordinary people nor the ruling elites in imperial China possessed the spirit of unity against the monarch, akin to the British aristocracy during the Glorious Revolution. Throughout imperial history, significant changes never arose from the joint initiative of high-ranking ministers, but instead always necessitated direct approval from the emperor. The Hundred Days' Reform, which occurred towards the end of the last dynasty, served as an example. At that time, the political elites were roughly divided into four groups: The two groups within the court were the conservative nobles of the Manchu minority and reformist officials of Han ethnicity and a few Manchu, while two outside the court were royalist reformers, represented by Kang Youwei, and emerging revolutionaries. Had the conservative and reformist factions within the court collaborated, akin to the Tories and Whigs during the Glorious Revolution,[15] and exerted pressure on the imperial family to embrace change, China could have potentially achieved a constitutional monarchy by the late nineteenth century, which might have endured until the present day.

Unfortunately, China never seemed to have the fortune required for such circumstances. The obstinate Manchu nobles consistently rejected any reforms that threatened their vested interests and firmly held veto power over political reforms, thus becoming an incorrigible impediment to social progress. In such a situation, successful reforms required the leadership of

[15] Miller, "The Glorious Revolution," 545–55; Weingast, "The political foundations of democracy and the rule of law," 252–5.

reformist officials within the court, joined by moderate reformers outside the court, effectively marginalizing both the conservative forces within the court and the radical revolutionaries outside the court.[16] For reformers outside the court, such as Kang Youwei, Liang Qichao (梁启超), and Tan Sitong (谭嗣同), it was more effective to remain outside the court and focus on educating and mobilizing the people. By solving the "coordination dilemma" at the popular level,[17] they could create social pressure for constitutional reform while leaving institutional and policy reforms to their reformist counterparts within the court.

The intellectual reformers led by Kang Youwei, however, did not content themselves with staying outside the system. They managed to enter the Qing court and assume important positions, which ironically contributed to the downfall of the reform movement. As outsiders to the court, these reformists lacked power resources beyond the personal support of the emperor. Fortunately, they encountered an enlightened emperor, Guangxu, who was committed to reform. Yet their unilateral and hasty actions ultimately led to the demise of the enlightened emperor and the reformist forces. During the Hundred Days' Reform, over a hundred reform documents were issued in the name of the emperor, which accelerated long-overdue institutional reforms impeded by vested interests. However, it also directly heightened the conflict between the Emperor's Faction (帝党) and the Empress Dowager's Faction (后党), representing the conservative forces that safeguarded vested interests.

The radical reforms not only threatened the interests of the conservative court, predominantly composed of the Manchu minority, but also aroused jealousy among enlightened officials of Han ethnicity. The various enlightened factions within the court should have united with the social forces supporting reform to negotiate and resolve their differences. Initially, reformist officials such as Zhang Zhidong and Yuan Shikai did support the intellectual reformers. Unfortunately, they eventually pursued separate paths, failing to form a strong and cohesive coalition capable of countering the conservative forces led by the Empress Dowager. The solitary advancement of the radical reformers only provoked a powerful backlash from the conservative forces. After the suppression of the Hundred Days' Reform, the reformist forces both within and outside the Qing court were unable to effectively regroup and form a viable counterforce.

16 Samuel P. Huntington, *The Third Wave: Democratization in the Late 20th Century* (University of Oklahoma Press, 1991), pp. 163–74.

17 Weingast, "The political foundations of democracy and the rule of law," 261.

Nor were the reforms outside the imperial court able to form a coalition with the relentless revolutionaries, who were increasingly numerous after the reform failed. After Kang Youwei and other key reformers fled to Japan, Sun Yat-sen went to London seeking revolutionary support. Some Japanese sympathizers of the Chinese reform had hoped that the two forces would join hands, but the constitutional monarchists and revolutionary democrats quickly went their separate ways, reaching a point of irreconcilable rivalry. The constitutional monarchists believed that the nature of the polity (政体) was more important than the form of the state (国体), and improving upon the existing system was easier than radically altering it. The revolutionaries, on the other hand, insisted that fundamental transformation was in order, believing that "it is hopeless to reform the Qing government."[18] Of course, the critical question was whether the Qing government was willing and able to establish a constitutional monarchy, the affirmative answer to which would have settled the dispute between reform and revolution. While the Qing government was forced to prepare for constitutional reform, it became increasingly corrupt. As the nation grew increasingly outraged by the backlash against reform, revolutionary appeals gained more national sympathy, with radical newspapers spreading throughout the country. As the appeal for reform waned, many reformers even joined the revolutionary forces.

Revolutionary violence, of course, can never produce any kind of contract. As Mao Zedong put it, "Revolution is not a dinner invitation … It is riot, namely, a violent action by which one class overthrows another class."[19] It is about life and death. Between you and me, only one survives. How can we possibly reach an agreement? How can any contract be negotiated between mortal enemies who refuse to share the same sky? Amid fire and gunshots, even the lives of all parties are not worthy of respect. What else can be honored and respected? Only in countries with deeply rooted contract-based political traditions like Britain, can rivals return to the negotiating table from the battlefield, which is too much to expect for China. Despite the misleading title of "China's Glorious Revolution," the Xinhai Revolution in 1911 marked the beginning of the end of China's experiments with republican democracy. In less than a decade, the political revolution gave way to a more radical cultural revolution that systematically introduced totalitarian ideals and practices to China.

[18] He Haiming, "It is the peace that will destroy China," 《大江报》 (July 11, 1911).

[19] Mao Zedong, "Hunan Peasant Movement Investigation Report," (March 1927), www.marxists.org/chinese/maozedong/marxist.org-chinese-mao-192703.htm.

2.3 THE FAILURE TO ESTABLISH A SOCIAL CONTRACT THROUGH IMPERIAL REFORM

2.3.1 *A Belated Reform Forced by Revolutionary Threat*

After the failure of the Hundred Days' Reform and Emperor Guangxu's loss of power, the hardliners led by Empress Dowager Cixi (慈禧) emerged from behind the scenes and took center stage in politics, signaling the impending downfall of the crippled constitutional reform. Under domestic and international pressures, the conservative-dominated government was still compelled to continue with reforms, but the movement of "implementing constitutionalism by imitation" (仿行宪政) was initiated half-heartedly. Just half a month before their deaths in 1908, Cixi and Guangxu issued four constitutional edicts in a single day, including the Outline of the Imperial Constitution, rules for establishing a parliament and its election, a list of items to prepare for enacting a formal constitution within nine years, and the Charter of Urban and Rural Self-Governance.

The Outline of the Imperial Constitution was established on the traditional authoritarian model, implying unchallengeable imperial authority that contradicted modern constitutionalism. The year 1911 witnessed the establishment of the "Royal Cabinet" (皇族内阁), which was filled with Manchu nobles, radically altering the policy of ethnic parity between Manchu and Han in previous cabinets. All of these developments indicated that imperial reform had come to an end at the very moment when the Hundred Days' Reform failed. Without revolution, constitutional progress was impossible. As a result, support for the revolutionary forces had been steadily growing since 1898. A decade later, the death of the Empress Dowager further fueled the revolutionary momentum. The success of the revolution in 1911 simply shattered any hope for a social contract even before it had a chance to take shape.

Within a month of the Wuchang Uprising on October 10, 1911, over half of the southern provinces declared independence. The imperial court was forced to negotiate only after its power was fatally weakened. As the situation quickly became critical, the Qing court had to reappoint Yuan Shikai, a key minster who had been dismissed earlier, and convened an emergency meeting of the Advisory Council (资政院). The majority of the Council proposed the abolition of the Royal Cabinet, the non-interference of royal relatives in politics, some form of popular consent to be acquired for the new constitution, and the immediate lifting of bans on political parties. These proposals were reluctantly accepted by the Qing court under pressure. On October 29, local military officers led by Zhang Shaozeng (张绍曾), Lan Tianwei (蓝天蔚) and

Wu Luzhen (吴禄贞) initiated the Luanzhou mutiny as "military remonstrance" (兵谏), which proposed a twelve-point constitutional outline and threatened to march on Beijing, the imperial capital. While the Qing court was initially reluctant to act, Shanxi province declared independence on the same day, suddenly putting Beijing in a situation of facing attacks from both the front and back. As a result, it was forced to issue decrees abolishing the Royal Cabinet, implementing a responsible cabinet, authorizing Yuan Shikai as the Prime Minister to organize the cabinet, lifting the ban on political parties, and granting amnesty to political prisoners criminalized for advocating reform or revolution, including Kang Youwei, Liang Qichao, and Wang Jingwei (汪精卫). On November 3, the Advisory Council drafted, based on the twelve-point outline, the Nineteen Articles on Major Constitutional Principles (宪法重大信条十九条), which was immediately promulgated by the Qing government.[20]

The Nineteen Articles did not specify the rights of the people, but substantially limited the imperial power, implementing the republican ideal with a "figurehead monarch" (虚君) proposed by reformers in the late Qing dynasty. While the monarchy was preserved, such a system would fundamentally reform the tradition of absolute monarchy that had ruled China for millennia. Although the Nineteen Articles still stipulated that "the imperial throne of the Great Qing Empire shall forever be passed down from generation to generation" (Art. 1), and "the sacredness of the emperor shall not be violated" (Art. 2), the imperial powers were substantively limited:

The emperor's power is limited by the constitution. (Art. 3)
The constitution is to be decided by the Advisory Council and promulgated by the emperor. (Art. 5)
The right to propose constitutional amendments belongs to the Congress. (Art. 6)
The prime minister is elected by the Congress and appointed by the emperor. Other state ministers are recommended by the prime minister and appointed by the emperor. Members of the imperial family shall not serve as prime minister, other state ministers, or provincial governors. (Art. 8)
The system and regulations of officials shall be determined by law. (Art. 13)
The grand ordinances of the imperial family shall not conflict with the constitution. (Art. 16)

[20] Gao Quanxi, *The Constitutional History of China*, vol. 1 [in Chinese] (Hong Kong: City University of Hong Kong Press, 2022), pp. 140–3.

While the army and navy are under the command of the emperor, "its internal use shall abide by the specific conditions determined by the Congress, beyond which no dispatch shall be permitted" (Art. 10). "International treaties shall not be concluded without the decision of the Congress"; a declaration of war or peace made during Congressional adjournment shall be confirmed by the Congress after it reassembles (Art. 12). The Congress also decides on the annual budget and the expenses of the imperial family (Arts. 14 and 15).

If the Outline of the Imperial Constitution, imitating the authoritarian Bismarck Constitution of 1871 and the Meiji Constitution of 1889, merely reflected China's long tradition of absolute monarchy, the Nineteen Articles were close to the British constitutional monarchy after the Glorious Revolution. In fact, as the Wuchang Uprising and Luanzhou mutiny played similar roles to that of the Glorious Revolution, the Nineteen Articles could be seen as China's Bill of Rights that established its constitutional monarchy following the British model. As Shang Binghe pointed out: "The Nineteen Articles deeply embodied the spirit of the British constitution, using representative institutions as the pivot of national politics. If implemented, popular governance can be achieved. Regrettably, it was released too late."[21]

After the promulgation of the Nineteen Articles, Prime Minister Yuan Shikai organized a new cabinet that swept away the royalist influence of its predecessor, with the vast majority of its members being Han Chinese. Everything seemed so hopeful, except that it all came too late to stop the footsteps of the revolution. Although the Qing government still held absolute military advantage, it had irreversibly lost all popular support. While Yuan Shikai's army recaptured Hankou and headed straight for Wuchang, the temporary seat of the revolutionary government, he decided to cease the attack and instead reached a compromise with the revolutionary army through negotiation. In mid-December, with the mediation of the British ambassador, Yuan Shikai sent a representative of the Qing government, Tang Shaoyi (唐绍仪), to Shanghai for the North–South Peace Negotiation with the revolutionaries, represented by Wu Tingfang (伍廷芳). Yuan's condition was to preserve the Qing court as a symbolic power, while he himself exercised substantive executive power. The southern revolutionary party outright rejected the proposal and insisted on establishing a republic, in which Yuan was promised to be appointed as its founding president if he succeeded in persuading Emperor Puyi to abdicate.

21 Quote from Chen Ruxuan, *Constitutional History of China* [in Chinese] (Taipei: Wenhai Press, 1985), p. 65.

During the North–South Negotiation, Sun Yat-sen returned to China. Representatives from various revolutionary provinces in the south gathered in Wuchang to form the Nanjing Provisional Government of the Republic of China and draft its Organizational Outline (临时政府组织大纲). After much debate, the representatives adopted Sun Yat-sen's proposal, which followed the American model of presidentialism and separation of powers. This involved establishing a senate and a provisional president, who would serve as both the head of state and the chief executive, as well as the commander-in-chief, to be elected by the provincial representatives.[22] On the first day of 1912, the Nanjing Provisional Government declared the establishment of the Republic of China, and inaugurated Sun Yat-sen as the provisional president. By the end of January, representatives from most provinces had taken their seats in the Nanjing Senate, thus formally constituting the Provisional Senate, which then began to develop the Provisional Constitution (临时约法).

Preceding the Weimar Constitution by seven years, the Provisional Constitution introduced one of the earliest mixed, dual-head system in the world. Departing from the earlier presidential model, it established a unicameral legislative body with investigatory and impeachment powers, as well as a prime minister, who was expected to cosign the presidential edicts. The aim was to incorporate the advantages of both presidential and parliamentary systems by keeping the two powers in balance. On the other hand, the *Provisional* Constitution was evidently incomplete, with numerous loopholes that left the powers of the parliament and cabinet largely undefined. For example, it failed to address the parliamentary vote of no confidence and dissolution. The prime minister essentially served as an assistant to the president, whose power was checked solely through the prime minister's authority to cosigning laws and orders. Unfortunately, the provisions regarding co-signature were ambiguous due to hasty drafting, which ultimately enabled Yuan Shikai to evade parliamentary control.[23]

[22] Jing Zhiren, *Constitutional History of China*, p. 161.

[23] In June 1912, Yuan Shikai disputed with the revolutionary party over the appointment of Wang Zhixiang (王芝祥) as the Governor of Zhili (now Hebei) province. Yuan issued an order to appoint Wang as a peace envoy to the southern army, but Prime Minister Tang Shaoyi refused to cosign the appointment letter. Misinterpreting the co-signature provision to oblige rather than empower the prime minster, Yuan went ahead and issued the appointment letter without Tang's co-signature. Yuan's abuse of power prompted Tang to resign from the post. See Jin Chongji and Hu Shengwu, *Manuscript on the History of Xinhai Revolution, Vol. 4: Success and Failure of Revolution* [in Chinese] (Shanghai: Shanghai People's Publishing House, 1991), p. 314.

On February 12, 1912, the imperial court issued the Qing Emperor's Abdication Edict (清帝退位诏书), abdicating the throne in exchange for the security and decent treatment of the imperial family. The Edict granted:

> Yuan Shikai the full power to organize a provisional republican government and negotiate with the revolutionary military. The objective is to secure the peace and stability of the people, unify the five ethnicities of Manchu, Han, Mongol, Uighur and Tibetan, and safeguard the territory and establish a great Republic of China.[24]

The following day, Yuan Shikai announced the establishment of a unified republic through a public notice for organizing the provisional republican government. On February 14, Sun Yat-sen declared his intention to resign from the position of provisional president, laying out three conditions: The capital should be located in Nanjing, where Yuan Shikai's oath of office would be taken, and the observance of the Provisional Constitution being drafted by the Nanjing Provisional Senate. The next day, Yuan was unanimously elected as the provisional president by the Senate. After several rounds of political struggles and compromises, however, the capital was ultimately located in Beijing, where Yuan took the oath of office. On March 10, Yuan Shikai formally assumed the office, while Sun Yat-sen, who had not officially resigned as the Provisional President, promulgated the Provisional Constitution adopted by the Provisional Senate. On March 16, Yuan formed a cabinet, which received approval from the Provisional Senate.

In a short span of two months, the millennia-old imperial government in China came to an end with a relatively bloodless transfer of power to the republican government. However, the manner and speed of the power transfer raised concerns about the fate of the republic.

2.3.2 *Was the Xinhai Revolution "China's Glorious Revolution"?*

Scholars such as Guo Shaomin and Gao Quanxi argue that the abdication of the "Last Emperor" was tantamount to a Chinese version of the Glorious Revolution, and the Abdication Edict amounted to a "contractual transfer" of power from the old monarchy to a democratic republic. To be sure, the Abdication Edict did provide China with another chance to embrace constitutionalism without violence. The peaceful abdication of the Last Emperor, the agreement reached between Yuan Shikai and the revolutionary

[24] Quoted in Guo Shaomin, "The great transformation: Imperial system, republic and the national transition of modern China," 《中外法学》, no. 5 (2011), 903–26, 903–4.

party to establish a republic, the smooth unification of the northern and southern regions, and the graceful handover of power by Sun Yat-sen to Yuan Shikai – all these were impressive achievements that demonstrated the spirit of politics based on contract.

However, such categorization tends to exaggerate the perception, foresight, and capabilities of the child emperor on the one hand, and the integrity of Yuan Shikai and the revolutionary party on the other. By 1912, the Qing court had lost many prominent figures, leaving behind only Puyi (溥仪), a six-year-old emperor, and his aunt Empress Dowager Longyu (隆裕). They were easily manipulated by Yuan Shikai, who was granted full authority to negotiate with the revolutionary army. Yuan opted to trade the throne of his master in return for his own presidency in the republic. In comparison, the Nineteen Articles issued after the Luanzhou mutiny were much closer to the Glorious Revolution, as they aimed to establish a constitutional monarchy similar to that of Britain. Unfortunately, Sun Yat-sen staunchly rejected this compromise on behalf of the revolutionary party, making constitutional monarchy unattainable in China. The failure of constitutional monarchy foreshadowed subsequent failures in compromises between the revolutionary party and the remnants of the old regime led by Yuan Shikai, which were carried over to the new republic.

While the Last Emperor, Yuan Shikai and the revolutionary party seemed to have effectively resolved the "coordination problem" that often plagues political transitions,[25] the limitations of such elite compromises became evident. First, the revolutionary party maintained an unwavering stance against monarchism in favor of republicanism, abruptly ending any possibility of constitutional monarchy and setting a negative precedent for elite compromises in the early republican period. To be sure, the downfall of the Qing government was well deserved, as it was a just retribution for their stubborn refusal to implement constitutional reforms. Since the failure of the Hundred Days' Reform, the Qing government had adopted a stern outlook to mask its lack of confidence. By intensifying suppression of widespread discontent, it closed off the path to peaceful reform, which could have extended its reign. After the revolution broke out and the imperial army unleashed brutal violence, even moderate reformers like Zhang Jian (张謇) abandoned the idea of constitutional monarchy. Zhang not only declined to serve as a minister of commerce in Yuan's cabinet, but openly supported the republic. At this point, with the loss of popular support, the downfall of the Qing court became inevitable.

[25] Weingast, "The political foundations of democracy and the rule of law," 261.

Unlike a revolution, however, constitutional reform relies more on reason than on impulse. For a legitimate revolution to occur, the necessary condition is the ruling group's repeated rejection to reform. Once the Qing court, for whatever reason, was willing to relinquish its previously unlimited power and accept constitutional limitations, the revolutionary legitimacy would have significantly diminished. In fact, the revolution had already achieved considerable success by pressuring the Qing court to release the Nineteen Articles. As Liang Qichao pointed out, both the revolutionary and monarchist movements were mere means to an end, with constitutionalism being the ultimate goal.[26] Constitutionalism could have been attained through reforming the monarchy, and the rational strategy would not have been to overthrow the monarchy, but rather to transform its political system while maintaining the monarchical structure. This approach was advocated by reformers both within and outside the court, such as Yuan Shikai and Kang Youwei. If the Chinese revolutionaries had displayed the self-discipline of the British nobility during the Glorious Revolution in 1688–89, they would have been content with a constitutional monarchy when victory was within their grasp. They could have reached a compromise with the reformers to implement parliamentary politics. The social contract embodied in the Nineteen Articles would have taken root in China, and the path to constitutionalism would have been much smoother compared to the revolutionary course it ultimately took.

In fact, had the monarchy persisted, Emperor Puyi could have cultivated favorable sentiments from the still significant royalist faction for the revolutionary party and helped to maximize consensus for the constitutional transformation. He might have even served as a mediator in the political struggle between the revolutionary party and Yuan Shikai, preventing both sides from engaging in unrestrained clashes. Once the Nineteen Articles were rendered defunct by the imperial "abdication," the social contract lost its political foundation, and the constitutional transformation became deadlocked. Unfortunately, the revolutionary party lacked a spirit of compromise, causing China to miss the opportunity to establish a social contract. The constitutional reform began with an arrogant and obstinate imperial court that clung to political power and resisted reforms, and ended with an equally stubborn revolutionary party that refused to compromise and insisted on one-party rule, leading to clashes with the authoritarian warlord, Yuan Shikai, who ultimately self-destructed by restoring the monarchy. Although the late Qing

[26] See Liang's debate with the revolutionaries, e.g., Liang Qichao, "On enlightened despotism," 《新民丛报》, no. 76 (January 1911).

dynasty's transformation began with the opportunity created by the Nineteen Articles and a bloodless abdication, it was soon lost in relentless power struggles among uncompromising factions. This outcome was hardly surprising, as Chinese society generally revered power and had an inherent aversion to negotiations. While compromises were viewed as weakness, naked rules of the jungle such as "the winner takes all" and "one mountain cannot accommodate two tigers" (一山不容二虎) were accepted as natural laws. Without the support of power, specifically military strength, political authority would cease to exist, and the regime would inevitably collapse. Under the dominance of a power-worshipping culture, an experiment to establish social contract is almost destined to fail.

Second, the political compromises during that time primarily revolved around the specific allocation of power between rival parties and individuals. Unfortunately, these negotiations often resulted in a zero-sum game, making it difficult to reach mutually beneficial agreements. Sun Yat-sen yielded the provisional presidency to Yuan Shikai on the condition that the capital be relocated to Nanjing, where Yuan would take the oath of office. Apart from the general adherence to the Provisional Constitution, most of the compromises between rival parties focused on specific power allocations. Even the Provisional Constitution itself was a product of power struggles. While Sun Yat-sen strongly believed in the American presidential system, which served as the basis for the Organizational Outline of the Provisional Government promulgated by the Nanjing Provisional Senate, the Provisional Constitution underwent abrupt changes in its fundamental design once it became evident that Yuan Shikai would assume the presidency. The Provisional Constitution was hastily drafted within a month in order to restrict Yuan's power through a parliament and cabinet controlled by the revolutionary party. It was promulgated the day after Yuan took office. In an attempt to render Yuan a president without real authority, the Provisional Constitution transformed the presidential system into a mixed system with dual heads. If the Organizational Outline was personally tailored to suit Sun Yat-sen, the Provisional Constitution was specifically aimed at limiting Yuan's power. Both documents can be considered "personal laws" (对人立法) enacted by the revolutionaries-dominated Nanjing Provisional Senate.[27]

To be sure, it can be beneficial for institutional changes to arise from power struggles, something that had been notably lacking in China's long political history. It is well known that major American constitutional innovations, such as bicameralism, were established through political compromises (e.g., the

[27] Jing Zhiren, *Constitutional History of China*, p. 227.

Great Compromise) during the framing period in the 1780s.[28] To produce a sustainable constitutional system, however, the compromises reached must be genuine. Although Yuan Shikai pledged to abide by the Provisional Constitution that was directed against him, it was clear that he was unwilling to be sidelined by a prime minister who was appointed by and loyal to the revolutionaries. This also explains his deep concern regarding the candidacy of Song Jiaoren (宋教仁), the de facto leader of the Nationalist Party founded through the coalition of revolutionaries in August 1912, who declared his intention to run for prime minister. When Song was assassinated in March 1913, suspicions arose that Yuan was the mastermind behind the plot, prompting Sun Yat-sen to launch a "second revolution" against Yuan. In response, Yuan ordered the complete banning of the Nationalist Party. While one can blame Yuan for being power-hungry and inconsistent, from his perspective the revolutionaries had broken the agreement first. As Yuan had long desired the presidency, the unhindered presidential system outlined in the Organizational Outline represented his "legitimate expectation." Without seeking his consent, however, the revolutionaries unilaterally changed it to the dual-head system by hastily enacting the Provisional Constitution, which significantly weakened presidential power. Therefore, the Provisional Constitution was essentially the result of one party's imposition, rather than an agreement between both parties. Without mutual trust and respect, opportunistic compromises are bound to fail. Given the political tension and deadlock between the Nationalist Party (KMT) and the Northern government (北洋政府) dominated by warlords, the dual-head system seemed to be the only option acceptable to both parties. However, it was not a viable solution. Attempting to sideline a rival president through a prime minister accountable to the Nationalist-dominated Congress would only intensify political frictions, soon leading to the total collapse of multiparty cooperation.

In retrospect, a viable option at the time may have been a presidential system with a separation of powers similar to the American model. While the Northern government would be responsible for administration, the KMT would control the parliament. However, even with this arrangement, ensuring a peaceful separation of powers would still have been challenging, as political conflicts between the president and Congress would have been inevitable. Even in the American model, the legislative, executive, and judicial branches are far from independent entities operating in isolation, but involve intricate checks and balances between each other. For instance, Congress has

28 Bruce Ackerman, *We the People, Vol. 2: Transformations* (Boston: Harvard University Press, 1998), pp. 50–1.

significant influence over the president, as the Senate's confirmation is required for cabinet appointments. If the Senate, under Nationalist control, repeatedly declined to approve Yuan Shikai's cabinet nominees, the president would face a desperate situation.

More important, the acceptance and sustainability of a constitutional design resulting from political compromises relies on a rough balance of political capacities among the parties involved, creating uncertainty about the future outcomes of political struggles. In a way, the parties engaged in the institutional agreement are placed in a "veil of ignorance" regarding the political consequences of the power dynamics within the institutions. For instance, the American constitutional system enjoys bipartisan support because both the Democrats and Republicans have a fair chance of winning presidential and congressional elections. However, this support would likely diminish if one party consistently dominated all branches of government. In contrast, during the early days of the Republic of China, the KMT had a clear advantage in political mobilization compared to the warlord factions in the Northern government and third parties like the Progressive Party, which primarily emerged from late Qing reformers. As the Northern government lacked effective mechanisms for political mobilization to win elections, the Nationalist Party held an absolute majority in the Congress. Given the circumstances, the warlords had little choice but to rely on force to seize and maintain power, leaving the Nationalist Party with no alternative but to use force to regain control. This power struggle and the absence of a balance in political capacities ultimately hindered the peaceful resolution and stability of the constitutional system.

This illustrates the impossibility of a complete transition from monarchy to a genuine republic before the social contract has a chance to take root. Regrettably, China has never had such an opportunity. While the Qing dynasty relied on power, ultimately the military power, its successor, the Northern government led by Yuan Shikai, still had to rely on force. Nor did the revolutionary party, which emerged from the same political soil, hesitate to use force to seize power. Power sharing found no room between the successors and destroyers of monarchy, as they confronted each other on the ruthless battlefield, aiming to determine the ultimate winner and turning everyone into a believer of the creed that "political power grows out of the gun barrel."[29] After several rounds of unlimited conflicts, all political issues were resolved through the use of force, leaving no chance for the social contract to take root.

[29] Quoted from Mao Zedong's speech about the necessity of armed struggles at the CCP emergency meeting on August 7, 1927, after the KMT decided to clean the party and began to slaughter the Communists.

2.3.3 *Returning to Military Politics*

Before his assassination, Song Jiaoren, the major proponent of parliamentary politics within the KMT, led the party to a resounding victory in the parliamentary election. Strongly critical of Yuan's policies, Song pledged to lead the formulation of a British-style constitution and establish a one-party cabinet, where the president would serve as a mere figurehead. He also proposed Li Yuanhong, the vice president, to replace Yuan Shikai as the president, directly challenging Yuan's presidency. Song's assassination on the fateful night of March 20, 1913, however, completely shattered the already vulnerable cooperation between the KMT and Yuan Shikai. In July, after failed attempts at judicial trial and political settlement, seven southern provinces announced their secession from the Northern government and initiated the "second revolution" with the aim of overthrowing Yuan. However, Yuan Shikai swiftly suppressed the uprising, forcing Sun Yat-sen and other organizers to seek refuge in Japan. He arrested and executed some Nationalist participants, and eventually dissolved the Congress while repealing the qualifications of Nationalist members. Without the institutional constraints of the KMT, Yuan acted with increasing arrogance and greed, steadily consolidating his power until he embarked on the ill-fated path of restoring the monarchy in 1916. This reckless action not only led to his own downfall, but also dealt a significant blow to the young republic.

From the tumultuous early years of the republic to the brief period of monarchy restoration, the failures of the early republic severely undermined the credibility of republicanism. While China experienced a superficial peace during Yuan's era, it descended into a decade of warlord chaos after his demise. Although Chinese academics have recently begun reevaluating warlord politics, the fundamental nature of military rule remained unchanged. As the great warlord Yuan Shikai was replaced by smaller ones like Duan Qirui, Feng Guozhang, Cao Kun, Wu Peifu, and Zhang Xun, all of whom were Yuan's former subordinates, military involvement in politics became commonplace. With the absence of a common master, these petty warlords eagerly sought to unify a nation divided by military power, each vying for a seat in the presidential chair. The numerous abuses of power during this period do not require further elaboration.[30] An authority rooted in the military is inevitably at odds with elected institutions. When Yuan Shikai held the presidency,

[30] See Zhang Qianfan, *Introduction to Constitutional Law: Principles and Applications*, 3rd ed. [in Chinese] (Beijing: Law Press, 2014), pp. 105–28.

conflicts arose between the presidency, the Congress, and the cabinet. Now that the warlords controlled the Cabinet, political conflicts shifted to the struggle between the Cabinet and the Congress. In both cases, the only means of resolving conflicts was resorting to violence through blatant disregard for basic rules.

In April 1917, the government led by Prime Minister Duan Qirui (段祺瑞) summoned the provincial military governors (督军) to Beijing for discussions on military affairs and the declaration of war on Germany. While the military governors unanimously advocated declaring war on Germany and submitted the proposal to the House of Representatives, the KMT, constituting the majority in Congress, opposed the declaration, believing that Duan's true intention was to appease Japan, from which he had accepted a secret loan. Fearful of failing to achieve his objective, Duan followed in the footsteps of Yuan Shikai and organized a "citizens' petitioning team" consisting of several thousand individuals. They were commanded by the Ministry of the Army to surround the Congress and physically assault its members, coercing them to pass the resolution on that very day before being allowed to leave. The House of Representatives was outraged and shelved the resolution. Subsequently, the military governors jointly criticized the constitution, claiming that provisions such as the vote of no confidence and the Senate's approval of congressional dissolution were inappropriate for China's situation, and petitioned the President to dissolve the Congress. Taking the side of Congress, President Li Yuanhong issued an order dismissing Duan as prime minister, which was cosigned by the foreign minister.

Under attack from the military governors, Duan was forced to reject the validity of the dismissal order, arguing that the presidential dismissal, according to the Provisional Constitution, could only take effect with the co-signature of the prime minister himself, who was the very target of dismissal. All the military governors chimed in and announced their secession from the national government. To protect himself, Li urgently summoned Zhang Xun (张勋), a loyalist to the Qing dynasty known as "the general with a pigtail" (辫子将军), to Beijing to counter Duan's forces. As Zhang Xun led his troops northward, he made the dissolution of Congress a condition. Despite the absence of provisions for congressional dissolution in the Provisional Constitution and other laws, Li was compelled to issue an illegal order, making it the second time, after Yuan Shikai, that Congress was dissolved. Zhang Xun then invited old loyalists such as Kang Youwei to Beijing to carry out a restoration, during which the deposed Last Emperor issued a decree proclaiming, "listening to politics in the court and reclaiming power to initiate a new era with the people." As Duan Qirui and most of the military governors opposed the restoration, Zhang's army was swiftly defeated, bringing an end to the short-lived farce that lasted only twelve days.[31]

The defining events of political chaos in the early Republic, from the assassination of Song Jiaoren to the attempted restorations of Yuan Shikai and Zhang Xun, dealt fatal blows to the public confidence in constitutional democracy. These events were particularly disheartening for intellectuals who had advocated for republican democracy, as the vast divide between their ideals and the grim reality became increasingly apparent. In just a few years following the establishment of the Republic in 1911, the chaotic political landscape demonstrated that Chinese elites, disregarding the democratic rules of political game, readily resorted to violence as a means to achieve their goals. Professor Jing Zhiren accurately highlighted this phenomenon, stating:

> Every society consists of two opposing forces: conservative and radical. In countries with relatively democratic systems, not only does society possess a solid legal foundation, but the conservative and radical factions also share basic ideals. As a result, their conflicts can be resolved within the framework of the law, without resorting to violence. However, in countries lacking a democratic foundation, conflicts between these two sides often persist and escalate to the point of violence, disregarding the principles of the law.[32]

The Republic of China, unfortunately, fell into the category of "countries lacking a democratic foundation," where neither the elites nor the general population had embraced the habit of adhering to the rules of political games. In essence, it is crucial for the people to reach a basic agreement among themselves regarding the fundamental rules of power dynamics before they can expect those in power, whether it be Yuan Shikai or Sun Yat-sen, to abide by these rules. Had the people shown their support when the KMT was suppressed by Yuan Shikai, even a powerful warlord like him would not have dared to openly violate the law. Nor would he have gained the ignoble reputation of a "tyrant and thief" (独夫民贼) in Chinese history due to his egregious abuses of power.[33] The political landscape of the early Republic could have entered a virtuous cycle.

Since China had only recently overthrown absolute monarchy, however, it had yet to establish a contract-based liberal democracy. While the entire nation was united in opposition to the rule of the Manchu minority, there was a lack of knowledge and consensus regarding the fundamental principles by which the country should be governed. The ideas of constitutional

[31] Ibid., pp. 116–17.
[32] Jing Zhiren, *Constitutional History of China*, p. 268.
[33] *Mengzi*, 1B4.

democracy had not taken root in the hearts of the people, let alone been put into practice. If ordinary citizens failed to understand and insist on the rules, compelling the elites to abide by them, the elites would simply disregard the rules of democratic politics in the absence of external constraints. If a ruling group is not held accountable for violating the rules, their arrogance and thirst for power will only grow, surpassing every constraint. Yuan Shikai serves as a typical example of his time. From coercing parliamentary members to vote for his presidency to abolishing the Provisional Constitution and dismantling the Congress, his series of flagrantly illegal actions failed to incite significant social protests, further encouraging him to indulge in even more severe and self-destructive abuses of power.

The transition from monarchy to the Republic of China failed to eradicate the deep-rooted winner-takes-all tradition, where political struggles were still governed by the law of the jungle, where victory was determined by sheer violence. The establishment of the Republic did little to change the core nature of court struggles, which continued to be decided by the relative strength of different factions, often relying on military power alone. To be sure, the Republic aimed to change the culture of power worship that had made those in power arrogant and unscrupulous, and had driven power seekers to employ any means necessary to achieve their goals, such as the persecution of reformers like Kang Youwei and Liang Qichao, Yuan Shikai's restoration and persecution of the KMT, and the ruthless conflicts between the KMT and the Communist Party. Regrettably, the republican political practices had not sufficiently transformed the underlying political culture. The resulting turmoil and chaos in the early Republic quickly led to widespread disillusionment with democracy. Observing the disorder of the republican era, the Chinese public hastily concluded that Western-style democracy was unsuitable for China. Furthermore, the West itself was experiencing its own decline, as it was deeply embroiled in the devastating World War I. Europe, in particular, seemed to be in an irreversible decline, both in terms of its capitalism and democracy. Even an intellectual as wise as Liang Qichao, who had traveled through Europe in 1919, cheerfully declared that "Western civilization has gone bankrupt."[34]

Just around this time, the October Revolution presented a seemingly quick and attractive solution to China's desire to break free from its impoverished and humiliating past. The socialist revolution in the neighboring country provided an inspiring blueprint for building a strong nation. Why should

34 Liang Qichao, *Reflections on the Trip to Europe* [in Chinese] (Beijing: The Commercial Press, 2014), p. 15.

China follow the well-trodden path of Western empires, which were not only corrupt but also unjust? As the World War I reached its conclusion, Chen Duxiu, the founder of the Chinese Communist Party (CCP), joined other intellectuals in celebrating the defeat of Germany as a triumph of "justice over power." However, the disappointment caused by the Peace Treaty of Versailles led to a complete reversal in their attitude towards the West.[35] As late as 1918, Chen still criticized the Boxer Rebellion as a product of ignorant traditional culture. Yet, when confronted with a similar rebellion in 1921–24, he glorified it as a heroic "anti-imperialist struggle."[36] Following the May Fourth Movement in 1919, intellectuals who veered left became thoroughly disillusioned with the West and its liberal democracy. As they sought new institutions and forces to transform China's cultural and political traditions, the country quickly found itself being drawn into the grip of totalitarianism.

2.4 FATAL CHANGES: PUBLIC OPINION AROUND THE MAY FOURTH MOVEMENT

If the Xinhai Revolution was China's last chance to establish a social contract, its path towards radicalism was essentially predetermined once this opportunity was missed. While the cooperation among political elites quickly disintegrated, the situation was no better among the ordinary people. As mentioned earlier, political elites were unbridled in violating the rules of the game precisely because the "public opinion" was next to nothing. The vast majority of ordinary citizens were apathetic towards politics, and did not believe they had the power to constrain the behavior of the elites. The intellectuals and young students who did care about politics had already become disillusioned with the corrupt state of republican politics and began searching for fundamental solutions. The New Culture Movement (新文化运动), which took place in 1915–16 and attacked Chinese cultural traditions, did nothing to reverse or prevent a more radical trend in the years to come. In fact, its radical criticism of tradition laid the ideological groundwork for the May Fourth Movement that occurred three years later. Some cultural conservatives argued that the relentless criticism of the Confucian tradition led the nation to lose its moral compass (国是) and fall prey to various "demons."[37]

35 Jin Guantao and Liu Qingfeng, *Study on the History of Concepts: The Formation of Important Political Terms in Modern China* [in Chinese] (Beijing: Law Press, 2009), pp. 410–12.

36 Ibid., pp. 413–14.

37 Du Yaquan, "The confused modern mind," 《东方杂志》, 15, no. 4 (1918).

On the other hand, simply reverting to the past orthodoxy was not a viable solution. Faced with "the unprecedented changes in the past three millennia,"[38] China's political elites were obligated to shape a new national consensus within a limited historical window. This new consensus could not be imposed by political power but had to be freely negotiated among elites representing different interests. Unfortunately, consensus-based politics was foreign to China, and numerous opportunities for cooperation were squandered in irreconcilable confrontations. The failure to establish a liberal social contract between 1911 and 1919 left the people increasingly frustrated with warlord politics. Popular dissatisfaction continued to accumulate, waiting for a spark to ignite a full-blown explosion.

That spark was ignited by a telegram from Paris in late April 1919, revealing that the Western powers in the peace negotiations intended to transfer the right to lease the Jiaodong Peninsula from Germany to Japan instead of returning it to China. Since China was at least a symbolically victorious nation in World War I, the decision highlighted the perceived unfairness and betrayal by Western powers, even though its actual harm to China might have been exaggerated, particularly from the retrospect that China successfully recovered full sovereignty at the Washington Conference in 1921–22.[39] As the news was widely covered by the media, it destroyed the last goodwill that Chinese intellectuals had for Western liberal democracy and sparked a wave of patriotism and outrage, particularly among the young students who set fire to Zhao's Mansion during demonstrations on May 4, 1919.

The May Fourth Movement marked a turning point in the mindset of Chinese intellectuals towards Western liberal democracy. In China's long history, intellectuals have always been considered as the barometer of national sentiment in China. Their expressions not only reflect the collective mentality of a particular period, but also have a profound impact on the broader public, whose opinion determines the direction towards which the nation will develop. In a liberal society that upholds freedom of speech, the nurturing of a rational and tolerant national spirit allows its people to be well informed, participate in

[38] A phrase used by Li Hongzhang (李鸿章), the prime minister in the late Qing dynasty, in his petition to Emperor Tongzhi (同治) in June 1872, advising that "the proposal on ship building should not be withdrawn." Although the petition was about shipbuilding during the Self-Strengthening Movement (洋务运动), which focused primarily on importing the Western industrial technologies, Li's remark indicated the awakening of a few Chinese intellectuals and officials at the time. It took another two decades for the majority of them to realize that the fundamental impediment to China's reform was its absolutist imperial institution.

[39] Xu Xin, "Preliminary discussion on Gu Weijun's diplomatic achievements during the Beijing government of the Republic of China," 《西部学刊》, 119 (July 2020), 123–5.

self-governance, and gradually address social issues through democratic processes. In contrast, an authoritarian regime stifles free speech, deprives people of opportunities for self-governance, and suppresses avenues for gradual improvement, thereby fostering a poorly informed, narrow-minded, and frustrated public opinion, which is prone to bursts of anger and unrest with even the slightest provocation. The patriotic sentiment triggered by the Paris telegram largely resulted from the systematic repression of free speech and press, which had long prevented the emergence of a rational public opinion in China.

The suppression of rational proposals for political reform by the imperial court during the Qing dynasty indeed played a significant role in fueling revolutionary sentiment among the Chinese public. The Xinhai Revolution did not bring an end to revolutionary discourse. Instead, the disillusionment with the practice of republican politics and the failure to establish a stable and democratic system only heightened the desire for a more radical and thorough revolution. Following the May Fourth Movement, China's mainstream ideology shifted towards radicalism, and revolutionary totalitarianism began to dominate public discourse. The new ideology advocated for comprehensive state control over every aspect of society, including politics, the economy, speech, thought, and belief. Advocating to use state violence and control to bring about social transformation, it represented a total departure from the concept of a social contract freely formed by the people.

2.4.1 *The Characteristics of Chinese Public Opinion in Late Qing and Early Republic*

In the first two decades of the twentieth century, a critical period that would determine China's destiny, the Chinese public opinion exhibited several characteristics. First, the number of newspaper readers was low in comparison with its over 400 million population at the time. The newspaper sales reached a peak during the Xinhai Revolution, but it was still less than 1 percent of the population. In six months after the Wuchang Uprising, the number of newspapers in the country increased from over 100 a decade before to over 500, with a total circulation of 42 million copies.[40] The number should stand for annual rather than daily circulation, as even the best-selling newspapers at the time printed only around 10,000 copies per day.[41] Since the vast majority of

[40] Ge Gongzhen (戈公振), *The History of Study on Chinese Press* [in Chinese] (Shanghai: The Commercial Press, 1927), Ch. 5, p. 4.

[41] The Reformist newspaper – *Current Affairs* 《时务报》 once reached a peak circulation of 17,000 copies per day, setting a record as the highest circulation among domestic newspapers at that time.

newspapers had a daily circulation of less than 1,000, the daily sales of over 500 newspapers would be at most several million copies, less than 1 percent of the population. This was unsurprising because, when the Nine-Year Plan for Constitutional Preparation was launched in 1906, it was estimated that the literacy rate in China was less than 1 percent, which was unlikely to rapidly increase in the next decade. In other words, those who fought fiercely on the battlefield of media, be they the revolutionaries, reformers, or conservatives, constituted together only a small minority of elites, while the vast majority of the nation remained completely ignorant and indifferent to the dynamics of public opinion that would determine the direction of the national development.

Second, the Chinese news media at the time lacked the tradition of independent journalism based on objectivity and impartiality. The influential newspapers, whether run by reformers or revolutionaries, were essentially "party newspapers" whose finance and personnel depended on particular political parties or factions. Their primary function was to promote specific political positions and opinions rather than provide political information to the general public. As a result, it was almost inevitable for them to slander or spread rumors under political directives. For example, *Hui Bao* (汇报), one of the first Chinese newspapers founded in 1874 by a Chinese, Rong Hong (容闳), known as the very first Chinese student studying abroad, was accused by *Shun Pao* (申报), the oldest Chinese newspaper owned by the British, of being "frequently false" and was discontinued within a year and a half of its publication.[42] Instead of reaching an agreement on objective facts, these newspapers constantly attacked each other, making it difficult for ordinary readers to judge what to believe and to cultivate the civic habit of impartial rationality. Since most citizens were predisposed, prejudiced, and ignorant about simple facts, China was full of mutually opposed radical sentiments, making it impossible to reach basic political consensus, much less a social contract.

Third, during the late Qing dynasty, the media industry was heavily influenced by state violence, effectively fueling radical public opinion and promoting the development of revolutionary forces. In 1894, when Sun Yat-sen founded the Society for Reviving China (兴中会) in Honolulu, it initially attracted few responses in the first five years. In comparison, when Kang Youwei established the Royalist Society (保皇会) overseas in 1899, the response was overwhelming, with donations exceeding US$1.6 million.

[42] Fang Hanqi, *The History of Modern Chinese Press* [in Chinese] (Taiyuan: Shanxi Education Press, 1981), p. 63.

When they founded the influential *Times* (时报) in 1904, they were able to take out 100,000 yuan to start the newspaper immediately. However, as time went by, the balance of power gradually tipped towards the revolutionary forces. The reformers found fundraising increasingly difficult to the point that when Liang Qichao traveled to Taiwan in 1911 to raise the same amount for another newspaper, he returned with nothing.[43]

The popular support for the royalist faction was weakened not so much by the revolutionary party as by the imperial court's stubborn refusal to reform. The reformers, represented by Kang and Liang, demanded constitutional reform and a limited monarchy, essentially to maintain the stability and longevity of the Qing dynasty. Despite their mildness, the reformist views were repeatedly suppressed. In July 1907, Liang secretly returned to Shanghai to establish the newspaper *Political Commentary* (政论), with the aim of "implementing a parliamentary system and building a responsible government" so that the reformers could offer advice on policies regarding the Congress, finance, currency, and local autonomy. As these pieces of advice would be entirely constructive, such a newspaper would obviously benefit the imperial rule in the long run. In August 1908, however, the Qing government banned the Political News Society (政闻社) on the grounds that it would "rally partisans and plot to incite disturbances and disrupt public security under the name of studying current affairs."[44] As a result, *Political Commentary* ceased publication. In February 1910, Liang founded the *National Morale Daily* (国风报) in Shanghai. While mildly praising the imperial court for its effort to prepare for constitutional monarchy, having experienced repeated delays and repressions by an insincere and incompetent court, he could not help but express harsh words such as that "the country will fall into chaos within three years, to the point of demise."[45] Between 1898 and 1911, at least fifty-three newspapers were banned, accounting for more than a third of the total newspapers at the time. In connection with this, twenty-five people were arrested and two were killed.[46]

Since the Qing government stubbornly refused to establish a constitutional monarchy, the moderate reformist position was vulnerable to attacks and ridicules from the revolutionary party, which often emerged on the winning side of debates. Its repeated rejection of reform had made revolution the only viable means to realize constitutionalism. As pointed out by a revolutionary,

43 Ibid., p. 580.

44 Ibid., pp. 576–7.

45 Chang Jiang, "On the government's fault in obstructing the Congress," 《国风报》, no. 17 (1910).

46 Fang, *The History of Modern Chinese Press*, pp. 594–6.

"the authoritarian regime is a sharp axe that harms the public interest of the nation and exploits the rights of the people. Therefore, born in a civilized world, where justice is clear and the rights consciousness is strong, everyone will seek to overthrow the despotic regime."[47] Revolutionary newspapers such as the *People* (民报) did everything they could to ridicule and insult the reformers. They not only made attacking social reformers their top priority, but also scorned every measure of constitutional reform taken by the Qing court. One of its articles accused the Qing government of "covering the people's ears and eyes by borrowing the empty name of constitutionalism."[48] Another revolutionary newspaper, *Public Opinion* (民心), insisted on "engaging in revolution without being swayed by constitutionalism."[49]

The stubbornness of the imperial court not only led to the general radicalization of public opinion but also radicalized the revolutionary faction itself. Initially, the conflicts between the revolutionary and reformist factions were not irreconcilable. In January 1900, the revolutionary party established its official newspaper, *China Daily*, with the expectation of cooperating with reformers such as Kang and Liang, and even the enlightened Qing officials, such as Li Hongzhang, for whom it expressed much praise. However, radical anti-Manchu speeches soon emerged. Zou Rong's *Revolutionary Army* (革命军), the most influential revolutionary pamphlet of the time, opened with a call to kill all five million Manchus "who wear furs and horns."[50] Written by an eighteen-year-old youth, the radical pamphlet was published in more than twenty editions, totaling over 1.1 million copies. In 1903, Chen Tianhua's *Fierce Turn* (猛回头) also expressed strong racial revanchism. As anti-Manchu sentiments grew more intense, the revolutionary forces continued to expand. After the establishment of the Alliance Society (同盟会), the number of students studying in Japan reached up to 20,000 per year, of which Sun Yat-sen claimed that 80–90 percent supported the revolution. Revolutionary violence had become a popular trend, as reflected in the popularity of the press. Whenever newspapers reported news about armed uprisings, such as the one taking place at Yellow Flower Hill (黄花岗), "sales would greatly increase until all copies were sold out, while a newspaper carrying any derogatory speeches about the revolution would find no buyers."[51]

47 Yuan Sun, "The Lucia Nihilist Party," 《江苏》, no. 4 (1903).

48 "Manchuria preparing for constitutionalism," 《民报》, no. 19 (1908).

49 "Public opinion for the government," 《民心》, no. 5 (1911).

50 Fang, *The History of Modern Chinese Press*, pp. 591–2.

51 Liang Jingqiu, "The story of Guangzhou Revolution on March 29," in Guangdong Provincial Research Committee on Cultural and Historical Materials ed., *Historical Materials on Xinhai Revolution in Guangdong* [in Chinese] (Guangzhou: Xinhua Bookstore, 1962), pp. 2–3.

By the eve of the Xinhai Revolution, the Chinese public had become desperate about the prospects of imperial reform, and revolution was seen as the only remaining option for China. In July 1911, two influential short commentaries published in the *Great River Daily* (大江报) reflected the prevailing sentiment at the time. One argued that only revolution could save China, dismissing other methods of promoting imperial reform such as "no acknowledgment" or "no tax payment" as pedantic and futile.[52] The other commentary, written by the celebrated scholar Huang Kan (黄侃), asserted that peaceful reform was impossible, and that "great chaos" was the only "magic medicine" to save China:

> China is in a situation where everything appears hopeless, and every path leads to a dead end. The terminal disease is already incurable. Yet everyone is intoxicated and dreaming, unaware that the time of death is approaching. Long days feel like years, wasted in lethargy. Everyone is sick like a paralyzed flower. In such a time, only a tremendous shock and radical reform can awaken the 400 million people from their slumber. They are all happily wearing the official title of slaves to a doomed nation (亡国奴) without even realizing it. Since peaceful reform has been rendered impossible by the logic of things, the ensuing great chaos without rules will cause deep wounds and great pains to the people, pushing them to the brink of destruction. But it will also make them suddenly abandon their slavish mentality towards a doomed nation and open up the possibility of hope in the absence of a better alternative. Therefore, the great chaos is truly the magic medicine to save China today.[53]

The establishment of the Republic did not substantially improve the state of press freedom. On the contrary, the suppression of the press became even more severe under warlord rule than during the Qing dynasty. Soon after the Republic was established, northeastern newspapers such as the *Three Northeastern Provinces' People* (东三省民报) were physically destroyed, and the editors and managers were beaten up. The Minister of the Interior, Zhao Bingjun (赵秉钧), and the Infantry Commander led over 200 soldiers to surround the office of the Central News (中央新闻) and arrested 11 persons. *Civil Rights Daily* (民权报) in Shanghai was harshly accused by the Public Concession for its criticism of the finance minister for raising foreign debt. Its chief editor, Dai Jitao (戴季陶), was arrested and fined on charges of "inciting assassination" and "disturbing order." Vice President Li Yuanhong closed revolutionary newspapers such as the *Great River Daily* (大江报), *Public*

[52] He, "It is the peace that will destroy China."

[53] Huang Kan, "Great chaos is the magic medicine to save China," 《大江报》 (July 26, 1911).

Opinion (民心) and *Liberty Daily* (自由报) in Wuhan on charges of "fabricating rumors" and "bewitching people's mind." Even enlightened constitutionalists did no better once they were in power. The military governor of Hunan, Tan Yankai (谭延闿), allowed local officials to ban newspapers such as *Yueyang Daily* (岳阳日报), which exposed officials' malfeasance and disturbance of local people. The acting military governor of Guangdong, Chen Jiongming (陈炯明), banned the *Public Speech Daily* (公言报) and killed two journalists. *Aurora People's Daily* (震旦民报), founded by Zhang Zhenwu (张振武), the chief of staff of the Hubei military governor's office, published the "Hero Hiding under Bed" and other articles satirizing Li Yuanhong,[54] who instigated Yuan Shikai to assassinate Zhang after he was lured to Beijing. Han Yan (韩衍), a member of the Alliance Society and the founder of the *Anhui Ship* (安徽船) and *Youth Army News* (青年军报), was assassinated as soon as he published his views openly opposing Sun Yat-sen's transfer of presidency to Yuan Shikai.[55]

When Song Jiaoren was assassinated in March 1913, newspapers affiliated with the Nationalist Party extensively alleged that Yuan Shikai was the mastermind behind the assassination. In November, after Yuan dissolved the Nationalist Party, many newspapers against the president were confiscated, and the newspapers in concessions were banned from sale. By the end of the year, only 139 domestic newspapers were still publishing, a decrease of more than 300. Not only were newspapers with strong anti-Yuan sentiments banned, but even moderate newspapers such as the *New Current Events* (时事新报) in Shanghai, *Great Han Daily* (大汉报) in Wuhan and *New National Daily* (国民新报) in Chengdu were accused of "spreading unfounded rumors" and "confusing military spirit" for occasionally offending Yuan's faction, and were closed or prohibited from delivery. Some journalists were even shot, mostly on the charges of "confusing military spirit" and "secretly aiding the partisans, with the plot to overthrow the government." The editor of the *People Stand Daily* (民立报) was accused of opposing Yuan simply for writing a eulogy for Song Jiaoren, and was immediately bound for execution without trial. During Yuan Shikai's presidency from 1912 to 1916, at least seventy-one newspapers were banned, forty-nine were interrogated, and nine were destroyed by the military police, with at least twenty-four journalists killed and sixty imprisoned.[56]

54 It was rumored at the time that Li was pulled out from underneath the bed by the revolutionary army to be its leader after the Wuchang Uprising broke out.

55 Fang, *The History of Modern Chinese Press*, pp. 694–6.

56 Ibid., pp. 719–20.

In March 1916, after Yuan Shikai's imperial ambition failed, the previously banned newspapers and periodicals were allowed to resume publication. In July, the Interior Department of Beijing Municipal Government ordered the lifting of bans on twenty-one publications. By the end of the year, the number of newspapers had recovered to 289 nationwide. The situation did not last, however. In June 1917, Li Huiquan (李汇泉), the editor and publisher of the *Southern Canton Daily* (南越报) in Guangzhou, was executed without trial for opposing gambling. In June 1918, Chen Gengfu (陈耿夫), a journalist for the Guangzhou-based *Democracy Daily* (民主报), was arrested by the Guangxi military warlords for attacking their control of finances and undermining the rule of law, and was executed on charges of "inciting mutiny." In October 1918, the Anhui military warlords enacted the Newspaper Law, imposing strict and detailed regulations on content, and incidents of newspaper closures and journalist arrests continued to occur. Between 1916 and 1918, at least twenty-nine newspapers were banned, and seventeen journalists were punished under criminal law.[57]

Not only were the media suppressed by the state, but newspapers representing different political views often attacked each other personally, sometimes even escalating into a "spectacular warfare of beating up persons and destroying newspapers."[58] Dozens of staff members from seven newspapers affiliated with the Beijing Alliance Society once destroyed the *National Gazette* (国民公报) and assaulted its chief editor. The *Hunan Gazette*, a publication of the Republican Party in Changsha, was destroyed by the *Changsha Daily*, affiliated with the Nationalists. Both sides were prepared for armed conflict, to the point where "each reporter carried a handgun when coming and going."[59] Journalists from various Nationalist newspapers sent to Beijing, governed by warlords, were also armed for self-defense. While the revolutionary party initially advocated for freedom of speech and press, they abandoned their original promise once they had gained political power and, like their predecessors, used state power and violence to suppress different viewpoints. In the highly tense media atmosphere, the political natural law of free press was repeatedly disregarded. Since the partisan struggles knew no limits, it was impossible to peacefully practice contract-based politics.

57 Ibid., pp. 726–7.
58 Ibid., pp. 702–4.
59 *Shun Pao* (May 25, 1913).

2.4.2 *The Public Opinion Change in 1911–1919: A Quantitative Illustration*

From 1911 to 1919, the setbacks in the political practices of the early Republic of China explained the radical shift in national sentiment, which was reflected in the public opinion of national newspapers during this period. Inspired by the work of Jin Guantao (金观涛) and Liu Qingfeng (刘青峰), I used the Modern Periodicals database in the National Newspaper Index developed by the Shanghai Library to search for keyword frequencies.[60] Although the quantitative indicators are somewhat crude, they can intuitively demonstrate the social impact of related concepts. Taking the word "constitutionalism" (立宪) as an example, it had the highest frequency of appearance in the first decade of the twentieth century. During the first five years of the 1900s, when the constitutional reform of the imperial court was in slumber, "constitutionalism" was not popular in the newspapers. In 1905, however, when the Qing government sent five ministers to study constitutionalism abroad and announced to "implement constitutionalism by imitation," the word suddenly surged to its peak, reflecting the sharp increase in social awareness of constitutionalism. Afterward, the number of articles discussing "constitutionalism" gradually decreased, indicating that the concept had faded from the Chinese social vision (see Figure 2.1).

A related concept is "republicanism" (共和), and its comparison with "democracy" (民主) is particularly thought-provoking. As pointed out by Jin Guantao and Liu Qingfeng, the concept of "republicanism" declined after 1919, while "democracy" became increasingly more frequent, with its meaning shifting from people's rule to "democratic dictatorship" (民主专政) and its core values settling on political and economic equality.[61] This transformation did not happen immediately, however. As shown in Figure 2.2, while the

[60] Jin and Liu, *Study on the History of Concepts*, pp. 280–2. The data here are derived, however, from the Database of Article Titles in Late Qing Periodicals (1833–1911) and the Database of Article Titles in Republican Periodicals (1911–49) provided by the Shanghai Library. In other words, the statistics here count the number of articles containing the keywords in their titles, rather than the frequency of the keywords appearing in the articles. To be sure, some relevant articles may not have the keywords in their titles, and therefore are not included in the statistics. Counting by frequency may give too much weight, however, to longer articles or those with frequent keyword appearances. While longer articles often have more impact, the length of an article is not necessarily proportional to its impact. Overall, the number of related articles can more accurately reflect the influence of a particular concept than its frequency of appearance.

[61] Ibid., pp. 282–3. It is worth noticing that, prior to 1920, the influential *New Youth*《新青年》magazine had a positive evaluation of democracy. However, negative evaluations started to emerge afterwards. After the establishment of the Communist Party in 1921, *New Youth* became the official journal of the CCP, which often criticized "democracy" as a product of capitalists and social democratic parties. Ibid., 286.

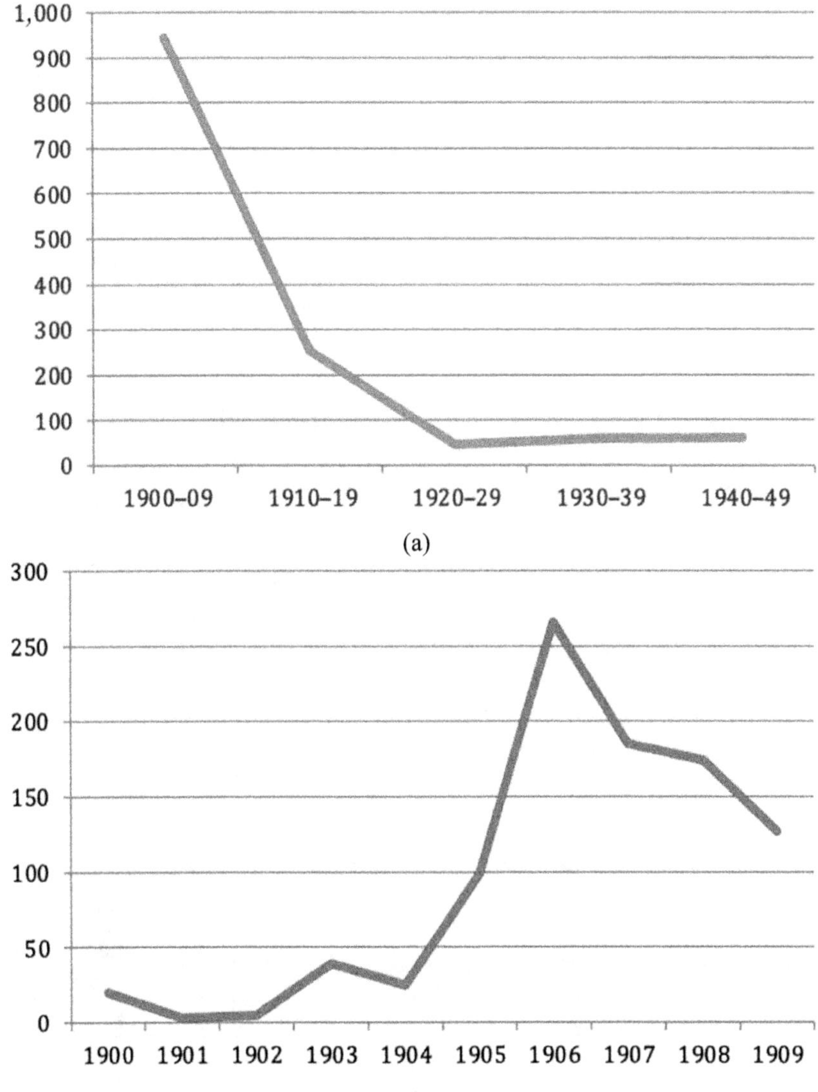

FIGURE 2.1 The total number of articles with titles containing "constitutionalism" (a) by decade, 1900–1949 and (b) annually, 1900–1909
Source: All data are derived, from the Database of Article Titles in Late Qing Periodicals (1833–1911) and the Database of Article Titles in Republican Periodicals (1911–49) provided by the Shanghai Library.

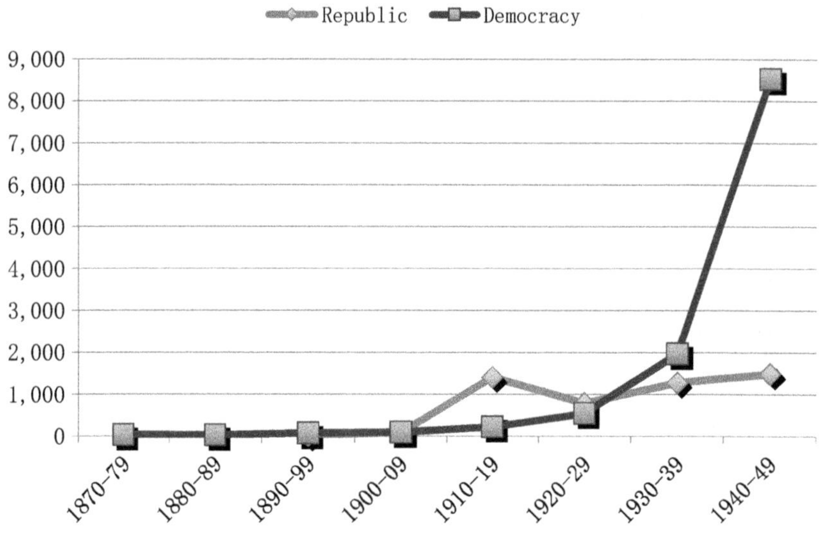

(a)

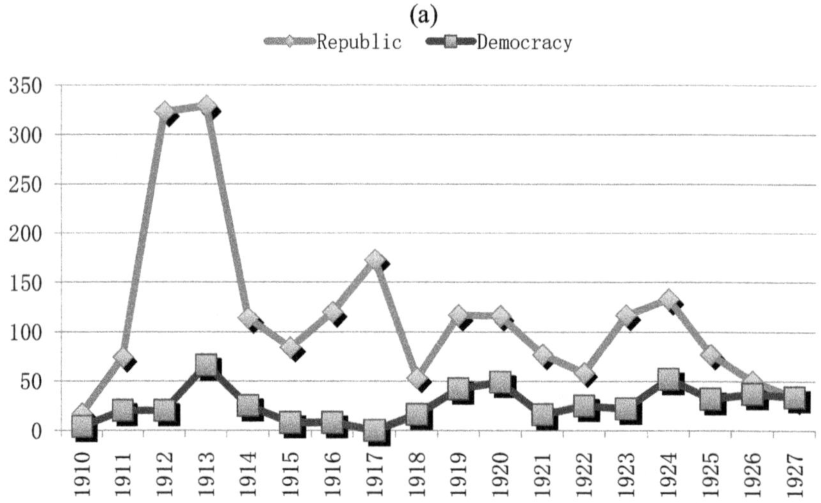

(b)

FIGURE 2.2 The total number of articles with titles containing "republic" (共和) or "democracy" (民主) (a) by decade, 1870–1949 and (b) annually, 1910–1927

Note: The number of article titles for "democracy" has excluded that for the "Three People's Doctrine" (三民主义).

Source: All data are derived, from the Database of Article Titles in Late Qing Periodicals (1833–1911) and the Database of Article Titles in Republican Periodicals (1911–49) provided by the Shanghai Library.

frequency of "republicanism" peaked in 1912 to 1913 and sharply declined thereafter, it still exceeded "democracy," a trend undisturbed by the May Fourth Movement. The transformation took place only in the 1930s, when the frequency of "democracy" began to skyrocket, and far surpassed "republicanism" in the 1940s, symbolizing the complete dominance of populism in Chinese public opinion. In the database of the Shanghai Library, the top three periodicals with the most numerous titles containing "democracy" were all left-wing publications: *National Information* (国讯), *Times Magazine* (时代杂志) and *News Classification* (新闻类编).[62]

Compared to popular terms such as "democracy" and "republicanism," terms of "social contract" (社会契约) or "civil covenant" (民约) were negligible. In the Shanghai Library's database, this concept first appeared in the periodicals around 1900, but in the following half-century, there were only thirty-one articles with titles bearing these terms. After reaching two small peaks in 1913 to 1914 and 1929,[63] this concept declined and disappeared altogether (see Figure 2.3). More important, most of the discussions at the time focused on Rousseau's social contract theory, which had conceptual flaws and produced serious harms when put into practice, particularly for underdeveloped countries such as Russia and China.[64] Little attention was given to the social contract theories of Hobbes and Locke. A rare article about Locke discussed his theory of sovereignty rather than the social contract itself.[65] Indeed, the primary focus of these articles was not social contract, but rather the more concrete problem of constitutional designs, which ought to be based on the social contract.

Liang Qichao, a prominent figure who strongly promoted Rousseau's theory, served as a typical example.[66] While he published a series on the Study of Rousseau (卢梭学案) in his own newspaper, the *China Discussion*

62 They carried 346, 303, and 218 articles, respectively, among which *News Classification* was a newspaper published by the Soviet Embassy in Chongqing.

63 Since each of these years had only four relevant articles, the fluctuation in the number of titles was subject to a great deal of contingency. If the minor peak in 1913–14 was possibly related to the establishment of the Republic of China, the contributions in 1929 all came from a single person, Hu Gongxian, who serialized four articles in the same journal: "Social contract theory and its critics,"《社会科学论丛》, 1, no. 3 (1929), 11–27; "Social contract theory and its critics: An analysis of the content of social contract theory,"《社会科学论丛》, 1, no. 4 (1929), 64–78; "Social contract theory and its critics: A critique of the value of social contract theory,"《社会科学论丛》, 1, no. 5 (1929), 54–61; "The logical fallacy of social contract theory,"《社会科学论丛》, 1, no. 6 (1929), 67–78.

64 Zhang, "Against the holistic temptations," 370–80.

65 "Locke's theory on sovereignty,"《新民丛报》, 42–43 (1903), 28–31.

66 Liang Qichao, "The theory of Rousseau, a great social contract scholar,"《新民丛报》, 2, no. 3 (1900), 39–71.

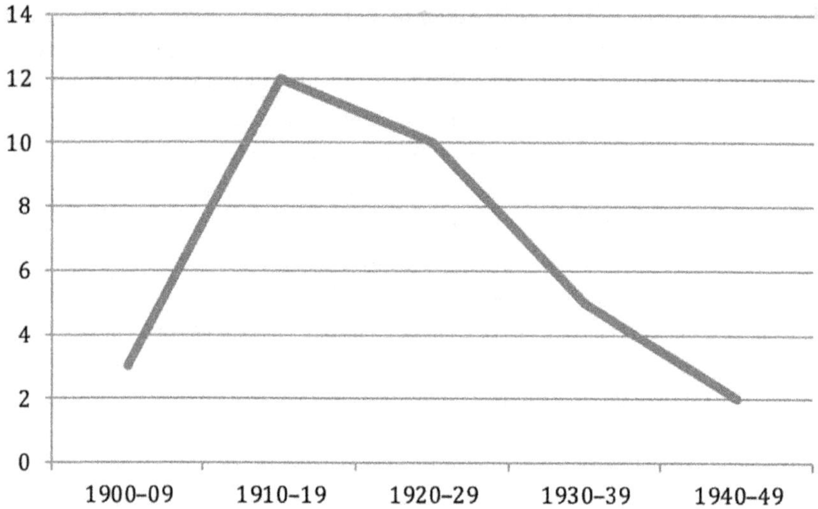

FIGURE 2.3 The combined total number of articles with titles containing "social contract" (民约) and "social covenant" (社会契约) by decade (1900–1949)
Source: All data are derived, from the Database of Article Titles in Late Qing Periodicals (1833–1911) and the Database of Article Titles in Republican Periodicals (1911–49) provided by the Shanghai Library.

(清议报), he did not truly grasp Rousseau's theory. As evidence, he used the egalitarian social contract as the basis of his argument for constitutional monarchy in a debate with the revolutionary leader Wang Jingwei about the desirable form of a political system, which ultimately ended in failure.[67] Only many years later did Liang realize the radical implications of Rousseau's theory and its dangers to China's constitutional reform.[68] If even Liang Qichao, known as the "first person" to enlighten China with modern

[67] Sun Hongyun, "The 1905–1907 debate between Wang Jingwei and Liang Qichao on racial revolution and its relation to J. K. Bluntschli's theory of the state,"《学术研究》, no. 6 (2002); Ren Ze, "Wang Jingwei's refutation of Liang Qichao's view on Rousseau,"《经济观察报》(July 8, 2018).

[68] Liang Qichao, "What I have for serving my country from now on," *Collection of Ice Chamber Papers, Set* 30 [in Chinese] (Beijing: Chung Hwa Book Co., 1936), p. 54; Yan Deru and Han Liqun, "The gradually banished Rousseau: Focusing on Liang Qichao's understanding,"《北京科技大学学报（社会科学版）》, no. 2 (2011). These contributions did not significantly alter the overall assessment of Liang Qichao's lack of understanding of the social contract. Although he recognized that Rousseau's theory of the social contract was not feasible for China, his shift seemed to be from Rousseauism to Hegelianism. In his article, "Observations on the 'Chinese nation' in history," *New People's Gazette*, no. 17 (1905), Liang introduced the concept of the "Chinese nation" (中华民族) as a multi-ethnic state, which was indeed a significant intellectual contribution. However, without a foundation of the social contract as the basis for the relationship between ethnic groups, it is difficult to avoid the risk of centralized unity and the oppression of ethnic minorities.

Western theories, had such a limited understanding, it can be inferred that the general public had even less comprehension of the social contract theory. Needless to say, a political practice based on the consciousness of social contract had never existed before or after the republican revolution.

After the establishment of the Republic, the New Culture Movement made little intellectual progress in propagating the social contract ideas, and the May Fourth Movement marked the very end of the liberal enlightenment in China. Even Hu Shih, a recognized leader of China's liberal movement, never took interest in the topic. In 1917, as the October Revolution shook Chinese intellectuals, the term "revolution" (革命) experienced a small surge in popularity. After 1919, the radical student movement and the rapid spread of left-wing ideology further diminished the interest in the social contract. In contrast, the number of articles discussing "revolution" skyrocketed, far surpassing the peak reached during the Xinhai Revolution (see Figure 2.4). In fact, throughout history, except for the last decade of the nineteenth century, the popularity of "revolution" consistently outweighed that of "reform," aligning with the research of Jin Guantao and Liu Qingfeng.[69]

From the outset, revolutionary magazines closely followed the events of the Russian Revolution and displayed a strong interest in revolutionary violence. For example, the periodical of the revolutionary party, *Jiangsu*, advocated for violent revolution, asserting that the Russian Revolution succeeded because the Russian people were "good at revolt! Good at killing officials, killing the monarch, killing foreign nationals!!!"[70] In addition to promoting revolutionary violence, these periodicals also demonstrated great interest in radical left-wing ideologies such as communism. Interestingly, it was not the Communist Party but the revolutionary party led by Sun Yat-sen that initially introduced socialist and anarchist ideas. As early as 1903, the editorial of *Jiangsu* praised the "communist doctrine of equalizing wealth and poverty."[71] Another revolutionary journal, *Zhejiang Tide* (浙江潮), criticized capitalist inequality and exploitation, predicting a "purely socialist world at the turn of the nineteenth and twentieth centuries."[72] Believing

69 Before 1900, the frequency of reform was noticeably higher than that of revolution. In 1903 and 1906, two small peaks of revolution occurred. The former was due to the publication of *Revolutionary Army* by Zou Rong, leading to the rise of radical intellectuals. The latter was attributed to the *Minbao* 《民报》 newspaper that established the revolutionary faction, with Zhang Taiyan (章太炎) as the editor-in-chief and Chen Tianhua (陈天华) arguing for the legitimacy of revolution in the inaugural issue. See Jin and Liu, *Study on the History of Concepts*, pp. 382–5.

70 Fang, *The History of Modern Chinese Press*, p. 222.

71 Editorial, "New soul of nationals," 《江苏》, no. 5 (1903).

72 Dalu zhimin, "History of recent great changes in the century," 《浙江潮》, no. 6 (1903).

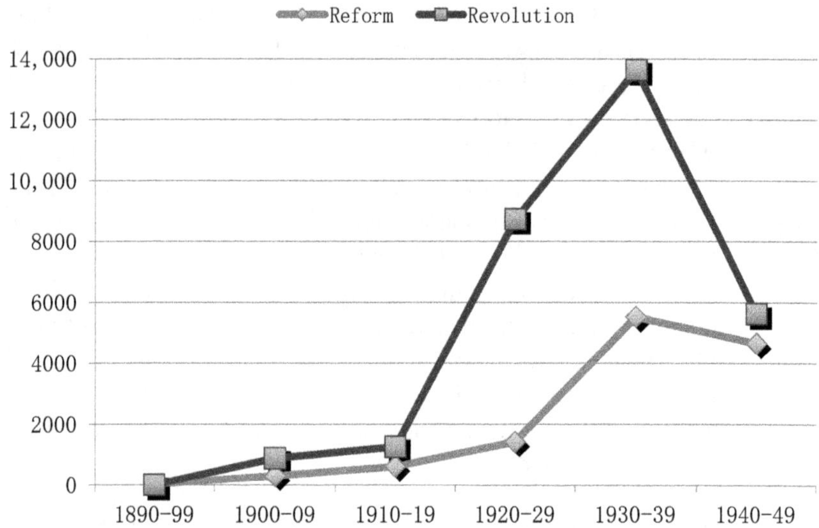

FIGURE 2.4 The total number of articles with titles containing "reform" or "revolution" by decade (1890–1949)
Note: The number of article titles for "revolution" excludes the articles containing "National Revolutionary Army" (国民革命军), which frequently appeared in various government announcements.
Source: All data are derived, from the Database of Article Titles in Late Qing Periodicals (1833–1911) and the Database of Article Titles in Republican Periodicals (1911–49) provided by the Shanghai Library.

that "socialism will increase the happiness of mankind and eliminate misfortunes," it called for the abolition of private ownership and property inheritance.[73] In 1905, during the first Russian Revolution, the *Chinese Times* introduced various Russian factions such as the Decemberists, Social Democrats, and anarchists. Through authors like Liao Zhongkai (廖仲恺) and Song Jiaoren, it systematically translated and compiled socialist doctrines, including the *Communist Manifesto*. Translations of the Manifesto's preface and main text were continuously published in *Heavenly Justice* (天义报), an anarchist-oriented revolutionary newspaper.[74]

The May Fourth Movement in 1919 was not intentionally initiated by the left-wing forces in China at that time, but was triggered by the opportunistic propaganda of the marginalized Study Society (研究系) in an attempt to

[73] Dawo, "A theory of a new society," 《浙江潮》, no. 8 (1903).

[74] *Tianyi Bao*, Combined Collection of no. 15 (January 15, 1908) and nos. 16–19 (March 15, 1908). To be sure, although revolutionary party newspapers and publications despised the various problems associated with capitalism and envisioned socialism, they generally did not believe that proletarian revolution was necessary.

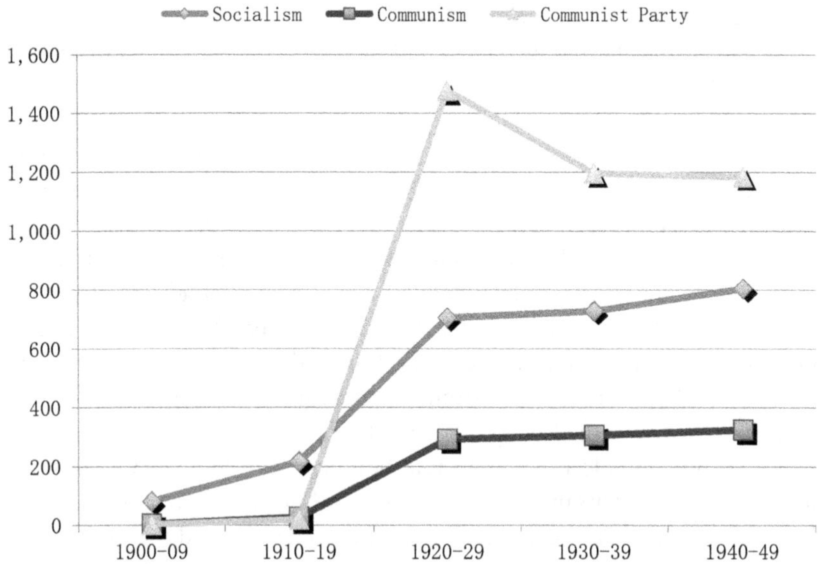

FIGURE 2.5 The total number of articles with titles containing "socialism," "communism," or "Communist Party" by decade (1900–1949)
Source: All data are derived, from the Database of Article Titles in Late Qing Periodicals (1833–1911) and the Database of Article Titles in Republican Periodicals (1911–49) provided by the Shanghai Library.

regain political prominence.[75] However, it became a necessity due to the prevailing radical sentiment, and fundamentally reshaped the national political landscape, marking a watershed moment in modern Chinese history. The year 1919 witnessed the emergence of several key concepts and events. From this point on, words such as "Marx," "Lenin," "Soviet," "Communist Party," "Socialism," and "Communism" all experienced explosive growth (see Figure 2.5). "Socialism" had a minor peak in 1912, thanks to Sun Yat-sen's introduction of the concept. "Communism" enjoyed a small surge in 1914, but was associated with "anarchy" at the time. After 1919, however, all these concepts received contemporary orthodox interpretations.

[75] In late April 1919, while Liang Qichao was traveling in Paris, he learned that the negotiations regarding the Shandong issue had failed at the Peace Conference. Upon receiving this information, Liang telegraphed Lin Changmin, who promptly responded by mobilizing the Study Society. On May 2, Lin published a provocative article titled "A diplomatic alert warning the nation" in the Study Society's *Morning Post* 《晨报》. The article exaggeratedly declared that "Jiaozhou is lost, Shandong is lost, the nation is no more! May our 400 million compatriots swear to die for it!" This article successfully stirred up the students' sense of national salvation, leading to the burning of Zhao's Mansion the following day. See Ma Jianbiao, "The euphemistic alliance: Peking University and the Study Society during the period of the May Fourth Movement," *Fudan University Journal*, no. 5 (2018): 61–70.

Indeed, the May Fourth Movement not only gave birth to the Communist Party, but also revitalized the Nationalist Party that was declining in vitality.[76] The terms "Lenin" and "Soviet" experienced a small peak in frequency in 1923–24 when Sun Yat-sen reorganized the Nationalist Party based on Soviet principles (Figure 2.6a). From 1927 to 1949, the "Three People's Principle" experienced a long-lasting climax (Figure 2.6b), corresponding to the era of the one-party rule (党治) after the success of the Northern Expedition and, serving this purpose, the beginning of the deification movement of the "founding father" (国父). Following the advice of Soviet advisors, Sun Yat-sen completed in 1924 the reorganization of the Nationalist Party in Guangzhou. In the following year, the Guangzhou government was transformed into the "National Government" through the National Government Organization Law, establishing the earliest form of party rule in China.

According to Article 1 of the Organization Law, "the National Government handles national affairs under the command and supervision of the Nationalist Party." From the beginning, the Organization Law adopted the principle of "one authority" without clearly defining the powers and limits of the National Government. It appeared to be a comprehensive body that combined legislative, executive, and judicial powers. Although subsequent modifications gave it the rudimentary form of a "five-powers constitution" (五权宪法), the government functioned merely as an instrument of the party, subject to its command and supervision at all times. The government's role was to reflect the party's will and implement its power. Party resolutions or commands were often directly copied into official government documents and ordinances. Even after several revisions to the Organization Law following the victory of the Northern Expedition, the principle of party rule remained unchanged throughout the constitutional-making process of that period. As advocated by Hu Hanmin (胡汉民), a right-wing leader within the Nationalist Party, strict one-party dictatorship was to be implemented during the entire period of "tutelage politics" (训政):

> There is not only no party outside the party, but also no politics outside the party ... all powers are concentrated by the party and carried out by the party. The party is responsible for babysitting the government, so it leads the government and supports the government ... Only the party could represent the entire nation and undertake the task of nation-building, and only the

[76] Hu Shih observed that the purpose of the Nationalist reorganization in 1924 was "to fully absorb the youth who emerged in the New Cultural Movement," Ma, "The euphemistic alliance," 69–70.

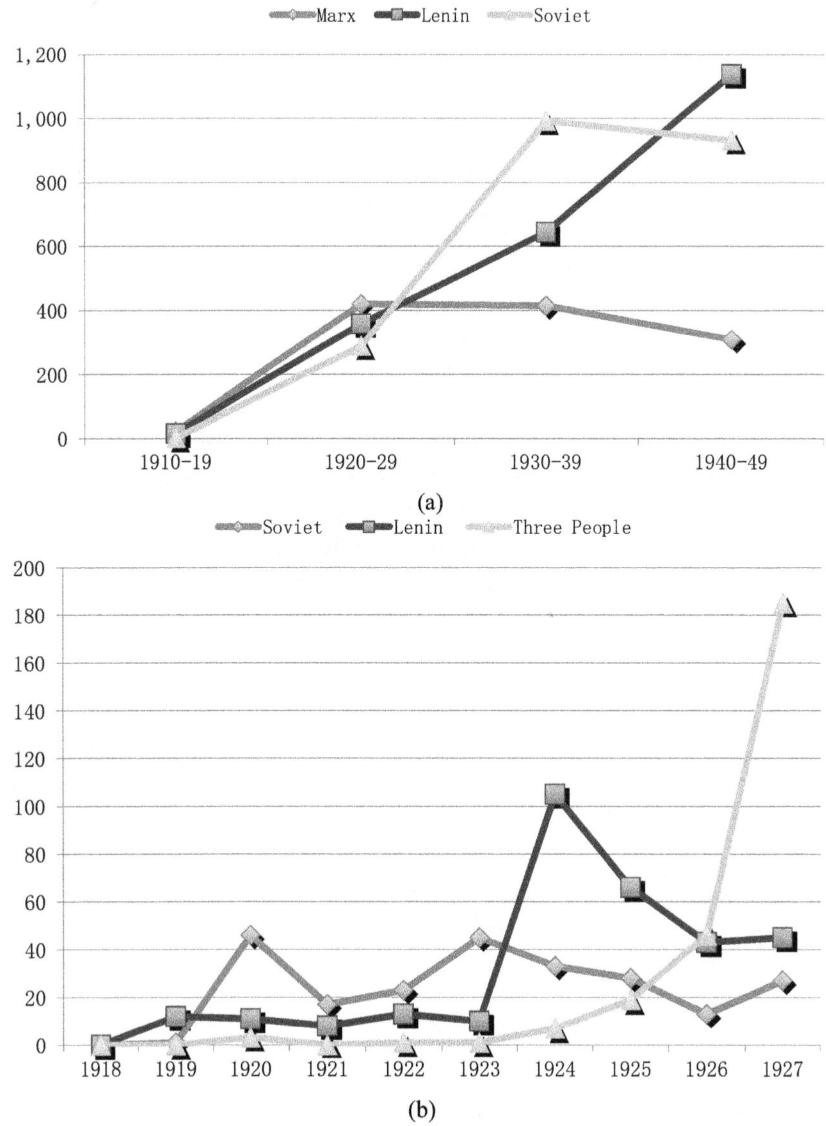

FIGURE 2.6 The total number of articles with titles containing (a) "Marx," "Lenin," and "Soviet" by decade, 1910–1949 and (b) "Soviet," "Lenin," and "Three People's Doctrine" annually, 1918–1927

Source: All data are derived, from the Database of Article Titles in Late Qing Periodicals (1833–1911) and the Database of Article Titles in Republican Periodicals (1911–49) provided by the Shanghai Library.

> party could guide the people of the entire nation towards realizing the Three People's Principle.[77]

As Chinese history has repeatedly shown, the result of implementing one-party dictatorship in society inevitably leads to personal dictatorship within the party. Chiang Kai-shek concentrated party, government, and military powers in his hands. The system of party dictatorship created the necessary and often sufficient political conditions for personal dictatorship.

The vicissitudes of the political concepts such as "constitutionalism," "republicanism," "democracy," "social contract," "reform," "revolution," "socialism," "communism," and the "Three People's Principle" from 1911 to 1919 illustrated that the Chinese intellectual elites and the general public were ignorant about the contract-based politics, dissatisfied with the political chaos brought by republic constitutionalism, skeptical of the Western liberal democracy, and yearning for Soviet revolution and communism. As a result, the Leninist totalitarianism gained widespread popularity in China. After 1919, totalitarian revolutionary extremism dominated China's mainstream ideology. Both the Nationalist and the Communist parties were advocates of totalitarianism. In that sense, China's destiny was already foreclosed by 1919, awaiting only a military victory for the formal ascendence of a totalitarian regime. With the Nationalist reorganization in 1924 and the success of the Northern Expedition in 1927, the one-party dictatorship system finally entered the historical stage, with the Nationalist creed of the "Three People's Principle" taking over as the new orthodoxy, which completely eliminated all remnants of the failed contract-based politics of the early Republic. By the time when the cooperation between the two revolutionary parties broke down again in 1946, and the Nationalist was defeated in the ensuing civil war, an even greater totalitarian Leviathan was established, under which China has been governed to this day.

2.5 CONCLUSIONS

If the past of modern China is too painful a lesson to look back on, what about its contemporary situation, after a century of travails is over? On the one hand, since 1978, China has experienced another opportunity for reform that lasted for forty years. Although political reform suffered a major setback merely a decade later and stagnated, as the Hundred Days' Reform did in 1898,

77 Zhang Guofu, *The Constitutional History of the Republic of China* [in Chinese] (Beijing: Sino-Culture Press, 1991), p. 263.

economic reform continued shortly. In a few years, market-oriented reforms injected enormous vitality into Chinese society, and private contracts became prevalent. The Chinese economy gradually shifted from a state-controlled planned economy to a market economy led by private contracts. On the other hand, the contract-based economy has not transformed into a contract-based politics. Like a century ago, China today still lacks minimal awareness of social contract. None of the five political natural laws – freedom of religion and belief, freedom of speech, equal protection (especially against ethnic discrimination), electoral democracy, administrative impartiality, and judicial independence – has been implemented. While judicial reform, the least politically sensitive reform, was put on the agenda after 1999, it reached an impasse only after two decades, by which time even "judicial independence" had become a "sensitized word" (敏感词). The other four principles were not so blatantly violated in the four decades since 1978 as they were in the first three decades after 1949, but they have not been implemented to any degree. While elections of the basic-level people's congresses (基层人大) were once active in the early 1980s, they have remained stagnant ever since, to the point that every congressional election in China is heavily controlled and manipulated by the ruling party. Since substantive political reform cannot move forward, China today has returned to the debate between reform and revolution found prevalent in the late Qing dynasty.

To be sure, as discussed in the next chapter, the basic freedoms of ordinary people have improved significantly as a matter of fact over four decades of reform. Especially in the past twenty years, with the rapid development of internet technology, people's ability to express opinions and receive information has greatly increased, and civil society has grown rapidly. If contemporary China is any different from itself a century ago, it is that the people's right to know, legal knowledge, and the awareness of participation have achieved a quantum leap, which is the precondition to transition from totalitarian regime to a polity based on social contract. While the actions of political and social elites are no doubt important in regime transition, it is easy to overlook the role of ordinary people in establishing the social contract. The lessons of Chinese modern history repeatedly show that, if the general public remains unenlightened, the elite behaviors will not adhere to the basic rules of political game, as violation of the rules will go unpunished. In fact, since all reformist elites were removed from the system since 1989, progressive forces can only emerge from an enlightened and self-conscious community of the people. If their demand for reform is broad and strong enough, a horizontal alliance may result from the process of forming a consensus for reform, leading to a social contract.

It must be acknowledged, however, that the civil society in China, growing out of the thawing totalitarian iceberg, is still feeble. Civilian alliances not only face oppression from the state, but also lack solidarity among themselves. Under top-down fragmentation and disintegration, horizontal connections are easily shattered. Compared with the late Qing dynasty, China today faces a much deeper political dilemma. If the reformist elites have disappeared or at least cannot appear publicly, is the civilian alliance alone sufficient to reach a social contract? The prospects for such an outcome are slim today. Not only are factions within civil society intolerant of each other, but even within the liberal camp, the moderate and radical factions have little common ground. Similar to their predecessors such as Kang Youwei and Liang Qichao a century ago, moderate reformists today are ridiculed and mocked by radical proponents of revolution in an environment where the party-state stubbornly refuses to reform and harshly suppresses free speech. It cannot be predicted whether China can break free from the vicious cycle of failed reform and revolution. However, it is certain that if it continues to fail in reaching a social contract centered on political natural laws, and if both its elites and general public continue to indulge in power worship and the jungle logic of winner takes all, China is destined to remain trapped in the vicious cycle that has persisted for two millennia.

3

The Rise and Fall of Totalitarianism

The Cultural Revolution and Beyond

3.1 INTRODUCTION

The twentieth century was known for its extreme polarization. In some countries, liberal democracy was expanded and consolidated, while in others, authoritarianism reached its peak, even turning into totalitarianism. World War I led to the downfall of the Russian Empire and, in its place, the Soviet Union was established in 1917 as the very first totalitarian regime. After the Great Depression of 1929, fascism rose in Europe and Japan almost simultaneously, once again plunging the world into the horror of a great war. Shortly after the end of World War II, the socialist bloc consisting of countries under Soviet control or influence, such as Eastern Europe, Cuba, China, and North Korea, successively established totalitarian regimes, causing immense suffering for their people. As a consequence of the totalitarian rampage, the Chinese Communist Party (CCP) initiated political movements after seizing power from the Nationalists in 1949, culminating in the Great Famine, euphemistically referred to by the party as the "three years of natural disaster" (三年自然灾害) from 1959 to 1962, and the Cultural Revolution from 1966 to 1976. The Cultural Revolution, in particular, is seen as a significant human catastrophe and the peak of Mao's totalitarianism. However, it is a gross mischaracterization, indicating a fundamental misunderstanding of the working mechanisms of totalitarianism in general and the nature of the Cultural Revolution in particular. For countries like China, which are desperately seeking a way out of totalitarian dictatorship, it is particularly necessary to explore the structure and mechanisms of totalitarianism, both in its construction and deconstruction.

Totalitarianism is the most profound political revolution in human history, with its original purpose to transform human nature through state machinery. Prior to 1917, any government in the world, whether democratic or authoritarian, aspired primarily to regulate the behavior of its people. In contrast, a totalitarian regime seeks to control not only behavior but also the very motives behind behavior, including thoughts and beliefs. While a typical authoritarian regime is satisfied with keeping social actions within bounds, a competent totalitarian regime aims to instill the official ideology in every individual and convert them into ardent supporters of a regime that enslaves their very souls. It obliterates the distinction between inner and outer, mind and action, thus erasing the primordial separation of powers in human history, namely the separation between God and Caesar. To be sure, absolutist regimes such as the Chinese and Russian empires did have an official ideology or religion, but the fusion of the secular and spiritual rulers was far from complete. Modern totalitarianism, on the other hand, aspires to dismantle any "wall of separation" between the powers that control beliefs and those that regulate behavior by centralizing all power in the state, ultimately placing it in the hands of one person, the supreme leader who also serves as the highest priest of the nation.

Although theocracy, in theory, is capable of achieving a similar integration between the state and religion, it is often a lesser harm compared to a totalitarian regime. In a theocratic regime under Islam, for example, the religious leader is usually unable to assume complete control over every secular detail, despite claiming the supreme title in both the secular and spiritual worlds.[1] Furthermore, since the church outlives any particular regime, political power typically cannot fully infiltrate the church hierarchy before the regime's lifespan comes to an end. More important, the church itself represents a form of organizational power, wherein religious believers are never isolated from one another and can always expect the protection of their peers, making it difficult for a theocratic regime to establish a personal rule of a supreme leader.

[1] It is no coincidence that, among fifty-seven nations in which Muslims constitute the majority of population, only a few, such as Iran, Afghanistan, and Brunei, can be characterized as pure theocracy. Contrary to common belief, Saudi Arabia is not a pure theocracy since its monarch is not the highest religious leader, even though Article 1 of its 1993 Constitution declares that "Holy Quran and the Sunnah of His Prophet … are its constitution." Even in Iran, there is a degree of separation of powers between the president and the highest spiritual leader, leading to shifting balance between reformers and hard-liners. See Wilfried Buchta, *Who Rules Iran: The Structure of Power in the Islamic Republic* (Washington, DC: Washington Institute for Near East Policy, 2002), pp. 31–48.

In contrast, a secular state like Confucian-dominated imperial China is more vulnerable to a totalitarian takeover. The absence of a religious tradition allows an ascending totalitarian regime to create a secular religion seemingly out of thin air and implant it into every mind through a state-controlled propaganda apparatus. For a community that previously had a strong religious tradition, the risk of a totalitarian takeover increases as it becomes secularized. In fact, totalitarianism itself is a secularized form of "political religion,"[2] which replaces waning spiritual worship with new power worship based on secular "truth." As Talmon pointed out, after the Renaissance and the Enlightenment, the traditional European order gradually collapsed, and the church began to lose its intellectual support and emotional attachment. As the feudal society based on status was replaced by an egalitarian society of isolated individuals, utilitarianism became the dominant standard for measuring institutional validity, and the secular state replaced the church as the sole guardian of the moral order.[3] After the religious worldview transformed into a rationalist secular worldview, religious power evolved into state power, combining strength with truth.

This part elaborates on the concept, characteristics and conditions for the construction of totalitarianism, and discusses the causes and potential paths of totalitarian transformation. It was originally written in 2016, half a century after the outbreak of the Cultural Revolution. Its purpose was not to examine the revolution itself, however, but rather to analyze the nature and process of totalitarianism, of which the Cultural Revolution was a bitter fruit. When the trauma finally ended with the fall of the Gang of Four (四人帮) in 1976, significant institutional progress was made, including the establishment of term limits for major party leaders. This progress was necessary because the personal worship of Mao Zedong (毛泽东), who had previously served as the President of the State from 1954 to 1959, was seen as a primary cause of the Cultural Revolution. However, with the constitutional amendment in 2018 removing the term limit for the President of the State, China appears to be rapidly reverting to its totalitarian past. To prevent a similar tragedy from recurring, it is crucial to study totalitarianism and explore possible ways to avoid it. The most effective way to remember the Cultural Revolution is to learn from its lessons, through which the recurrence of similar tragedy can be avoided.

[2] A. James Gregor, *Totalitarianism and Political Religion: An Intellectual History* (Stanford: Stanford University Press, 2012), pp. 3–5.

[3] J. L. Talmon, *The Origins of Totalitarian Democracy* (New York: Praeger, 1960), pp. 1–3.

3.2 DEFINITION AND PATTERNS OF TOTALITARIANISM

3.2.1 *Definition*

Totalitarianism refers to a form of regime where an all-powerful state exerts comprehensive control of every minute detail of life over all individuals within its jurisdiction. As defined by Conquest, "In a totalitarian regime, the state recognizes no limits and seeks to control every aspect of public and private life to the fullest extent possible."[4] Although a totalitarian regime does exert their power to the extreme in its effort to control all aspects of human affairs, its essence lies not in how much it actually controls, but in its unbridled ability to control whatever comes into its purview. Since the power of the state is without limit, it can control whatever it wants and in whatever way it chooses, depriving individuals of all rights to autonomy and self-defense. Before the state, individuals are entirely powerless to defend themselves. In its heyday, the totalitarian regime controls not only every body and its action, but also every soul and its thoughts.

If I may use an electrical circuit as an analogy, totalitarianism can be likened to a perfect conductor with zero impedance, where social resistivity is nonexistent and the current flow of power reaches infinity when any voltage is applied. This abnormal political condition is analogous to a short circuit in an electrical system, which can burn out its components. Similarly, the unrestrained power of a totalitarian regime will inevitably burn out its social fabric. In a highly centralized totalitarian state, "society" as an autonomous entity ceases to exist, as demonstrated by the political catastrophes like the Cultural Revolution. In fact, totalitarianism not only causes a power "short circuit," but also uses the massive state "generator" to charge and indoctrinate every individual within its grip. Deeply harmed by the totalitarian regime, these individuals should have risen up to resist against the regime in order to protect and preserve themselves. Once they have been transformed into "mini-batteries," however, they not only accept their abject condition of slavery, but positively abet the regime to more deeply enslave themselves. When the totalitarian "generator" itself is running out, each "mini-battery" may supply the source to prolong its lifetime.

The essence of totalitarianism is to collectively short-circuit the minds of an entire nation through the short-circuiting of political power. The double short-circuiting of state power and national consciousness reinforces each

[4] Robert Conquest, *Reflections on a Ravaged Century* (New York: W. W. Norton & Co., 1999), p. 74.

other. The totalitarian regime is at risk of collapse as long as there is a single citizen who maintains independent thinking, as it indicates that the state power has not achieved the perfect condition of zero or even "negative" impedance.

Indeed, while totalitarianism as a distinct concept emerged in modern times, it can be traced back to certain characteristics present in traditional authoritarian regimes. The idea of constitutional limits on state power is a relatively recent development. In traditional societies such as imperial China, if a king remained inactive for some reason, the state might limit its own power within a moderate range, but there was nothing to prevent a tyrant from seizing power and expanding it without constraints. The signing of the Magna Carta in 1215 by King John of England marked a significant moment in history, as it represented a balance of power between the king and the nobility.[5] This balance, however fortuitous, placed limits on the exercise of state power, a condition rarely found in traditional regimes. In absolute monarchies, where the power of the monarch knows no bounds, the potential for totalitarianism can easily be realized. When a monarch is supported by an appealing ideology that legitimizes unlimited state power, along with a powerful party capable of exercising that unlimited control over all aspects of life, an absolute monarchy can evolve into a totalitarian state. The absence of fully developed totalitarian states in premodern societies can be attributed to the limitations of bureaucratic machinery and technical conditions of the time. The organizational infrastructure required for mass political parties, along with their political programs and propaganda instruments, was lacking in efficiency in premodern societies. As a result, the emergence of a fully-fledged totalitarian state was hindered by both the technical challenges and customary constraints.

The rise of modern mass parties created the political conditions for totalitarianism. While mass parties first emerged in the United States in the 1830s, they were unrelated to totalitarianism, which had to await the emergence of fascist ideology on the European continent to gain momentum and ferment in the harsh economic and social climate of the Great Depression.[6] As early as 1923, Mussolini declared that totalitarianism is a political system that politicizes every aspect of human existence, both material and spiritual: "Everything within the state, nothing outside the state, nothing against the

5 William Sharp McKechnie, *Magna Carter: A Commentary on the Great Charter of King John*, 2nd ed. (New York: Burt Franklin, 1960), p. 4.

6 Daron Acemoglu and James A. Robinson, *Economic Origins of Dictatorship and Democracy* (Cambridge: Cambridge University Press, 2006), pp. 287–95; Sebastian Haffner, *Von Bismarck zu Hitler*, trans. Zhou Quan [in Chinese] (Nanjing: Yilin Press, 2016), pp. 160–3.

state."[7] In 1927, Carl Schmitt elaborated on the concept of the "total state."[8] To be sure, as early as 1917, the Soviet party-state had already begun implementing these ideas, but Marxism was considered a marginal theory by the Western academic community at the time and did not attract widespread interest. It was not until after European fascism was physically defeated and the postwar world entered the Cold War that the concept of totalitarianism was also applied to Soviet-style communist regimes. Although one was defined as extreme left and the other as extreme right, both variants of totalitarian regimes share essential common features.

In their definitive study of totalitarianism, Friedrich and Brzezinski summarized six basic features of totalitarianism: a comprehensive dominant ideology, a single mass party usually led by a dictator, a system of intimidation using secret police and state violence, a monopoly on the military and weaponry, a monopoly on mass communication, and centralized control of the economy through national planning.[9] In other words, totalitarianism is a symbolic representation of a series of institutional and cultural control mechanisms. A state becomes totalitarian primarily because its people have accepted, voluntarily or not, an ideology that promises to achieve great goals and a political party that claims to be the only one that is "correct" in whatever sense it means and is capable of fulfilling these promises. The other characteristics are inherent in the nature of the totalitarian regime, either as the natural consequences of its political and ideological monopoly, or as the necessary means of maintaining such regime.

3.2.2 *Totalitarianism and Authoritarianism*

If we consider "authoritarianism" as a general typology for undemocratic regimes, with various degrees of differentiation, totalitarianism represents the pinnacle of the authoritarian pyramid, distinguishing itself from the less extreme autocracies beneath it. While the latter are generally limited to political dictatorship, manifested through manipulative electoral practices and the suppression of speech and press freedoms, a totalitarian regime exercises comprehensive control over all aspects of human affairs. To be sure, political dictatorship often produces "spillover effects" beyond the political sphere. For instance, an authoritarian regime may establish crony capitalism,

7 Stanley G. Payne, *Fascism: Comparison and Definition* (Madison: University of Wisconsin Press, 1980), p. 73.

8 Carl Schmitt, *The Concept of the Political* (Chicago: University of Chicago Press, 1996), p. 22.

9 Carl Friedrich and Z. K. Brzezinski, Totalitarian Dictatorship and Autocracy, 2nd ed. (New York: Praeger, 1967), pp. 3–12.

characterized by extensive nepotism within state-owned or private monopolies. However, since an ordinary authoritarian regime lacks the ideological underpinnings of totalitarianism, it typically has no ambition to control the economy and society comprehensively, allowing a certain degree of freedom for its people. In countries like Chile during the authoritarian phase of the 1970s and 1980s, dictators like Pinochet even actively promoted free-market economies.[10]

Friedrich and Brezinski argued that ordinary authoritarian regimes lack three distinct features of totalitarianism: (1) a totalitarian ideology, (2) a ruling party supported by secret police, and (3) monopolistic control over the industrial mass society.[11] While an authoritarian regime often commits police brutality against political opponents and restricts them from openly competing with itself through the occasional use of secret police, it lacks an official ideology to control the minds of its citizens, upon which its legitimacy is based. As a result, "thought crimes" as a generic category do not exist. Nor does the regime typically employ secret police on a daily basis as a means of maintaining control, usually limiting its target to opposition leaders who pose a direct threat to its political power monopoly. In fact, partly because an authoritarian government or ruling party does not monopolize the discourse over "truth," "correct," or "great," it often allows the de facto existence of opposition groups and even parties.[12]

To begin with, it should be noted that the term "secret police" in a totalitarian regime does not necessarily mean that they are secret or even formal police in the traditional sense. It refers to amorphous entities responsible for monitoring people's thoughts and reporting to the state authorities. They often operate behind the scenes, but can also openly establish regular contact with their monitoring targets. In China, there is a special section within the Public Security bureaus, known as the police for domestic security protection (国保). In addition to the professional police, there are numerous part-time employees or informants who may have other full-time professions, but dedicate part of their time to collecting information or monitoring public opinion for the state. Furthermore, there are revolutionary masses, nicknamed "Chaoyang district masses" (朝阳群众), who report to the authorities any activities they find suspicious. For instance, in 2002, based on information provided by the masses, the police in Xi'an raided and detained a young

10 Alan Angell, *Democracy after Pinochet: Politics, Parties and Elections in Chile* (London: Institute for the Study of the Americas, 2007), pp. 32–3.

11 Friedrich and Brzezinski, Totalitarian Dictatorship and Autocracy, pp. 8–11.

12 See, e.g., Juan J. Linz, "An authoritarian regime: Spain," in eds Erik Allardt and Stein Rokkan, *Mass Politics: Studies in Political Sociology* (New York: New Press, 1970), pp. 152–83.

couple who were watching an explicit movie in their own room.[13] In a vibrant totalitarian regime, in principle, everyone is potentially an active informer, if not a "secret police" as strictly defined.

If totalitarianism is included in the authoritarian typology as its extreme variant, it can be labeled as "Authoritarian 3.0," which distinguishes it from the ordinary variants labeled as "Authoritarian 1.0." The level of dictatorship is proportional to its authoritarian version. Using the circuit metaphor again, a democratic regime itself has no "voltage," and the "voltage" of the entire nation derives from the "voltages" of all individuals who exhibit high "impedance" against impositions and infringements from the state. On the other hand, an authoritarian regime inherently possesses a high "voltage" itself and reduces its citizens to weak "resistors" by depriving them of their political rights. Authoritarian 1.0 is typically characterized by one-party dictatorship with a leader within the ruling party. The relationship between superiors and subordinates may be adjusted by the rules of the game among elites or factional power balance, allowing for the tolerance of social or political forces outside the party, albeit with limited political influence. While the people's voting rights may lack substance, and freedom of the press is subject to considerable restrictions, at least they are not completely indoctrinated and enjoy a limited degree of free speech, personal freedom, property rights, and economic freedom.

In comparison, a pure totalitarian regime not only carries itself with ultra-high "voltage," but also completely deprives the people of all basic rights, reducing them to a state of almost "zero impedance." It is essentially a superconductor through which the command from the very top of the power pyramid instantly reaches every single individual of the nation with perfect execution. In fact, it transforms its subjects into thoroughly indoctrinated "mini-batteries" that serve as a reserve army constantly resonating with and nourishing the totalitarian regime. As the 3.0 version of authoritarianism, perfect totalitarianism is characterized by strict one-party dictatorship, intense leader worship both within and outside the party, highly efficient indoctrination of the entire population through powerful propaganda machinery, and a pervasive army of secret police apparatus to effectively identify and eliminate opposition forces. Furthermore, not only are people deprived of political rights and freedom of expression, but their personal freedom, property rights, and economic freedom are also severely restricted through measures such as nationalization and public ownership of the "means of production,"

[13] Jiang Xue, "Husband was put under criminal detention for watching obscene video at home," 《华商报》 (October 25, 2002).

particularly land, making them highly dependent on the state for property, personal, and psychological security.

As the sublimation of Authoritarian 1.0, perfect totalitarianism is built upon the more primitive versions of authoritarianism, which prepares the necessary political and social psychological conditions for its emergence, such as a prevalence of uninformed masses, weak civil society, and the popular fascination with charismatic leaders, serving as the starting point for the evolution to the higher version of authoritarianism. Conversely, in the process of democratization, the transition from Authoritarian 3.0 to 1.0 is an inevitable path. After reaching the climax of dictatorship, a totalitarian regime will decline and retreat to a more typical authoritarian system, giving rise to a peculiar "post-totalitarian" regime that falls somewhere between Authoritarian 1.0 and 3.0. Decaying from version 3.0, Authoritarian 2.0 is characterized by a weakened leader worship, a challenged and paralyzed orthodox ideology, a largely failed propaganda machine, a partially disintegrated public ownership, a limited protection of private property and respect for the rule of law, an increasing de facto (though not institutionally protected) freedom of expression in private space, and a rapidly growing civil society actively participating in addressing public issues.

While authoritarianism provides the political soil for totalitarianism, not all authoritarian regimes will evolve into totalitarian states. Totalitarian regimes only take root in countries with inherent political and cultural traits that are uniquely indicative of totalitarianism. A primary example is absolute monarchy, a common outcome of absolutist traditions that often acquires totalitarian characteristics during rapid industrial modernization. In early eighteenth-century Russia, for instance, Peter the Great swiftly established modern military, industrial, taxation, educational, and even secret police systems. Since these modern achievements were often made possible only by the absolute authority of a charismatic leader, the personal decisions of a strong monarch played a decisive role in the national modernization, which in turn further strenghened the absolute authority.[14] Historically, absolute despotism originated with the construction of centralized nation-states in the West, which coincided with economic and social integration, such as national self-determination, unified taxation, established legal and political institutions, centralized administrative procedures, standing armies, and rationalized bureaucracy as essential tools for maintaining the regime. However, the most

[14] Andrey N. Medushevsky, *Russian Constitutionalism: Historical and Contemporary Development* (London: Routledge, 2006), pp. 61–81.

significant characteristic is the ideology that establishes the principle of a single unified sovereignty.[15]

To be sure, the absolute monarchy of Peter the Great was an "enlightened despotism" (开明专制), characterized by centralized power, the rule of law, and social modernization achieved through top-down reforms. Nevertheless, enlightened despotism is a form of despotism after all, and is often associated with the "police state," implying comprehensive state intervention in public life and social relations through legal and administrative means. While enlightened despotism may be seen as a historical progression towards national modernization, such "progress" can potentially serve as a decisive step towards totalitarianism.

By the first quarter of the eighteenth century, Peter the Great had essentially completed the construction of absolute monarchy. Akin to the English situation during the time of the Magna Carta, the Russian nobility did still retain some traditional control over the monarchy. Peter's successors, Catherine I and the underaged Peter II, lacked the charismatic qualities necessary to fully exercise the power bestowed by absolute monarchy. Unfortunately, the Russian social structure differed fundamentally from that of medieval England, as the Russian nobility had not formed a political community capable of mustering a sufficiently strong force to solicit concessions from the monarch. In 1730, when Empress Anna Ivanovna came to power, a group of nobles demanded that she respected their rights and privileges, but ultimately failed in their efforts. On February 25, approximately 800 nobles arrived at the Kremlin with a petition requesting the establishment of a representative body composed of one or two representatives from each noble household. However, the palace guards and officials unanimously shouted for an immediate return to absolute monarchy. Another representative then presented his petition making the same demand, and Anna publicly tore up the nobles' petition. Although the nobles' demands for reduced military service were gradually met, there was nothing to impede the imperial centralization of power. By abolishing the Supreme Privy Council upon the nobles' own request, Anna successfully restored absolute monarchy that disregarded all limitations.[16]

Once a nation is unfortunate enough to be infected by absolutism, its influence becomes deeply ingrained. After the February Revolution of 1917, which overthrew the Tsarist regime, the provisional government and the representative assembly introduced universal suffrage, preparing to draft a

15 Ibid., pp. 61–3.
16 Ibid., pp. 72–3.

constitution. However, the constitutional plan still carried remnants of absolute monarchy. The constitution established a strong presidency, granting the president powers akin to those of the Tsar, including legal immunity and the authority to dissolve the parliament. The National Assembly was scheduled to commence operations in December, but before the mechanism for transferring power from the provisional government could be established, the October Revolution erupted,[17] plunging Russia and the world into an unprecedented totalitarian movement.

3.2.3 *Totalitarianism and Democracy*

If absolutism is understood broadly as standing for all regimes denying that the sovereign power can be limited by any power other than itself, then both monarchy and democracy can be absolutist. Although totalitarianism typically grows out of an authoritarian regime rooted in absolutist soil, it often emerges in the form of "democracy." While the Nazis came to power through democratic elections, socialist regimes boasted about making "the people the master." As early as 1960, Talmon even treated "totalitarian democracy" as a form of democracy, which is divided into two subcategories: liberal and totalitarian.[18] Totalitarian democracy began with Rousseau's concept of the "general will," a holistic notion that confuses fact with value and reason with faith. The secular state became the embodiment of ultimate good and absolute truth. The relentless pursuit of the "general will" led to the Jacobin "reign of terror," which can be seen as the embryo of totalitarian democracy, later consummated by economic communism and one-party dictatorship.[19]

Indeed, totalitarianism almost always has to go through a form of mass democracy in order to succeed. Although an authoritarian regime may also acquire considerable popular support, it typically lacks the ambition to control the thoughts of its people or the intention to conceal its naked tyranny of the minority. In contrast, the totalitarian ideal is to use a set of self-proclaimed, unchallengeable "truths" to transform and control every individual soul. Thus, although totalitarian regimes have without exception come to power through revolutionary violence by a tightly organized minority, their enthusiasm for mass movements has been persistent. Having completed the brainwashing of the entire nation and consolidated its dictatorship, the totalitarian regime does indeed gain the support of the vast majority. Whether out of sincere belief or

[17] Ibid., pp. 126–8.
[18] Talmon, *The Origins of Totalitarian Democracy*, pp. 1–3.
[19] Ibid., pp. 5–6.

opportunistic calculation and fear, the appearance of popular support is an undeniable force in maintaining the totalitarian machine.

Of course, the fact that totalitarianism often takes on a democratic form does not legitimize any democracy-phobia. It merely implies that democracy is a necessary but insufficient condition for good governance, which is premised on both democracy and liberty. If the liberal democratic option is, for some reason, closed to a nation, its best remaining option is authoritarian tyranny, which in itself becomes a breeding ground for totalitarianism. Totalitarian "democracy" is obviously a misnomer for a novel form of dictatorship, as no one in that regime - neither the majority nor the minorities, often not even the dictator himself – is free to think, know, speak, or choose. In what sense can a regime based on an unreflecting mass of brainwashed automatons be called "democratic"?

On the other hand, liberal democracy is equipped with corrective capacities that prevent it from developing totalitarian vices. The touchstone that distinguishes totalitarian "democracy" from liberal democracy is periodic elections and freedom of speech, which are sufficient to prevent a democracy from becoming totalitarian. Although a majoritarian democracy may occasionally experience the "tyranny of the majority,"[20] such a possibility is more often the product of democracy-phobia rather than reality. The occasional "tyranny of the majority," if ever likely to occur, can be prevented through corrective mechanisms such as separation of powers and judicial review. A democracy may also centralize power, and the national legislative power is unlimited unless it exceeds its constitutional authorization. However, the centralization of power in a liberal democracy differs fundamentally from totalitarian omnipotence. British constitutionalist A. V. Dicey once claimed that the House of Commons could enact any legislation except to turn a man into a woman or a woman into a man.[21] If the British Parliament were to exercise unlimited regulatory power, it would become an omnipotent state. Fortunately, since Britain is a liberal democracy, its members of Parliament are politically accountable to voters through periodic elections, and most British voters are rational in the sense that they will not use the power of the majority to deprive minorities of their basic rights.

As sociologist Barrington Moore observed, democracy encompasses three aspects: constraining the caprice of powerholders, establishing fair and

[20] Alexis de Tocqueville, *Democracy in America*, trans. George Lawrence (New York: Harper & Row, 1969), pp. 435–6.

[21] A. V. Dicey, *Introduction to the Study of the Law of the Constitution*, 8th ed. (London: Macmillan, 1915), p. 39.

rational governance, and enabling the majority to participate in lawmaking.[22] The primary condition to democracy is the balance of social powers. During the sixteenth and seventeenth centuries, European countries began to develop powerful central governments with the purpose of restraining aristocratic forces. In the early modern period, the power of the monarchy and the aristocracy was roughly balanced, allowing the aristocracy to enjoy a de facto independent status – a prerequisite for parliamentary democracy. Other indispensable conditions for modern democracy include the emergence of urban residents and the bourgeoisie as independent classes. If the bourgeois revolution fails or never takes place, the liberal movement of the aristocracy is likely to veer towards fascism, whereas peasant or plebeian revolutions would tend to lead to communism.[23]

3.2.4 *Left and Right Totalitarianism*

Although both communism and fascism came to power under the banner of democracy because the "masses" had to take the political stage, they differ markedly in terms of ideology and organization. In contrast to communism on the left, right-wing fascism represents a form of conservative populism that upholds hierarchy, discipline, and obedience as its motto. It emerged as capitalism encroached upon agricultural economies and became more entrenched in regions with heavy industrial development. Consequently, fascism found limited popularity in China and Russia but had deep roots in the histories of Germany and Japan. Both landlords and farmers in these countries fiercely opposed the capitalist development that compromised their interests. As early as 1894, the German Agricultural Union displayed clear Nazi tendencies. In the July 1932 election, the Nazis obtained a rural support rate of 37.4 percent, reaching as high as 80–100 percent in some areas.[24]

Unlike its left-wing counterpart, right-wing totalitarianism is based on individualist atomism and rationalism, with history, race or "organism" serving as its foundation, rather than the universalist collectivism embraced by the left. As a special variant of pragmatism, right-wing totalitarianism denies the universality of human values. Furthermore, while the left-wing ideology believes in the inherent goodness of human nature and its potential for perfection, the right wing insists that human nature is corrupt and weak,

[22] Barrington Moore, Jr., *Social Origins of Dictatorship and Democracy: Lord and Peasant in the Making of the Modern World* (Boston: Beacon Press, 1966), p. 414.

[23] Ibid., pp. 417–18.

[24] Ibid., pp. 447–9.

necessitating the use of force to maintain order and discipline the poor.[25] As fascism recognizes the legitimacy of social hierarchy, it has not reached the pinnacle of totalitarianism. It is also less inclined towards ideological transformation and systematic brainwashing compared to the left, as it perceives human nature as inherently evil. For instance, after World War I, fascism began to spread from Italy to Central and Eastern Europe, but Mussolini was primarily focused on establishing a personal dictatorship and one-party rule, rather than striving to create a complete totalitarian regime.

When compared to its right-wing counterpart, left-wing totalitarianism appears to be more comprehensive and "authentic." Left-wing ideology is built upon an optimistic view of human nature and promises the realization of a utopian paradise with a harmonious society. Intellectuals during the eighteenth-century Enlightenment rejected the notion of an irreconcilable conflict between freedom and virtue. Some even believed that freedom itself *is* a virtue. These political messiahs positioned themselves as embodiments of freedom and virtue, suppressing any dissenting voices. As Rousseau's "general will" was internalized, reason transformed into a public passion that claimed absolute truth. This provided the theoretical basis for the Jacobin Terror, ultimately leading to economic communism and one-party dictatorship.[26]

At least in the economic dimension, left-wing totalitarianism surpasses its right-wing counterpart, resulting in more profound consequences during the subsequent transition process. Fascism has far from realized "perfect" totalitarianism in the economic realm. The role of the fascist state is largely limited to macroeconomic intervention and cooperation through the inducement or bribery of employers and labor organizations. It does not involve direct confiscation of private property or micro-level interference in economic activities. In contrast, communism brings about a comprehensive transformation of the national economic system. It implements industrial nationalization and agricultural collectivization by confiscating private property, transforming the market economy based on private ownership into a centrally planned economy based on public ownership. The deprivation of property rights and economic freedom also strips individuals of their economic foundation for personal independence. Public ownership intensifies economic and psychological dependence on the state, greatly facilitating state control over society and the maintenance of a totalitarian order. Following the decline of totalitarianism, fascist regimes like Germany and Japan primarily faced challenges posed by political transformation, while socialist regimes such as the

[25] Talmon, *The Origins of Totalitarian Democracy*, p. 7.
[26] Ibid., pp. 5–6.

former Soviet Union and Eastern Europe had to address both political and economic transformation.[27] This dualistic aspect significantly increased the difficulty of reform.

3.3 THE POLITICAL COMPONENTS OF TOTALITARIANISM

Since totalitarianism stands for a radical condition in which the social "impedance" against the abuse of state power is near zero, a totalitarian regime must create a series of radical political and social conditions for its own establishment and maintenance. First, totalitarian regimes are invariably constructed through violent takeovers via revolutionary conspiracy rather than free and democratic elections. Even in Russia in 1917 and Germany in 1932, when popular support for totalitarianism was exceedingly strong and people were not intellectually or psychologically immune to the brand new totalitarian "virus," the totalitarian parties still failed to gain majority support. Both the Bolsheviks and the Nazis ultimately came to power through coups. Once the totalitarian party successfully seized power, it established a strict one-party dictatorship within the nation and cultivated a cult of personality for the dictator through political struggles within the party. Second, through systematic brainwashing by the propaganda machine, the regime consolidated the totalitarian order of "one doctrine, one party, one leader," a succinct and accurate characterization by Sun Yat-sen, the first totalitarian leader in China. Finally, by depriving individuals of their freedom of thought, belief, speech, person, and property, the totalitarian regime made individuals completely dependent on the state, creating a morally dehumanized nation and laying a socio-psychological basis for the reign of terror in which the masses were induced to collaborate in political crimes.

3.3.1 *Ideology as the Hallmark of Totalitarian Trinity*

In the current global communist recession, the communist ideology may appear to be nothing more than a laughingstock in daily life. However, ideological control is the most distinctive characteristic and lasting legacy of totalitarianism, setting it apart from ordinary authoritarianism. It also contributes to the relative stability of a totalitarian regime compared to an ordinary authoritarian regime, where a small minority of ruling elites, lacking a solid mass base, holds power and maintains order primarily through the use of naked force. In contrast, a totalitarian regime is capable of indoctrinating the

[27] Medushevsky, *Russian Constitutionalism*, pp. 236–7.

entire population with a grandiose ideology and a powerful propaganda machine, thereby causing the vast majority to sincerely believe in a single "truth" and accept the ruling party and its leader as the sole embodiment of such "truth." At least until the ideological bubble bursts, such a society will be highly unified and stable. Totalitarian dictators like Chairman Mao can effortlessly employ the Daoist practice of "governing without action" (无为而治), without the need for state violence. Contrary to popular belief, perfect totalitarianism is the most peaceful and harmonious regime of all, with everyone thinking and chanting in unison. The few dissenters who fail to conform can be swiftly dealt with by the state apparatus without disturbing the public. Or even better, they can be exposed in mass assemblies, where their reactionary thoughts or beliefs will be thoroughly excoriated, and their fate will serve as a painful lesson to those who dare to indulge in similar thoughts. Such instances may involve some violence, fury, and excitement, but they are deemed worthwhile for the sake of ideological reactivation, pervasive fear, and the ensuing prolonged peace.

Ideological control is an essential element of a totalitarian regime, not only because the very essence of totalitarian omnipotence implies the ability of the state to control people's thoughts and beliefs, but also because all dissidents must be eliminated to achieve totalistic control. It is important to acknowledge that such control is difficult, if not impossible, as it goes against human nature. Humans are primarily self-interested rather than selfless, as the communist ideology advocates, and they often hold differing opinions rather than unanimous agreement. Due to individual uniqueness in identity, interests, preferences, and prejudices, differences among individuals are bound to be prevalent. If individuals are allowed to make independent judgments, their opinions are so unique that even twins will not take exactly the same position on all issues. Even with endless debates, certain differences are deeply rooted and cannot be bridged. However, the totalitarian regime is predicated on one correct "truth," one grand goal, and one legitimate party led by one great leader, demanding unconditional acceptance of all these "ones" from everyone. Therefore, a totalitarian regime cannot be established through liberal democracy and rational persuasion, but only through revolutionary violence or deceptive conspiracy that deceives voter support, as Hitler did in 1932, followed by the violent suppression of opposition after coming to power.[28]

Compared to typical authoritarian regimes, a totalitarian regime places significant importance on its ideological legitimacy, which forms the basis of

[28] Ralf Dahrendorf, *Society and Democracy in Germany* (New York: W. W. Norton & Co., 1967), pp. 365–96; Haffner, *Von Bismarck zu Hitler*, pp. 172–83.

its popular support. The ability of a totalitarian ideology to gain popularity and dominance is closely linked to the social environment in which it emerges. Like an epidemic virus, extreme ideology exists in every society, but its outbreak depends on the immunity of a particular nation. Even in mature democracies such as the United States, where the liberal foundation is strong, it is impossible to exclude individuals with extreme thoughts and antisocial behavior. The essence of liberal democracy is precisely to tolerate their existence, but they will never represent more than a minority in a free society where the majority of citizens are capable of rational thinking and informed judgment. In contrast, despotic regimes are invariably characterized by poverty and ignorance. The lack of political freedoms in these societies denies people the opportunity to exercise and develop the skills necessary for self-governance, resulting in uninformed and immature political judgment. Since the majority lacks the ability to discern truth from falsehood in practice, they are particularly susceptible to believing in utopian promises and accepting them as unquestionable "truth." As Popper pointed out, unlike the open society in a liberal democracy, totalitarian states are completely closed, with highly unified and simplified views and limited sources of information. The foundation of totalitarian ideology lies in the belief that history is progressing towards an eternal and unchanging grandiose goal, governed by laws of historical progress that can be mastered by humans, at least by a few revolutionary vanguards.[29]

All totalitarian regimes have their own political culture as an ideological resource, often rooted in a utopian moral and political tradition. Moral despotism typically establishes a grand social objective, which is considered the sole "correct" ideological dogma, while everything else is deemed wrong and treacherous, and naturally should be prohibited by the state. The mission of the state is not only to forbid harmful words and actions but also to guide the entire nation towards the pursuit of "luminating the luminous virtues" (明明德) and "arriving at the ultimate good" (止于至善).[30] Thus, the moral origins of totalitarianism can be found in traditional ideologies such as Confucianism. In the face of a great state, every individual is rendered insignificant. Selfish "small men" (小人) are clearly undeserving of enjoying any "rights," and there is no need to restrain public authority that regulates them on behalf of the public interest. Admittedly, Confucian ethics did impose some moral constraints on officials, but such constraints were clearly

[29] Karl R. Popper, *Open Society and Its Enemies* (Princeton: Princeton University Press, 2013), pp. 83–114, 283–320.

[30] *Daxue* [*Great Learning*], sec. 1.

insufficient to institutionally prevent the abuse of state power. While the Confucian state did not transform into a true Leviathan due to various physical constraints such as limited regulatory capabilities of the bureaucratic system, underdeveloped transportation and communication, and the inability of an agricultural society to support burdensome public finance, the potential for a totalitarian culture has always been present.

In reality, even if the old regime is overthrown and the old orthodoxy is rejected, moral and political despotism may not only persist but also intensify. After all, Confucian ethics are inherently aristocratic, advocating moral autonomy, at least for the "gentlemen." Regardless of the extent of imperial power, it was expected to be constrained by Confucian principles, at least in theory. The bureaucracy established on Confucian ethics also formed a self-sustaining vested interest that often resisted the unlimited expansion of imperial power. Historically, imperial China was never a totalitarian state when dominated by Confucians, whereas occasional periods of Legalist dominance, which rejected Confucian ethics, brought it perilously close to the abyss of totalitarianism. Once the new regime succeeds in dismantling traditional ethics, eliminating the aristocratic class, and replacing the relatively inefficient traditional bureaucracy with a highly developed party apparatus, the full potential of totalitarianism is unleashed. At this point, political power not only controls all tangible state machinery but also monopolizes the intellectual and moral resources that provide legitimacy to the regime. From then on, the regime becomes self-legitimizing; the same group that exercises power determines the legality and legitimacy of its actions, possibly with some internal division of labor. Under the grand illusion of the utopian ideal, any abuse of public power can be justified, and any criticism will be silenced by the state machinery and submerged by mass movements. Once the impedance to state power approaches zero, the highest directives will permeate down to the grassroots through the pervasive tentacles of the party. From the top to the bottom, no obstruction to supreme command is allowed throughout the country.

Therefore, totalitarianism is more likely to succeed in countries with theocratic or atheistic traditions. Theocratic regimes consolidate power by merging spiritual and secular authority, while atheist regimes exclude spiritual worship, which could have provided organized resistance against state-controlled orthodoxy. Independent organizations in civil society, whether religious or otherwise, pose insurmountable obstacles to totalitarianism. China's totalitarian rule under both the Nationalist and Communist parties became possible only after the Confucian moral order had been significantly weakened. Admittedly, the Nationalists tolerated and even relied on the gentry to govern local communities, implying limitations on their dictatorial power as a right-wing party. Similarly, Nazi Germany and Fascist Italy maintained cooperative relationships with the Catholic Church, revealing imperfections in Nazi and fascist totalitarianism, which could not simply dominate the religious realm. In contrast, atheist communism could easily "sweep away all the ghosts and snakes" (牛鬼蛇神), completely breaking down barriers between the secular and spiritual worlds, and eliminating any obstructive forces in either realm. Recent examples include the pledges made by various religious associations in China, apparently under coercion or pressure, declaring "patriotism" and obedience to the Communist leadership.[31]

Whether atheistic or theocratic, a totalitarian order consists of three essential components: one doctrine, one party, one leader. The first component is a utopian ideal. Totalitarian parties exploit national pride to establish a vision of national rejuvenation or universal unity. Nations that embark on the path of totalitarianism often have experienced periods of humiliation in their history, which contrasts strongly with their feelings of national, racial, or cultural superiority. China's repeated defeats since the Opium War and Germany's enormous indemnity for World War I were but examples illustrating how great damage in the sense of national dignity stimulated the strong desire for revenge. To achieve utopian goals such as ethnic revival, national development, or social equality, the totalitarian ideology advocates the establishment of an all-powerful Leviathan, easily captivating many people.

The second component is a perpetual ruling party that acts as a vanguard to implement the utopian ideal. Given that the reality of the totalitarian state falls far short of its proclaimed ideal, the realization of this ideal requires diligent efforts under the guidance of a revolutionary vanguard. The totalitarian ideology theoretically elevates the "people" to the status of divinity, albeit existing solely in a conceptual realm. Once it returns to reality, the totalitarian regime views the actual populace as ignorant, troublesome, and potentially dangerous masses in need of constant indoctrination. Although the May Fourth Movement overturned traditional Confucian culture, the new Marxist–Leninist doctrine proved even more elitist. If the traditional model involved a small number of "gentlemen" leading the vast majority of "small men," the lofty Communist ideal could only be attained by the "proletarian vanguard" leading and eventually eliminating all classes.

The third component is the cult of personality surrounding the party leader. As the totalitarian party serves as the vanguard of an advanced ideal, it must be

[31] Mimi Lau, "China orders clergy to toe Communist Party and socialist line," *South China Morning Post* (February 19, 2021), www.scmp.com/news/china/politics/article/3122253/china-orders-clergy-toe-communist-party-and-socialist-line.

led by thinkers and statesmen capable of grasping the truth. A totalitarian regime cannot tolerate democracy within or outside the party because there is only one correct version of the "truth," which can be embodied by only one person. Totalitarianism demands strict uniformity of thought and opinion, yet individuals are naturally diverse in their perspectives. In cases of disagreement, opinions must be unified under a single position. Hence, a totalitarian party must be led by an all-knowing, all-powerful, and unchallenged supreme leader, reminiscent of the Platonic philosopher-king. Indeed, the legitimacy of the party ultimately rests on this individual. If other leaders within the party begin to question his authority, divisions in the party's stance arise, leading to the erosion of the myth of a unified "truth." Any challenge to the ideological supremacy also undermines the legitimacy of the ruling party and its unchallenged leadership over external forces. The cult of personality not only naturally emerges within a totalitarian regime, but also serves as the linchpin that holds the pieces of the totalitarian logic together. Ultimately, it is this one great leader who maintains the cohesiveness of this one great party, dedicated to the pursuit of his vision of this one great ideal.

Indeed, the "trinity" of totalitarianism is nothing more than a myth fabricated by totalitarian ideology and can only be sustained through lies. As Arendt observed in her seminal study, however, totalitarianism possesses a unique ability to transform lies into reality.[32] Totalitarian leaders are always portrayed as infallible and never admit their mistakes. This is not because they possess superhuman qualities, but rather because the structure of totalitarian power allows them to continually manipulate and shape reality to align with their own narratives. For example, they can employ state violence to eradicate classes considered degenerate, thus turning their predictions into self-fulfilling prophecies. A totalitarian regime is full of lies because the masses believe that facticity depends on the power of the fabricator. Immersed in so many lies and having lost their sense of reality, the masses start to disbelieve their own eyes and what is clearly visible in their own experience, but only believe in the guided imagination through which they derive satisfaction. The totalitarian regime meet the needs of human thinking by providing them with perfectly consistent lies, even though they defy common sense: "Totalitarian propaganda can outrageously insult common sense only where common sense has lost validity."[33]

[32] Hannah Arendt, *The Origins of Totalitarianism* (San Diego: Harcourt Brace Jovanovich, 1979), pp. 341–63.

[33] Ibid., p. 352.

3.3.2 *Leader Worship and Psychological Control*

To ensure absolute control over every individual, a totalitarian regime must satisfy certain social psychological conditions. One crucial condition is the absolute obedience of all individuals to the omnipotent state, which establishes and enforces its power to ensure such obedience. Humans are not inherently inclined to agree with and blindly obey others; on the contrary, they possess natural differences in interests, needs, beliefs, and perspectives that make them inherently resistant to submission. Overcoming this natural resistance requires the exertion of Herculean external forces. In order to maximize individual fear and control, a totalitarian regime must reduce each person to a helpless solitary figure, devoid of any ability to resist tyranny. Every individual perceives others around them as potential informers under the control of an enigmatic force, who will be readily mobilized against him at the slightest sign of disobedience. The expansive state machinery isolates and subdues each individual, leaving them in a constant state of fear and submission.

To be sure, a perfect totalitarian state is not ruled solely by terror, but rather by the insidious mechanism of brainwashing, a feature that sets totalitarianism apart from ordinary authoritarianism. While an authoritarian regime relies on intimidation, leaving individuals outwardly obedient but harboring disobedient thoughts, a perfect totalitarian regime achieves genuine obedience through the tight control of propaganda and educational apparatus. The ideal state seeks to indoctrinate every individual with a single ideology, fostering willing obedience to the party's leadership and unconditional loyalty to the supreme leader. While such a state of affairs may have existed fleetingly in history, such as during the early stages of the Cultural Revolution when Chairman Mao received tearful adoration from the Red Guards in Tiananmen Square, or in the enduring decades-long regime of North Korea where the masses express their gratitude to their supreme leader as the "loving father" (慈父), it represents an exceptional and normally transient state. As Arendt observed, once people are infected with the totalitarian toxin, they suffer from an almost incurable delusion of leader worship. This delusion, exemplified by the unwavering devotion to leaders like Stalin, Hitler, and Mao, plays a pivotal role in creating and perpetuating the legendary success of totalitarian regimes.[34]

[34] Ibid., pp. 309–25.

According to Arendt, the ultimate goal of totalitarian movements is to turn everyone into politically indifferent and non-participating masses.[35] Participation itself is dangerous since politics begins with distinguishing between "yours" and "mine," implying the formation of self-awareness and the beginning of the end of the totalitarian order. When the Nazi and European communist movements emerged after 1930, the masses they recruited were clearly indifferent and inept gangsters, who were believed to be worthless and thus abandoned by other political parties. These newcomers to the political stage adopted a completely new method of political propaganda, disregarding altogether the arguments of political opponents and directly using death threats to achieve their outcomes. The SS, recruited by Heinrich Himmler, took no interest in daily drudgery that concerned their personal interests but were preoccupied with the "ideological questions of importance for centuries."[36]

The situation was similar in China during the Cultural Revolution, when everyone on the street seemed to be preoccupied about the "ultimate truth" as contained in the "little red book" of *Chairman Mao's Quotes*. Unlike Arendt's prediction, however, China under Chairman Mao did not seem to be concerned with the mass participation. On the contrary, Mao was fond of launching one mass movement after another, apparently with total confidence that the mass participation was under firm control, given his immense popularity among the masses. After thorough brainwashing through repeated "thought reforms," the masses worshipped Mao as their demi-god and naively believed the official propaganda to be absolute truth.

Ultimately, the success of totalitarian ideology lies in its unique ability to satisfy the oversimplified social psychological structure. In a moderately sophisticated world, the concepts of good and evil are never clear-cut. For a nation that has never developed a habit of independent judgment, however, evaluating complex social issues becomes a daunting and tiresome task. The function of an ideology is to simplify the judgment of right and wrong, thus saving time and effort in daily assessments. Totalitarian ideology simplifies the world into sensational dichotomies such as "good" versus "evil," "people" versus "enemy," "advanced" versus "backward," with the working class portrayed as the "leading class" versus the "landowners, rich, reactionaries, villains and rightists" as targets to be suppressed by the proletarian dictatorship. These simplistic dichotomies not only cater to the jealousy and vanity of the masses struggling with poverty, but also resonate with their everyday language

35 Ibid., pp. 347–54.
36 Ibid., p. 324.

and thinking style, prompting them to wholeheartedly participate in political movements that aim to suppress those labeled as "evil" or "enemies." The obvious course of action is to strike them down and administer summary justice without due process. On the other extreme, the totalitarian ideology elevates a figure to the deified status of a moral paragon, to be worshipped by all. In the one-dimensional evaluative framework of totalitarianism, the "bad" are unforgivable sinners, while the "good" are perfect angels.

This angelic figure is none other than the totalitarian leader himself, the embodiment of every virtue, hailed as "high, great and comprehensive" (高大全). Chairman Mao was not only the greatest revolutionary, statesman, and military strategist, but also the greatest philosopher, poet, and calligrapher. No one in the vast history of China could possibly rival him in art or literature, let alone surpass his profound philosophical insights as expressed in works like *On Contradiction* (矛盾论) or *On Practice* (实践论). Every word he uttered was truth, and "one sentence of his was worth ten thousand of others."[37] Arendt was right in stating that, in a perfectly totalitarian regime, everyone becomes one person. Mao was *the* perfect man in every aspect, serving as a role model for all to admire and emulate. Other models, such as Lei Feng (雷锋), may exist, but their purpose is to demonstrate how to "learn and apply Maoist thought in real life." As the models of studying that true model, they are created as examples for the purpose of "making god." Of course, there can only be one "true god."

In fact, the practices of "god making" (造神) remain pervasive even after the totalitarian regime has partially transformed into what is known as "post-totalitarianism." These practices are not exclusive to the left but are shared by many liberals who have emerged since the decline of strict totalitarianism. Partly driven by the need to counter the leftist god-making propaganda and partly influenced by the long-lasting effects of totalitarian indoctrination, liberals in China today also engage in the act of deification by creating perfect idols in their imagination, assuming their anti-totalitarian stance still qualifies them as "liberals." They vehemently oppose the leftist political position, but share the habit of thinking inherited from the totalitarian legacy. When the strict Marxist–Maoist monotheism decays, it is replaced not by pluralism but by polytheism, with different "gods" in each ideological camp. Although their positions may oppose each other, these little "gods" break down all

[37] Lin Biao's famous quote shortly before the outbreak of the Cultural Revolution. See News of the Communist Party of China, http://cpc.people.com.cn/GB/64162/64164/4416081.html.

professional barriers in their own camp, as "gods" – whether liberal right or totalitarian left – do not recognize professional distinctions.[38]

One example is Hu Shih, an influential Chinese liberal during the republican era. While Hu initially started as an intellectual, he assumed administrative positions such as the President of Peking University and the ambassador to the United States (1938–42), which interrupted his intellectual career. Yet, in China today, he is still regarded by many liberals as one of the greatest scholars in modern China, with his collection of political comments considered almost a bible, surpassing all intellectual contributions of that era.[39] Undoubtedly, there were genuine scholarly contributions even at that time, when natural and social sciences were first introduced to China. However, few Chinese today seem to be interested in pure scholarship. No matter how exceptional someone is in a particular field, they are destined to pale in comparison to a popular idol, and the liberals are no exception, despite their seemingly resolute opposition to leader worship pervasive in the existing regime. After decades of totalitarian education, politically immature individuals dismiss any division of labor and bestow all halos upon the idols they create without paying attention to the laborious details of professional achievements. Like its totalitarian opponents, the liberal version of idol worship has neither patience nor respect for nuanced reasoning; all they want is simply one person whom everyone seemingly loves with irresistible passion. While idol worship of a figure from the past like Hu Shi may appear harmless, such a habit can easily misguide judgments. For instance, during the 2020 US presidential election, many Chinese liberals, driven by idol worship, became fanatical supporters of the presidential candidate, Donald Trump, and enthusiastically spread fake news asserting election "frauds."[40]

Apart from the impact of totalitarian brainwashing on people's habits of thinking, another factor that consistently contributes to the maintenance of totalitarian control is pervasive monitoring and the resulting fear. While the leader of a totalitarian regime can initiate waves of "thought reform" (思想改造) movements to maintain ideological control during its heyday, such frenzied conditions cannot persist indefinitely. Especially after the charismatic leader passes away and society becomes weary of successive movements and economic disasters, ideological mobilization loses its effectiveness.

[38] As ex-reporter Lu Yuegang (卢跃刚) points out, professionalism is the nemesis of despotism. See Lu Yuegang, "Non-fiction writing in a fictional state," www.chinesepen.org/blog/archives/151626.

[39] Hu Shih, *Toleration and Freedom* [in Chinese] (Beijing: Law Press, 2011).

[40] Yu Zhi, "Did massive fraud exist in the 2020 American Election?," 《联合早报》 (January 11, 2021).

After all, people are not fools and will not indefinitely cooperate with totalitarian movements that treat them as puppets. Reflection and challenges will inevitably arise. Even during the peak of totalitarian terror, courageous thinkers such as Yu Luoke (遇罗克), Lin Zhao (林昭) and Zhang Zhixin (张志新) openly criticized the totalitarian ideology and practices. Opposing voices will be swiftly punished and suppressed, but each forced silence contributes to the erosion of totalitarian legitimacy and may even facilitate the spread of heresy. As the efficacy of brainwashing diminishes, the focus of totalitarian control shifts towards the reign of terror.

At this stage, the totalitarian regime fully utilizes its machinery of violence to establish micro-control over society. Arendt observed that a common characteristic of totalitarian regimes is their reliance on secret police forces, which often surpass the military in power and influence. The advantage of the police lies not only in their ability to suppress domestic disorder but also in facilitating ideological control. The Nazi SS, for example, was essentially a police force rather than an army, with the ultimate goal of integrating the military and police under the jurisdiction of the SS. Stalin's seizure of power in 1929, on the other hand, was achieved through a coup orchestrated by the secret police. Once in power, he swiftly purged the leadership of the police department. Behind the bewildering power shifts and apparent inefficiencies of totalitarian regimes, there lies the super efficiency of the secret police as the core of state power. By the 1930s, both the Soviet and German totalitarian regimes had eliminated open and secret organized resistance, effectively eradicating true enemies of the regime. However, after this initial phase, they began hunting for "objective enemies" who were not genuine "reactionaries" actively attacking the regime, but merely individuals occasionally critical of the measures taken by the regime. To eliminate potential competitors, totalitarian regimes regularly employ provocative strategies such as the "drawing out of snakes from their hideout" (引蛇出洞), as Mao did in 1957 when he encouraged intellectuals to criticize the party-state through the movement of "letting a hundred flowers bloom" (百花齐放) and "letting a hundred schools of thought contend" (百家争鸣).[41] Under the guise of achieving utopian goals, the totalitarian regime successfully implements what is essentially a reign of terror.

While a reign of terror is a characteristic of ordinary authoritarianism, a totalitarian regime pushes this mode of governance to its extreme. If the regime fails to genuinely garner the support of the people for the orthodoxy

[41] Roderick MacFarquhar, *The Origins of the Cultural Revolution, Vol. 1: Contradictions among the People, 1956–1957* (New York: Columbia University Press, 1974), pp. 218–49.

propagated by the propaganda machine, it will seek to transform everyone into a "refined egoist" (精致利己主义),[42] a selfish individual masquerading under a sanctimonious cloak, devoid of moral responsibility, mutual trust, and the desire for collective action, let alone the feeling for their own political and legal rights. The regime uses vaguely defined and broad "sack crimes" (口袋罪) as loosely outlined in criminal law to encompass all human activities, manipulating the interpretation of the law so that anyone can be punished at any time under the pretext of legality.[43] This ensures that individuals obediently kneel before the state machine, which holds legislative, judicial, and executive powers in its grasp. Tempted by the prospects of promotion and threatened with demotion or even more severe punishment, the vast majority of people become morally apathetic. Since accepting the orthodoxy poses no harm and may even bring benefits, while openly criticizing it leads to certain and immediate repercussions, they choose to accept it, at least in words. Before long, most individuals become thoroughly assimilated into the totalitarian system. Though they lack emotional attachment to the orthodox doctrine and care little about its meaning, the vocabulary of orthodoxy becomes internalized as their standard mode of expression, effectively hindering them from pursuing meaningful beliefs.

As Hannah Arendt observed, a totalitarian regime not only erodes the moral sentiments of its people, but also actively encourages their participation in organized crimes. Despite its professed ideology of seeking global harmony, the regime's actual practice revolves around a philosophy of perpetual struggle, where certain individuals are constantly victimized and sacrificed on the altar of power. To lead a nation down the path of mutual persecution and self-destruction, the totalitarian regime manipulates the masses into committing violent crimes under the guise of lofty ideological goals. Totalitarian leaders often begin by glorifying their past crimes and meticulously outlining their criminal plans. The Nazis, for example, believed that people are naturally tempted towards evil.[44] This natural allure of evil seems to captivate mass mobs, such as the Red Guards during the Cultural Revolution, who willingly become sacrificial victims and aid the regime in persecuting themselves. Indeed, the very purpose of instilling "revolutionary ideals" is to legitimize crimes and absolve the perpetrators of any sense of guilt.

[42] A term coined by Qian Liqun (钱理群), which quickly became popular in China. See Qian Liqun, "The absolutely delicate egoists in universities," www.rfa.org/mandarin/zhuanlan/fuyouluntan/women-01062017144854.html.

[43] Zhang Qianfan, "The application of criminal law shall adhere to the spirit of the constitution: Taking the judicial interpretation of picking quarrel as an example," 《法学》, no. 4 (2015), 3–9.

[44] Arendt, *The Origins of Totalitarianism*, pp. 327–38.

Under the grandiose banner of totalitarian ideals, any heinous crime can be forgiven and justified, or even mandated by the regime. During the height of the Cultural Revolution in 1968, when the Red Guards of Beijing Normal University Affiliated Middle School publicly beat Principal Bian Zhongyun (卞仲耘) to death, they likely believed that their violent action was necessary to demonstrate their revolutionary spirit. The totalitarian ideology incites individuals to abandon their sense of self in service of grand ideals, creating a moral framework where they can commit any act, including organized crimes, without moral guilt or legal accountability.

3.3.3 *One-Party and Personal Dictatorship*

To be sure, to establish and maintain such a terrifying regime is far from easy. Even in a country with an absolutist tradition, it requires the right circumstances and opportunities to transform into a modern totalitarian state. As James Madison pointed out in the Federalist No. 10, freedom inherently gives rise to remarkable individual and group differences, which are accompanied by strong self-esteem and jealousy, making it impossible for people to unanimously embrace a single ideology or unconditionally submit to the leadership of a single group without an overwhelmingly dominant force that eliminates all freedoms.[45] In other words, unless a normal society is distorted and suppressed by such a dominant force, it naturally possesses significant resistance to totalitarian control, implying that a totalitarian regime cannot possibly be established through liberal democratic processes. Indeed, even a hereditary autocracy cannot completely suppress all human freedoms. The traditional bureaucratic hierarchy and local gentry in imperial China were too slack and inefficient to construct a massive, efficiently organized apparatus capable of implementing iron-fisted control at the mass level. Therefore, a totalitarian regime must start with a tightly organized militant vanguard, which is often a small and inconspicuous party. Such a small party necessarily relies on major domestic or international upheavals to seize power through revolutionary violence or electoral fraud. After achieving success, it invariably evolves into a one-party system and personal dictatorship.

Initially, the totalitarian vanguard is established by gravitating around a central figure rather than a team, as any team, no matter how small and tightly knit, is prone to internal differences that can weaken the effectiveness of the vanguard, or at least damage its appearance of unity. The Soviet,

[45] Alexander Hamilton, James Madison, and John Jay, *The Federalist Papers*, ed. Clinton Rossiter (New York: Penguin, 1961), pp. 77–84.

founded in 1898, started as a loosely organized group, with most of its party members being tolerant Mensheviks. However, the Bolshevik faction, centered around Lenin, maintained strong cohesion. After Lenin's death in 1924, Stalin legitimized his rise to power by positioning himself as Lenin's successor. It took two decades of purges and assassinations for him to exterminate political rivals and establish supreme personal authority within the party.[46] In China, the first revolutionary and totalitarian party was the Nationalist Party, which revered Sun Yat-sen as *the* "founding father" and granted him absolute personal authority within the party. After Sun's death in 1925, various factions emerged within the party. It was only after the victory of the Northern Expedition in 1927 and the Japanese invasion crisis in 1931 that Chiang Kai-shek consolidated his personal authority within the Nationalist Party. Similarly, the early Communist Party witnessed factional rivalries among various "hills" (山头) within the party, such as the native faction and the Moscow faction, the Soviet region and the Nationalist-occupied regions. Mao Zedong established his supreme leadership within the party after two decades of armed struggles that decimated the Communist top leadership and through internal purges, culminating in the Yan'an Rectification Movement (延安整风运动) in 1942.[47] For a totalitarian regime, only when personal leadership remains unchallenged can a politically cohesive and militant team be established.

Such a team is characterized from the outset by its small size, ideological unity, and highly focused target, which is the seizure of power by arms. The only way for such a small vanguard to seize power is through armed struggle, as its chance of winning through the ballot box is negligible. Even the highly popular Nazis did not come to power purely by voting but intermittently used conspiracy and riots. Indeed, the vanguard would find it difficult to seize power even through revolutionary violence unless aided by major domestic or international changes that provide them with unusual opportunities. The Bolsheviks were able to gain power because the Tsarist regime was brought to the verge of collapse by World War I, while the Nazis won considerable popular support because defeated Germany was burdened with massive war reparations, exacerbated by the Great Depression of 1929. Similarly, the Chinese Communists defeated the Nationalists in the Civil War of 1946–49 largely due to the damage inflicted on the Nationalist military during the

46 Sheila Fitzpatrick, *The Russian Revolution: 1917–1932* (Oxford: Oxford University Press, 1982), pp. 100–18, 153–7.

47 See Gao Hua, *How the Red Sun Rose: The Origin and Development of the Yan'an Rectification Movement, 1930–1945*, trans. Stacey Mosher and Guo Jian (Hong Kong: The Chinese University of Hong Kong Press, 2019), pp. 330–64.

preceding eight years of Japanese invasion, which provided the Communists with an opportunity to recuperate and expand.

Once the totalitarian party seizes power, the way it controls the nation is largely determined by the way it governs itself. If a totalitarian party leader cannot establish absolute authority within the party before taking power, nor can it effectively implement totalitarian control after taking power. Party control over the nation is usually shaky shortly after the establishment of totalitarianism, confronting challenges from both within and outside the party. Only massive purges are capable of physically eliminating the remaining dissent and resistance forces, thereby creating a powerful deterrent for everyone. Of course, since the ruling foundation is unstable, a cautious totalitarian party will practice the strategy of divide and conquer, redefining each time the scope of the "United Front" (统一战线) and limiting the targets to a "small handful" (一小撮). By slowly narrowing the "front" while expanding the scope of targets, it is able to eliminate anyone outside the ruling party, who might potentially challenge its legitimacy. In China, this pattern was followed in a series of political movements launched by Mao in the 1950s, such as the "industrial and commercial reform" (工商改造) and "Anti-Rightist" (反右) movements.

At the same time, the totalitarian party will further strengthen unity and leader worship within itself. Although the leader's supreme authority was usually established within the party before coming to power, such authority was not absolutely unchallengeable. Particularly, since those party elders who shared weal and woe with the supreme leader during the revolutionary era have earned military or other merits as capital, the "emperor" has to share power with these "barons" within the leadership group. In the eyes of the "emperor," however, the threat from the "barons" next to him is always far greater than any opposition outside the circle, only that the urgency to deal with the common external threats suppresses the internal struggles and temporarily maintains the peace and a degree of collective leadership within the party. Once the totalitarian party cuts off all social forces that are capable of challenging it and effectively eliminate the external threats, the party elders have helped to remove the greatest barrier that used to protect themselves, and the ephemeral collective leadership will transform into severe personal dictatorship. Stalin's Great Purge in 1937 and Mao's Cultural Revolution beginning in 1966 shared essentially the same purpose. Both were movements designed to cleanse potential power contenders and consolidate the authority of the supreme leader, who somehow felt insecure. Once his absolute authority is established, the nation will submit to one party, which in turn will submit to one person, whose caprice will bring the nation to ruin so long as he lives.

As Arendt observed, totalitarianism should not be confused with one-party dictatorship, which establishes the political foundation for totalitarian practice, but is itself only a negative form of totalitarianism where the ruling party prohibits any opposition and freedom of political speech. After the party seizes state power, the government and military under the control of party members begin to function normally. Having transferred its power center to the government, the ruling party no longer has its own power center. On the other hand, a totalitarian regime continues to use mass movements to govern the country after seizing power, striving to keep the movements above the state and prevent the revolutionary institutions in charge from being absorbed by the state. Therefore, totalitarianism often begins with a one-party dictatorship, but goes far beyond simply replacing a multi-party system with a one-party system. It transforms classes into masses and replaces the party-state with mass movements. The power center is transferred from the military to the secret police, which directly answers to the supreme leader. During the Soviet Civil War, as the secret police became a Bolshevik rather than a Soviet institution, the government lost its power and influence. While the Soviet was the highest constitutional authority, its practical power was exercised by the Bolsheviks, who were recognized as the "leading party," but were actually controlled by the secret police. Completely obedient to the will of the supreme leader, only the secret police know the next target to eliminate in the leader's scheme.[48] The totalitarian regime is then reduced to thorough personal dictatorship.

As a result, the seemingly irrational and incomprehensible cycle of purges in a totalitarian state is but the natural consequence predetermined by the nature of the regime. Despite the totalitarian ideology often advocating for "mass democracy," the combination of strict one-party rule, government by secret police, regularized mass movements and the radical deification of the leader inevitably leads to the extreme of personal dictatorship. In a political culture that insists on one "truth" represented by one party, which is led by one leader, it is impossible to institutionalize "collective leadership" (集体领导) according to the procedures of "intra-party democracy" (党内民主). As the one-party dictatorship has already transformed the masses into a group of puppet spectators, intra-party elite struggles are bound to be highly imbalanced power games. Even in ordinary authoritarian regimes, such elite struggles can easily lead to violent competitions without observing any rule of games, such as coups, persecution, and assassination. In a totalitarian regime, even if the supreme leader has long lost the majority support within the party leadership, he can still turn the tables by launching mass movements to eliminate potential challengers.

[48] Fitzpatrick, *The Russian Revolution: 1917–1932*, pp. 153–6.

The most typical example was the Cultural Revolution initiated by Chairman Mao in 1966. After the humanitarian disaster caused by the Great Leap Forward, a politically motivated economic movement that resulted in the Great Famine from 1959 to 1962, Mao's prestige within the party plummeted to its lowest point, forcing him to publicly apologize at the 7,000 Cadres Meeting (七千人大会) in 1962 and relinquish substantive powers.[49] However, a totalitarian leader could never tolerate any humiliation or diminution of his absolute authority. Within four years, Mao managed to mobilize the masses to "smash" state institutions and imprison potential leading challengers such as Liu Shaoqi, leaving him to die solitarily of terminal disease. Ironically, Liu was the chief culprit for making Mao the "Red Sun" of China through the Yan'an Rectification Movement in 1942. Relying on a highly personalized culture of leader worship to gain efficacy and seize power, the totalitarian party is bound to rule the country according to the same pattern once it comes to power. By excluding the possible constraints of social forces on the ruling party, the same totalitarian regime has also excluded any checks and balances within the party, creating the natural conditions for the personal dictatorship of totalitarian leaders.

3.3.4 *The Construction and Destruction of the Totalitarian Trinity*

Therefore, the establishment of a totalitarian state is a violent process filled with uncertainties, even in countries with a long absolutist tradition. The Russian and Chinese communist regimes were by no means the necessary outcome of any inevitable "historical laws," but rather the convergence of various factors, including the dogmatic nature of traditional political culture, the impact of modernization bringing new ideas and interests, geopolitical influences from neighboring countries, uncontrolled international events such as wars and foreign invasions, and even personal traits of revolutionary leaders. While the rise of Russian communism was directly influenced by World War I, the CCP benefited from almost all of the factors mentioned above. The fervent spread of communist ideology since the May Fourth Movement in 1919 would not have been possible without the stupendous efforts of the new Soviet Union, which sought to establish a friendly regime in its eastern neighbor. The CCP would also not have survived the relentless

49 Roderick MacFarquhar, *The Origins of the Cultural Revolution, Vol. 3: The Coming of the Cataclysm, 1961–1966* (New York: Columbia University Press, 1987), pp. 140–62, 461–73; Sima Changfeng, *The Beginning and End of the Cultural Revolution* [in Chinese] (Hong Kong: Baiye Book Store, 1976), pp. 51–8.

sieges launched by the Nationalists after their decision in 1927 to eradicate all Communist remnants derived from their previous cooperation, had it not been for the full-scale Japanese attacks on China in 1937, which reinitiated the Nationalist-Communist cooperation. The Japanese invasion disrupted the Nationalist control over China, weakened its military forces, and provided an opportunity for the Communists to recuperate. While the Japanese invasion and domestic challenges from the Communists prevented the Nationalists, the first totalitarian party in China, from descending into strict personal dictatorship, partly due to the early death of their founding father, Sun Yat-sen, the Communist Party, settling in the secluded region of Yan'an, was able to launch a deification movement in 1942, establishing the absolute authority of Mao Zedong Thought within the party. As aptly described by Gao Hua, the "Red Sun" had risen in the revolutionary base,[50] where the trinity of one doctrine-party-leader had already been established. It only took a national victory in 1949 to replicate the same model across the nation.

Of course, the consolidation of the totalitarian regime after seizing power was far from easy, as the totalitarian trinity was fundamentally at odds with human and social nature. While the idealistic ideology attracted capable youths to dedicate their lives to the revolutionary cause and gained popular support from peasants and intellectuals alike, there were numerous real or perceived enemies that needed to be eliminated before the regime could truly solidify its control over the nation. Although the Common Program (共同纲领) was enacted in 1949 by a new Political Consultative Committee (政治协商会议) consisting of a broad leftist alliance, the leadership of the CCP was unquestioned. After the beginning of the Korean War in 1950, which framed the struggle against American imperialism, successive political movements were implemented to carry out systematic social transformations. Capitalist industries were gradually nationalized, private landowners were expropriated, and land was distributed to peasants as promised in the Communist agenda. However, in a few years, peasant land was collectivized into People's Communes. The radical egalitarianism, known as the "big rice pot" (大锅饭) system, in which people in the same commune worked and ate together regardless of their productivity, led to a decline in the work ethic of peasants and quickly depleted food reserves in the less-than-abundant year of 1959, causing a devastating famine in the subsequent three years, during which at least 35 million people died of starvation.[51] In fact, within a few years of the Communist takeover, intellectuals were already deeply

[50] Gao Hua, *How the Red Sun Rose*, pp. 605–45.

[51] Yang Jisheng, *Tombstone: A Documentary Report on China's Great Famine in 1960s* [in Chinese] (Hong Kong: Cosmos Books, 2009), p. 11.

disillusioned by the widespread bureaucratism and numerous privileges enjoyed by the new vested interests, which starkly contradicted the pristine Communist ideals. Their disappointment turned into anger when Chairman Mao invited them to criticize official bureaucratism in 1957, only to be labeled "rightists" and suppressed in the ensuing "Anti-Rightist" movement. Thus, while the CCP largely achieved one-party dictatorship in the first decade of coming to power, it was never completely free from challenges.

As the one-party dictatorship was consolidated, so was Mao's personal supremacy within the party. While the Communists had to maintain a pretense of liberal democracy during the Yan'an period to garner international, particularly American, sympathy and support, they could now unleash their propaganda machine to cultivate the worship of Mao. The complete control of the media can be observed from the fact that during the three years of the Great Famine, which was exacerbated by the media's grossly exaggerated crop yields, there was not a single report or criticism of Mao's disastrous Great Leap Forward policy, which directly led to the famine. When Defense Minister Marshall Peng Dehuai mildly questioned Mao's policies and their impact on peasants at the Mount Lu Conference in 1959, he and a few other officials who shared a similar opinion were swiftly suppressed as an "anti-party bloc" (反党集团). Even though high-ranking officials such as Liu Shaoqi, Zhou Enlai, and Deng Xiaoping actually agreed with Peng, they not only failed to support him, but also aided Mao in the political persecution. It was only after the tragedy of the Great Famine had passed that Liu dared to complain to Mao, but this time it was Liu's turn to be persecuted by the Great Leader he had helped deify during the Yan'an Rectification Movement in 1942. Although Mao's policy was widely discredited within the party, his personal supremacy remained unchallenged. As the Red Sun of China, his personal popularity among the grassroots was unmatched, and he effectively used this social resource to eliminate Liu, Deng, and other "capitalist roaders" within the party by launching the Cultural Revolution.

The Cultural Revolution then, while demonstrating Mao's immense personal popularity as a result of successive worship movements, was far from the pinnacle of the totalitarian moment. On the contrary, it was a desperate attempt to safeguard Mao's personal authority within the party, which he believed was at risk. In other words, it marked the first crisis of the totalitarian order, where the trinity began to crumble. While the Communist ideology and one-party dictatorship remained intact, the grave policy mistakes inherent to such a regime had a detrimental effect on the unquestionable authority of the Great Leader (伟大领袖). Unwilling to be sidelined by rivals within the party, Mao decided to overthrow both the rivals and the party itself (which he had built with his own hands but no longer seemed to align with his views) by mobilizing the grassroots. Throughout the Cultural Revolution and numerous smaller movements, ideology was at the center. These struggles were of course not naked power struggles driven by self-interest, but were always framed as battles between different "lines" or "roads" (路线), between right and wrong. Liu was removed from his position as a "traitor," unconstitutionally, and imprisoned because he was deemed to be pursuing the wrong path that would lead the nation astray. The Cultural Revolution did not stop with the purge of Liu and his "bloc," but escalated into a quasi-civil war in which various factions of Red Guards zealously persecuted their teachers and party cadres, engaging in deadly battles among themselves.[52] It was a massive catastrophe that resulted not from the deliberate operation of a perfectly designed totalitarian machine, but from the desperate efforts of its top leaders to prevent its collapse and recreate an unconditionally loyal party by first shattering it through an unprecedented mass movement.

While the Cultural Revolution seemed equivalent to the Great Purge in the 1930s by which Stalin cleansed his imagined political threats within the party, the two movements differed in nature. As dictators never feel secure, they cannot help periodically rotate their successors and close collaborators through constant movements to mitigate potential threats, since the closer they are, the greater the threat, whether real or illusory. Unlike Mao after the Great Famine, however, Stalin's grip on power within the party remained strong despite the great famine in Ukraine caused by his disastrous collectivization policy in 1932–33. Having already expelled major rivals like Trotsky in the 1920s, the party was firmly under his control. Since the potential threat he sensed from within the party was largely born out of his paranoia,[53] he could easily purge the party through its own organizational machinery without needing to initiate a mass movement from outside the party. Since the Great Purge primarily involved court struggles within the party, rather than a social revolution that devastated the entire nation, its damage was confined to the party itself. Only when the dictator fears that the political resource within the party is out of his control, will he resort to his ultimate resource – the fanatic mass support accumulated through decades of totalitarian brainwashing – to eliminate political opponents, as Mao did through the Cultural Revolution.

52 Gao Gao and Yan Jiaqi, *Ten-Year's History of the Cultural Revolution, 1966-76* [in Chinese] (Tianjin: Tianjin People's Publishing House, 1986), pp. 209–80, 430–53.

53 Fitzpatrick, *The Russian Revolution: 1917–1932*, pp. 154–7.

Of course, the Cultural Revolution did not and could not put an end to the endless power struggles inherent in the totalitarian regime, especially ones between the dictator and his hand-picked successor, who was viewed as the greatest threat due to their close proximity to power. Within two years after the death of Liu Shaoqi, Mao's second appointed successor, Lin Biao, who helped Mao to launch the Cultural Revolution, also met his demise in a plane crash while attempting to flee to Mongolia after being defeated in a deadly struggle against Mao. Lin was similarly labeled as the center of an "anti-party bloc" and thoroughly condemned, along with the symbolic condemnation of Confucius (referring to Premier Zhou Enlai, Mao's second-hand man), in another ideological mass movement. It was the death of Lin, who was once seen as Mao's loyal successor, that led some individuals in the masses to question their blind devotion. Exhausted and disillusioned by the endless political movements since 1949, they began to feel deceived and their feelings towards the Great Leader shifted from love to hatred. The demystification of the charismatic leader marked the formal collapse of the totalitarian trinity.

3.4 THE DECLINE OF TOTALITARIANISM

Since a totalitarian regime is a hysteria that blatantly defies human nature in every respect, its peak is bound to be short-lived. After the madness subsides, it will eventually evolve from Authoritarian 3.0 to the more ordinary version 1.0. Some aggressive totalitarian states were defeated by external forces because they posed a threat to global peace. For example, after they were defeated in World War II, Germany, Italy, and Japan underwent regime transformation under the supervision of victorious liberal democracies. The transition of other totalitarian regimes, however, would have to wait for the awakening of their own people, while the international environment would serve as a background factor facilitating reform. The transition of these regimes was usually slower and more painful, with uncertain outcomes. Even after three decades of transition, Russia and Central and Eastern Europe, for example, still display significant disparities in their progress towards democratic reform. Indeed, countries like Russia under Putin have largely reverted back to authoritarianism. Despite its failure of political reform in 1989, China managed to continue its economic reforms, which transformed it into a post-totalitarian regime.

3.4.1 *The Inevitable Decline of Pure Totalitarianism*

Although the totalitarian victory has never been the result of its ideological superiority, ideology is the keystone that distinguishes totalitarianism from ordinary authoritarianism, and the totalitarian transformation usually starts with the ideological bankruptcy. Since the lofty and unattainable ideals are impossible to realize, it is only a matter of time for them to be reduced to deceptive jokes and moral poison that makes everyone cynical. The totalitarian ideology is necessarily based on the myth of a "great, glorious and correct" (伟光正) totalitarian party, whose officials are incorrigibly corrupt because their power is not subject to any supervision from the people. Every corrupt official repeats the ideological gibberish while speaking on the stage, and poisons the people's conscience each time they are taken off the stage. Finally, everyone realizes without expressing the daily norm of saying one thing and doing another. Everyone is indignant when pointing fingers at others but never faces the interrogation of his own conscience. More seriously, everyone knows that he is nothing but an insignificant hypocrite and purely selfish villain, speaking more beautifully even than singing. At this point, the totalitarian ideology as a belief system goes completely bankrupt. In fact, since the totalitarian regime has established a highly visible and supposedly lofty interest group whose power and privileges have been out of control since the first day it was established, the glaring rupture between the ideal and the reality will surface and grow quickly, soon leading to an ideological crisis. As early as 1957, a mere eight years after the Communist takeover, Chinese intellectuals were already so disappointed with the new regime that when Chairman Mao encouraged them to criticize bureaucratic corruption in order to attack his political rivals, the "contest and bloom" (鸣放) movement quickly triggered a flood of "malicious attacks" (恶毒攻击), which had to be abruptly stopped and hastily transformed into the Anti-Rightist Movement.[54]

When a society has lost its moral baseline and surrendered itself to the reign of power, the most efficient way to govern is through the terror of the police. To be sure, terror is nothing alien to a totalitarian regime, which begins with revolution, the greatest terror on earth. Once it seizes power, it continues the reign of terror through "continuing revolution" (继续革命) under the proletarian dictatorship – political movements that eliminate enemies and instill fear in the masses. During the initial period, the reign of terror is truly untouchable, like high-voltage electricity, usually resulting in the physical annihilation of enemies. At the same time as the ideological fever subsides, the reign of terror becomes institutionalized and, to some extent, humanized. As the "high voltage" gradually decreases to "low voltage," the cost of challenging the power decreases, and so does the people's fear of the state and its

[54] Sima Changfeng, *The Beginning and End of the Cultural Revolution*, pp. 32–8.

supreme leader. Although the vast majority still do not dare to stand up and fight for their own rights, unwilling to face reality and reflect on the legitimacy of the regime, they no longer take the revolutionary ideology seriously and make it their guide to action. Since pure totalitarianism is nothing short of ephemeral madness, it will sooner or later enter a more rationalized phase of a "post-totalitarian" state. Compared to typical totalitarianism, a post-totalitarian regime is usually more resilient and lasting because it can carry out more cost-efficient management of terror and effectively use state-monopolized violence to punish and deter various instabilities. While the post-totalitarian regime still engages in ideological propaganda, it increasingly relies on legalized terror to maintain its power.

Once the totalitarian ideology no longer holds the people's hearts, the totalitarian legacy is not so much about brainwashing with positive propaganda as it is about cultivating the habit of dishonesty among the people. Growing up in lies and deceit, the people in the post-totalitarian regime no longer believe in the totalitarian ideology, but are nevertheless forced to be indoctrinated and publicly acknowledge its truth and legitimacy. Apart from fostering a cowardly and morally defective personality, such open confession and spiritual distortion also exaggerate the power of the regime and intensify personal inner fear. This creates an illusion that everyone, except oneself, seems to support the system – an illusion that persists until the very eve of the totalitarian collapse. Despite internal and external troubles, the totalitarian regime still appears unshakable on its seemingly pristine surface. Since it never allowed any independent social group to organize and govern themselves, or even discuss various models of governance until its very collapse, the entire society runs the serious risk of instantly falling into a dangerous state of power vacuum and disorder once it does collapse. Before long, the resulting chaos will strongly call for another omnipotent regime to replace its predecessor.

3.4.2 *The Inherent Difficulties in Totalitarian Transformation*

Before discussing the possibilities of totalitarian transformation, we cannot exclude the worst possibility. Although pure totalitarianism is doomed to be short-lived, an unfortunate country that happens to be trapped in the totalitarian dictatorship may never gather enough wisdom and courage in order to break its spell. In fact, even an ordinary authoritarian regime usually fails to reform itself until it is overthrown by an angry people through revolutionary violence, which may lead the nation to an even more catastrophic path towards totalitarianism. The history of imperial China had already served as a good lesson. While peaceful reform is not impossible, it always takes a small probability miracle such as the ascendance of a Gorbachev or Chiang Ching-kuo (蒋经国) to make it happen. China had its chance when the enlightened Emperor Guangxu came to power during the Hundred Days' Reform in 1898, but quickly lost it. Most authoritarian rulers are mediocre, myopic, and fatally arrogant. Since they have neither the will nor the interest to reform themselves, they can only be swept away by the storm of revolution. Whether and when revolution will occur depends, however, on the balance of power between the regime and its opposition forces. The deeper the totalitarian oppression, the stronger and steadier the totalitarian regime, the weaker the popular resistance, and the graver the social crisis. Only when the people are degraded to such a dire condition that they have nothing to lose and the regime is so fragile as to be on the brink of collapse, will they rise to replace it. In other words, if a totalitarian regime is left to itself, liberal democratic transformation may never happen. It is perfectly possible that a post-totalitarian regime is permanently stuck somewhere between Authoritarian 1.0 and 3.0.

In a post-totalitarian regime, the power is still highly imbalanced. While the abuse of public power by the selfish and capricious ruling group is inevitably rampant, the powerless society can do nothing to protect itself. To be more precise, the totalitarian regime has an omnipotent state without a society as such. It is composed of atomized individuals without faith, organization, and mutual trust. Everyone is a "prisoner" in the Prisoner's Dilemma, helplessly facing the totalitarian behemoth alone. Even someone who occasionally wants to do something cannot muster enough moral courage, or quickly sinks into despair before the pervasive collective inaction. Particularly, in a regime where the official ideology is centered on economy, everyone is turned into a purely economic animal. Such is a necessary condition for the maintenance of the post-totalitarian regime, where everyone must learn to follow the pragmatist rule preaching that "follow the system, or perish."

Nor is reform within the ruling party a likely event. As Arendt observed, the totalitarian regime is characterized by the conspicuous absence of successful or abortive coups because it is not governed by a faction or group, but by the totalitarian leader over a flock of completely atomized individuals.[55] Such an atomized state is not limited to the masses, but extends all the way to the highest level of the totalitarian order. Within the ruling party, the supreme leader prohibits any "factions and cliques" (团团伙伙),[56] and will replace any

[55] Arendt, *The Origins of Totalitarianism*, pp. 323–4, 392–3.

[56] Article 52 of the CCP Regulations on Disciplinary Actions, enacted in 2015, makes it sufficiently clear: "Engaging in cliques and factions within the party, forming factions for

top confidants suspected of engaging in factional activities at any time. Indeed, the absence of an institutionalized ruling group has made the peaceful succession of the leader impossible for the totalitarian regime. While Hitler repeatedly designated and replaced his own successors, the succession of Stalin was full of breathtaking suspense, and Mao even killed twice his hand-picked successors who were suspected to be conspiring against him.

As a result, even if a totalitarian regime has rotted, no one dares to challenge its legitimacy. There are so few who dare to break away from it that they will easily be eliminated, or at least quickly marginalized. Most people are either blind or too scared to see the evils that the regime brings them daily. The elites are easily bought off to comply with the regime or even knowingly assist it in committing evil, until the living space of the grassroots is squeezed to the brink of exhaustion, reducing them to truly proletarian revolutionaries who have "nothing to lose but their chains." As an intensified version of authoritarianism, however, a totalitarian regime enjoys abundant social resources and a profound popular base. Only when the rich totalitarian resources are depleted is it possible to change the regime, by which time not only the totalitarian political resources but also the moral and natural resources will have suffered great damage. If the collapse of a typical authoritarian regime only results in "a broken nation, while the mountains and rivers remain" (国破山河在), the collapse of a totalitarian regime may well bring about the opposite predicament, with "broken mountains and rivers." Only when the social and natural environment is completely corrupted will it reach rock bottom, but surrounded by institutional, moral, and material crises, the society will also lose the ability to recover and rebound.[57] Even if the totalitarian regime eventually collapses all of a sudden, the hitherto deeply depressed society is powerless to turn back and avoid the irreversible state of destruction.

3.4.3 *Possible Paths towards Post-Totalitarianism*

Of course, these are worst-case scenarios, which are possible but not inevitable. If lucky enough, a totalitarian state is not necessarily doomed to a dead

personal gain, forming alliances and cliques, cultivating personal influence, or engaging in activities such as exchanging benefits and building a personal image to gain political capital shall be given a severe warning or have their party positions revoked. Those with particularly severe circumstances shall be placed under probation within the party or expelled from the party."

57 Sun Liping, "The Chinese society is accelerating towards a rout," 人民网 (February 16, 2011), https://cmcn.org/archives/22568.

end. While a totalitarian regime is extremely hard to establish, it is even harder to maintain. After the death of its supreme leader and, particularly, the first-generation vanguards, it usually passes its peak and starts to decline, making political reform a feasible option. China started its reform right after Mao died in 1976, and Khrushchev embarked on reform immediately after Stalin died in 1953. Although both reforms failed within a decade, they did open up new possibilities. After enduring the long, dull second-generation leadership, the third-generation leadership in the Soviet Union and Eastern Europe initiated Glasnost and Perestroika, which achieved limited success. Without external interference, small totalitarian regimes such as North Korea and Cambodia may establish stable rule, in which the dictator can effectively monitor the bureaucracy and the entire country through an absolutely loyal secret police force. The larger the nation, the more resources are at the disposal of the regime, making it harder to overcome its dictatorship. On the other hand, it is also more difficult to maintain such a regime in its pure form since both the power contenders inside the system and social interests outside are more diverse, and the pressure over the "one leader" scenario is greater than in a small monolithic state, making it less likely to be tolerated in the long term. With the grotesque failures of utopian experiments, social disillusionment, and dissatisfaction are bound to arise, exerting growing pressure over the ruling party. As a result, extreme personal dictatorship often dies with the death of the founding generation. As strict totalitarianism can no longer be maintained, the ensuing ease of control will open the nation up and prepare its transition to a more ordinary authoritarian regime.

First, the totalitarian ideology is among the first to face a major crisis, as the party-state can no longer explain the glaring gap between the ideal and the reality, especially given the irreconcilable disparity between the democratic promises pledged by the party before and the reality of extreme centralization after taking power. Second, as totalitarian regimes practicing public ownership and planned economy inevitably run into constant economic crises, enlightened leaders will relax economic control to a degree, allowing for limited private ownership and a market economy. This implies opening up the nation to the world, from which new ideas and doctrines will arrive together with new technologies and management models, making the orthodox ideology completely marginalized and reduced to the deceitful occupation of those in the Marxist schools.[58] Finally,

[58] Recent news are not particularly friendly to them, exposing several sex scandals in a row about faculties from the Marxist Schools of several major universities. See, e.g., Xu Sir, "Zhengzhou University scandal," www.163.com/dy/article/I4FACT4C0544QVMF.html.

in order to promote a market economy, the ruling party is obliged to actively embrace the rule of law, even though effectively limiting the power of the ruling party is unrealistic in a post-totalitarian state that rejects genuine democracy and judicial independence. Particularly given the painful lessons most first-generation vanguards suffered during the Cultural Revolution, they had every incentive to advocate the rule of law in order to prevent similar tragedies from recurring.

Although the ruling party will never attempt to reform the political system on which its power depends, nor will it change its ideology or even seriously criticize the personal dictatorship of the supreme leader, such as Mao, reform is like Pandora's Box, which cannot easily be closed once it is opened. As social interests and ideas become increasingly diversified, more individuals are becoming economically independent. The orthodox ideology is increasingly reduced to a mere formality, ridiculed by an increasing number of liberals as a lie and a joke. More importantly, the ruling party itself is more differentiated in interest and opinion. Although there is "no party outside the party," factions within the party have never ceased to exist and are bound to multiply as the external environment softens. Any top leader must consider factional balance rather than acting alone. In other words, whether inside or outside the party, personal dictatorship under pure totalitarianism is no longer possible. The typical totalitarian regime is evolving, willingly or not, into an ordinary authoritarian one, although it is unlikely to change directly from Authoritarian 3.0 to version 1.0.

On the other hand, while the totalitarian regime is no longer at its zenith, its three "magic weapons" (法宝) are still at its disposal: one-party dictatorship, brainwashing propaganda, and reign by terror. The goal of reform is to maintain the one-party dictatorship by improving the performance of the party-state through rationalized policies. This shift will effectively move from totalitarianism to ordinary authoritarianism and from personal dictatorship to some form of collective leadership. Although there will always be a "Big Boss" at any given time, their power is no longer unlimited since major policies need to be decided through agreements with other major leaders. Brainwashing will no doubt continue, but its effectiveness will continue to decline. Reign by police terror is indispensable but will be carried out under the banner of "rule of law." The ruling elites expect this to protect themselves from mass mob movements and personal authority, but in vain. They have forgotten the pain once the scar is healed and have forfeited its protection through their own abuses. Overconfident when in power, they maximize abuses by constantly intervening in the judiciary for the sake of personal interests, reducing the rule of law to a useless facade when they themselves need its protection against arbitrary persecutions.[59] Depending on the level of political crisis, the urgency of suppressing opposing voices, and the historical positioning of their own mission in the eyes of the post-totalitarian leaders, they may, at times, be more lenient, allowing a degree of free social activities without fully utilizing the three "magic weapons." The essence of post-totalitarianism lies in the fact that the complete totalitarian panoply is still present, but it is operated ineffectively, like a rusted machine unplugged from the wall. Conscientious rulers such as Gorbachev are not even interested in playing with the totalitarian magic weapon, while mediocre rulers merely follow the game of "drumming while passing the buck" (击鼓传花), hoping that the regime will not collapse within their term.

As the control of the party-state over society weakens, social freedom increases. The role of brainwashing is no longer about positively educating anyone to accept the official ideology but rather about filling the blank of people's faith with a set of hypocritical teachings, which are believed by a constantly decreasing number of followers, and preventing them from embracing more authentic beliefs. People are increasingly focused on their own immediate interests and are less concerned with the state and political preaching. Cynicism is very common both inside and outside the system. Officials are eager to use the remaining power and resources under their control to seek rent, while people are keen to exploit every market opportunity to earn money. As moral and political ethics seem to be constantly declining, society appears to be on the verge of disorder. In this seemingly chaotic process, however, society is growing in its "impedance" against the state, and the "zero impedance" condition characteristic of totalitarianism is gone forever. Using a magnetic field as an analogy, the irresistible magnetic force of the totalitarian regime used to polarize every individual "magnet" in its field, aligning each orientation in its direction. After the decline of the totalitarian magnet, the individual magnets undergo chaotic "Brownian motion," randomizing the individual magnetic distribution or developing them towards neutral "insulators" of weakened magnetism. The post-totalitarian state shares similarities with Authoritarian 1.0 in that, after the official ideology is no longer capable of commanding people's beliefs, it is mainly maintained by the one-party dictatorship and reign by terror.

59 For example, Bo Xilai was infamous for undermining the rule of law, while serving as the party secretary of Chongqing, but complained about judicial injustice when it was his turn to be incarcerated, tried, and sentenced to life imprisonment. See Zheng Hanliang, "Bo Xilai angrily yelled that the judgment was unjust and unfair after hearing the sentencing," RFI (September 23, 2013), www.rfi.fr/cn/中国/20130923-薄熙来闻判后怒喊裁决不公不义.

3.4.4 *China after the Cultural Revolution*

This is precisely what has happened to China since 1949 when the national replication of the Yan'an Rectification model established the absolute authority of Mao and his "thought" throughout the nation within a few years after the Communists took over power. By 1954, the first constitution of the People's Republic, drafted by Mao, was unanimously passed by the National People's Congress, symbolizing the consolidation of the totalitarian trinity of "one doctrine, one party, one leader." To be sure, in a regime that ostensibly practices "democratic centralism" (民主集中制), the social condition of "zero impedance" to such authority is never truly reached. Besides constantly initiating political movements for brainwashing and weeding out nonconformists, the ruling party had to deal with intellectual dissatisfaction, exemplified by the Anti-Rightist Movement in 1957. Even without substantial challenges from outside the party, the dictator constantly felt a legitimacy crisis for maintaining dictatorship within the party and was pressed to manufacture achievements to sustain his absolute authority. Hence the race to the ceiling on promises of speedy development that led to the catastrophic Great Leap Forward in 1958.[60] The ensuing Great Famine substantially challenged Mao's absolute leadership within the party, a challenge that a dictator could never accept. Regardless of whether Liu Shaoqi and his colleagues had any real ambition to replace him, Mao felt a sense of crisis that he had never experienced at least since 1942. The Cultural Revolution was launched in 1966 under the ruse of "struggles over paths" (路线斗争), but its essence was obviously a power struggle through which Mao used the still fanatical worship of the masses to destroy his political rivals within the party. While the one-party dictatorship remained largely intact, the crisis of the one-leader element in the totalitarian trinity ultimately undermined the Communist ideological unity. Mao's absolute authority was rescued at the expense of his party and the totalitarian order as a whole.

After the Cultural Revolution ended with Mao's death in 1976 and rural reform was initiated in 1978, the totalitarian regime quickly entered its "post-totalitarian" phase. On the whole, the early stages of China's reform seemed to proceed much more rapidly than its neighbor and teacher, the Soviet Union. In fact, it proceeded so fast that within a decade, the reform clashed with the vested interest groups again. Unfortunately, although Mao was dead, the first-generation revolutionary vanguards such as Deng Xiaoping, Chen Yun, and Li Xiannian were still alive and active in the political arena. By 1989, like

60 MacFarquhar, *The Origins of the Cultural Revolution, Vol. 1*, pp. 218–25, 281–90, 311–17.

Empress Dowager in 1898, these patriarchs had largely retired to the second line by joining the Central Advisory Committee, but their actual political influence remained. When the protesting students held a prolonged hunger strike on Tiananmen Square, the reformers within the party had to face off against the conservatives backed by the patriarchy. Without suspense, the patriarchy crushed the social demand for political reform and consolidated their control ability through the centralization of power within the party. A generation has passed since the crackdown, without a single sign of political reform within the party. On the other hand, Deng Xiaoping's Southern Tour in 1992 restarted economic reform, making officials' rent-seeking the "contract" within the ruling party and the resulting enormous vested interest the fatal obstacle to political reform, which has lost both its social basis and moral resources. Despite the intensification of ideological brainwashing, the official ideology has long become a self-deceptive facade, behind which is a completely cynical officialdom, in whose eyes only personal interest counts, and its greatest interest is to maintain power.

In comparison, the Soviet Union launched political reform only after almost seven decades of taking power. In three generations, the authoritarian regime was in its twilight. As the October Revolution succeeded more than three decades before the Chinese Communists seized power, the first-generation leaders, headed by Stalin, had mostly passed away by the 1950s. In the next decade, the second-generation leader, Khrushchev, attempted to correct Stalin's excesses but failed. In another two decades, while domestic political freedom was severely suppressed, the power struggle within the party continued. With a stagnating economy, the political legitimacy of the Soviet dictatorship was almost depleted by 1985, when it was fortunate enough to encounter a young and enlightened reformer, Gorbachev.[61] The lack of economic reform also accounted for a weaker vested interest group. To be sure, the party cadres always enjoyed various privileges, which were nevertheless not so significant as to make them deadly enemies of political reform. On the contrary, as the ruling party had a relatively strong ideological flavor and limited rent-seeking opportunities, most grassroots party members were unsophisticated, without realizing that economic reform without its political companion could have allowed them to earn as much rent as their Chinese

[61] Gorbachev's rise to power was "fortunate" because it was not guaranteed in any way, even though he was the youngest and most capable member of the Politburo, perhaps the only one at the time who could bring hope to the Soviet Union. However, in a post-totalitarian country where the principle of "bad money drives out good" is prevalent, there is obviously no mechanism to ensure that such a person will come to power by necessity.

counterparts did after Deng Xiaoping's Southern Tour. With the Communist die-hards gone and without an unshakable vested interest barrier against reform, Soviet political reform proceeded naturally and achieved a degree of success. Had second-generation political reformers such as Hu Yaobang or Zhao Ziyang come to power a decade later, when the first-generation patriarchs like Deng Xiaoping and Chen Yun died in the 1990s, the balance of power between reformers and conservatives would have been remarkedly different, leading to a completely different outcome of political reform.

From 1989 to the present day, China has been caught in a post-totalitarian mode, oscillating between Authoritarian 1.0 and 3.0. On the one hand, economic reforms have greatly improved the people's material lives, leading to liberalization in almost every aspect of human life, including economic freedom, personal freedom, and freedom of belief and expression. With the development of the Internet, people have gained a significant degree of de facto free speech. Although freedom of speech is not institutionally protected, its limited de facto existence demonstrates that the social resistance against state encroachment has increased substantially. Starting with the Sun Zhigang incident in 2003, online speech has entered the public sphere and, on occasion, has been powerful enough to push for national institutional reforms.[62]

On the other hand, the Sun Zhigang model only works sporadically. Most of the time, public opinion still cannot influence the state. The people lack the power to decide on laws, policies, and resource allocation that affect their daily lives, nor can they effectively protect their rights from the infringement of the still-powerful state. In fact, the post-totalitarian state has consolidated its legitimacy to a great extent through economic growth, enabling it to invest more resources in maintaining the lingering totalitarian order. From the "firewall" (防火墙) that restricts internet access to online monitors, the "internet navy" (网络水军) and the "50-cents Party" (五毛党) who spread disinformation under official commands, from the "Chaoyang district masses" (朝阳群众), the nickname for active informers who report suspicious activities to public security, to the increasingly enhanced stability maintenance forces across the nation, micro-level social control by the state has reached unprecedented levels. In this sense, a post-totalitarian regime often contains "neo-totalitarian" elements, both mechanisms for preserving, repairing, and strengthening the existing totalitarian order.

[62] Zhang, "A constitution without constitutionalism?," 961–6.

3.5 CONCLUSIONS

To recap, a totalitarian regime is driven by the logic that it must be under the absolute dictatorship of one leader. Any degree of genuine "collective leadership" within the party would inevitably lead to divisions among leaders along policy lines, undermining ideological unity and the party-state's comprehensive control over society. These divisions within the party would immediately threaten the one-party monopoly, as party leaders would seek political alliances with various social forces to bolster their power and position within the party, thus enabling society to develop some "impedance" against state power for self-protection. Conversely, excluding competition from social forces outside the party has provided great convenience for personal dictatorship within the party. In both China and the former Soviet Union, the top leader was able to purge political rivals within the party under the pretense of "struggles over paths," anti-privilege and anti-corruption campaigns to maintain their unchallenged position. Once the absolute authority of the "one leader" can no longer be sustained, the totalitarian regime inevitably collapses.

A totalitarian regime is a massive Leviathan that is difficult to construct, and once it is established, its immense inertia makes it challenging to halt. Perhaps time is the only effective decelerator that can slow it down. As it gradually becomes weary and its primary components begin to crumble, a turning point may eventually arise. If it is on the verge of collapse, there is a possibility for self-reflection and repair. By repairing, updating, and strengthening certain components, it can continue to function and prolong its existence. While totalitarian transformation is difficult enough, China's transformation is further complicated not only by a tradition of absolute monarchy spanning over two millennia but also by its massive size and abundant resources at the regime's disposal. Compared to smaller regimes like North Korea, it is much more arduous for a vast country like China to remain totalitarian because the condition of "zero impedance" can be disrupted at any point, significantly raising the cost of upholding the totalitarian trinity of "one doctrine, one party, one leader." This partly explains why North Korea remains a rigid totalitarian regime, while China has progressively moved towards nationwide reforms since 1978 through local experimentation. Once China settled into Authoritarian 2.0, however, it gained significant advantages in maintaining domestic stability and resisting international pressures. While authoritarian power is naturally organized and centralized, social forces are inevitably scattered and sporadic, making it easier to defeat them individually.

The transformation of China presents itself not only as a question for the century, but also as a global challenge. Its tradition, scale, and institutional inertia all point to the conclusion that China is the most difficult country to transform. On the other hand, it is evident that China's transformation is not impossible. Historically, China's absolutist tradition played a role in the failure of imperial transitions, eventually leading to the establishment of a totalitarian regime. However, its failure was also influenced by international developments at the time, particularly the emergence of the first Soviet regime following World War I and the invasion of militarist Japan. Undoubtedly, the international landscape has fundamentally changed today. Coupled with economic prosperity and national strength, liberal democracy has become the mainstream international consensus since the end of World War II. Although the infiltration of liberal democratic ideas alone is insufficient to change China, and its scale and economic success enable it to remain aloof from external pressure, a peaceful and reform-friendly external environment at least makes sustained domestic reform possible. In the past four decades, China has transitioned from Authoritarian 3.0 to a more relaxed version of 2.0. Although recent attempts have aimed to revert some progress, it is impossible to return to the era of the Cultural Revolution. To be sure, the reform process is currently stuck, and the path ahead is filled with challenges and uncertainties. With the right timing and favorable conditions, however, there is no reason why China cannot eventually break free from the curse of totalitarianism.

Ultimately, the key lies in the hands of the Chinese people, as the sustainability of totalitarianism depends on their strength and courage. For those who possess the courage like the participants of the White Paper Movement, national transformation is not only a difficult political mission, but also a true test of their wisdom, dedication, and human potential. It is also a rare opportunity to apply the experience, knowledge and resources accumulated over the past four decades to achieve a historical milestone for a nation constituting one-fifth of the world's population – something that has eluded it for the past two millennia.

4

The Vicissitudes of a Crippled Reform

1978–Present

As the revolutionary hysteria was eventually put to an end with Mao's death and the fall of the Gang of Four (四人帮) in 1976, China entered once again the phase of reform. The first decade since 1978 was truly the "golden age" of reform since the CCP leaders represented by Deng Xiaoping (邓小平), Hu Yaobang (胡耀邦), and Zhao Ziyang (赵紫阳) adopted a balanced approach between economic and political reforms. With the demotions of Hu in 1986 and Zhao in 1989, however, the reform has become crippled ever since the crackdown of the democratic movement in Tiananmen Square in June 1989. Although Deng reignited economic reform through the Southern Tour in 1992, political reform has since been indefinitely shelved, putting China back to the imperial time when the constitutional reform lacked genuine momentum. The crippled reform is not necessarily a *good* reform in the first place, creating high speed of economic development with huge social cost, nor can it prevent a totalitarian revival as witnessed in the recent decade. Despite the failures of political reform and recent backlashes towards neo-totalitarianism, however, the first three decades of Reform and Opening had not only nurtured a reasonably strong private sector, but also introduced new ideas and social forces that might thwart an uninhibited rise of neo-totalitarianism and sustain reform when the political environment is improved in the future.

4.1 REFORM: FOR BETTER OR WORSE?

In January 1992, Deng Xiaoping visited southern cities such as Shenzhen and Shanghai, and delivered the Southern Tour (南巡) speech, reinitiating the reform that had been stagnated since the crackdown of the Tiananmen Square protests in 1989. In the first two decades, the significance of the Southern Tour was positively recognized both within China and internationally. In the next two decades, however, the effects of reforms restarted by the Southern Tour have become increasingly ambivalent. On the one hand, the economy once enjoyed rapid development, together with significant government financial expansion and continuous growth in urbanization and infrastructural construction. On the other hand, the Chinese society has increasingly been troubled by issues such as "advancement of the state at the expense of private sectors" (国进民退), rampant official corruption, forced land taking and house demolitions, growing disparity in wealth, and severe damage of the environment and natural resources. While the economic reform has relaxed restrictions on society and brought about vitality, it also multiplied rent-seeking opportunities for officials and stimulated their zeal for corruption and power abuses. The ambivalent impact of the reform has led the grassroots as well as liberal and left-wing elites to question its legitimacy, prompting more people to reflect on and reevaluate the significance of the Southern Tour and to explore China's future path of reform.

I have previously argued that "reform" is not necessarily a commendatory term. Even in democracies where political and legal reforms take place continuously, retrogression can occur due to mistakes such as cognitive biases of political elites and the general public. In authoritarian regimes, where the general public cannot hold political elites accountable through periodic elections, systemic flaws are commonplace, making benign reforms that benefit the public is an urgent need of society. Paradoxically, in such a society where reform is urgently needed, benign reforms are often poorly implemented and may not even make it to the agenda, thus becoming trapped in a pervasive feasibility dilemma at every turn. In fact, while benevolent reforms are infeasible, feasible "reforms" often turn out to be malevolent.[1] In other words, reform may not necessarily mean a change for the better (改良); it is entirely possible that it is heading towards a change for the worse (改恶).[2]

Examining reforms from China's own experiences, it becomes clear that a benign reform requires at least two conditions. First, reform must be conducted with moderate participation from the general public, with ordinary people having the right to say "no" to policies that harm their interests. Second, political elites must be sufficiently open-minded and well-intentioned, welcoming (at least tolerating) public participation and voluntarily implementing benign reforms under social pressure for the sake of their

[1] Zhang Qianfan, "Why will the reform keep getting worse?," *China Digital Times* (September 15, 2010), https://chinadigitaltimes.net/chinese/104972.html.

[2] Indeed, "*gai'e* (改悪) [reform for the worse] is an available term in the Japanese vocabulary.

long-term political interests. In democracies, the second condition is largely redundant since the powerholders are obligated by the votes to engage in reforms for the better. For authoritarian regimes, however, it is necessary for benign reforms to take place. To be sure, there is also a fortunate scenario where enlightened leaders consciously implement reforms that benefit the public without its substantial participation. In fact, I believe that the reforms in China before 1989 can largely be characterized as such a fortunate scenario. However, while such a scenario is not entirely impossible, opportunities bestowed by rulers are undoubtedly rare and destined to be short-lived. The necessity of the Southern Tour itself suffices to demonstrate the transitory nature of such fortunate reforms.

In the absence of the aforementioned conditions, a nation is left with two less fortunate choices: either no reform or "reform" for the worse. Prior to 1978, from people's communes to state-owned enterprises, China stagnated everywhere. While corrupt officials did exist during that time, they were indeed fewer in number due to the pervasive poverty that afflicted the entire nation. Every household lived near or below the poverty line, struggling for basic sustenance, leaving little resource for corruption. To be sure, no society can possibly implement absolute egalitarianism. Mao's era was no exception. Behind the facade of the "big rice pot" (大锅饭), officials at all levels enjoyed various privileges accessible only through their special status. While local cadres were strictly controlled by their superiors, they possessed immense discretion over the daily lives of ordinary people. Beneath the stagnant surface of the planned economy, there were still many exploitable gaps. In life-and-death situations, these gaps could even provide life-saving opportunities. It should not be forgotten that tens of millions of peasants died during the Great Leap Forward, while few city residents suffered from the same fate and starving cadres were unheard of.[3] A few handfuls of rice taken from the grain stores might seem insignificant, but were enough to save the lives of a whole family during the period of starvation. This was the privilege enjoyed by a cadre at the lowest level of the power pyramid. The various "exceptions" that occurred before the reform can only illustrate one rule: In an authoritarian regime, any opportunities, wealth or resources that are available for seizure will be seized by those in power who are situated in advantageous positions. In a poor society that is suffocated by regulation (一管就死), these resources

[3] Even the guardians of the grain stores were able to preserve their families. For recollection of survivors, see Cai Shankang, "Personal experience and memory specimen in the age of hunger," 《新三界》 (March 27, 2018), https://posts.careerengine.us/p/5e607ed716582d20f74923a5.

are so scarce, and information so underdeveloped, that disparity in wealth does not appear as glaringly alarming. The ordinary people are aware of almost nothing that actually happens in their country, apart from how much of their own salary is left by the end of each month.

The purpose of the reform is precisely to break the stagnant "big rice pot" policy, adding vitality and momentum to social development. The main theme of the reform is "delegation" (放权) – the central government delegates power to the local authorities and, overall, the state surrenders some power to the people. The colossal wheel of reform has been set in motion, through which every stratum of society has gained greater economic freedom, accompanied by social wealth that is quickly rolling in. However, it immediately raises a question: As the government relaxes its control to allow people creating wealth, who gains the wealth? If the structure of political power remained unchanged, the "exceptions" before the reform become the "norm" thereafter: The wealth of the people may grow, but the growth rate is inevitably far behind that of the government and all vested interest groups capable of approaching and sharing its power. Economic reform without its political companion not only laid the foundation for Deng Xiaoping's Southern Tour in 1992, but also creates new difficulties that subsequent Chinese reform is bound to face.

4.2 HOW IS A BENIGN REFORM MADE POSSIBLE?

4.2.1 *One Reform or Two Reforms?*

Political scientist Wu Guoguang proposed the theory of two reforms, instead of one, suggesting that the reforms between 1978 and 1989 and from 1993 to the present are completely different in terms of objectives, nature, driving forces, and results.[4] One key indication is that officials had fundamentally different attitudes towards the two rounds of reforms. In 1978, while grassroots such as the villagers of Xiaogang (小岗村), Anhui Province, collaborated with the reformers in the national government to promote reforms that benefited the people, they encountered resistance at various local levels (中梗阻). Government officials generally lacked enthusiasm for the reforms and even passively impeded the implementation of central policies through various "countermeasures." In contrast, the reforms restarted in 1992 sparked unprecedented interest and enthusiasm among officials at all levels. From massive

4 Wu Guoguang, "On Reform and 'Second Reform,' 爱思想 (August 4, 2004), www.aisixiang.com/data/3821.html.

land requisition to rapid "old city renovation" (旧城改造), from arduous investment solicitation to fervent infrastructure construction, officials seemed to transform overnight from obstacles to the driving force of reform.

To verify the theory of two reforms, I reviewed the documents of the CCP Central Committee (中共中央, hereinafter CCPCC) and the work reports (工作报告) of the Central People's Government (中央人民政府, hereinafter CPG) from various years in an attempt to identify different governing approaches between the two rounds of reforms.[5] Although I agree that the reform initiated in 1978 should be divided into two or three stages, and the driving forces and effects of different stages are completely different, I failed to discover any fundamental differences in the reform approaches or institutional designs apart from the short-lived proposal for the separation of the Party and government. Therefore, my basic judgment is that the reform from 1978 to the present is continuous as a whole. The only difference is that by 1989, the comprehensive implementation of core programs such as the reform of state-owned enterprises had not been fully carried out. The significance of the Southern Tour speech layprecisely in restarting the unfinished reforms. Of course, the second reform that has taken place since 1992 did occur in a completely different political environment. However, its objectives and original intentions are not fundamentally different from the first reform that has been interrupted since 1989.

First, I examined the origin of the much criticized "merit system" (政绩体制) and the GDP-dominated mindset since the reform started in 1978. It is generally believed that the merit system is a root cause of the GDP-dominated mindset, blind development, and numerous social conflicts caused by land acquisition and demolition. The top-down control mechanism of officials was certainly not a unique invention of 1949. It has existed in China since ancient times, and cannot be viewed as a product of the post-Southern Tour system. In fact, as early as 1979, the Central Organization Department (中组部) issued a Notice regarding Opinion on Implementing the Cadre Assessment System.[6] To be sure, the cadre standards of that era had ideological components. In addition to work effectiveness (工作成效), they also included political thought, organizational leadership ability and "democratic working style." In 1983, however, the central government held a national conference on

[5] The CPG is the highest administrative organ, also known as the State Council (国务院), which submits its work report to the National People's Congress during its annual convention, usually held in early March each year.

[6] CCPCC Department of Organization, Notice Regarding Opinion on Implementing the Cadre Assessment System (November 21, 1979), www.pkulaw.com/chl/a43b6e34befa663ebdfb.html?keyword=关于实行干部考核制度的意见&way=listView.

organizational work, specifying the assessment content in four aspects: virtue, ability, diligence, and performance. The focus was on assessing specific work achievements, thereby establishing the dominant position of work effectiveness in the evaluation system. In 1988, the Central Organization Department introduced a highly systematic Annual Work Assessment Plan for Leading Cadres in Local Government Departments (Trial Implementation),[7] which detailed the procedures and content of cadre assessments. Essential items for evaluation included the local industrial output value, agricultural output, infrastructure investment, tax revenue, and other digitized indicators. The Explanation for implementing the assessment plan determined the assessment format as a system, in which "the leadership of the superior level takes responsibility, while assisted by the party committee of all members and the standing committee of the people's congress at the same level."[8] The assessment was concluded with "the leader in charge (主管首长) evaluating the reported work of the person to be assessed, with evaluation divided into four levels, classified as 'good,' 'relatively good,' 'average' and 'relatively bad.'" Therefore, the top-down performance management system and the developmentalist mindset centered on GDP had already been established long before 1989.

After the Southern Tour in 1992, the central government implemented a series of controversial policy reforms, including the fiscal decentralization system, state-owned enterprise restructuring, the commodification of housing, farmland protection system, land requisition system and urban demolition regulations. However, most of these measures were the result of years of deliberation and planning, rather than innovations after the Southern Tour. Taking fiscal decentralization as an example, in the early 1980s, both proportions of the central government revenue to national revenue and the national revenue to GDP had been steadily declining. From 1978 to 1982, the share of fiscal revenue in national income dropped from 37.2 percent to 25.5 percent.[9] The insufficiency of the state fiscal resources had long been a concern for the central leadership. As early as the twelfth CCP Congress in 1982, then General Secretary Hu Yaobang proposed to "adjust the distribution ratio of the central and local fiscal revenues and the proportion of enterprise profits

7 CCPCC Department of Organization, Annual Work Assessment Plan for Leading Cadres in Local Government Departments (Trial Implementation) (June 6, 1988), www.pkulaw.com/chl/3eb44a1812bf5cc5bdfb.html?keyword=地方政府工作部门领导干部年度工作考核方案&way=listView.

8 Ibid.

9 Zhao Ziyang, Government Work Report of the State Council in 1983 (June 6, 1983) [in Chinese], www.gov.cn/test/2006-02/16/content_200823.htm.

retained."[10] In the government work report of 1983, Zhao Ziyang, the then Premier of the State Council, pointed out that the "most prominent problem facing us is the inadequate national fiscal resources and severe fund dispersion," and it was necessary to "unify thinking and take resolute and effective measures to bring about rapid change."[11] In 1987, Zhao Ziyang, now the new party General Secretary, earnestly proposed in the report of the thirteenth CCP Congress to "implement the fiscal decentralization system on the premise of a reasonable division of the central and local fiscal revenues and expenditures."[12]

Although the State Council did not promulgate the Regulation on the Transformation of Operational Mechanism of the Industrial Enterprises Owned by the Whole People until 1992,[13] the reform of state-owned enterprises had started as early as 1980 with the trial experiments of "enterprise autonomy" (企业自主权). As Zhao Ziyang explicitly proposed in the government work report of 1987,

> according to the principle of separating ownership from management, earnestly implement various forms of contractual management responsibility system, so that enterprises truly become relatively independent economic entities with autonomous operation and self-financing.[14]

This fundamental idea was directly reflected in the constitutional amendment of 1993, found its legacy in the "16-character principle" (十六字方针) of state-owned enterprise reform established in the mid-1990s, namely "clear property rights, defined rights and responsibilities, separation of government and enterprises, and scientific management."[15] The main contribution of the Southern Tour was to completely resolve the debate over whether the reform should be "socialist" or "capitalist" in nature, and to determine the direction of establishing a "socialist market economy" (社会主义市场经济), thereby removing the obstacles to continuing the economic reform in the aftermath of the

10 Hu Yaobang, Report on the 12th National Congress of the CCP (September 1, 1982) [in Chinese], http://cpc.people.com.cn/GB/64162/64168/64565/65448/4526430.html.

11 Zhao Ziyang, Government Work Report of the State Council in 1983.

12 Zhao Ziyang, Report on the 13th National Congress of the CCP (October 25, 1987) [in Chinese], http://cpc.people.com.cn/GB/64162/64168/64566/65447/4526368.html.

13 The State Council, Regulation on the Transformation of Operational Mechanism of the Industrial Enterprises Owned by the Whole People (July 23, 1992) [in Chinese], www.pkulaw.com/en_law/4f987c00d4b595e7bdfb.html.

14 Zhao Ziyang, Government Work Report of the State Council in 1987 (March 25, 1987) [in Chinese], www.gov.cn/test/2006-02/16/content_200857.htm.

15 Li Peng, Government Work Report of the State Council in 1995 (March 5, 1995) [in Chinese], www.gov.cn/test/2006-02/16/content_201109.htm.

Tiananmen crackdown. However, even here, traces of the pre-1989 era can be found, as the theory of the "primary stage of socialism" (社会主义初级阶段) defending the market economy had already been proposed in the report of the thirteenth CCP Congress China in 1987.[16]

Finally, the problems confronted by the two rounds of reform were largely similar. As Zhao Ziyang acknowledged in the government work report of 1983, "while the national fiscal revenue declined, off-budget funds increased significantly, from 37.1 billion yuan in 1978 to 65 billion yuan in 1982, an increase of 75.2 percent over four years."[17] Off-budget funds (预算外资金) and various "unauthorized fees" (乱收费) that emerged in the 1990s had greatly increased the burden on farmers, and later evolved into various forms of "land finance" (土地财政) at local levels. For example, in the government work report of 1985, Zhao pointed out the prevalent corruption at that time: "random distribution of bonuses, goods and subsidies; arbitrary price hikes for profiteering; exploiting power for buying and selling scarce goods; and the growth of improper practices such as treating guests and giving gifts, and giving and accepting bribes."[18] Compared to the later corruption and bribery, the improper practices of that time, such as using official positions for profiteering (官倒), seemed insignificant, but their nature was essentially the same. The lower amount of corruption at that time was also due to the fact that the rent-seeking opportunities for officials were limited during the early stages of reform, indicating that different stages of reform shared not only similar strategies, but also the same root causes.

4.2.2 *Why Is the Reform Benign in 1978?*

Although the second phase of reform initiated by the Southern Tour was largely continuous with the previous reform that began in 1978, it is undeniable that the effects of the two reforms differed remarkably. Reading Zhao Ziyang's government work report of 1981 makes one feel that the government at least intended to work for the people. Further, unlike the neo-totalitarian regime today, it openly acknowledged its shortcomings. Entitled "Current Economic Situation and the Guidelines for Economic Development in the Future,"[19] the report thoroughly discussed economic issues without focusing

[16] Zhao Ziyang, Report on the 13th National Congress of the CCP.

[17] Zhao Ziyang, Government Work Report of the State Council in 1983.

[18] Zhao Ziyang, Government Work Report of the State Council in 1985 (March 27, 1985) [in Chinese], www.gov.cn/test/2006-02/16/content_200841.htm.

[19] Zhao Ziyang, Government Work Report in 1981 (November 30, 1981) [in Chinese], www.gov.cn/govweb/test/2006-02/16/content_200802.htm.

on GDP. Zhao made impressive comparison of economic data between 1952 and 1980: While the total output value of industry and agriculture increased by eight times, the fixed assets of industry grew by twenty-six times, the national income (国民收入) only quadrupled and the average consumption level only doubled.[20] He continued with words that sounded almost moving today because, in the subsequent four decades of reform, not only did the government completely change tunes, but even the vast majority of "mainstream" economists also speak in very different voices:

> Our growth rate of national income in the past 32 years is much lower than that of the total output value of industry and agriculture, and the improvement in people's living standards is far below the growth rate of national income. The effectiveness of our economic development is far from ideal, while the improvement in people's living conditions does not correspond to the labor they put in.[21]

Due to the strong emphasis on national income by the central government, income growth in the early 1980s matched the growth in industry and agriculture output. According to Zhao Ziyang's government work report in 1982, the growth rate of the total output value of industry and agriculture was set at 4 percent per year for the Sixth Five-Year Plan, while the per capita consumption level of urban and rural residents was to increase by 4.1 percent annually. The actual growth rate far exceeded the plan, but national income growth closely followed the growth in domestic output value and fiscal revenue. From 1979 to 1983, the average annual growth rate of industry and agriculture output was nearly 8 percent, with a 14.2 percent increase in 1984 compared to the previous year, while national income and fiscal revenue also grew by 12 percent compared to the previous year. After deducting the inflation factor, urban per capita income increased by nearly 7 percent on average each year during the five-year period, while farmers' per capita net income increased by 13.7 percent.[22]

There are several reasons why the reform initiated in 1978 achieved good results, or at least was widely perceived to have done. First, after the tumultuous periods of the Great Leap Forward, the Great Famine, and the Cultural Revolution, the Chinese people had little left, and their expectations were as low as the starting point when the reform took off. As a result, any reform was likely to improve their conditions. Particularly, as the urban reform had just

[20] Ibid.

[21] Ibid.

[22] Zhao Ziyang, Government Work Report in 1982 (November 30, 1982) [in Chinese], www.gov.cn/govweb/test/2006-02/23/content_208652.htm.

begun, substantive reforms were primarily focused on rural areas. The rural population had already been stripped of their land property under the people's commune system and had virtually nothing. They were like a "blank sheet of paper, ready to be written with new and beautiful words or painted with new and beautiful pictures."[23] It was they, rather than urban workers, who were the proletarians having "nothing to lose but their chains." Any reform with basic rationality would improve their situation. Rural reform could only proceed by returning rights to the peasants rather than further centralizing power since they had nothing that could be concentrated in the hands of the authorities, except for a small amount of "private plots" (自留地). The People's Communes had centralized almost all the land, and without a land market at that time, rural cadres could not exploit the land as a profitable asset. As land had little value in the communes or in the hands of the cadres, its value could only be realized through peasant labor. The household responsibility (包产到户) system initiated in rural areas, such as Xiaogang village in Anhui, delegated land use rights to farmers, naturally bringing enormous benefits to hundreds of millions of farmers.

Second, as the institutional reform of state-owned enterprises had not yet started during this period, the reform was limited to improving and expanding their operational autonomy, allowing enterprises to be responsible for their own profits and losses, and partly separating ownership rights from management rights, while urban economic reform was limited to legalizing private economic activities such as self-employed businesses (个体户).[24] Similar to rural reform, the essence of such reforms was to untie enterprises and society, granting private entities greater economic freedom, with the result of injecting social vitality and accumulating private wealth. The reform of state-owned enterprises witnessed a universal paradox of reform: The degree of economic freedom was directly proportional to the opportunities for corruption. While reforms were limited in scope and impact, so was the potential for corruption. Although poorly performing state-owned enterprises underwent limited reforms, they continued to provide basic welfare benefits to workers such as basic housing, healthcare, and education, without creating major issues such as large-scale layoffs or the widening of wealth disparities.

[23] Mao Zedong, Introducing a Cooperative (April 15, 1958) [in Chinese], www.yhcw.net/famine/Documents/mzdwg/d070076.html.

[24] In 1988, the amendment finally supplemented Article 11 of the Constitution with the following provision: "The state allows the existence and development of the private economy within the scope prescribed by law. The private economy is a supplement to the socialist economy of public ownership."

Third, after experiencing the catastrophe of the Cultural Revolution, the national leaders had a deep aversion to the ultra-left (极左) path that seriously violated human rights and the rule of law. Therefore, they genuinely pushed for benign reform that would benefit the nation and the people. This may be somewhat difficult to explain from the perspective of the rational choice theory. However, the phenomenon seems to have become a pattern: In modern Chinese history, crises and challenges almost always stimulate a generation of leaders to aspire for benign reform. Like Emperor Guangxu during the Hundred Days' Reform, leaders such as Deng Xiaoping, Hu Yaobang, and Zhao Ziyang, having suffered from a tumultuous decade of the Cultural Revolution, were determined to govern with wisdom and determination. Behind this seemingly "fortunate" pattern lies the still-existing moral resources. Whether rooted in Confucian principles or Communist beliefs, the leaders of the transitional period were keenly aware of their political responsibilities and genuinely desired to lead the nation onto the right path. For leaders like Deng Xiaoping and his generation, this was also their long-standing aspiration that had remained unfulfilled since 1949. Although the 1950s witnessed a period of rapid industrialization, China subsequently experienced political turmoil. After 1978, they believed that the opportunity for peaceful development had finally arrived. In their view, this hard-won opportunity should not be abruptly interrupted by another political movement arriving within a decade.

4.3 THE LIMITS AND DEFECTS OF CHINESE REFORM

4.3.1 *A Reform That Never Went Through*

The goodwill and courage of the top leadership were no doubt necessary to initiate the reform, but they alone are insufficient to consolidate and sustain benign reforms. For reform to continue in a positive direction, it must gain institutionalized political momentum. Returning to the first condition mentioned earlier, constructive reform requires the sufficient participation of society at large, without which the reforms cannot continue to be in the best interests of the people. While rural reform in 1978 was indeed initiated by local experiments such as the one in Xiaogang village, and voices for reform did emerge in civil society, overall the reforms in China after 1978 were led by the government. The calls for reform from civil society were not only fragmented and weak, but also failed to fully develop due to the highly restricted social environment in the absence of political democracy and freedom of speech. Particularly after the Cultural Revolution, the post-totalitarian regime remained highly vigilant and suppressive towards social movements, resulting in a passive people who were largely receptive to whatever major policies decided by the party-state. In the first decade of the reform, this situation was acceptable because the reform was buttressed by a proactive central leadership. As the reform progressed, this inherently authoritarian state of rule by man became increasingly unsustainable. In fact, without popular participation, even good central policies were difficult to implement. During this stage, it was common to observe phenomena that were apparently perplexing for a highly centralized totalitarian regime, such as "policies from above, countermeasures from below" (上有政策，下有对策) and "decrees cannot reach beyond the Central South Sea" (政令不出中南海).[25]

Under such a situation, the CCPCC timely raised the issue of political reform. On October 14, 1987, General Secretary Zhao Ziyang first proposed the "separation of the Party and government" (党政分开) in his speech at the preparatory meeting of the CCP Seventh Plenary Session of the Twelfth Congress:

> The centralized regime was formed during the era of revolutionary wars and strengthened during the frequent political movements. It was tailored to the planned economy model characterized by highly centralized commands. Now the situation is different. The construction for modernization needs to bring into play the initiative of various organizations and from every aspect, and requires the establishment of a normal order of various organizations. The wartime regime no longer fits the need during peacetime, just as the mass movement regime no longer fits the need of modernizing construction, and the highly centralized regime no longer fits the need of developing the commodity economy.
>
> The lack of separation between the Party and government has made the party committee (党委) itself the executor [of decisions]. Only the separation of the Party and government can make the party committee truly equipped with the supervisory function. The administrative system must be strengthened [to] improve efficiency, but precisely for the same purpose, it must strengthen supervision. One cannot supervise oneself. If you monopolize the administrative works, you will lose the qualification for supervising the administration.[26]

25 As the symbol of the supreme power in China near Tiananmen Square, Zhongnanhai (中南海) is the location for the offices of the CCPCC and the State Council. The phrase suggests that benign central policies cannot be faithfully and effectively implemented by the local governments because their implementation would harm the vested interest of the party-state.

26 Zhao Ziyang, On the Separation of the Party and Government, Speech on the Preparatory Meeting for the Seventh Plenary Session of the 12th CCPCC (October 14, 1987) [in Chinese], www.china.com.cn/ch-80years/lici/12/12-7/1.htm.

As the basic premise of separating the Party and government, the Party and government should be divided in labor and responsibilities. Zhao Ziyang believed that the Party should assume a detached position in formulating major policies, while the government should primarily be responsible for their concrete implementation: "The Party is the political leader and should engage in the work of political leadership. Dividing money and goods, deciding projects and approving applications should all be the daily affairs of administrative departments."[27] Therefore, the benefit of separating the Party and government lies in "allowing the Party to assume a detached position, handle conflicts and have an overall view, thus playing a leadership role in 'coordinating all parties.'"[28] Based on this characterization, the role of the ruling party mainly involves decision-making, supervision, and coordination.

The problem is that, while the authority to formulate major policies is undoubtedly lofty, it is destined to be a "clear water office" (清水衙门) – truly clean, uncorrupted, and non-profit, as long as it does not involve implementation. Policy implementation is not only a burdensome obligation, but also a source of substantial power that can provide rent-seeking opportunities to those involved in the enforcement process. In this sense, the Party-government separation strikes at the heart of the party-state. However, would the ruling party, which is already highly centralized, be willing to step back, give up tremendous temptations for personal gain and live a "clean water" life? While the separation proposal is benevolent, its feasibility is evidently a major issue that even the General Secretary may not be able to decide.

In the report to the thirteenth CCP Congress on October 25, 1987, Zhao Ziyang proposed the long-term goal of reform as "establishing a highly democratic, legally sound, efficient and vibrant socialist political system." The separation of the Party and government was identified as a key step in this regard:

> The Party has led the people in enacting the Constitution and the laws. It should act within the bounds of the Constitution and the laws … The party leadership is by its nature political leadership, i.e., the leadership in terms of political principles, political direction and important major decision-making, as well as reflected in recommending important cadres to the power organs of the state. The Party's main way of exercising political leadership over state affairs is to transform the Party's propositions into the will of the state through legal procedures, mobilize the masses through Party organization activities and the exemplary role of Party members, and implement the

[27] Ibid.
[28] Ibid.

> Party's line, principles, and policies. The Party and the state organs have different natures, functions, organizational forms and ways of work. The Party leadership system should be reformed, the functions of the Party organization and state authority should clearly be demarcated, and the relationship between the Party organization and the People's Congresses, the government, the judiciary, mass associations, enterprise institutions and various forms of social organizations should be straightened out, so that each entity exercises its own duty and gradually moves towards institutionalization.[29]

If the aforementioned proposal of Party-government separation could be implemented, China's governance model would bid farewell to the era of personalized rule and enter the era of rule of law. As a complementary aspect of the separation reform, the report to the thirteenth Congress also put forward the principles of separating central and local functions and local autonomy:

> All matters suitable for handling at lower levels should be decided and implemented by those lower levels. This is a general principle. In the relationship between the central and local governments, while ensuring the unity of national decrees, the responsibilities of the central and local governments should be gradually clarified, with local matters managed locally, and the central government responsible for formulating major policies and conducting supervision.[30]

Like the Party-government separation, these proposals demonstrate foresight. The consequence of the Party-government fusion is inevitably the fusion of central and local powers because the leadership of the Party is essentially a top-down approach. The Party-government fusion means that the central government can monopolize all local affairs, and local governments must obey the leadership of higher-level Party organizations in everything they do. In contrast, the Party-government separation creates space for decentralization of power between the central and local levels and local autonomy. Of course, it also presents requirements. Once the Party-government separation is implemented, as the government is freed from organizational control by the ruling party, the relationships between various levels of government are no longer simply based on commands and obedience, but are transformed into relationships between different levels of legal norms, making it necessary to define the legislative powers of the Party and government at various levels. While major legislations and decision-making are undoubtedly the responsibilities of the central government, given the significant disparities between regions in

[29] Zhao Ziyang, Report on the 13th National Congress of the CCP (October 25, 1987) [in Chinese], http://cpc.people.com.cn/GB/64162/64168/64566/65447/4441804.html.

[30] Ibid.

China, a one-size-fits-all (一刀切) approach from the central government is clearly inappropriate, and local authorities should have the autonomy to meet the changing needs of the local people. In the exercise of local autonomy, local governments should be subject to the supervision of local people's congresses elected by local voters, as stipulated by the 1982 Constitution. Through bottom-up elections and the representative mechanism of the people's congresses, the reform measures of governments at various levels are held accountable to the people in their respective jurisdictions. Therefore, to promote sound reform, it is crucial to clarify the boundary between central and local powers, institutionalize the relationship between the Party and government and between the central and local authorities based on the rule of law, and reform the electoral system to make various levels of power accountable to the voters.

Unfortunately, the political aspirations of the thirteenth National Congress were not implemented before it was permanently shelved after June 1989. Deng Xiaoping's Southern Tour speech itself negated the path of political reform and set the tone for subsequent reforms: "We have found that our generation cannot solve the problem of long-term stability and security, so we recommended other people, genuinely looking for the third generation. But the problem was not solved, both of them (i.e., Hu Yaobang and Zhao Ziyang) failed. They stumbled not on economic issues, but on the issue of opposing bourgeois liberalization."[31] As a result, subsequent reforms took place without political reform. However, politics and economy are like two wings of reform, each being unable to proceed far without the other. After political reform came to a complete halt, the economic reform inevitably took a devious path, on which the state power was out of balance.

4.3.2 *The Reinitiation and Consolidation of Reform, 1992–2002*

The absence of political reform inevitably means the absence of the popular participation throughout the entire reform process, rendering the first condition for constructive reform invalid. As the reform progressed, the second condition also began to go unfulfilled, resulting in fundamental changes in the nature, effects, and trends of the reform. It is worth noting that such changes do not require assuming a fundamental shift in the stance and expectations of the leaders towards the reform. They may still expect the reform to benefit the people, but once they firmly insist on a "correct"

[31] Deng Xiaoping, "The Southern Tour Speech in 1992," 求是理论网 (January 29, 2018), www.71.cn/2018/0129/984317_3.shtml.

direction such as "development is the hard principle" (发展是硬道理), without considering the actual sentiments of the people or allowing their effective participation, seemingly constructive reforms invariably yield counterproductive effects. For example, Premier Zhu Rongji (朱镕基) became known for his bold reform measures and iron-fisted approach in dealing with corruptions during his tenure (1998–2003). However, even if disregarding the resistance from officials at various levels, the reform itself did not necessarily align with the public opinion. In fact, if there were still officials resisting reform in the 1990s, they were simply too stubborn to see the changing perspective that would provide them with huge opportunities for corruption. Once the key to reaping the benefits of reform became common knowledge, officials at all levels became enthusiastic supporters of "reform" and "development," only that the meanings of these terms had radically changed.

The Southern Tour speech itself did not imply specific directions for reform, but rather initiated an economic reform with an uncertain future. Due to domestic and international pressures in the early 1990s, the speed of economic reform was not only related to China's social development and the well-being of its people, but was elevated to the height of socialist superiority (社会主义优越性) and international competitions. As General Secretary Jiang Zemin stated in the report to the fourteenth Congress in October 1992,

> The essence of current international competition lies in the comprehensive national strength based on economic and technological capabilities. Many countries around the world, especially some neighboring countries and regions, are accelerating their development. If our economic development lags behind, the consolidation of the socialist system and the long-term stability of the country will face great difficulties. Therefore, whether our economy can accelerate its development is not only a significant economic issue but also a major political issue.[32]

Under this context, the annual growth rate of the national GDP was raised from the original target of 6 percent to 8–9 percent.[33] In March 1993, Li Peng's government work report proposed an average annual growth of 15 percent in the total industrial output value for the next five years, "aiming to achieve an average annual real growth of around 5 percent in per capita disposable income for urban residents and an average annual real growth of

[32] Jiang Zemin, Report on the 14th National Congress of the CCP (October 12, 1992) [in Chinese], http://cpc.people.com.cn/GB/64162/64168/64567/65446/4526308.html.

[33] Ibid.

4–5 percent in per capita net income for rural residents."[34] However, the 1994 government work report indicated that the per capita net income of peasants had only grown by 3.2 percent from the previous year. Although the performance assessment system and the GDP-centric thinking in government work exhibited significant historical continuity, the new government's allocation of importance differed greatly from the past even in terms of GDP figures, resulting in a noticeable widening of the gap between the growth of the national income and domestic (especially industrial) production value.

In November 1993, the Third Plenary Session of the fourteenth Congress passed the Decision of the CCPCC on Certain Issues Concerning the Establishment of a Socialist Market Economic System.[35] This decision set the agenda for the next decade of reforms and marked the beginning of a new phase. The immediate priority of the reform was fiscal decentralization. Although fiscal deficit had not occurred since the mid-1980s, the Decision still identified tax system reform as a short-term focus: "By developing the economy, improving efficiency and expanding financial resources, gradually increase the proportion of fiscal revenue in the GDP, and reasonably determine the proportion of central and local fiscal revenue."[36] In a single-party regime where the central authority enjoyed unchallengeable supremacy, "reasonable determination" naturally implied a tilt of fiscal revenue towards the central government.

In December 1993, the Decision of the State Council on Implementing the Tax-Sharing Fiscal Management System emphasized that "the state's financial resources are biased towards dispersion, hindering the reasonable growth of fiscal revenue. Particularly, the continuous decline in the proportion of central fiscal revenue has weakened the macroeconomic regulatory capacity of the central government."[37] The tax-sharing system (分税制) fundamentally reversed this trend, leading to an abrupt rise in the proportion of central fiscal revenue in total fiscal revenue from around 30 percent to about 55 percent. The proportion of total fiscal revenue to domestic production value initially declined every year from over 30 percent in 1978 to around

[34] Li Peng, Report on the Work of the Government in 1993 (March 15, 1993) [in Chinese], www.gov.cn/test/2006-02/16/content_200926.htm.

[35] The Third Plenary Session of the 14th National Congress of the CCP, Decision of the CCPCC on Certain Issues Concerning the Establishment of a Socialist Market Economic System (November 14, 1993) [in Chinese], www.gov.cn/test/2008-08/13/content_1071062.htm.

[36] Ibid.

[37] State Council, Decision on Implementing the Tax-Sharing Fiscal Management System (December 15, 1993) [in Chinese], http://fgcx.bjcourt.gov.cn:4601/law?fn=chl044s002.txt.

10 percent in 1994–95, then gradually increased to nearly 20 percent.[38] The growth rate of fiscal revenue was nearly twice that of GDP. In the process of the "second reform," more of China's growing wealth ended up in the government's coffers rather than in the people's pocket. Fortunately, compared to welfare states in Western Europe, China's share of fiscal revenue in GDP is not considered high. In a country where the electoral system is not sufficient to ensure that "what is taken from the people is used for the people" (取之于民，用之于民), a wealthier government inevitably means poorer citizens.

Until the Tang Fuzhen incident that occurred in 2009, the public evaluation of the tax-sharing system was overall positive. After all, it is hard to imagine that such a large country could sustain a centralized unitary tax system for decades. Some form of tax-sharing scheme, in which the national and local taxes were divided according to certain criteria, was undoubtedly necessary. However, it seemed perplexing that the apparently decentralizing fiscal reform, eulogized by scholars as "China's fiscal federalism,"[39] encountered stubborn resistance from local governments. It was only under strong pressure from the central government and after lengthy negotiations that the local resistance was resolved. The reason was actually simple: While the tax reform was an institutional experiment in favor of local decentralization, its effect was fiscal centralization, which occurred almost necessarily under the centralized unitary system. The tax reform started with local decentralization but ended with fiscal centralization, by which the central government effectively consolidated greater fiscal power.

Of course, as Premier Zhu Rongji pointed out in his book,[40] a considerable portion of central fiscal revenue was returned to local governments through transfer payments, implying that local governments should be well provided for. In a country where the democratic accountability is absent, the question of whether local governments lack funds is always a murky issue. Since voters cannot hold officials accountable, government finances are more likely to be spent on "three public expenses" (三公消费), namely, official receptions, official vehicles, and overseas trips, rather than public welfare. If local governments manage their funds well, they may not lack money. Even in that unlikely situation, it does not negate the centralized nature of the tax reform, as transfer payments themselves are a sign of the central power. Moreover,

38 Ibid.

39 Li Qingxia, "Fiscal federalism with Chinese characters: Debates and reflections," 《财政研究》, 25–7, no. 3 (2011).

40 Zhu Rongji, *Zhu Rongji on the Record: The Road to Reform, 1991–1997*, trans. June Y. Mei (Washington, DC: Brookings Institution Press, 2013), pp. 155–70.

transfer payments often take the form of project funding, which not only fails to address the daily public welfare expenses of local governments, but also exacerbates what Premier Zhu himself admitted as "rushing to central departments to get money" (跑部钱进) since the central government is responsible for approving the fundings of local projects.

At the same time, the urban and rural land policies also roughly determined the direction of the reforms. The aforementioned Decision of the State Council stated, "Since China has a large population and limited land, it is necessary to cherish and reasonably use land resources by strengthening land management, protecting cultivated land effectively and strictly controlling the conversion of agricultural land into non-agricultural land. The state monopolizes the primary market for urban land."[41] Enacted in 1997, the joint Notice of the CCPCC and the State Council on Further Strengthening Land Management and Effectively Protecting Cultivated Land reiterated the basic policy of "focusing on protecting cultivated land and strictly controlling its occupation":

> Except for state requisition, the use rights of collective land shall not be transferred or used for commercial real estate development, nor shall they be transferred or leased for non-agricultural construction ... Collective-owned wasteland shall not be used for non-agricultural construction through methods such as auctioning or leasing land use rights.[42]

To be sure, it is necessary to properly protect China's agricultural land resources since they are so scarce. Therefore, the policy of protecting arable land seems to be infallible. However, in an institutional framework where the discriminatory urban–rural system has largely remained and the institutionalized poverty in agriculture has not fundamentally changed, the mandatory prohibition of developing agricultural land without proper compensation means depriving the vast rural areas and peasants of their right to development. Even more serious is Article 10 of the 1982 Constitution, which lays down the scheme of a dualist land ownership: While urban land is owned by the "whole people" (全民), rural land is owned by the collective (集体), i.e., villages. Since the 1990s, it has been mistakenly interpreted that the urbanization of agricultural land must first be subjected to government requisition before entering the primary market for land transactions.

41 State Council, Decision on Implementing the Tax-Sharing Fiscal Management System.

42 CCPCC and State Council, Notice on Further Strengthening Land Management and Effectively Protecting Cultivated Land (April 15, 1997) [in Chinese], www.mohurd.gov.cn/gongkai/fdzdgknr/zgzygwywj/200106/20010614_155380.html.

As a result, compulsory requisition has become a necessary condition for urbanization. As the key element of the "China model," rural land must be taken by the government in order to become urban. To my knowledge, such a developmental model is unique in the world, making China a country most enthusiastic about land taking under the ruse of "development." In fact, under the strong land-taking impulse of local governments, the protection of arable land has become empty talk. Subsequently, land taking and resale have become the favorite of virtually all local governments, as it could not only increase local GDP, but also enrich local finances and officials' wallets. The only regret is that, if the government and officials are so pleased, the people are bound to be unhappy. As arable land is only a small part of agricultural land, prohibiting the free circulation of agricultural land without distinguishing between different types unjustly discriminates against farmers' property rights and greatly restricts urban residential and commercial access to land, resulting in a shortage of urban land supply and skyrocketing housing prices.[43]

In 1994, the State Council issued a Decision on Deepening the Reform of the Urban Housing System, calling for an end to the welfare-based distribution of housing in the planned economy era and a "shift from the use of housing as a welfare distribution towards a monetary wage distribution system based on labor."[44] Like the reform of state-owned enterprises, housing reform was also aimed at "getting rid of burdens" (甩包袱) to the state. The reform of state-owned enterprises did improve the competitiveness of enterprises to an extent, but created tens of millions of laid-off workers (下岗工人) who were not properly resettled. Housing reform activated the real estate market and, on the whole, improved living conditions. As a result, however, urban housing prices remain abnormally high due to combined effect of the government monopoly on urban land supply, the prohibition of rural "small property houses" (小产权房) under the pretext of "strictly protecting arable land,"[45] and the large population density in metropolitan areas like Beijing and Shanghai, which enjoy various privileges in terms of wages, welfare, and education. As a result, the majority of residents endure multiple pressures in their lives, such as inability to afford housing, medical care, and education.

[43] Zhang Qianfan et al., *The Protection of Peasants' Land Rights in the Process of Urbanization* [in Chinese] (Beijing: China Democracy Legal System Publishing House, 2012), pp. 9–15.

[44] State Council, Decision on Deepening the Reform of the Urban Housing System (July 18, 1994) [in Chinese], www.gov.cn/zhuanti/2015-06/13/content_2878960.htm.

[45] See Zhang et al., *The Protection of Peasants' Land Rights in the Process of Urbanization*, pp. 15–24.

In 2001, the State Council promulgated the Urban Demolition Regulation,[46] which further facilitated the government requisition of residential houses, leading to numerous tragedies similar to the Tang Fuzhen incident across the country, all in the name of "development."[47]

In summary, in the decades following the Southern Tour speech, the restarted reform has continued and strengthened the developmental strategy aligned with economism. Under the squeeze of centralized fiscal power and the attraction of developmentalist urbanization strategy, local governments at all levels resorted to "land finance" through excessive land taking. The huge price difference earned by the government during the process of land taking or house demolition replaced various illegal fees and became the "black hole" for local governments to swallow people's wealth. If the increase in the proportion of government finance to domestic output is a sign of "the advancement of the state at the expense of private sectors," then the land finance outside the regular budget has become a convenient means for the government to plunder social resources. Under the mindset preoccupied by "development," Chinese society is becoming increasingly more polarized between two irreconcilable extremes. As the proportion of central government finance keeps increasing, local finance is squeezed; as local governments and officials are making a fortune through land finance, the people are enduring expensive housing and education, as well as low coverage of health insurance and social security. As a result, a considerable number are forced to become displaced, engage in endless petitioning (上访), with some even resorting to extreme behaviors such as self-immolation. While the GDP index soared every year, the people did not seem to be happier. The rapid economic development has left behind highways and high-rises, but has also displaced workers and peasants, caused environmental pollution, ecological destruction, and resource devastation.

To a large extent, China today is still living under the shadow of the developmentalist model established in the decade after the Southern Tour. After 2003, the Hu Jintao (胡锦涛) and Wen Jiabao (温家宝) regime put forward the concepts of "treating human as the basis" (以人为本) and building "harmonious society" (和谐社会) in order to partially correct the numerous aftermaths left by the developmentalist strategy while continuing the reforms. However, these limited efforts have not been able to slow down the

[46] State Council, Regulation on the Administration of Urban House Demolition and Relocation (June 13, 2001) [in Chinese], www.gov.cn/gongbao/content/2001/content_60912.htm.

[47] Zhuo Yuan, "Tang Fuzhen's self-immolation reflects China's inherent dilemma," *FT Chinese* (December 11, 2009), www.ftchinese.com/tag/唐福珍.

tremendous inertia of "reform" and "development" pushed by officials at all levels. Meanwhile, the negative consequences of "development" have become more pronounced. The CCPCC Decision on Improving the Socialist Market Economy System, passed at the Third Plenary Session of the sixteenth CCP Congress in 2003, continued the "strictest arable land protection."[48] At the same time, it proposed to reform the requisition system, improve the requisition procedures in accordance with the principles of safeguarding farmers' rights and controlling the scale of requisition by strictly defining public-interest and commercial construction land. Requisition must comply with the overall land use planning and land use control, and provide farmers with reasonable compensation in a timely manner.[49]

After the Sun Zhigang incident in 2003, the new government promptly abolished the Custody and Repatriation Regulations. Although the incident gave rise to the mainstream model of rights defense in contemporary China, it is limited by fundamental problems such as indirect public participation, high costs of rights defense and uncertain outcomes. The tragic self-immolation of Tang Fuzhen in late 2009 was a replica of the Sun Zhigang model. Faced with tremendous public opinion pressure, the State Council eventually abolished the Urban Demolition Regulation (城市拆迁条例) and promulgated in its place the Regulations on Housing Requisition and Compensation, which improved the procedures and compensation standards for urban housing requisition. However, it failed to resolve the problems of local land finance and the pattern of power imbalance in a reform that is exclusively concerned with economic development. Although Premier Wen Jiabao openly advocated political reform on several occasions, substantial institutional improvements have never been initiated.

4.3.3 *The Impact of Political System on Economic Reform*

In the absence of political reform and popular participation, it is easy to explain the seemingly strange phenomenon that the reform tends to make things worse instead of better. From the cadre assessment and tax-sharing system to farmland protection and state-owned enterprise restructuring, a series of reforms initiated after the Southern Tour speech were the result of decisions made in the first decade of reform. Why did they produce

48 CCPCC, Decision on Several Issues Regarding the Improvement of the Socialist Market Economy System (October 14, 2003) [in Chinese], www.gov.cn/gongbao/content/2003/content_62494.htm.

49 Ibid.

completely different effects after being restarted in 1993? In fact, all these reforms could have achieved better results. The tax-sharing reform could have reasonably allocated financial powers according to the division of responsibilities between the central and local governments, instead of centralizing fiscal power and leading to "rushing to the central departments to get money" and "land finance." Farmland protection could have implemented effective land use control and properly redistributed residential, industrial and agricultural land in China, rather than simply prohibiting the circulation of agricultural land and tying urbanization to government land acquisition. Urban redevelopment could have improved the urban living environment and housing quality for residents, instead of enabling the government to profit from land sales and evicting residents from their homes. State-owned enterprise restructuring could have implemented a more competitive employment system and developed a skilled workforce, instead of resorting to mass layoffs without appropriate compensation. Economic development could have improved people's lives and effectively protected the environment while increasing comprehensive national strength, rather than simply pursuing GDP numbers. Most important, cadre assessment did not need to become a catalyst for "performance project" (政绩工程), arbitrary land acquisition, and the buying and selling of official positions; it could have genuinely played a role in democratic supervision. However, if the path of political reform is completely blocked and the people are excluded from decision-making, "reform" inevitably becomes the exclusive domain of vested interests such as officials and their affiliates, and all these good intentions can only remain as mere fantasies. Under different political frameworks, economic reform agendas of the same nature have yielded completely different results.

In fact, economic development has not only been the consistent focus of government work since the beginning of the reform in 1978, but also the primary governing objective that has remained unchanged since 1949. From the first government work report by Premier Zhou Enlai in 1954 to his last report before the Cultural Revolution a decade later, they all placed economic development at the center without exception. Although these reports occasionally included political language such as "class struggle" or "world revolution," their overall structure was no different from the government work reports of 2012 or any year after reform. Even during the decade of the Cultural Revolution, the only government work report at the time (1975) emphasized the comprehensive modernization of agriculture, industry, national defense, and science and technology within the twentieth century, aiming to make China's national economy at the forefront of the world.

Of course, successive political movements during Mao's era had prevented the ruling party from consistently pursuing these goals. After Mao's death in 1976 and the downfall of the Gang of Four, China finally entered a period of peace and stability.

In many ways, 1978 marked a return to the early 1950s, when the ruling party could finally focus on construction without distraction. The suppression of political movement in 1989 further solidified this situation, and the Southern Tour speech laid the track for China's economic development for the next few decades. While the ruling party could no longer claim a lack of opportunity to achieve its developmentalist goals, the final outcomes of the "development" are far less optimistic than anticipated in 1978. Had China not experienced the setbacks of the Great Leap Forward and the Cultural Revolution, it is likely such a result would have arrived in advance. As early as 1957, only eight years after the ruling party took power, the bureaucratic corruption had become so serious that the Hundred Flowers campaign suddenly unleashed a flood of sharp criticism, far surpassing the liberal discourse of any "public intellectuals" in China today. Mao Zedong originally intended to suppress the arrogance of the powerful faction within the party by capitalizing on the dissatisfaction of intellectuals. Witnessing the extent of this momentum, however, he had to urgently put a stop to it, turning the Hundred Flowers campaign into a "trap to lure snakes out of their hideouts" (引蛇出洞).

Compared to Mao Zedong, Deng Xiaoping's greatest achievement lies in reinvigorating an apparently dysfunctional system. If Mao was a destroyer, willing to launch the Cultural Revolution to dismantle the entire system in order to maintain his personal power and status, then Deng Xiaoping was the restorer and rebuilder, whose legacy successfully carried on. During Deng's era, China faithfully followed the original design of the party-state, but was it really good for China? Mao launched one Great Leap Forward, which resulted in the death of tens of millions, leading to widespread opposition among the cadres. The developmental model established after Deng's Southern Tour was essentially to allow local governments to pursue numerous "small leaps forward" within the existing system, which was widely welcomed by officials at all levels. The secret behind the success of the contemporary China Model lies in aligning the logic of politics with that of economy by inventing the assessment mechanisms such as the unique "local GDP" indicator, tolerating and encouraging rent-seeking, and mobilizing officials at all levels to promote "reform" and stimulate "development." This approach is characterized by full motivation, immense momentum, and enormous social cost. Every government is engaged in land appropriation, construction projects and investment solicitation because they have become part of the production chain that benefits officials' positions and wallets. The projects thus launched are necessarily associated with poor quality, resource waste and environmental pollution, as they seek to maximize personal benefits with minimal investment, efficiently converting public interest into personal gains of a few. The question is, which is more harmful – one Great Leap Forward or numerous "small leaps forward"? The disaster of the Great Leap Forward was indeed unprecedented, but the destructive energy of a single individual is ultimately limited. On the other hand, under the banner of "reform" and "development," officials of all sizes are engaging in destructive actions, with almost boundless destructive potential.

The Southern Tour speech in 1992 brought us to the present day. How should the path of reform in China be pursued in the future? This is an urgent question that should concern every contemporary Chinese. In fact, the answer to the question is not difficult to find because what Deng Xiaoping restored was not the Constitution established in 1982, which he himself presided over, but rather the "latent rules" of the party-state. Only when the institutions such as the people's congresses stipulated in the Constitution are truly put into practice can China's reform take the right track.

The above was originally written in 2012, during the leadership transition of the CCP. At the end of the year, the author drafted the Initiative for Consensus on Reform, proposing reforms in six areas: implementing democracy within and outside the Party, advancing grassroots elections, safeguarding freedom of speech, deepening the market economy, achieving judicial independence, and establishing a constitutional review. Aiming to foster consensus on the future direction of reform in Chinese society, the Initiative was published on the Christmas Day of 2012 with seventy-two initial signatories and it received active responses from numerous scholars, lawyers, and media professionals. Since 2013, however, except for limited progress in judicial reform and the promotion of informal constitutional review, all these areas have experienced significant setbacks. To paraphrase Sun Yat-sen, as the reform has not yet succeeded, comrades still need to make efforts.[50] The Initiative is reproduced below for reference, discussion, and critique by friends of reform.

[50] Sun's famous remark was extracted from his testament, referring to "revolution" instead of "reform." See Yan Zenghua, "The last days of Sun Yat-sen," 《人民文摘》, no. 9 (2013), http://paper.people.com.cn/rmwz/html/2013-09/01/content_1307470.htm.

4.4 INITIATIVE FOR BUILDING CONSENSUS OVER THE CHINESE REFORM

Over the first three decades of reform, China has experienced phenomenal economic growth accompanied by severe social problems. Rampant official corruption, serious abuses of public power, and an expanding gap between the rich and the poor have contributed to mounting social dissatisfaction, largely due to the lack of synchronized political reform. Popular demand and expectation for reform continue to increase, but reform measures lag far behind, obstructed by the vested interest. More fundamentally, although people generally resent various forms of social inequity, they have failed to reach a consensus among themselves concerning the necessary measures to eradicate institutional causes of social injustice. This has led to the diversion of the already weak forces driving China towards reform. In the absence of sufficient external pressure for reform, the system has little internal motivation to change. Constant hindering of institutional reform will cause official corruption and social injustice to accumulate to a critical mass. Upon reaching that point, China will once again lose the opportunity to achieve peaceful transformation and will face the possibility of being permanently mired in the tumult of violent revolution.

The November 2012 Report of the eighteenth CCP Congress expressed aspirations for political reform. On December 4 of the same year, in a speech commemorating the thirtieth anniversary of the 1982 Constitution, the new General Secretary Xi Jinping emphasized the necessity of enforcing the Constitution. These events have revived the prospects for reinvigorated constitutional reform. At a time when China's reforms have come to a crossroads, Chinese society desperately needs to reach a consensus regarding the fundamental principles and general direction of change. This consensus will necessarily include constitutional principles shared by modern civilizations, such as electoral democracy, the rule of law, and respect for human rights. To facilitate the formation of a consensus, we hereby present six basic proposals: (1) promoting constitutional government; (2) realizing electoral democracy; (3) respecting the freedom of expression; (4) deepening the transition towards a market economy; (5) protecting judicial independence; and (6) safeguarding the legal effects of the Constitution. We believe that these proposals should constitute the basic consensus of China's reforms, agreeable to every rational citizen.[51]

[51] Translated by Bryan Flannery and Qiuye Yi with minor adaptions. For a brief report of the event, see "Prominent Chinese scholars push for consensus in hope of mild political reform, not revolution," www.foxnews.com/world/prominent-chinese-scholars-push-for-consensus-in-hope-of-mild-political-reform-not-revolution.

4.4.1 *Promoting Constitutional Government*

To date, China's reforms have been conducted under the CCP leadership. However, the experiences and lessons of thirty years of change have demonstrated the impossibility of implementing and deepening reforms without first reforming the highly centralized political structure. In its early days, during a period of revolution and war, the Party attracted many idealistic individuals who sought justice and detested corruption. They joined the revolution because the Party promised democracy, but in reality, the Party had long functioned as a top-down organization. At that time, highly centralized power might have promoted operational efficiency. After 1949, however, the ruling Party failed to keep its promise of returning power to the people.

In a political system with highly centralized power, it is difficult to restrict the ruling power, making it impossible to prevent or correct errors in decision-making. The decision-makers are easily trapped in perpetuating minor errors, which ultimately lead to gross catastrophe, a familiar phenomenon in China's recent past. The Anti-Rightist Campaign and other political movements stifled the conscience and courage of intellectuals. In 1958, the Great Leap Forward resulted in more than thirty million deaths by starvation. The 1966 Cultural Revolution lasted for ten years and caused hundreds of millions of innocent people to suffer assault and persecution, leaving the country on the brink of civil war. These tragic lessons show that a ruling system with highly centralized power bordering on dictatorship is not fit for the daily administration of society in peacetime. It is thus time for the ruling Party to make good on its promises of the past.

The Third Plenary Session of the 11th Central Committee in 1978 created a favorable situation for Reform and Opening. The report of the thirteenth Party Congress expressly required, as early as in 1987, the separation between the Party and administration. The reports of the sixteenth and eighteenth Congresses stressed time and again that internal democracy is the lifeline of the Party. However, the problem of excessive centralization of power remains fundamentally unresolved because reform of the political system has yet to be addressed. Today, the problem manifests itself in three respects.

First, the Party functions are highly confused with the government functions. Absent a clear division of rights and responsibilities between the Party and government, the Party interferes in and replaces government functions without any institutional restraint.

Second, decision-making power within the Party is highly centralized. Small minorities or even a single individual frequently make important decisions and personnel arrangements. Therefore, it is easy for the highest local official to become a petit emperor, unrestrained by the laws of man or the divine. For example, Bo Xilai (薄熙来), the ex-Party secretary of Chongqing Municipality, was able to act according to his personal whims in a number of different positions because, as the highest local authority, his power faced few effective restrictions.

Third, internal Party election procedures have been neither normalized nor practiced in accordance with law. Party congresses do not play a true role in the process because leading Party cadres are almost always chosen at the next level up rather than elected by representatives. Such a system readily causes separation of leading cadres from Party members and the masses, allowing one person to call all the shots. In turn, the selection process opens a convenient gateway for the buying and selling of official positions and the abuse of public power.

The only route to maintaining both long-term stability of the state and a harmonious society is transformation of the revolutionary Party into a true ruling party, clarification of the divisions between Party and government, establishment of a ruling system governed by law, and democratic elections at every level of the Party. Democracy within the Party, which will ensure its integrity and continuous rule, manifests itself in four ways.

First, it is necessary to reasonably define the relationship between the Party and the government. The Preamble of the 1982 Constitution does call for "leadership of the Communist Party," but "leadership" is not tantamount to taking on all or directly interfering with government affairs. The "leadership" required by the Constitution means political leadership by the ruling Party, accomplished primarily through democratically determining fundamental policies, implementing them as law and state policy via the legislative procedures of the National People's Congress, and recommending cadre candidates for state positions. Leadership also includes supervising Party members to ensure compliance with the law. Accordingly, the ruling Party needs to depart from its old course of strictly controlling cadres, as this leads to direct interference with the decisions of government personnel or involvement in administrative and judicial affairs, especially in the disposition of specific cases.

Second, to ensure democratic decision-making and prevent excessively centralized power, the ruling Party must strengthen its development of internal democracy. The Party must practice internal democracy as required by the Party Charter, beginning with Party elections for grassroots village organizations, residential communities, townships, and counties or cities. All Party representatives must be elected directly by Party members with no interference from higher-level Party committees.

Third, Party representative congresses at all levels must participate in everyday leadership and supervision. All levels of Party member representative congresses should have complete power to elect and supervise their corresponding Party committees. Disciplinary inspection committees at the various levels should both accept the leadership of and bear responsibility to Party representative congresses.

Finally, it is essential to implement fundamental reforms of the accountability system for the highest local officials. Such a system has greatly aggravated the problem of centralized power within the Party. A collective leadership system must be implemented at all levels to establish a system of checks and balances within the party.

Democratic reform within the Party must be coupled with transparency in Party and government affairs as well as extensive citizen participation. Reforms must also include a system requiring public officials to disclose personal assets and a strong push for transparency in Party and government budgets. Important decisions or projects that influence the livelihood of citizens, such as land acquisitions, should include hearings that guarantee citizens the right of participation and an understanding of the facts surrounding final decisions.

4.4.2 *Implementing Electoral Democracy*

Article 2 of the 1982 Constitution clearly states that "all power belongs to the people." The key to implementing this "sovereignty of the people" principle lies in standardizing the election of people's congresses at every level and in allowing congresses to play an actual role in supervision and representation. The various levels of people's congresses are intended, in the design of the 1982 Constitution, to serve as the basic mechanism allowing citizens to participate in the administration and discussion of state affairs. Whether elections of people's congresses are standardized and whether representatives are willing and able to actively carry out their intended duties are questions that directly determine the fundamental nature of the state, the basic relationship between the government and the people, and whether the fundamental interests of the majority are protected. The multitude of massive protests in the recent decades have seriously undermined China's social stability and the Party's ruling legitimacy, and their root cause is the failure of the people's congresses at various levels to exercise their constitutional mandated functions.

At present, China's system of people's congresses has two types of problem. First, there is a severe prevalence of mere formality in the elections at the various levels of people's congresses, plagued by government interference, bribery, and other malpractices. This does not allow the representatives to represent the opinion of the people. In fact, most of the representatives fail to actively carry out their duties and are invisible at important public events. The few representatives who actually act selflessly, enthusiastically, and actively on behalf of their constituents are considered strange. Some are even assaulted or otherwise persecuted.

Second, the role of representatives as set forth in the Constitution remains superficial. Because most of the representatives and committee members serve part-time, they have little time, energy, or money to invest in constitutionally mandated legislative, budget-making, and supervisory functions. Thus, much of the people's congress work is merely rubber stamping, with representatives simply raising their hands in support of whatever proposal that the Party and the government put in their agenda.

Changing the current situation must begin with reform of direct elections of people's congresses in townships and counties. At present, most social problems are at the grassroots level. Standardizing the election of grassroots people's congresses can address these problems at the source, thereby consolidating the basis of ruling and defending the authority of government. Therefore, the Party Central Committee must strictly forbid local Party and government interference in nomination and campaign activities of candidates for local people's congresses.

At the same time, the Party must guarantee that people's congress representatives at all levels effectively perform their constitutional functions. Articles 34 and 35 of the Constitution and the Law on Elections grant citizens freedom to participate in elections of representatives for grassroots people's congresses. The laws prohibit using accusations of "disturbing social order" to interfere with or restrict free exchanges between candidates and voters. According to the general rules of constitutional states, a candidate naturally becomes legitimate when he gains sufficient support from voters. Our current electoral law, however, sets up an opaque process involving "exploratory discussions" and "consultations," which gives local election committees unfettered freedom of discretion. This provides the opportunity for the local Party and government to internally choose candidates, an evil that must be eradicated at its source.

With standardizing elections for people's congresses as a foundation, it is next necessary to enhance the function of all levels of congresses and push for representative specialization. Reform of congress organization should begin at the standing committee, with an increase in full-time committee members every year. We recommend a 10 percent increase in full-time committee members per year in an attempt to achieve 50 percent full-time committee members in five years. We further suggest a 5 percent increase in full-time congress representatives per year with the goal to have 25 percent of the representatives full-time in five years. Representatives themselves should have discretion to choose their own methods of performing their duties without interference of the local Party or government, as long as the methods are lawful.

Village committee elections and homeowner committee elections are the latest experiments in Chinese grassroots democracy and they too need institutional protection. In recent years village committee elections have been subject to extensive interference by the higher-level Party and government. Bribery and corruption have also become increasingly pronounced. Village committees have sold villagers' land and other vital interests without villagers' consent, such as in the Wukan case in Guangdong. To effectively resolve land disputes in Chinese rural areas and maintain stability in Chinese society, interference in village committee elections by the local Party and government must be clearly prohibited. At the same time, the election of village committees and villagers' representatives must be standardized and a series of checks and balances must be established among village level organizations like village committees, villagers' representative congresses, and election committees.

4.4.3 *Protecting Freedom of Expression*

Article 35 of the Constitution states that "citizens enjoy freedom of speech, of the press, of assembly, of association, of procession, and of demonstration." In three decades of reform, great progress has been made in developing the freedom of speech and of the press. With the advent of the internet, more and more members of the media are courageous enough to expose corruption all over China. This has greatly increased knowledge of public incidents at both the Central Government and grassroots level. Undeniably, however, many unnecessary restrictions remain, as seen by the following specific examples.

First, internet speech has experienced unnecessary restrictions. Internet postings are frequently deleted and blogs banned, and citizens are occasionally convicted under the education through labor program or even imprisoned for their speeches.

Second, there are too many restrictions on the freedom of the press. Not only are publishing organizations subject to strict examination before establishment, but books, newspapers, and magazines are further censored before publication. The press is also subject to many restrictions in daily operations. These restrictions conceal scandals of corruption that should be exposed to the public and severely obstruct citizens' rights to access truth. The phony and devastating "Chongqing model" thrived precisely in the background that the local Party chief was able to suppress the media and covered up all the mischief.

Third, the freedom of assembly is unnecessarily restricted. Although many countries with the rule of law require government approval for assembly and procession, in China the approval procedure has disintegrated into an excuse to prohibit the assembly of citizens. Indeed, it is nearly impossible to receive local government approval for an application for peaceful assembly.

Finally, there are also unnecessary restrictions on the freedom of association. The establishment of voluntary associations is subject to many stringent requirements and entails strict examination before and after establishment. Furthermore, farmers may not establish associations, and workers' union representatives are not elected by the workers, leaving their interests unrepresented.

We recommend the gradual abolition of unnecessary restrictions on the freedom of speech, a complete transformation of social administration from political control to the rule of law, and a shift from substantive to procedural management. This transformation includes four aspects.

First, control of Internet speech must be thoroughly eliminated and local government must be prohibited from using criminal sanctions or education through labor (劳教) as punishment for Internet expression.[52]

Second, with regards to the press, management must shift from political interference prior to publication to *post facto* judicial control for the purpose of investigating the legal liability of those publishing unlawful information. As to the establishment of publishing organizations and their publications, substantive examination should shift to a procedural review. The establishment of a record management system for magazines and newspapers can provide for legal supervision of publishing organizations after publication. Since to date the Constitution has not been effectively implemented and the rights granted under Article 35 have not been effectively guaranteed, it is necessary to establish a Press Law that substantially strengthens guarantees of freedom of speech and of the press and clearly defines the legal limits of these freedoms. Neither the Party nor the government should interfere with speech permitted by the Constitution and other laws.

Third, examination and approval procedures for demonstrations must shift from content review to procedural examination. The purpose of the

[52] The education through labor system, which empowered local administration to incarcerate individuals up to three years without judicial trial, was abolished at the Third Plenum of the eighteenth CCP Congress in 2013.

examination is not to restrict citizens' freedom of expression, but to prevent violence, traffic jams, and other incidents that disturb public order. Officials at all levels should adopt the fundamental constitutional principle that freedom of speech is the rule and restriction is the exception. So long as there is no sufficient evidence to suggest that an assembly will become violent, the assembly should be presumed peaceful and the local government should not be permitted to reject the application on the grounds that it will "disturb social order."

Finally, the examination and approval of citizen applications for association should also shift from a content review to a procedural one. The establishment of an association record management system should accompany this transformation. An association found in violation of the Criminal Law should be duly punished and have its association registration revoked. In 2011, new rules published in Guangzhou loosened the restrictions on associations and have had a positive social effect. Experimentation of this type should be promoted nationwide.

4.4.4 *Deepening Market Economy*

Since the beginning of China's opening policy, the market economy has been the basic national policy and has played an irreplaceable role in thirty years of development in Chinese society. The 1993 amendments to the Constitution granted constitutional status to the market economy. Of concern, however, is that the lack of synchronization with political reform has become a serious hindrance to the deepening of economic reforms. Under the politically influenced mindset of "GDP first," Chinese-style "growth" has become a derogatory term synonymous with corrupt officials, encroachment on people's interests, destruction of the environment, and the waste of resources. Moreover, the phenomenon of "state advancing, society retreating" (国进民退) has become increasingly pronounced, as seen in the following respects.

First, the monopoly status of state-owned enterprises has become increasingly prevalent while private enterprises have been elbowed out. This is especially true when considering market entry, bank loans, and other financing issues in which the environment for fair competition has been severely hindered. This in turn has obstructed the economic vitality of Chinese markets.

Second, China has seen increases in state revenues far in excess of increases in national gross product, with a continued rise in the proportion of state revenue relative to GDP.

Third, state finances are used increasingly for the purpose of "stability maintenance" (维稳) and armaments at the expense of investment in public benefits such as welfare, education, social insurance, and environmental protection. This has caused an ever-increasing gap between the rich and poor that has led to ordinary people struggling under the crushing burden of medical care, education, and housing expenses.

Finally, after the implementation of the "revenue sharing" scheme, the proportion of finances for the central government relative to those for local governments has dramatically increased. Thus, local governments do not have sufficient funds to support local public welfare using normal taxation alone. This fact, coupled with motivation from the "GDP first" mindset and rent-seeking officials, has led to the advent of "land finance," by which cities use a loophole in Article 10 of the Constitution to confuse urbanization with land taking without adequate compensation. This has severely injured farmers' interests and social stability.

To completely curb the phenomenon of "state advancing, society retreating," return the wealth to the people, and allow market economy reform to fully benefit the majority rather than minority interest groups, the following measures should be promptly taken:

First, the state must ensure constitutional equality for private enterprises (including private schools and universities) and loosen control over private capital and non-government funded education.

Second, state finances must be limited with a clear requirement that increases in government revenue at all levels must not exceed those in national income, because the actual tax burden on Chinese citizens is already quite heavy.

Third, reasonably distribute expenditures with increased investment in people's livelihood, such as education, medical treatment, basic welfare, and environmental protection. Other investments should include the realization of regionally equal compulsory education and university admission, establishment of an all-citizen medical insurance system, and the provision of bottom-line insurance for low-income individuals.

Fourth, reasonably distribute central and local finances and unify the powers of office with the powers of finance. At the same time, the mindset of "GDP first" must be fundamentally reversed. Local governments should devote themselves to local welfare, such as public order, education, livelihood, and environmental protection rather than infringing on citizen interests and creating opportunities for corruption under the guise of "development."

Finally, the land management system must be reformed. This includes implementing the just compensation principle laid out in the

Constitution and strictly restraining land taking within the domain of "public interest." In the mean time, restriction on the use of farmland must be loosened so that land right is returned to farmers, and urbanization should be separated from land taking.

4.4.5 *Upholding Judicial Independence*

The market economy and political democracy are inseparable from the basic order based on the rule of law, which in turn cannot be constructed without teams of just and independent lawyers and judges free from political interference. Article 126 of the Constitution clearly mandates that "the people's courts shall, in accordance with the law, exercise judicial power independently and are not subject to interference by administrative organs, social organizations, or individuals." Judicial independence is a reform demanded by the Constitution, and it is the route China must take to realize the rule of law. After ten years, however, China remains far from its goal of a just judiciary. Although there has been some judicial reform, corruption from within the judiciary and administrative interference from without remain prevalent. The slowing and even reversal of judicial reform has been especially noticeable since 2008, placing further reform at a crossroad with no clear direction.

At present, the many drawbacks of the Chinese judicial system are reflected chiefly in the following three respects. First, courts lack independence and are subject to political and administrative interference during the course of trial. The independence of trial as stipulated in Article 126 of the Constitution has not been realized in judicial practice. The administration of justice cannot avoid interference from the local Party and government, which commonly intervene in specific cases, because personnel, finances, and court functions and powers are not independent. Although internal court institutions such as the court president responsibility system, adjudication committees, management via ranks, and various assessment systems perhaps help in the monitoring of decision-making by judges, they also constrain the development of the independent character of the judge.

Second, judicial corruption is rampant and it is not uncommon for judges to accept bribes from both parties in the litigation. Judicial corruption is particularly easy because trials are not transparent, sentencing is not public, and court verdicts do not focus on reasoning.

Finally, the Party and government at all levels often unlawfully interfere with the judicial process by undermining the rights of lawyers to handle cases. This leads to extortions, torture, and other cases in which people are unjustly and falsely sentenced despite repeated prohibitions imposed by the higher authority. An example of this was seen in the Chongqing crackdown on organized crimes under the leadership of Bo Xilai.

The only way to improve the quality and dignity of the Chinese judiciary is to recommit to substantial judicial reform. Court functions must return to the judiciary in order to establish institutional guarantees of judicial fairness and rulings governed by law. First, the ruling Party must conscientiously defend judicial independence and proactively avoid interference with specific cases. According to the requirements of separating the Party from the state, the functions of the ruling Party lie in selecting cadres and determining fundamental state policies. Party functions do not include interfering in the judiciary and directly imposing its own will on specific rulings. Allowing the Party to do so leads directly to the rule of man rather than the rule of law, thus violating the laws, policies, and principles laid out by the ruling Party itself. Currently, interference by political-legal committees at all levels is especially rampant and such organizations must be dissolved, beginning at the bottom levels.

Second, constitutional design must strengthen vertical management of the judiciary to reduce courts' reliance on local governments for personnel and financial support and to restrain local protectionism. Doing so will create a better institutional environment for the courts to independently hear cases and issue rulings in accordance with the law.

Third, political and administrative control must be reduced to give judges maximum ability to issue rulings independently and in accordance with the law. Administrative control is not a remedy for judicial corruption. On the contrary, it creates a hotbed for increasing such corruption. The ideals of restraining corruption and increasing judicial independence run parallel, not in conflict, with each other. Reform measures such as open trials, open sentencing, and improving the quality of reasoning in verdicts will compress the space for corruption and, at the same time, enhance judges' professional qualities and credibility in society.

Fourth, the basic function of the court must return to trial and sentencing by law. Judges must be responsible to the laws and their trial work should recognize the supremacy of the law. The level of popular satisfaction with trial and sentencing is influenced by a variety of factors and, therefore, should not serve as a standard for appraising judicial work. The courts can carry on some conciliation work, but they should avoid overly emphasizing conciliation as a priority. Most conciliation and arbitration work should be diverted outside of the courts to judicial administrative departments. For small lawsuits, simplified judicial procedures can be designed to increase efficiency and lower costs, but no flexible measures should permit the judiciary to stray from its fundamental role of deciding cases by law.

4.4.6 *Safeguarding Constitutional Supremacy*

None of the above proposals are innovations in any sense of the word. In fact, they are all based on the language of the 1982 Constitution. If the Constitution is taken seriously, promotion of constitutional governance, standardization of elections, freedom of speech, market economy, and judicial independence will naturally come about. However, these requirements of the current Constitution have yet to be realized because the mechanism for implementing the Constitution remains incomplete. Thus, the Constitution has decayed from the fundamental law of the state to a useless facade, unable to have the "supreme legal effect" promised in the Preamble to the Constitution.

To rectify this situation, a complete constitutional implementation mechanism must be established that will allow the realization of constitutional requirements guaranteeing the rights of citizens and the supervision of state power. In fact, the essence of institutional reform is to realize the requirements of the current Constitution. On December 4, 2012, at a conference commemorating the thirtieth anniversary of the current Constitution, General Secretary Xi Jinping stressed that "both the life and authority of the Constitution lie in its enforcement."

Article 67 of the current Constitution states that the Standing Committee of the National People's Congress is empowered to "interpret the Constitution and supervise its enforcement." The Constitution has now been in place for thirty years, but the Standing Committee has never exercised the powers of Article 67 despite numerous constitutional problems occurring during this period. This demonstrates the ineffectiveness of the constitutional enforcement mechanism. It is not an accident that the incomplete system design has caused constitutional review to have an empty record.

Requiring the Standing Committee to interpret the Constitution flies in the face of the principles of democracy and the rule of law, because this system overrides the power of the NPC and causes the Standing Committee to interpret laws that it has passed itself. Having the Standing Committee interpret the Constitution also violates the principle of reasonably distributing responsibilities. The Standing Committee is in essence a legislative body, while interpreting the Constitution and laws is judicial work. The amount of legislative work undertaken by the Standing Committee is already strenuous, leaving it no time to interpret the Constitution in specific cases.

The only way to make the current Constitution useful is to apply it in the daily political life of the state. Countries with the rule of law have generally applied three methods of enforcing the constitution: (1) the American model with enforcement by common courts; (2) the German-Austrian model with enforcement by constitutional courts; and (3) the French model with enforcement by a constitutional council. Even if the American and German-Austrian models do not fit China at the present, it is essential to reform the constitutional enforcement mechanism by establishing a special committee as early as possible. For the time being, this committee could be established within the NPC and made responsible to Congress, though personnel and operational procedures must be relatively independent to truly give effect to the Constitution.

Finally, the key to constitutional review lies not in controlling the constitutionality of National People's Congress legislation, but in ensuring the constitutionality and legality of regulations, ordinances, rules, and other normative documents that are often found in violation of fundamental rights and liberties. Constitutional review should further serve to balance the relationship between local and central legislatures to guarantee a harmonious and unified Chinese legal system that takes into account the need for variation and innovation across the vast territory of China. Provided they comply with the Constitution and other laws, various localities should be permitted to freely experiment in order to foster healthy competition. In fact, the past thirty years of reform resulted from local experimentation, begun in 1978 by Xiaogang Village in Anhui, that was eventually adopted by the Central Government. Future reform requires the introduction of new mechanisms from local experiments and competition in the areas of democracy within the Party, grassroots elections, judicial practice, and review of legal norms.

As Sun Yat-sen pointed out: "The trends of the world rush forward with mighty vigor; those who go with the flow will flourish, while those who go against it will perish." Democracy, the rule of law, respect for human rights, and constitutionalism are irresistible trends of the world today. China's hundred-year course of blood and fire, especially the agonizing lesson of the Cultural Revolution, demonstrates that moving against these trends necessarily results in the people's suffering, social unrest, and instability of the regime. We sincerely hope that the new leaders will grasp the historic opportunity that lies before them, transcend ideological constraints and the seduction of short-term interests, and move resolutely with progressive reform for the long-term interest of the state and the Party itself.

More important, we hope that the people will recognize global trends and the true interests of this nation, without being disturbed by narrow nationalism, stand for rational and gradual domestic institutional reform, and come to the foundational consensus on promoting constitutional governance, standardizing electoral democracy, respecting freedom of expression, deepening the market economy, realizing judicial independence, and safeguarding the constitutional effect. They shall then take actions to spread, promote, and accomplish these ideals. Let us rise above divisions to the left or right, ignore distinctions between the ruling and the ruled, and make joint efforts to establish a constitutional China committed to democracy, rule of law, and respect for human rights.

4.5 NEO-TOTALITARIAN REVIVAL AND ITS LIMIT

Unfortunately, in the recent decade, China has moved to the opposite direction and shown inclinations towards neo-totalitarianism in areas such as intensified centralization of party power, regular use of disciplinary committees in the name of anti-corruption, and various forms of public opinion control. Although these measures cannot return China to the Maoist era, they further divide and weaken the still nascent and severely suppressed civil society, diminishing the impetus and pressure for political reform. Unless there are major unexpected events or sustained systemic factors that significantly alter the balance of power between the state and society, China will continue to hover around the vicinity of Authoritarian 2.0 as explained in Chapter 3.

4.5.1 *The Possibility of Neo-Totalitarianism*

To be sure, the unfortunate wrong turn is nothing surprising. Certainly, the process of totalitarian transformation is far from guaranteed, nor is there any assurance that a post-totalitarian regime will not reverse course and become a neo-totalitarian one. The full panoply of totalitarian machinery is still there and actively employed daily, albeit with reduced efficacy due to wear and tear. The nascent civil society is simply too weak to protect itself, leaving no barrier to prevent an ambitious dictator from revitalizing and sharpening the party-state machinery. As the totalitarian machinery is tightened once again, increasing tension and confrontation are bound to arise between the state and society. While the "three magic weapons" of one-party dictatorship, reign by terror, and brainwashing propaganda are old tactics, the totalitarian "magnet" has significantly intensified its influence in order to restore each individual to a "polarized" state.

Despite practical difficulties, a neo-totalitarian regime would fully utilize its propaganda and state machinery to suppress dissenting opinions and information. It would establish and maintain various "firewalls," virtual or real, to restrict freedom of expression and association, while employing a massive army of the "Fifty Cent Party" to spread disinformation and manipulate public opinion, creating a false belief that the old orthodoxy still has significant support. Undoubtedly, a considerable proportion of individuals who have grown up under the influence of brainwashing education remain ignorant and willingly serve as the "self-employed Fifty-cent Party" (自干五) to help sustain the regime. While the effectiveness of the totalitarian power generator has significantly diminished, there are still numerous individual "batteries" that, after being charged by decades of brainwashing, willingly contribute to prolonging the lifespan of the very regime that keeps them in slavery.

Therefore, compared to a typical authoritarian regime, the totalitarian transformation is a more volatile political process. While a totalitarian regime is a single-source power system, where all powers ultimately come from one supreme leader, liberal democracy is a multi-source power system, where the source of the state power ultimately comes from every citizen. The transition from totalitarianism to constitutionalism follows a diagonal path, which is bound to be more difficult than a relatively simple transition from ordinary authoritarianism. Before this process has completed (regardless of the past achievements in the liberation of the state control over thoughts and speech, the development of market economy and the diversification of social interests), it can never be ruled out that the post-totalitarian regime will revert to the old days. After decades of totalitarian dictatorship, the people's moral values, courage, sense of responsibility, and dignity have all suffered great damage. The post-totalitarian reform begins with a tenuous social foundation where social resistance against totalitarian control was originally non-existent and grows slowly. Within the party-state, officials at all levels have long been accustomed to a culture of submission to superiors and concealment from subordinates. Outside the officialdom, independent social forces have grown from scratch under totalitarian suppression, while suffering from internal factionalism and lack of cooperation. The vast majority of people remain aloof from political participation. In this situation, a political strongman can easily revive the totalitarian "magic weapons" and bring the rusted totalitarian machine back to effective operation without facing effective resistance from within and outside the regime.

Since Xi Jinping became the General Secretary of the CCP in late 2012, China has witnessed a totalitarian revival, with efforts to reestablish the totalitarian trinity. This has been achieved through intensifying crackdowns on civil society and restricting free speech, effectively strengthening the one-party monopoly over all public affairs. In 2013, the party outlined "seven taboos" (七不讲) in an unpublished file called Document No. 9 (九号文件), which included subjects such as press freedom, universal values, civil society, civil rights, and judicial independence. These topics were deemed off-limits for discussion in any media.[53] The July 9 Incident of 2015 marked a significant event when the police raided the Beijing Fengrui (锋锐) Law Firm, resulting in the arrest and subsequent imprisonment of over twenty lawyers across the country, accusing them of inciting subversion against state power. In the following months, more than 200 lawyers nationwide were summoned or interviewed by authorities to aid in criminal investigations.[54] Since then, over a dozen civil rights lawyers have had their licenses revoked, as ordered by various local Justice Bureaus, prohibiting them from practicing.

The new regime has also intensified efforts to isolate China's civil society from foreign social and cultural influences. In April 2016, the Standing Committee of the National People's Congress passed the Law on the Administration of Domestic Activities of Overseas NGOs, imposing strict restrictions on the establishment and activities of foreign NGOs within mainland China, effectively making it nearly impossible for them to assist domestic civil rights groups. In December 2018, the authorities raided the Early Rain (秋雨) Covenant Church in Chengdu and arrested Pastor Wang Yi (王怡) along with more than 100 members. Wang received a prison sentence of nine years for inciting subversion of state power.[55] In fact, as early as 2014, Zhejiang province initiated a movement to demolish crosses on Christian churches.[56]

In the meantime, Xi Jinping has significantly concentrated powers within the party, primarily through the anti-corruption campaigns and the establishment of the National Supervision Commission. Widespread corruption provides him with a convenient tool to selectively purge high-ranking officials who have not shown absolute loyalty to him personally, thereby creating space for promoting his own trusted allies. Ironically, two deputy ministers of the

[53] The seven taboos were made known to the public in early May 2013 by the *weibo* (microblog) of Zhang Xuezhong (张雪忠), a law faculty at the East China University of Political Science and Law. Zhang was soon removed from his teaching post. Independent correspondent Gao Yu (高瑜), who harshly criticized Xi for suppressing freedom of speech, was convicted on the alleged crime of "leaking state secrets" to foreign media. "Veteran Chinese journalist Gao Yu jailed for seven years for leaking state secrets," *South China Morning Post* (April 15, 2015), www.scmp.com/news/china/society/article/1768290/veteran-chinese-journalist-gao-yu-jailed-seven-years-revealing.

[54] "709 Crackdown," https://en.wikipedia.org/wiki/709_crackdown.

[55] https://en.wikipedia.org/wiki/Wang_Yi_(pastor).

[56] "The fight for the holy cross in Wenzhou," DW (September 5, 2014), www.dw.com/zh/温州的十字架之战/a-18141254.

Public Security Ministry, Fu Zhenghua (傅政华) and Sun Lijun (孙立军), both being responsible for persecuting lawyers in the July 9 Incident, were removed from their positions and received suspended death sentences on various charges, including corruption and organizing "political groups" (政治团伙).[57] More recently, both the Foreign Minister Qin Gang (秦刚) and Defense Minister Li Shangfu (李尚福), two confidants holding key positions, were also removed under apparently similar charges.

As the State Council and Premier Li Keqiang (李克强) were sidelined and the state authority was increasingly transferred to the party organs, the party has intensified propaganda efforts to promote Xi's absolute authority and cultivate a personality cult. In March 2018, Xi successfully removed the term limit for the President of the State through constitutional amendment, symbolizing his personal supremacy within the party and overturning a significant political achievement of Deng Xiaoping, who aimed to limit personal rule (人治) in a one-party system. In 2020, Professor Xu Zhangrun (许章润) was dismissed by Tsinghua University for sharply criticizing Xi, while Ren Zhiqiang (任志强), a prominent entrepreneur, received an eighteen-year prison sentence under the pretext of "corruption" for voicing similar views.[58]

China's media is easily controlled as all newspapers, magazines, televisions, and cable networks are owned by the government, with their leadership appointed and changed at will by the party-state. While the internet media, which have become increasingly significant, are owned by private entities, they are tightly regulated and infiltrated by the state security force, which actively searches for and deletes "sensitive" (敏感) content. The party-state also intensifies its indoctrination efforts, particularly in universities. The Central Propaganda Department has organized the Marxist Project for textbooks, effectively mandating that every university use official textbooks in each subdiscipline of law, humanities, and social sciences. In January 2019, the popular textbook *Introduction to Constitutional Law* was ordered to be removed from bookstores nationwide based on an informant's report claiming it contained "harmful materials."[59] In the following months, five central

57 Xiao Shan, "Who are those in the political group constructed by Sun Lijun after the 19th Party Congress," RFI (September 26, 2022), www.rfi.fr/cn/中国/20220926-孙立军19大后组建的-政治团伙-都是些什么人.

58 Tan Jingxiang, "The reasons why Ren Zhiqiang was sentenced to eighteen years in prison," 《亚洲周刊》, no. 39 (2020), www.yzzk.com/article/details/特別報道/2020-39/1600917266288/任志強判刑18年來龍去脈.

59 James Miles, "China tries to stop academics from taking its constitution literally," *The Economist* (February 16, 2019), www.economist.com/china/2019/02/16/china-tries-to-stop-academics-from-taking-its-constitution-literally.

organs collaborated to organize a thorough review of over 100 constitutional law textbooks and identified eight as "problematic," six of which were mine. Such a move has been unprecedented since the Reform and Opening was initiated in 1978. In May 2021, as part of the effort to ensure a smooth centennial celebration of the founding of the CCP, Central Inspection Teams (中央巡视组) were sent to more than thirty major universities nationwide, with the additional task of "political inspection." At Peking University, known for its (relatively) liberal and tolerant policies, Professor He Weifang (贺卫方) and I became the primary targets of "political inspection." As a result, we have been prevented from teaching classes and recruiting new graduate students.

The zero-Covid policy implemented nationwide from 2020 to 2022 is another manifestation that the totalitarian mechanism has retained full vigor in China. Through the strict top-down command system, aided by the high-tech information such as the Health Code (健康码) and widespread implementation of the face recognition system, the party-state was able to rigorously carry out the central commands through layers of governments to the very bottom of the social units, namely the resident communities and villages, even though many of these commands proved grossly unreasonable. Similar to the Great Famine sixty years ago, the people were locked at home for months, required to take nucleic acid amplification testing on a daily basis, transported to the often poorly equipped modular hospitals (方舱医院) if tested positive, and prevented from traveling without a green sign on their health code.[60] Despite rare and sporadic protests, one cannot help but marvel at the efficiency of the state that can be achieved nowhere but in a totalitarian regime, even though a popular movement did eventually reverse the "zero-Covid" policy after it was strictly implemented for almost three years.

4.5.2 *The Limits of Totalitarian Revival*

All of these bewildering measures implemented during the past decade remind one of the Cultural Revolution. Given that the situation and mood of society have fundamentally changed, however, it is nearly impossible to put the unleashed genie of social diversity back into the Maoist Pandora's Box, as it has extensively multiplied. Attempting to revert to intensifying brainwashing and indoctrination in order to suppress diversity would be akin to violating the

60 Murong Xuecun, "China's 'zero Covid' policy was a mass imprisonment campaign," *The Guardian* (April 18, 2023), www.theguardian.com/commentisfree/2023/apr/18/china-zero-covid-policy-xi-jinping.

second law of thermodynamics, which dictates the impossibility of decreasing the "entropy" of a closed system.

Despite the neo-totalitarian revival in China today, such efforts are ultimately doomed to failure because totalitarianism goes against human nature. Without exception, the totalitarian regimes that have been established so far are based on extremely adverse political and economic conditions and the popular ignorance of the great harms that a totalitarian regime brings. The maintenance of such a system necessarily relies on intense ideological brainwashing and state violence as a stability maintenance mechanism, exerting unbearably high pressure through incessant political movements and purges of high-level cadres, among other tactics. Any slight misstep may threaten a sudden collapse of the ruling foundation. Even if the neo-totalitarian regime exerts its utmost effort and operates according to a perfect plan, it can only maintain the status quo. It is almost impossible to repolarize the depolarized "magnets." Moreover, what is the driving force behind the neo-totalitarian repolarization? Every totalitarian state has learned a painful lesson, the hugely negative assets that the regime desperately tries to conceal. They can only be whitewashed as "positive energy" (正能量) through systematic lies, which always pale before the truth, especially in the internet age. Truth to lies is like light to darkness, which is destroyed by opening a tiny door slit. Therefore, although the totalitarian "magnet" is operating at full force, its efficacy is necessarily limited. Brainwashing has long lost its hold on adults who have grown up in a relatively pluralistic environment. For those who reject lies or have personally suffered from the totalitarian dictatorship, repeated brainwashing can only produce aversion. Their beliefs are already fixed, and their existence is itself a fatal obstacle to neo-totalitarianism. The only way to make them disappear is physical elimination, as was done to Yu Luoke and Lin Zhao during the 1960s, but this is no longer a realistic option today.

Even within the system, it is difficult for a neo-totalitarian regime to return to the strict "one leader" era. While reign by terror is applied not only to control ordinary people, but also to strike political rivals within the party, the effective use of such power requires the new Boss to muster real power in personnel, party discipline, as well as police and judiciary, and to buttress such power by prominent achievements and prestige within the party, without which the relationship between superiors and subordinates is merely naked interest. Such relationship cannot be sustained in the long run, unless he is in control of massive resources as temptation or secret police with absolute loyalty as a deterrent. The apparent obedience of subordinates is never absolute, but conditioned on the ability of the superior to meet their expectations of positions and benefits. If this condition is not met, subordinates will either shirk their responsibilities or retire from the system to pursue better opportunities. When the resources plundered by the regime are sufficient for distribution within the system, the powerholders will peacefully share the spoils and be united against external threats. However, if the spoils are no longer sufficient to meet everyone's expectation or its distribution is obviously uneven, then cracks will emerge within the regime.

To be sure, Xi Jinping has been rather successful in his effort of reviving totalitarianism through expansive anti-corruption measures, which "kill two birds with one stone" by both freeing up positions for redistribution and gaining the loyalty of newly appointed personnel, while exerting deterrence on the entire bureaucratic system. Both Stalin and Mao had used this strategy to consolidate their position in the party, but it remains to be seen how effectively it works today. Without the unrivaled merits and prestige derived from the act of state founding, the legitimacy of an undemocratic political power has always been a problem. The newcomer invariably seeks opportunities to establish his own merit, such as developing a new capital for future in Xiong'an or strengthening China's international clout through the "belt-road" (一带一路) initiative, but none has so far been a spectacular success.

4.6 THE FUTURE OF CONSTITUTIONAL REFORM

Needless to say, predicting China's future is a risky project since it involves balancing so many uncertain or even unknown countervailing factors.[61] Predicting the trend of China's neo-totalitarian development requires a psychological analysis of political behavior: If the political elites at various levels are aware that the regime is not morally legitimate and is maintained merely by the pervasive fear that the state violence creates, how long can such reign by terror as a strategy purely based on interest continue? What are the political and social conditions for maintaining such rule? As political legitimacy is commonly recognized as the social psychological basis for sustaining a regime, how far can a regime based exclusively on coercion and temptation go if its legitimacy becomes very thin? To be sure, after the repeated totalitarian catastrophes, the moral resources both inside and outside the regime are also scarce. Long used to the collective slavery under the totalitarian regime, most people lack the moral motivation and courage to openly resist the abusive public power. On the other hand, everyone has personal feelings, whether we approve what they think or how they behave. Although the people

[61] For the uncertainties of the future of totalitarian regimes in general, see Friedrich and Brzezinski, Totalitarian Dictatorship and Autocracy, pp. 300–3.

within the system dare not openly protest even when they are dissatisfied, they are good at passive shirking of duties or even creating obstacles.[62] Soon enough, the Big Boss will have to compromise and concede some decision-making power, leading to a de facto collective leadership in order to gain the support from his subordinates. At this point, the neo-totalitarianism is essentially moving back to post-totalitarianism.

In comparison with pure totalitarianism, however, a post-totalitarian regime may well be more resilient and can maintain stability for a considerable period of time. It not only violates human nature to a lesser extent, but also effectively exploits common human weaknesses, making the post-totalitarian transformation more difficult than a pure totalitarian one. The process of degeneration from totalitarianism to authoritarianism requires only the natural release of human nature without much proactive action. As long as people no longer believe in the lies fabricated by totalitarian propaganda, cease to worship the totalitarian leader, and stop actively participating in various organized political movements, the regime has largely degraded to Authoritarian 1.0. On the other hand, overcoming the authoritarian barrier requires positive political actions. To further enhance the social "impedance" against state power and organize themselves to express their collective will through ballots, citizens must acquire considerable courage to overcome the fear created by the authoritarian regime. At the political level, the authoritarian mechanisms of micro-social control and manipulation of fear are still operating. Whether such fear can be overcome depends on the balance of power between citizens and the regime. If the authoritarian leaders are determined to brutally suppress any protests and can effectively control the army and police, it is unrealistic to expect citizens to shed their blood in vain. The political environment within the party-state is undoubtedly crucial for constitutional transformation. The experiences of the former Soviet Union and Eastern Europe illustrate that a peaceful transition requires the regime to be dominated by moderate reformers who can tolerate social demands for political reform and effectively control the military to maintain neutrality during the confrontation between the state and the people.[63]

Ultimately, the key to breaking free from the totalitarian grip lies in individuals reclaiming their innate human nature and heeding the moral calling within themselves to become conscientious, dignified, and responsible

62 Xiao Shan, "It is rumored that Xi Jinping harshly criticized officials for faking illness or lying down on job to evade political risk," RFI (May 22, 2016), www.rfi.fr/cn/中国/20160522-传习近平严批官员装病或磨洋工逃避政治风险.

63 Zoltan Barany, "Democratic consolidation and military: The East European experience," *Comparative Politics* 30 (1997), 21–43.

citizens. To break away from the post-totalitarian regime, citizens need to actively strive for and exercise their political rights, which in turn are tolerated and accepted by the regime. As the hold of the totalitarian regime weakens, the cost of fighting for freedom diminishes, and courageous individuals become more numerous, further reducing the risk and cost of defending rights. With the continuous debunking of totalitarian myths, more people will come to recognize the inhumanity of the regime, and embrace constitutional democracy as a sensible idea. Meanwhile, suppressing different thoughts and expressions will become increasingly illegitimate and costly. As civil society gains strength and influence, enlightened reformers within the regime will seek it as an ally to bolster their own efforts. Although these reformers are not selfless like Lei Feng, they are astute enough to realize that constitutional democracy serves not only the nation's interest but also their own long-term well-being, providing a relatively safe and reliable exit for themselves.[64] At this stage, the transition to constitutional democracy is poised to take off.

China's current situation is mixed, as it has always been throughout history. While neo-totalitarian development continues and may well worsen in the coming years, its limit is equally obvious. Above all, we are here to stay. Although removed from teaching posts, Professor He (who just retired upon reaching the age of 63) and I remain university faculty. Fundamentally, unlike the 1950s and 1960s when everyone shunned "counterrevolutionary" (反革命) rightists as if they were plagues, we are warmly welcomed among our colleagues, students, and even the university leadership that is supposed to watch over us. The officials dare not speak out openly, but there are plenty of private complaints against leader worship and the current order of things. While teachers are generally required to use the typically low-quality textbooks produced by the Marxist Projects, the requirement is somewhat relaxed in major universities, where it can easily be sidelined by assigning additional "reference books" (参考书) – books that teachers really want to teach.

To be sure, the "die-hard" (死磕) lawyers were punished,[65] but the legal profession, comprising more than half a million lawyers today, is here to stay. Even if only a small fraction of them is courageous enough to openly defend

64 Tom Ginsburg, *Judicial Review in New Democracies: Constitutional Courts in Asian Cases* (Cambridge: Cambridge University Press, 2003), pp. 247–52.

65 Die-hard lawyers refer to those who vigorously defend the rights of their clients, particularly defendants in criminal trials. Since the 709 Incident in 2015, however, they have been defamed by official media as the protector of evil forces with foreign connections. See, e.g., "It is inevitable that the minority die-hard lawyers will stumble," 《环球时报》 (May 12, 2015), http://opinion.people.com.cn/n/2015/0712/c1003–27291548.html.

civil and political rights, the number is still significant. Compared to privately employed lawyers, China's media is a much less independent profession. Even though excellent correspondents emerged during the 1990s and 2000s, most of them are leaving this increasingly restricted field, with many preparing for judicial examinations, even though the judicial environment is deteriorating as well. When I teach the newcomers about freedom of the press once a year, their morale keeps descending as the restrictions continue to heighten. Near the end of the class, however, we are all encouraged. While they have learned how important and noble, albeit difficult, their profession is, I come to realize that they are so dissatisfied with themselves because they desperately want to do something, something that is consistent with the calling and dignity of their profession. The turnover rate may be high, but young talents will keep coming in. In other words, the media profession, as such, will stay here too.

I used to be turned down every once in a while by the unfortunate young generations of China today, who have to suffer through twelve years of tedious education that deprives them of a happy childhood and face intense competition in the job market upon graduation. When "involution" (内卷) and "lying flat" (躺平) are the catchwords of the day, depression and "hollow heart disease" (空心病) become a common symptom among them.[66] It seemed like a generation without ideals, motives and aspirations, until I was proven utterly wrong by the White Paper Movement (白纸运动) on November 26–27, 2022, the eventful night when I kept browsing my WeChat postings for protests popping up here and there. During this movement, long-depressed students and residents in various cities, furious at the fire incident in Urumqi that took away at least ten lives due to restrictive Covid policies, defied barriers, gathered in squares, and shouted "freedom," "democracy," "reform," "the rule of law," and even "no to dictatorship." As the latest example of the "Sun Zhigang model," it contributed to the sudden reversal of China's zero-Covid policy, which had been in place for three years.[67] Over a hundred protesters nationwide were detained, but most of them were released within a month. Perhaps equally significant, the Sun Zhigang model is still working in situations where people dare to collectively express their outrage, implying that the regime, despite its haughty disregard of every social "impedance" against it, is still concerned about the public opinion and its image after all.

[66] Xu Kaiwen, "The majority of those suffering from hollow heart disease have these seven symptoms," www.163.com/dy/article/H494269O0552IA4A.html.

[67] I was informed by a reliable private source that the White Paper Movement was *the* primary factor that prompted the sudden reversal of the zero-Covid policy.

The significance of the White Paper Movement is yet to be testified by history. Precisely six decades ago, the Great Famine took away at least 30 million lives. Like the Covid pandemic, it also lasted for three years, when millions of peasants were locked at their homes to starve to death. Unlike the pandemic, however, there had never been a White Paper Movement of any sort except sporadic resistances. For sixty years, that is a small progress, indeed, but it can be a decisive one for the future of China.

5

The Constitutional Manifesto

A Centennial Memorial to the Xinhai Revolution

5.1 THE PREDICAMENT OF CHINA

In 1911, the year of Xinhai (辛亥), the Wuchang Uprising made Qing (清) the last dynasty of China, bringing an end to the millennia of its imperial rule. However, the end of the imperial power was far from the beginning of a true republic. A century later, China is still stuck in an inescapable trap of absolute despotism, bureaucratic corruption, and social crisis. Throughout the past hundred years, China has suffered from wars, famines, and social turmoil, with repeated failures in the pursuit of constitutionalism. The Reform and Opening policy in 1978 brought a period of relative peace and allowed China to escape the threats of famine and political movements, enabling the nation to rejoin the civilized international community. However, the totalitarian power structure remained largely unchanged. Despite Mao Zedong's proclamation in 1949 that "the Chinese people have stood up from now on," in reality the people have never been the true masters of their own destiny for a single day.

One century after the Xinhai Revolution, China finds itself once again "reaching its most dangerous moment."[1] Without the protection of civil rights, public power will inevitably continue to expand infinitely. Acts of oppression, forced expropriation, violent demolitions, and disregard for human life are found everywhere. In a state where public power is supreme and unlimited, the government is bound to become the root cause of plunder and corruption.

[1] The phrase is quoted from the current national anthem, originally a movie song, the "March of the Volunteer Army《义勇军进行曲》," written against the background of Japanese invasion in the 1930s.

During the decades of reform, the central government relaxed its control, allowing people to pursue wealth and improve their lives. However, this also created abundant resources and opportunities for corruption among officials at all levels. As the fruits of people's labor are seized and distributed among a small number of vested interests, the growth of people's income inevitably lags behind the growth of fiscal revenue, and the gap between the poor and the rich continues to widen. On the one hand, the reform eroded the remnants of orthodox ideology among officials and the general public, leading to moral decay, unmitigated materialism, and rampant corruption. On the other hand, it has exerted immense pressure on China's natural resources and caused severe ecological damage at a rate surpassing sustainable development. As long as the current "merit-based" system (政绩体制) remains unchanged, this destructive cycle will continue, threatening everyone's basic survival. As a civilization with a long history, China has never before been so devoid of faith, moral judgment, courage, and the capacity for self-reflection and rectification. Corrupt officials have never been so numerous, the air and rivers have never been so polluted, food and medicine have never been so unsafe, and grasslands and lakes have never been shrinking so rapidly.

If the so-called China Model cannot be sustained domestically, China today is presenting a dangerous trend for the first time in its history towards external expansion. On the one hand, it exports cheap labor and products to developed countries by exploiting the domestic "rights-deficiency advantage" (低人权优势) to suppress workers' wages,[2] consume domestic resources, attract international investment, and sustain fast growth. In return, it expands the "rust belts" in developed countries like the United States, contributing to the electoral victories of charismatic leaders like Donald Trump. On the other hand, it also exploits the resources of even less developed countries, which usually suffer from constitutional problems similar to its own, in order to satisfy the domestic needs for raw materials. Whether for the purpose of diverting domestic crises or meeting the resource demands of an energy-consuming growth model, China has been approaching the world with a vindictive mentality no different from that of the Last Dynasty a century ago, but this time with the winner's pride and the expectation of seeking vengeance and recognition. Coupled with the international fear and hostility towards the "China threat," it is bound to experience frictions and conflicts with the world, further stimulating the "wolf warriors" (战狼) supported by populist patriotism.

2 The notion was first proposed by a Chinese sociologist and historian. See Qin Hui, "The human rights deficiency advantage of China's economic development," 爱思想 (April 14, 2008), www.aisixiang.com/data/16401.html.

Ever since the near complete collapse of the official Marxist ideology, the party-state has been eagerly seeking acceptable alternatives and soon finds the most convenient one – the remaining national pride among the ordinary people. Together with the distorted historical narrative shaped by prolonged brainwashing, the separatist dangers in Taiwan and ethnic minority areas, and the highly selective and misleading reporting of domestic and global events by a heavily controlled media, nationalist sentiment in China is spreading like wildfire. No matter how slightly is the territorial sovereignty challenged, extreme nationalist emotions are capable of rekindling overnight the sentiment akin to German or Japanese fascism in the 1930s. Behind the facade of peace and prosperity, China today is filled with explosives that are ready to ignite at any moment.

Whether it be the hardships of the past century or the dangers that lie ahead in the future, all evils are rooted in absolute despotism that has long enslaved the people on this land. Despotism is cunning and obstinate, however, and will not simply be destroyed by revolutionary violence. On the contrary, revolutions often establish stronger tyranny. The lesson to be learned from the fall of the Qing empire is that only by implementing constitutional reform in time can the tragedy of revolution be avoided. If the ruling group remains obsessed with its vested interest and repeatedly refuses to reform, not only will it dig its own grave, but the entire nation, trapped in a vicious cycle of revolution and despotic oppression, will fall with it into an irremediable abyss, where resources are exhausted, environment damaged, corruption rampant, and the people destitute. The vicissitudes of the past century have fully demonstrated that only constitutionalism can save China.

The termination of despotic tyranny can rely only on an enlightened people. To establish constitutionalism, the people must first establish their own dignity. The cultivation of a dignified personality is the very premise on which the success of constitutionalism is based. As Hu Shih pointed out decades ago, it is unimaginable that a nation of slaves ruled by slavish lackeys (奴才) can enact and implement a free constitution. The greatest sin of absolute despotism lies not only in daily trampling on human dignity, but also in depriving all subjects of the ability to restore their own dignity, making them willingly submit to tyranny. The fundamental dilemma of China's constitutionalism lies in the fact that the totalitarian regime has created a strange master-slave personality that is most favorable for its own survival, where everyone is a docile slave before the leviathan and a haughty master before the even weaker flock. The infinite expansion of public power and prolonged suppression of free personality form a steady pair of interdependent conditions. Only when the general public has awakened its consciousness as citizens can it bring itself out of the vicious cycle of tyranny.

One day, when the Chinese wake up from the nightmare of totalitarian enslavement, becoming conscious of the political corruption and moral decadence in which they are deeply trapped, and strive to restore the moral sense common to all humanity, they will eventually agree with the self-evident truths expressed below: Everyone has an inherent and inalienable dignity, the respect and protection of which are the duty of the state, to be fulfilled through an effective constitution. Any disregard or violation of dignity is illegal, and a government that has consistently disregarded or violated dignity is an illegal entity, whose only fate is to be abandoned by the people and dishonored in history.

5.2 THE SYNDROME OF ABSOLUTE DESPOTISM

Despotism is deeply rooted, however; its poison has long penetrated into the marrow of the nation and affected every crop that grows on that soil. To rid oneself of the despotic enslavement, one must soberly realize the harm caused by absolute despotism and the predicament in which it places its people.

Despotism (专制) refers to a type of regime in which the ruling group exercises state power without the consent of the governed, refusing to be held accountable to the people through constitutional mechanisms such as periodic elections. Absolute despotism refers to a despotic regime where the separation of powers is absent within the ruling group, resulting in absolute, unlimited power, usually held by a single despot. In such a regime, members of the ruling group, driven by self-interest, inevitably use their power to seize public resources that rightfully belong to the people. On the other side of the impervious ruling group are the oppressed and exploited subjects. In essence, despotism is a symbiotic entity composed of a flock of isolated subjects without political personality and a ruling group whose political power has been excessively bloated. The ruling group rules arrogantly over the obedient subjects, while the subjects allow themselves to be oppressed by the rulers, rising up only when they are deprived of the basic means of survival.

Revolutionary violence is, however, merely a sudden outburst after prolonged despotic oppression. It cannot change the personality of the subjects – more often than not, it makes the national character even more violent and volatile. It merely initiates a new cycle of tyranny, in which the revolutionary leaders, upon successful seizure of political power, become the new tyrants. Relying on the legitimacy bestowed by the revolution, they are capable of carrying out even more extreme tyranny until the legitimacy of the new regime is completely exhausted through successive abuses.

After more than a century of wars and revolutions, China's despotic order is once again facing challenge. However, the permanent scars it has inflicted upon the people cannot be healed overnight, and the historical cycle generated by its long despotic tradition is almost impossible to break. If the people cannot become the lion in control of their own fate, they will forever remain lambs to be slaughtered at will.

5.2.1 *Evils of Absolute Despotism*

While the harms brought by absolute despotism to its people are too numerous to list, the following are several main points:

A despotic regime sells off and claims as its own all the wealth of the nation, including labor, land, natural resources, and even water and air. The large part of national wealth either falls into the hands of a few corrupt officials or is openly squandered as public funds. The greater the scale of the state, the more resources are available for exploitation and squandering, leading to a more stable tyranny and greater suffering for the people. The ruling group, keen to present itself as the "savior" of the people, is apt to turn the fruits of their labor into its own political "miracle." In reality, it monopolizes enormous national wealth through the state machinery while coveting the fruits of the people's labor. Only out of fear that an aggrieved population may resort to desperate actions does it leave the people with bare means of subsistence.

A despotic regime holds the entire nation hostage and arbitrarily seizes national wealth to exchange with foreign nations. It uses the foreign exchange reserves accumulated through the exploitation of the domestic labor to "save" developed countries from economic crises, thereby gaining capital to safeguard its own rule. As a self-interested ruler, a despotic regime exploits and betrays the essential interest of the nation under its yoke. Depriving its own people and exchanging goodwill with other nations are not contradictory goals, but can be perfectly reconciled in the self-interest of the ruling group. As the Empress Dowager (慈禧) openly declared over a century ago, the imperial court would "measure the national wealth to win the hearts of other nations," as "it is preferable to give to friendly nations than to family slaves."[3] Dictators like Gaddafi and Mubarak were certainly not anti-American heroes

[3] Zhang Kaiyuan and Chen Huisheng, *Popular Reader of Modern Chinese History* [in Chinese] (Wuhan: Hubei People's Publishing House, 1983), p. 248. Although the phrases may be interpreted differently, it is indisputable that a despotic regime is inherently inclined to sell off the national interest to foreign nations. The most recent example is the party leader's unscrupulous granting of huge funds or waiver of debts to developing countries upon receiving superficial promises of acknowledging the "one-China" policy.

in any sense. On the contrary, relying on foreign support to sustain their last breath, they used their national resources to win over Western politicians and elites, with their offspring integrating seamlessly into the Western circles. If China were to go to war someday, the greatest obstacle would not be its people's love for peace, but the ruling elites' fear of jeopardizing their family interests overseas.

In a world where ideological commitment is globally declining, despotic regimes have long been intertwined with international capital. The latter needs to acquire cheap labor, reduce production costs, export environmental pollution, and evade domestic regulations and taxes, while the former is in desperate need of a continuous influx of international capital to maintain and expend domestic excess production capacity, maintain the illusion of prosperity and continuous growth, and sustain an export-oriented economy based on widespread poverty. If the exploitation of capital predicted by Marx has significantly been restrained by popular democracy in advanced capitalist countries, then it has found new outlet in the international market in the age of globalization, when democracy and dictatorship can join hands in exploitation. Through the deprivation of workers' rights by the domestic government, international capital realizes its profit maximization. The political power that was once established on the basis of Marxist ideology can now sustain itself only by relying on international investments and cheap exports, a situation deeply resented by Marx himself.

However, it is precisely such a traitorous regime that tirelessly whitewashes its "patriotic" image. Brainwashing its subjects with "patriotism," it constantly creates imaginary enemies and a sense of national crisis, making itself the guardian of the nation in a dangerous world with a deliberately distorted view of modern history. In order to maintain its rule, it even puts the entire nation on the crater of war. Under the banner of "national sovereignty" and security, all public misconduct appears insignificant, all criticisms of the government are easily labeled as "selling out the nation," and all spontaneous actions to defend rights and freedoms are attributed to the "international anti-China forces" and are prohibited due to their "serious disruption of social order."

It implements a highly repressive ethnic policy to maintain "national unity" and "ethnic solidarity," while distorting history by suppressing free communication between various ethnicities, thereby intensifying ethnic misunderstandings and hatred, and laying the ground for imminent national secession, which is used in turn as an excuse to maintain centralized dictatorship. A despotic regime that regards nationalism as its last life-saving straw will immolate itself in the surge of nationalist sentiment.

It instinctively envies any doctrine that is not in line with the official mainstream, and suppresses any organization independent of its control, thus effectively strangling all political and moral forces capable of replacing it. In dealing with religious forces, it seeks either to co-opt, domesticate and assimilate, or to exclude, suppress, and persecute. Such divisive practices not only create for itself national enemies due to arbitrary abuses, but also deprive the entire nation of faith. While the official orthodox dogma has long been a zombie, it still binds all bewildered souls, preventing them from freely accepting various beliefs, leaving them to die in the desert of nihilist desperation.

It prohibits free and open discussion of all essential issues, leaving the entire masses to live in ignorance, indifference, prejudice, and all the dangers arising therefrom. In the age of the internet, it has no choice but to allow the "uninformed" (不明真相) masses to whisper in private WeChat rooms. It condones if not positively abets false advertisements flying all over the sky; it even turns a blind eye to pornographic materials that pollute the minors. It earnestly wishes the entire nation to be immersed in vulgar flirtations and shoddy entertainment, but resolutely prohibits any serious and "sensitive" topics from public debate, thus reducing the nation's decision-making to a suicidal race of "blind men riding blind horses" (盲人骑瞎马).[4]

It deprives society of reason and its rational capacity, not only by arbitrarily imposing speech restrictions, making meaningful debates based on verifiable facts impossible, but also by making itself the paragon of imperious personality for the entire nation. A regime that is born out of the gun barrel can only be sustained and, ultimately, changed by the same.[5] All reasoning seems redundant, useless, even absurd. An imperious government has fostered an imperious nation, as a great dictator has fostered many puny dictators, whose daily lives are permeated with cynicism, snobbery, brutality, and power worship.

It allows bad laws to thrive, renders good laws void, turns judges into puppets, transforms laws of its own making into mere facade, and renders the constitutional declaration of "rule of law" a public mockery. Absolute despotism and the rule of law are inherently incompatible. Despotism, whether through individual or collective leadership, leaves no room for the rule of law. Laws are enforced if they benefit the rulers and shelved otherwise. Even if a few enlightened reformers sincerely seek to implement the law, despite their good intentions, they cannot overcome the massive vested

4 This is the first half of a Chinese idiom, followed by the second half: "approaching a deep pool at midnight" (夜半临深池).

5 It is Mao's famous aphorism that "power grows out of the gun barrel" (枪杆子里出政权).

interest opposed to the rule of law. Not to mention that, in a Prisoner's Dilemma where the nation will neither be saved by one person's integrity nor perish by one person's corruption, even enlightened reformers are members of the vested interest, and will not accept the constraints of law when it comes to their turn. When corruption has infiltrated every capillary of the social organism, a person of relative integrity will be purged in the name of "anti-corruption" because his presence impedes corruption.

However, its greatest sin lies in exterminating the free personality of its people, destroying their inner sense of dignity, and causing them to sprawl in its shadow under perpetual fear. Beside the all-powerful government is a group of incompetent plebeians who share the common trait of having lost their sense of dignity and shame. Officials feel no shame in exploiting and squeezing the people, while the people feel no shame in accepting enslavement. The people's abject cowardice buttresses the officials' arrogance and depravity, and the officials' haughtiness reinforces the people's fear and subservience. In a collectively depraved society, even the most absurd excesses are implemented without eliciting a single complaint. Everyone knows that the system is illegitimate, official propaganda is meaningless, and the ultimate consequence of unlimited "development" is inevitable collective destruction, yet all these do nothing to deter anyone from striving to join the party and pledging their worthless oath. As long as jobs are secured, homes remain standing, and there is still enough air and water to sustain subsistence, no one will rise up to resist despotic tyranny. After a century of turmoil and decades of "development," the moral horizon of this nation has sunk so low that everyone becomes a pure economic animal, indignantly observing every injustice they endure, while willingly serving as gears that faithfully perform their assigned duties in this massive totalitarian machine.

5.2.2 *Social Syndrome under Absolute Despotism*

While the state tyranny constitutes one half of absolute despotism, the other half is the apathy and cowardice of its people. At the same time as it makes a handful of unbridled and insatiable tyrants, it reduces the vast majority to submissive and servile subjects. Despotism breeds a pathological personality, which in turn perpetuates and reinforces despotism, leaving the nation in a permanent state of political disability, unable to stand on its own and govern itself.

The following are but the major symptoms that a despotic regime fatally inflicts upon society.

First, impudence. Absolute despotism stands as the most shameless regime in human history, and its model has been replicated countless times in its shameless subjects. To uphold its image, a despotic regime shamelessly praises itself and employs all means to suppress its critics. It not only crushes everyone's backbone with its unlimited power, transforming them into sycophants who bow and scrape before authority, willing to do anything for personal gain and remaining silent out of fear, but also sets a perfect example for all subjects. It forces them to see through the "emperor's new clothes," but obliges them to cover it up with their own lies, thereby eradicating their basic sense of shame, reducing everyone to shameless petty man (小人) who regards lying and faking as virtues.[6]

Second, cowardice. The maintenance of absolute despotism relies on the widespread fear among its subjects. The despotic tyranny reduces everyone to sorry creatures who are afraid and submissive in the face of their position, salary, fame, and family well-being. Totalitarian education consistently suppresses independent thinking and beliefs. Through a combination of less-than-noble lies and material inducements, it encourages children to lie and prevents them from confronting truth, questioning orthodoxy, and challenging authority when they grow up. The dictator replaces the beliefs of the entire nation with his own fabrication. Even after the inevitable decline of unquestionable orthodoxy, it still prohibits people from freely seeking and holding their own beliefs, thereby depriving the nation of any genuine faith. A group of unfaithful, unorganized, and isolated individuals is naturally terrified when facing a massive leviathan, whose mercy is considered life-saving grace. In a state where the state power permeates every corner, the superior is always equated with truth, obedience to superior orders is considered the supreme virtue and becomes the sole criterion for determining rewards and punishments, promotions and demotions. The expectation of the same obedience extends even to higher education institutions that claim to prioritize the pursuit of truth as their ultimate mission. Tyrannical power leaves no room for independent thinking and judgment, without which notions such as fault and responsibility are rendered meaningless. Everyone is following orders from a higher level, and superior orders will justify even the most lawless acts. A group of cowardly subjects cannot bear any responsibility, nor is there any responsibility for them to bear.

Third, radicalism. It is precisely in such a country that radical voices are sought after, while moderate proposals are neglected. Even if the latter exist, they are bound to be feeble and helpless, eventually submerged in a sea of

6 Indeed, Hegel noted this "great immorality of the Chinese" even during his time in the *Philosophy of History*. Carl J. Friedrich, ed., *The Philosophy of Hegel* (New York: Random House, 1953), p. 130.

vulgar laughter and vitriolic curses. Since a despotic regime prohibits free speech, breaking the imposed silence carries unpredictable risks, making courage the scarcest resource, bravery the primary virtue, and a fearless speaker the greatest hero. Regardless of one's political leanings, it is impossible to mobilize the cynical masses without resorting to radical expressions because, on the one hand, the reality in such a society is radical enough. With unchecked public power that is necessarily lawless and oppressive, social resentments quickly accumulate without finding an outlet. Any reported tragedy is enough to trigger a riot, which is prevented from erupting only through the powerful deterrent of the state machinery, leaving radical expressions as the only means of venting anger. On the other hand, the arrogance of absolute despotism reduces all reasoning to meaningless chatter, akin to "seeking skin from a tiger" (与虎谋皮). Even if the analysis is sound and beneficial to the people, it will at best encounter sneers from the ruling group, as it threatens their vested interests. Precisely due to the near impossibility of realizing any proposal in a despotic regime, the people never need to face the risks that radical proposals bring upon themselves. Since it remains no more than empty talking (空谈), social reform becomes a reserved topic for a few "public intellectuals." Irresponsible writers enjoy crafting grandiose plans to quench the social thirst, building illusory utopias with captivating words to win popularity, while the people revel in the psychological satisfaction they cannot attain in real life, similar to the pleasure of reading fictions about martial arts heroes (武侠), which give them the illusory experience of justice and chivalry. Radical proposals serve as stimulants to satisfy a peculiar social psychology rather than as prescriptions for curing institutional maladies. And stimulants are precisely what a depressed nation constantly needs in order to break free from its desperate monotony. In this way, a nation under despotism becomes a breeding ground for revolutionaries brimming with fantasies.

Fourth, naive arrogance. Subjects in a despotic regime often exhibit excessive confidence, credulity, willfulness, and arrogance. This is not only because they have been indoctrinated with a simplistic view of good and evil since childhood, taking it for granted as the sole truth, but also because public opinion is tightly controlled and information is selectively filtered, leading to an excessively singular worldview. As a result, they have neither need nor opportunity to confront clashes of different views and interests. Since they never had the chance to truly choose their master and decide his fate based on the free evaluation of his performance, they can only passively accept his deceptive and self-decorating public "philosophy," contenting themselves with identifying the master in front as their savior, despite repeated exposure of these lies by painful truths. In an environment where "sensitive" information is carefully shielded, nothing prevents the vast majority from taking for granted the a priori legitimacy of the existing regime.

Fifth, militancy. Weak and negligible individuals often harbor a strong sense of vanity, and hope to satisfy their ego through a powerful and illusory collective, while choosing to ignore the obvious dangers it poses. Since moral beliefs have disappeared, leaving behind an empty heart, external achievements such as GDP figures, space shuttles, and aircraft carriers become the only assets worth flaunting. The despotic regime never tires of instilling nationalist ideals in its subjects, prioritizing national sovereignty and territory as the supreme value above all else. Despite enslavement by their master, all subjects imagine themselves as unruly masters and sleepwalk in the "patriotic" values of sovereign supremacy. Since their fate as slaves will not change regardless of who rules, they have virtually nothing to do with the fate of their state, yet they are more enthusiastic than anyone else about serving as cannon fodder for the despot, even if it means sacrificing their and their family's lives, which are greatly devalued under absolute despotism. In a despotic regime, everyone is weak and vulnerable, yet all are resolute militarists.

Last, snobbishness. The subjects under absolute despotism are apt to grovel and kneel before the powerful, making them necessarily indifferent and haughty when facing truth and conscience. The lack of an independent personality is the regular condition in a despotic regime, which will eventually succeed in physically strangling independent thinking and set that as an exemplar, warning all subjects to speak cautiously and act with trepidation. When power becomes a universal currency that can purchase everything, all moral or legal rules appear utterly pale. In such a society, faith is for the paranoid, and principles are for the pedantic; only earthly interest is the eternal goal, and only power that can bring interest is worth pursuing. Everyone is thoroughly disciplined by rewards and punishments, turning himself into a slick, cynical opportunist who knowingly ignores his conscience and chooses to comply. The entire nation becomes a circus for the limitless pursuit of power and profits. Even knowing their participation in a national crime will not disturb their peace of mind, and finding an excuse is surely easy when their deeds are questioned: "I had no choice but to simply execute the orders of my superiors." That logic is exactly the same as that of a Nazi soldier escorting Jews to gas chambers, faithfully executing the führer's orders, with the only difference that the immediate consequences of daily derelictions of the despotic subjects are perhaps less conspicuous. The totalitarian machine turns the entire country into a colossal prison, where all prisoners are thoroughly tamed into arrant self-concerned animals. Freedom is surely a better choice for everyone, but since fighting for it comes at a heavy price when others decline to make the same choice, everyone willingly continues to embrace slavery. Even if the edifice of the nation is collapsing, no one dares to stand up and act, leaving it to crumble alone in the midst of storms towards collective destruction.

The combination of these symptoms has created an unfortunate personality. When most of the population is infected with such a syndrome, it creates an unfortunate nation, whose misfortune is much deeper than that of a person. An unfortunate individual may still be awakened by the awareness of his pitiful situation, while individuals in an unfortunate nation are neither obligated to personally face nor capable of changing the misfortune of their nation; even worse, they may move towards a dangerous abyss under the halo of national power and prosperity. It takes moral courage for individuals to face themselves, take personal responsibility as citizens and even endeavor to change their nation, while outsourcing all responsibility to the remote "imperialism" or "anti-China forces" (反华势力) is free from any risk. The despotic regime loves to see the popular forsaking of personal responsibility as the consequence of its persistent moral destruction. Under the nationalist discourse, the "patriotism" needs no reason, nor does "protecting the sovereignty" or silencing those dissident "traitors," who seem to be disloyal to the nation. On the other hand, the populist speeches cater well to the national psyche, helping the masses to cheerfully forget the humiliation of serving as state slaves and even gain the pleasure of playing the role of a master when the despot takes a tough stance against a weak nation or ethnic group. In the clamor of invincible nationalism, every "patriot" is relieved of his moral responsibility, seeking consolation in the self-indulgence of "anti-American" or "fighting Japanese" hysteria, taking pride in the "China miracle," ignoring the domestic crises constantly afflicting themselves and the conspicuous institutional roots, while celebrating the "developmental" model that brings destruction to the very land on which they live.

5.3 CHINESE MORAL AND POLITICAL PERSONALITY: A CRITIQUE

As a healthy nation is constituted of healthy individuals, the rejuvenation of China requires, first and foremost, the reconstruction of moral and political personalities (人格). For thousands of years, traditional moral culture represented by Confucian ethics had played an irreplaceable role in binding the Chinese society together. Due to the defects in its political personality, however, China has failed to fully transition into modern civil society. On the other hand, the Confucian tradition is not an obstacle to establishing civil society; instead, it can be a starting point for constructing a new personality. China's primary mission today is to restore and preserve the core values within its own tradition before integrating them with the mainstream civilizations of the world, thereby completing the double transformation of moral and political personality from "small man" to "gentleman" and from subject to citizen.

5.3.1 *The Confucian Personality and Its Defects*

In the history of human civilization, China's greatest intellectual contribution to the world has been its affirmation of the inherent value and dignity in every human being, a theory prevalent in classical Confucianism that was developed during the Axial Age. The classic Confucian teachings upheld the belief in the innate value of every human being, as embodied in the "four beginnings" (四端) for humanity (仁), righteousness (义), propriety (礼) and wisdom (智). While humanity makes one compassionate, righteousness makes one just, wisdom enables one to acquire knowledge of nature, humans, and society, and propriety stands for the reciprocal respect paid to others who equally possess inherent dignity.[7] Through learning the knowledge of propriety and consciously cultivating moral character, everyone can turn these potentials into actual virtues and grow into morally and intellectually mature "gentlemen" (君子). Confucian gentlemen represent the noble personality characterized by moral independence, righteousness, courage and fortitude: A gentleman "values righteousness above all,"[8] "neither oppress those beneath him nor seek favors from those above, and rectifies himself without beseeching others,"[9] and "is harmonious without being conformist, impartial without leaning to either side."[10] In the words of Mencius, a gentleman is to:

> dwell in the magnificent house of humanity, stand in the right place of propriety, and walk on the great path of righteousness. When he succeeds in obtaining an office, he practices his principles together with his people; when his effort is frustrated, he persists in practicing these principles alone. Wealth and honor cannot corrupt him; poverty and low status cannot sway him (away from righteousness); and power and force cannot subjugate him.[11]

7 The last aspect is my extension. See Qianfan Zhang, *Human Dignity in Classical Chinese Philosophy: Confucianism, Mohism, and Daoism* (New York: Palgrave Macmillan, 2016), pp. 17–29.

8 *Analects*, 17: 23.

9 *Zhongyong* [*Principle of the Mean*], sec. 14.

10 Ibid., sec. 10.

11 *Mengzi*, 3B: 2.

As the moral personality that served as a model for the traditional Chinese society, a gentleman was obliged to constantly examine his own behavior through self-reflection. If his conduct failed to conform to the principles of humanity and righteousness, thereby diminishing his own or others' inherent dignity, or hindering the normal development of their moral and intellectual potential, then he would feel ashamed. Confucius advocated "maintaining the sense of shame in one's own conduct"[12] precisely because a gentleman is aware of his own dignity. Every word or deed that undermines his dignity will be a degradation of his own person, and thus naturally arouses a sense of shame. Constrained by the sense of shame, a gentleman refrains from certain actions: "A person must first know what he ought *not* to do, before he can do what he ought to do."[13] He will not reduce himself, for example, to a thief or "court-hired scholar" (御用学者), who is hired by the government to flatter the powerful or even "play the jackal to the tiger" (为虎作伥) by positively abetting tyranny, thereby reducing himself to a parasite who survives on the tyrants and, like them, lives off harms caused to society. On the other hand, a petty man (小人) who remains morally immature cannot feel the shame since he fails to see that "everyone has something noble in himself."[14] Lacking sense of shame, the petty man will do anything with any means for petty gains. As Mencius warns, "One cannot be without a sense of shame. If one feels no shame, one is shameless to the extreme."[15]

For over two millennia, the Confucian virtues such as moderation (温), kindness (良), respectfulness (恭), frugality (俭) and humility (让) had cultivated generations of gentries, thereby maintaining China's moral and social order. On the other hand, it has to be admitted that the backward economy and education during the agricultural age made popularizing moral and intellectual cultivation nearly impossible. As a result, the Confucian gentlemen were limited to a small elite circle in the population. The vast majority of illiterate poor people were influenced by the Confucian customs, but might fail to cultivate an independent moral personality. Confucians thus believed that, although everyone has the potential to become a gentleman, most people cannot grow into gentlemen in reality and thus will remain morally immature and deficient. Even Mencius, a great liberal Confucian, claimed that gentlemen labor their minds, while petty men labor their bodies: "Those who labor their minds ought to govern others, those who labor their bodies are to be

[12] *Analects*, 13: 20.
[13] *Mengzi*, 4B: 8.
[14] *Mengzi*, 6B: 17.
[15] *Mengzi*, 7A: 6.

governed by others."[16] According to this seemingly logical reasoning, Confucians divided society sharply into the ruling and ruled classes, thereby excluding the possibility of political democracy – if the majority of people are selfish, myopic, and unable to self-govern, what will be the result of elections based on "one person, one vote"? To be sure, the traditional imperial examination (科举) system provided some social mobility for the lower classes, but the basic reality remained unchanged: The political opportunity was inevitably limited to a tiny number of elites. While Confucian ethics preached individual moral autonomy, it degenerated at the political level into a doctrine that justified despotism by depriving the moral freedom of the vast majority to choose the rulers.

Political despotism deprives not only the vast majority of their dignity and the right to develop their moral and intellectual capacities, but also Confucian elites themselves of the freedom to express their opinions and offer advices without fear. While the Confucian norm of "letting the king be king, the minister be minister" did impose obligations on both the emperor and his ministers,[17] such a relationship was clearly unequal and lacked effective mechanisms to compel the emperor to fulfill his obligations. Even though Mencius proposed a rebellious doctrine of revolution, claiming that "I had heard only about the killing of a tyrant called Zhou (纣), but nothing about regicide,"[18] Confucians were helpless before a tyrant who controlled the state machinery, and could do nothing more than what an evasive strategy would suggest: "Do not enter a state in danger, nor dwell in a state in chaos."[19] Although a handful of officials might be courageous enough to risk their life and family by admonishing and offending the supreme ruler, such courageous acts were bound to be the exception rather than the rule in a regime where the monarchic power was not institutionally constrained. Even if the gentleman is in office, he cannot help but restrict his own words and deeds out of fear of the unlimited power; if he is not in office, he is even more powerless to prevent the public power from arbitrarily trampling individual dignity and moral freedom. Such an image is clearly inconsistent with the original spirit of a Confucian gentleman, who is supposed to be fearless and upright in defending the public interest. The gentlemen cannot protect their own rights and freedoms from the encroachment of the imperial power above, nor can they guarantee that they will refrain from abusing their own power and

16 *Mengzi*, 3A: 4.
17 *Analects*, 12: 11.
18 *Mengzi*, 1B: 8.
19 *Analects*, 8: 13.

infringing upon the rights of the common people below. In depriving everyone of their political freedom, despotism turns all into political petty men.

The fatal defects in the Confucian political personality not only hindered the social development of China for over two millennia but also foreshadowed the depravation of the Chinese moral personality in the past century. Although the Confucian moral tradition played a limited role in combating imperial corruption and abuse of power, it was essentially a despotic moral order that could only be maintained by clinging to political despotism. After the republican revolution destroyed the imperial political order, it was only a matter of time before Confucianism was rendered a sacrifice for its deceased patron. Since Confucians distrusted the political judgments of the common people and refused to persuade the majority to voluntarily accept its doctrine through free debates and equal competition, but imposed its principles on all subjects through coercive state power, it was incapable of relying on the power of the majority and defending itself against the destruction by another despotic doctrine once the imperial political order collapsed. The ancient policy of "honoring Confucianism alone" (独尊儒术) did establish its dominant status as the state orthodoxy as early as 100 BC, but it also destined its decline after the May Fourth Movement in 1919 when a more thorough, totalitarian doctrine eagerly approached China.

Indeed, Marxism must have been felt intimate to those intellectuals who were vehemently against the despotic political culture in which they were steeped. From its demand for equality of wealth, sympathy for the masses, aversion to individual freedom, addiction to the love of collectives and the state, to the irresistible enthusiasm for "truth," "ultimate good" and self-proclaimed "correctness," all seemed so familiar. The only revolutionary promise that could not possibly be fulfilled was its republican dream because the revolution, carried out in the name of democratic republicanism, implemented in reality a much more systematic dictatorship under a single totalitarian party. It took successive political movements, claiming to cleanse everyone's soul, to thoroughly destroy the moral personality of traditional elites, before the public power could expand without limit in the name of "people," leaving behind a pile of unscrupulous worms that are recklessly nibbling away the material foundation of the nation's survival today.

5.3.2 *The Transmutation of Modern Chinese Personality*

If the imperial court could still maintain a degree of ease and magnanimity as long as its dominant position remained unchallenged, it was inclined to be stagnant and conservative in the face of continuous attacks from Western powers since the First Opium War in 1840. For more than two millennia, the Confucian-dominated civilization lacked substantial challenges from developed civilizations. As a result, China always considered itself the center of the world, treating neighboring civilizations with contempt and disdain. When confronted with more powerful Western nations, it naturally developed a hostile attitude towards the external challenges. The Qing government's repeated defeats and resistance to reforms not only diminished its legitimacy, but also made the Confucian tradition a scapegoat for failures. With the complete destruction of the moderate Confucian culture by the totalitarian regime, Chinese society lost the capacity for self-reflection, and became increasingly cynical and resentful. It blamed every defeat on the Western powers, desperately relying on a powerful state machinery to wash away imagined national humiliations. Statism, while dormant in the Confucian political personality, became the explicit emblem of the totalitarian regime, which eventually devoured the traditional moral personality, reducing all to the willing puppets of the state.

Contemporary Chinese history textbooks vividly reflect the decisive change in the national character. Since the Opium War, China's defeats and humiliation were certainly the result of the Western expansionism, but they were equally the consequence of obstinate resistance to institutional reforms by the imperial courts and conservative social forces, whose arrogance, xenophobia, and closed-mindedness greatly exacerbated the situation. While the Opium Wars were partly the result of the imperial court's persistent isolationism, the burning of the Old Summer Palace (圆明园) was caused by the slaughter of foreign missionaries by the Chinese officials and soldiers. Incapable of reflecting on itself, however, a failed nation would turn a blind eye to all its own improprieties. Contemporary history textbooks fail to mention a single word about China's own faults, and shift all the blame to Western "imperialism." Even worse, preaching "patriotism," these textbooks and official propaganda have made considerable success in instilling the people with hatred to Western liberal democracy. Although the Communist regime is not responsible for the past failures of the Qing government, it deliberately erased from official textbooks all the historical facts that were unfavorable to the China's image in order to portray China as a poor, innocent, bullied and weak nation begging for its "liberation." It embellished the history of the past century as a moving epic of continuous heroic struggle for China's sovereign independence, while depicting the Qing government as a corrupt and incompetent humiliation to the nation. The current regime is fond of escalating the foreign policy disputes such as the opium ban into an ideological struggle of "roads" (路线) between "patriotism" and "treason" (卖国), exaggerating the past national failures and obliterating the diplomatic achievements gained by the Republic of China. It makes full use of national vanity to sell its delusional militaristic view of history, and incites nationalistic sentiments against the West to sustain its own hostility towards liberal democracy. The Chinese often protest against Japanese history textbooks for denying facts such as the Nanjing Massacre, without realizing that their own history textbooks are many times worse. Never free from the imprint of political propaganda, contemporary Chinese history is in essence a "party history" (党史), cherry-picked to suit its own political purposes, giving rise to a pseudo history filled with self-glorification and cowardly shuffling of responsibility.

As Mencius wisely observed, "only after a man belittles himself will others belittle him; only after a family destroys itself will others destroy it; only after a country cuts itself down will others cut it down."[20] China had long been weak and helplessly beaten because, fundamentally, the despotic regime grossly enervated the free initiatives and creative capacities of its subjects. A country ruled by a group of slavish elites over mass slaves can never be truly strong. Political slaves will neither earn respect from others, nor treat others with equal respect, let alone protect the territory and sovereignty that do not belong to them in the first place. The root cause of the slaves' condition is obviously not Western "imperialism," not even the specific despotic regime that enslaves them, but ultimately themselves who willingly accept and help to maintain the bondage imposed by the state machinery over themselves. To make China truly stand up in the world and become a respected civilized power, the Chinese people must first stand up and become free and civilized people. A strong China obviously depends on the economic, industrial and technological developments, and certainly needs to learn from and draw on advanced political and legal institutions. The foremost foundation is, however, the construction and improvement of the moral and political personality of its people. Left alone, the Confucian capacities of self-respect, self-reflection and self-improvement contained in its moral personality would have sufficed to complete such mission as a proper response to the Western challenges.

In the Sino-Japanese War of 1894, Japan destroyed overnight the Beiyang Fleet that had been painstakingly built for decades of the Westernization Movement (洋务运动). The shockwave that stunned the imperial court and Confucian elites did not produce narrow nationalist hatred, but instead set off a tide of studying Japanese politics and legal institutions, an incredible miracle from today's perspective. By 1915–16, the disappearance of its imperial patron had made the Confucian orthodoxy defenseless against the New Culture

[20] *Mengzi*, 4A: 8.

Movement (新文化运动),[21] which began to comprehensively reflect on and attack the Confucian moral tradition. Unfortunately, it went too far. While the New Culture Movement aimed to correct the defects in the Confucian tradition, it exaggerated them and developed into a total negation of the traditional morality, which abandoned the essence of Confucian moral tradition, preventing China from relying on its own moral resources to accomplish its revival. As China's earliest "angry youth" (愤青) writer, Lu Xun (鲁迅) gained unrivaled eminence only because his leftist position was acceptable to the current regime. Although his critical consciousness is still valuable to contemporary China and is the very reason he continues to be admired by the young generation today, his scathing criticism that "preaching of propriety devours man" (礼教吃人) was but an extreme exaggeration that blamed all faults on "tradition."[22] After abandoning personal responsibility for self-reflection and self-undertaking, the radical individualism of the New Culture Movement opened up an unsettling era of fury and frenzy. Once Confucian tradition was completely abandoned, the moral personality of the nation underwent a fundamental change to its detriment. It was easy to unseat a child emperor,[23] but doing so not only failed to make the slightest change to the power-worshipping political personality, but brought in a dictator a hundred times stronger than the emperor once the moral personality was extinguished.

Sure enough, the good times were short-lived. The alleged betrayal of the Paris Peace Treaty against China's territorial integrity inadvertently sparked the fire that burned down Zhao's Building (赵家楼) on May 4, 1919. The long-suppressed anger and resentment in the hearts of the people finally found an outlet in nationalism and hit it off with Marxism, a revolutionary ideology that is hostile to the Western capitalist order.[24] After the May Fourth

[21] The New Culture Movement was initiated in 1915 by a group of liberal intellectuals centered at Peking University, advocating science and democracy. In four years, however, the liberals on the left and right parted their way, with the leftists leading the more radical "patriotic" May Fourth Movement, actively participated by students. Cheng Wei, "The New Culture Movement and May Fourth Movement: The entangled struggle between two 'spirits'," 《中华读书报》 (July 13, 2011), https://culture.ifeng.com/sixiang/detail_2014_01/13/32963795_0.shtml.

[22] Long labeled by the leftists as "the flag carrier (旗手) of the New Culture Movement," Lu Xun is regarded as the author of the first vernacular Chinese (白话文) novel, *A Madman's Diary* 《狂人日记》, published in 1918. He is still wildly popular in China today. See Li Oufan, *Shouting in the Iron House: A Study of Lu Xun*, trans. Yin Huimin [in Chinese] (Hong Kong: Sanlian Bookstore, 1991).

[23] The Last Emperor, Puyi (溥仪), ascended to the throne in 1908, at only six years old.

[24] Chow Tse-tung, *The May Fourth Movement: Intellectual Revolution in Modern China* (Boston: Harvard University Press, 1960).

Movement, under the active matchmaking of the newborn Soviet regime, China quickly moved from anarchism to totalitarianism. "Three Peoples Doctrine" (三民主义) and Communism successively replaced Confucianism as the national orthodoxy. It was only natural that a nation deficient in political personality failed to resist the invasion of variants of political despotism, the establishment and consolidation of which ultimately killed China's moral personality. The "patriotism" is in essence based on the hollowing out of individual personality. The phantom of the supreme state completely devoured individuals as moral beings, reducing everyone to mere dust without independent value or inner dignity, barely surviving under the patronage of an arbitrary state authority. Once individuals lost all human value and moral baseline, China opened its doors to massive destructions such as "revolution," rebellions (造反) and slaughter, with its people embracing the great dictator as their "great savior" and willingly obeying his orders to mutilate each other. A politically ignorant nation is bound to be wretched. Countless people will pay for their ignorance and depravity with their lives and blood.

China's greatest failure over the past century lies in its failure to reflect on the root causes of all failures, leaving the entire nation to linger in the petty grievances and frustrations. The Communists blamed all evil on Western "imperialism," domestic "feudalism" and "counter-revolutionary forces" plotting to sabotage the great revolutionary causes, while claiming itself to be the only "correct" and "advanced" (先进) force, thus justified in taking any means to eliminate the obstacles to the revolution. Under such a "theory," everyone who has accepted these "advanced" ideas becomes a god, who can only do the right things. As a result, any outrageous actions can be justified, while anyone who disagrees with "god" is an obstacle to "progress," thus a sinner against the nation and an enemy of the state, who must be removed to please the people. In essence, of course, these "revolutionary" doctrines are nothing more than a shield for criminal syndicates to seize state power through violence, while packaging their inflated personal desires under deceptive names such as "ideas," "theories" or "beliefs." They fully mobilize and manipulate human greed, arrogance, and fear, thereby completely freeing people from their inner sense of responsibility, for themselves and others, turning them into thugs who have no reverence except for power.

The revolutionary personality is repugnant to Confucian moral values. A revolutionary vanguard believes that they are gods who never err, while the people are, in reality, ignorant masses with low consciousness (觉悟) and limited abilities, who desperately need leadership and education, and the opponents are unforgivable enemies who must be physically exterminated. In their eyes, these "reactionaries" are no more than obstacles to social progress, devoid of intrinsic value and dignity, with nothing but evil inside them. If a speck of dust is merely insignificant, "counter-revolutionaries" are destined to do great evil; eliminating them not only removes a scourge for humankind, but also liberates and absolves themselves. As Chairman Mao astutely pointed out, "reactionary forces . . . will not voluntarily exit the stage of history."[25] Therefore, they must be destroyed by the "advanced" forces with violence. In the sanguinary rains of revolution and in the face of naked violence, personal dignity, and a sense of shame disappear without a trace, leaving behind only personal tyranny. Once they establish their rule, of course, such a ruling party "will never voluntarily exit the stage of history," nor is there any social or political force remaining to check and counterbalance the newborn supreme power. The "liberator" has become an unprecedented oppressor.

5.3.3 *The Depravation of Humanity under Absolute Despotism*

In a country where power overwhelms everything, moral corruption is an inevitable outcome. Power is by nature unrelated to morality – if anything, it inhibits moral motives and practices. The fact of holding power, especially through violent means, does not make it right or good. But once power becomes a social currency that is not only exchangeable for money, honors, and diplomas,[26] among other things, but also the source of its own legitimacy, then power becomes synonymous with truth, and society is bound to lose its basic moral standards. The monopoly of power over moral judgment is futile, however, not only because people's inner judgments cannot possibly be always consistent with the absolute orders of power, but also because power itself is highly fluid and unpredictable. One who sat on the high seat of party secretary yesterday, "preaching against corruption and advocating for integrity" (反腐倡廉), may well end up as a corrupt official in prison tomorrow. Such facetious scenes, increasingly common in the era of reform, cannot fail to confuse and dilute the moral conviction of common people, leaving behind ubiquitous worship of power and money. Everyone is eager to forget his moral nature and hollow out his inner self, reducing himself to a shell of emptiness cast by power, money, and desire.

25 Mao Zedong, Carry on the Revolution to the End (December 30, 1948) [in Chinese], www.marxists.org/chinese/maozedong/marxist.org-chinese-mao-19481230.htm.

26 Chu Heng, ed., "Why are officials keen on doctoral degrees?" 《瞭望中国》 (December 10, 2010), www.outlookchina.net/html/news/201012/2032.html.

Although the CCP claims to have faith in Marxism, Marxism is primarily a theory of political economy, not a moral doctrine about how humans *should* behave. Even if Marx himself might have been morally motivated in developing his theory, his theory is supposed to be purely empirical – in his word, "scientific" – with minimal moral sentiments. Indeed, he very much despised moral sentiments as shallow elements of mere "superstructure" (上层建筑), which is to be determined by the more profound economic basis (经济基础). In his "scientific" paradigm in which the non-human "productive forces" (生产力) dominate the entire human history, religious faith or moral belief were relegated to the vicinity of personal "superstition," serving as "spiritual opium" to delude the poor or palliate their sufferings. Since every despotic regime needs a unified ideology to buttress its legitimacy, however, the Chinese version of Marxism has become an all-encompassing sack of scientific truths, from which all nice things such as economics, political science, law, philosophy, even liberal arts conveniently derived their birth. Sadly, such a grandiose doctrine, claiming to "liberate all mankind," is based on a slave personality. In the "scientific" deterministic discourse of productive forces, productive relations (生产关系) and superstructure, a person is no more than a tiny screw on the mammoth machine of human history, which evolves according to the economic laws. Individual freedom is at most an occasional caprice committed by those who fail to understand the iron laws of economic development; self-determination is even more ridiculous, arrogant gibberish made in total ignorance of the profound "inevitable laws." Even the collective will of the vast majority is doomed to be futile in front of "laws" that dictate the necessary death of capitalism and inevitable victory of socialism. In this completely dehumanized economic world, it is hard to see any need to believe in anything, nor is there anything worth believing in, despite the official categorization of Communism and Marxism as "beliefs."

The greatest mistake of Marx was not that he failed to fully appreciate the decisive "counteraction" (反作用) of human consciousness on material development, but that his materialist framework of "existence determining consciousness" completely objectified and demoralized humans by binding the living to the "iron law" of economic development determined by the production forces. Unconditionally prioritizing one part of human activities – the economy – above all else, his "materialistic" theory submerged the entirety of a human being in the economic interest, reducing moral beliefs to "ideologies" subservient to their "economic basis." "Fair competition" is but a myth deliberately fabricated by mainstream bourgeois scholars; "getting rich through hard work" is either a lie that exploiters deliberately fabricated to deceive the exploited or an illusion of the latter to comfort themselves. Under the aegis of the ineluctable economic "laws," the "system" bears responsibility for everything. All virtues appear hypocritical, just as all vices become excusable. Poverty is deemed sufficient in itself to justify theft and prostitution. Even the exploiters, whose "capital comes dripping from head to foot, from every pore, with blood and dirt,"[27] can blame the vicious capitalist system for creating their insatiable greed. Since everything is the inevitable result of the productive forces, and every evil can be blamed on the institution hindering the development of productive forces, individual responsibility becomes utterly meaningless. Nor is there anything left for anyone to do. If China's lack of democracy is attributed solely to its GDP not reaching a mysterious "turning point,"[28] what can the Chinese people do to promote their country's political progress? Once Marxism transforms into an omnipotent "truth" capable of "explaining" everything, it is reduced to a sophistry for crime and depravation. Its rise as a state orthodoxy is destined to be accompanied by bloodshed and violence, while its fall will inevitably leave a fallen civilization of petty men preoccupied with material gain and unsatiable desires.

Once the "system" became the scapegoat for all evils, "smashing the murderous old world" naturally became the Marxist revolutionary program, as if everything could be saved simply by changing the system. When the Communist Manifesto asserted that "the proletarians have nothing to lose but their chains. They have a world to win,"[29] however, it forgot that every "proletarian" at least had a human life. It is morally unjust to goad the "proletariat" – if there is such a class – to risk their lives in order to eliminate the "bourgeoisie" through violence. From the Confucian perspective, no purpose, however noble, can justify such means because it destroys the very essence of human beings. Advocates of violent revolution ignore a commonsensical judgment: Institutions or collective behavior can never be solely responsible for individual choices. Ultimately, individuals who are free to choose are responsible for their own choice of action. In fact, despite the obvious significance of economic interest, individuals always have a degree of moral freedom. Even those living under a totalitarian regime still enjoy some spiritual and intellectual freedom. I simply fail to see why a capitalist cannot

[27] Karl Marx, *Capital*, in Tucker, Robert ed., *The Marx-Engels Reader*, 2nd ed. (New York: W. W. Norton & Co., 1978), p. 435.

[28] The notion of "middle-income trap" has caught much attention in the recent decade. See Michael R. Powers, "'Middle-income trap'? Perhaps a false proposition for China," *China Daily* (February 16, 2022), https://cn.chinadaily.com.cn/a/202202/16/WS620cec67a3107be497a0691f.html.

[29] Karl Marx and Friedrich Engels, *The Communist Manifesto* (New York: International Publishers, 1948), p. 44.

have minimal compassion or generosity towards the poor, as Engels generously supported Marx, or as many Chinese elites of wealthy birth led the Communist revolution initially intended to liberate the poor; or why every "proletarian" is necessarily so "selfless" as to sacrifice her life for a greater cause; or why a capitalist would wait foolishly for his fate, knowing that his "death knell" is bound to ring sooner or later, instead of negotiating with the "proletariat" to jointly establish a more humanized private ownership and market order through a democratic process. Much less can I understand why the Athenians and Romans could practice forms of democracy more than two millennia ago under slavery systems, and England and the United States could thrive through constitutionalism in agricultural ages centuries ago, while China, having at least entered the "primary stage of socialism" since its constitutional amendment in 1993, cannot afford to allow its people to become the real "masters of the house" (当家作主).

As the history of contemporary China has shown, the causal relation between theory and practice can occasionally be reversed. Marx never correctly predicted China's political and economic development, yet all the Chinese people have fallen into the trap of his economic determinism. In the past four decades, although the Reform and Opening effectively breached the planned economy that kept the people in servitude, the trap of economism has remained intact as China's dominant thinking pattern. The basic purpose of the reform is no more than "improving people's livelihood" or "enhancing the overall national strength," with the basic premise that the people are not only hopeless economic animals whose horizon never rises beyond their own subsistence, family wealth, or national GDP, but also incompetent economic animals who are incapable of breaking the chain of their servitude, predestined to rely on the state tutelage and endure its exploitation. The situation has fundamentally deteriorated since the crackdown on the democratic protests in 1989, when the reform was completely hijacked by the vested interest, which has since dominated the direction of China's development. Without popular participation, the "reform" can only benefit a handle of power holders at the expense of the long-term public interest, monopolizing and dividing among themselves not only wealth but also basic public goods such as land, environment, and natural resources. In an age where the revolutionary orthodoxy has lost its efficacy, the collective planned economy has proved to be a fiasco, and the statist "market economy" has monetized all public goods, everyone speeds up his transformation into a veritable economic animal.

Having first experienced the baptism of the "scientific" theory of Marxism-Leninism that effectively eradicated all faiths, followed by the collapse of the

Marxist-Leninist "faith" itself, the moral courage has come to near extinction in China today. The nation is reduced to a group of economic animals crawling under power and money. While the ruling group keeps amassing wealth with all means, the ruled, oppressed by multiple "mountains" of expensive housing, rising cost of living and education, and deficient social security, can hardly catch their breath.[30] Whether tempted by desires or pressed by survival, everyone seems to be inexplicably approaching the doomsday in the midst of "rapid development." While rural children can hardly see any hope for their tomorrow, the city children are hopelessly stuck in a marathon competition for one exam after another ever since their elementary school. In a nation of 1.4 billion people today, nobody seems to have the heart or leisure for their own moral cultivation. Serious discussions of the national future find interest only among a handful of disgruntled, idle literati. In a nation where the moral personality has been ruined, while the political personality has never taken shape and has suffered from serious malformation under decades of totalitarian education, the recurrent chaos witnessed today seems to be a predestined fate.

After experiencing the repeated ordeals of revolution and tyranny, China has entered an era without reflection, remorse, integrity, and sense of shame. An example is the contemporary spectacle of the "Fifty Cent Party" (五毛党), referring to a group that is paid – fifty cents per message, as rumored – by the state for distributing misinformation on the internet. China today is far from its revolutionary heydays in 1950s and 1960s. As a poet announced during the ceremonial protest on April 5, 1976, half a year before the fall of the Gang of Four (四人帮), "the people are no longer fools." "Fifty Cents" do not necessarily accept the official orthodoxy they help to propagate, and cannot use ignorance as an excuse for what they do. Adhering to the motto of "whoever having milk is as good as a mother," however, they willingly sell themselves to the devil in order to gain a small profit, thereby reducing their value to a few coins. The vast majority of China's academic "leftists" sound leftist not because they truly believe in the leftist policies or are unaware of their past consequences to China, but because they are seeking the best position to maximize their own opportunities within the existing ideological discourse system. In fact, there is hardly anything "left" about the Chinese leftists. Western leftists may hold disagreeable positions, but at least their integrity is unquestioned because the "left" stands for a minority who is often critical of

30 Much frustrated by "involution" (内卷) caused by heated competition and reduced opportunities, the Chinese young generation is increasingly inclined to "lying flat" (躺平), namely, doing nothing.

the government policies and the mainstream public opinion. On the contrary, China's leftists are either a group of brainwashed "angry youth" who have been thoroughly brainwashed by the nationalist historical education, or a more sophisticated faction, sometimes labeled as "New Left," who deliberately use the misleading historical views and manipulated public opinions to covet bigger rewards from the party-state. A group of impotent and opportunistic academics who cannot establish themselves in scholarship is apt to take advantage of shoddy "patriotism" to win popularity, or turn the critical theory of the West on its head to please the Chinese government. For an academic group that dedicates its soul entirely to the state, nationalism is its most natural and lucrative destiny. If the liberal voices, severely circumscribed by censorship, are not enough to counter the leftist incitement and radical populism, China is at great risk of repeating the fatal mistakes of the May Fourth Movement in 1919, while staging the fascist drama as Germany and Japan did in the same era.

Nationalism is in essence a deformity with its parts put together in a reversed order. It appeals to the construction of political state before the moral construction is properly completed. In China it originated from the historical sediment agitated by a group of marginal academics, who by themselves were unable to make it popular in a nation constantly beleaguered by domestic crisis. Under decades of distorted history education and heavy manipulation of public opinion by the party-state, however, the long depressed Chinese people have long nurtured a character of petty man, who is apt to bully the weak but yield to the power, and blame others for their own failures. As a result, they are easily inclined to take the imaginary and unreachable "international anti-China forces" as an outlet to vent their frustrations, often erupting into feverish waves of nationalism upon the slightest provocation of territorial disputes with the neighboring nations. The popular mood converges perfectly with the party-state's lofty "patriotic" posture. A ruling power thoroughly bankrupt in ideology can only play with the banner of "patriotism," surreptitiously swapping the notations of state (国家), nation (民族) and parties (政党), and proclaim itself as the representative of national interests by default, thereby binding everyone to the militaristic, self-destructive war chariot.

Ironically, in China today, government officials are among the most Westernized groups. They not only maintain frequent contacts with the West through regular state visits and "study" (考察) trips,[31] but also may have

[31] The word becomes a pejorative since many such "study" visits are little more than paid tourism for the power holders.

family members working or studying abroad, and have sizable deposits in overseas banks, making them most fearful of offending Western governments. Since indoctrinating militarism is tantamount to digging its own grave, a vested interest group of such a scale should serve as a secure assurance for China's "peaceful rise" (和平崛起). Unfortunately, as the human rationality is limited, decades of "patriotic" indoctrination of the party-state have added to the crater of radical sentiments, awaiting only an unexpected accident to ignite a national self-immolation. Originated from the desperate need for political legitimacy, nationalism may well be turned into a cause for subverting the very legitimacy it is supposed to defend. The nationalist sentiments kindled by the party-state have cradled a group of trumpeters ready to meet every nationalist demand, whose tireless clamoring will one day bring this insufferably arrogant nation to the brink of destruction.

To be sure, if international conflicts exacerbated by the "China rise" may still take time to ferment, the domestic conflicts have already been cropping up incessantly everywhere. The bustling events need no elaboration since, in the age of internet, someone who lives outside China can get a gist simply by browsing. They arise without exception from serious abuses of a public power completely out of control, which are well expected in a country that has suffered from decades of political disorder and moral destruction. In a society where political power has always been invincible, the power holders' ambitions, greed, and arrogance will necessarily inflate without bound, while the governed cower in fear and timidity, reluctant to stand up and resist until their own living is threatened. Even if the daily headlines are crowded with life-and-death events, more cunning exploitation. and encroachment on the public interest without necessarily involving the loss of life go unnoticed. In fact, surrounded daily by a plethora of fresh events, both the government and the governed have long developed fatigue and "adaptation" to the eventful living environment. As time goes by, they may even lose the common sense for moral judgment, taking abuses and tragedies for granted as normal part of life. When a nation loses its basic sense of right, wrong, and shame, to the point of ignorance of what is shameful (无耻之耻), then any event, however earth shattering, will fail to even raise curiosity. If China keeps "developing" in this trend, its millennia-old civilization will perish in the short span of a few generations, together with its great rivers and mountains. In a nation where the morals have decayed and the public power has never come under public control, the material foundation on which its survival depends will sooner or later crumble. Facing threats of resource depletion and environmental degradation, China has truly reached its "most dangerous moment."

5.4 THE RECONSTRUCTION OF CHINESE MORAL AND POLITICAL PERSONALITY

For China to return to the track of reason and peace, and away from the tyranny, revolutions, political movements and pseudo-"development" it has suffered for over a century, its people must first restore their moral dignity and sense of shame. To plunder the people's wealth is as shameful as a petty theft, as is abusing public finances for self-enrichment or extravagance, committing the nation to blind "development," depleting natural resources, polluting the environment, and bringing scourge to the people, all for the officials' own "merit projects" (政绩工程).[32] It is shameful to have great power but fail to fulfill the Confucian promise of "allowing the elderly to end peacefully, the middle-aged to contribute labor, the youth to grow up properly, and providing support to the widowed, the lonely, and the abandoned."[33] It is shameful to prohibit criticism of the poor governance, or manipulate elections in order to maintain the ruling power, or monopolize news media to fabricate a "great, glorious, and correct" image for the party-state. Equally shameful is the mutual harm and reckless disregard that people cause to each other by polluting the environment or producing poisonous food. It is shameful to ignore one's political rights stipulated in the Constitution, and resort solely to petitioning or begging when mistreated by the government. It is also shameful for the media to tell lies or fail to report the truth out of fear, and for scholars to remain silent before social injustice or preach lofty principles without practicing them, or flatter leaders with eulogies and lead the nation astray with radical nationalism.

Whether as an official or a private citizen, if everyone can recover the basic sense of shame, Chinese society would have avoided countless tragedies and travesties. To restore a sense of shame, the people must be conscious of their inner value and dignity, and stop regarding themselves as mere dust who are incapable of deciding their own destiny; stop degrading themselves into objects driven by power, interests, desires, and fear; stop serving as obedient slaves to the party-state, echoing without reflecting on its propaganda, and acting as "never-rusting screws" on the totalitarian machinery. A despotic regime is, in fact, one of the most fragile in the world, buttressed only by popular fear and reduced to nothing the moment when the majority wakes up and fears no more. Only after the people awaken can China stay away from

[32] More accurately, "face projects" (面子工程), which contribute nothing to the true benefits of the people but deceptive "merits" that officials need for their promotion.

[33] These are the Confucian ideals expressed in the *Book of Rites* 《礼记》, Ch. 9.

corruption, shame, fear, tyranny, insanity, collective cowardice, man-made tragedies, and crises of all sorts. For China to stand up in the world, the Chinese people must first stand up and establish themselves, restore their moral common sense, cherish their virtuous nature endowed by Heaven, and become fully conscious of their own dignity. This means that they need to complete the moral and political transformation from the personality of subjects to one of citizens.

5.4.1 *The Rebirth of Traditional Moral Personality*

While China's revival requires a new moral point of departure, the reconstruction of Chinese moral personality is not carried out in a historical desert, but can make full use of Confucian moral resources. As a moral tradition that has sustained Chinese civilization for more than two millennia, Confucianism is far from being an obstacle to constitutionalism; on the contrary, it embodies elements of constitutionalism itself. Admittedly, its moral dogmatism and political authoritarianism were incompatible with modern constitutionalism, making critical assessment and doctrinal adjustment necessary. Since education has been popularized in contemporary China, Confucians today can no longer claim the monopoly of cultivated moral and intellectual virtues by a few "gentlemen," while insisting on the moral immaturity of most people as mere "petty men." In the contemporary world where equality has long been a widely accepted idea and equality in education is a basic constitutional right, a roughly equal education confers everyone an equal opportunity to become a "gentleman" – that is, a competent citizen – and therefore, the equal right to participate in public affairs. After dispensing with the dogmatic and despotic elements, the Confucian theory on human dignity is capable of laying a solid foundation for the reconstruction of the Chinese moral personality.

Confucians believe that "Heaven endows virtues in me";[34] "all things are already complete in me. There can be no greater delight than to feel sincerity upon self-examination."[35] Confucian ethics aims to awaken human consciousness of inner dignity and help humans to gain moral autonomy and self-discipline. Since Heaven has endowed humans with health, courage, and moral and intellectual capacities, we should cherish this life and constantly strive for self-perfection, instead of giving up on ourselves or reducing ourselves to slaves of others or our own desires. As individuals, we are intelligent enough to understand things in the world, enabling us to make independent

[34] *Analects*, 7: 22.
[35] *Mengzi*, 7A: 4.

judgments without disturbances from the "Big Brother." Our moral maturity prevents shameful ideas from poisoning our minds, such as jobbery, bribing the powerful, or bullying the weak. With healthy and diligent limbs, we have no need to beg for alms, much less bow down to power. With enough confidence and courage, we can deal with people uprightly, handle things calmly, and speak candidly. If we have made a mistake, we must be brave enough to reflect honestly and take responsibility, rather than covering it up and evading our responsibility. Endowed with unique capabilities, we should strive to follow the model of Mencius' "great man": "to dwell in the magnificent house of humanity, to stand in the right place of propriety, and to walk on the great path of righteousness."[36]

Of course, the Confucian consciousness of innate dignity does not make anyone an omnipotent god. On the contrary, human dignity, properly understood, is partly reflected in one's sober cognition of his own limitations and equal respect for the dignity of others. Humans are noble in the sense that they are endowed with potentials for a sound conscience and capacities, but they cannot guarantee that everything they do necessarily aligns with their true selves. If they have not fully developed their virtues and capacities, they should reflect on themselves and constantly strive for improvement – a theme frequently found in Confucian teachings. As Confucius advises, "do not worry about not having a position, worry about that which establishes you for the position";[37] "a gentleman is like an archer, who first rectifies himself before shooting; if he misses the target, he reflects on himself rather than blaming others for defeating him."[38] As rational beings, humans can see their weaknesses and limitations as long as they are willing to sincerely face themselves, constantly reflecting on their words and deeds. Once they realize that their actions fall below their innate virtues, they should feel shameful and strive to improve their virtues.

Therefore, the first virtue of a gentleman is sincerity: "There is no greater joy than being sincere upon reflecting on oneself."[39] To be truthful to others, one must first be truthful to oneself. While one can deceive others, he can never truly deceive himself unless he chooses to escape from reality, refusing to face his own soul. If one will even deceive himself, there is no one in the world he cannot deceive. Confucians despise hypocrites who say one thing but mean another, as it not only leads to deceptive falsehood, but also forms a

[36] *Mengzi*, 3B: 2.
[37] *Analects*, 14: 30; 15: 19.
[38] *Mengzi*, 2A: 7.
[39] *Mengzi*, 7A: 4.

vice of escaping from reality. The ultimate escape for humans is escaping from themselves. Once a person begins to deny his inner value and dignity, refusing to face himself in reality, he will not only lose direction and motivation in life, but will blame all his faults and failures on external factors such as "imperialism," "anti-China forces," "the stage of social development," "institutional defects" or "the order from a superior." Ultimately, he will reduce himself to a petty man, complaining and making excuses all day without striving for improvement, with the inevitable result of "beginning with an error of one centimeter, ending with a blunder of a thousand miles." Without sincerity, all the other virtues, be they talent, eloquence, or diligence, will only lead him further astray.

Conscience (良知) and virtues (良能) that humans can feel within themselves also enable everyone to recognize that others are endowed with the same inherent value and dignity, requiring one to respect others before demanding respect from them. Even if one cannot follow the positive form of the Golden Rule: "establish others when you want to establish yourself,"[40] he should at least abide by the negative form of the Golden Rule: "Do not impose on the others what you do not wish others to impose on you."[41] Rousseau erred by taking reflection to be the source of evils such as jealousy, rancor, and greed among humans. While his "reflection" seemed to be no more than an unconditioned reflex derived from natural evolution,[42] Confucian reflection is rational introspection derived from contrasting one's own words and deeds, usually upon provocation of external events. Thus, if others show disrespect to me, I will first reflect on myself and examine if I have committed any fault, and follow what Confucius would do in like circumstances:

> On self-examination, if I find that I fail to be righteous, I would not threaten a single man, be he in an inferior status; but on self-examination, if I find that I *am* righteous, I will go forward even against a crowd of ten million men.[43]

Since all humans have equal inner dignity, it is particularly important to properly define the boundary between oneself and others. For a self-reliant, independent gentleman, it is obviously shameful to encroach on others' interests; knowingly doing so would reduce him to a petty thief. In principle, every economic and social interaction should be based on

40 *Analects*, 12: 2.

41 *Analects*, 15: 24.

42 Jean-Jacques Rousseau, *Discourse on Origin and Foundations of Inequality among Men*, trans. Maurice Cranston (New York: Penguin Books, 1984), pp. 36, 70, 101.

43 *Mengzi*, 2A: 2.

informed consent, and every cooperation must be a voluntary agreement by all parties without coercion or fraud. Conflicts that cannot be settled through mediation should be resolved through a transparent and impartial procedure agreeable to all parties.

If a modern gentleman is "not guilty upon introspection,"[44] then he *will* fight for his legitimate interests with moral confidence. Human dignity means that a person is more than the traditional subject of obligation; one who knows only selfless dedication is little more than a selfless slave without self-consciousness. Above all, human dignity is embodied in the consciousness of one's legitimate rights, the equal protection of which is the very purpose of establishing a legitimate nation with its constitution and laws. In a constitutional democracy, indeed, citizens not only compete for rights with each other, but also with the government for rights that properly belong to them. Tolerating state illegality is not only a manifestation of timidity, but also encourages officials to degrade themselves by degrading others.

In an unenviable setting where the morals decline daily, cynicism prevails, and material desires overrun everything, China today urgently needs to rebuild a self-conscious, self-disciplined, self-strengthening, and self-independent moral personality. The Confucian idea of human dignity not only lays the metaphysical foundation for China's moral reconstruction, but also helps to cure the prevalent slavish personality of power worship today by filling the moral voids left behind since the decline of Marxist orthodoxy and transforming Chinese moral personality from one of subjects into one of modern citizens.

5.4.2 *The Reconstruction of Contemporary Moral Personality*

The Confucian doctrine of dignity is not a high-pitched moral preaching but a practical norm that can directly guide ordinary life in China. In reformed Confucianism, even a poor farmer who can barely support himself can become a "gentleman" in modern society, while officials with high positions and heavy powers are more likely to fall into shameless "petty men" under the corrosion of uncontrolled powers. At the bottom, so many tragedies in China today occur because its people have failed not only to treat their compatriots as human beings but also to take their own dignity seriously. Since human dignity is equal in everyone, disrespecting others is equivalent to disrespecting oneself. To change this situation, people must face themselves seriously and act in a manner worthy of their noble nature. A Confucian gentleman will ask

[44] Ibid.

himself: As a person with inner dignity like others, what should I do and not do? How should I behave to comply with my noble nature? In an institutional environment that disrespects human dignity, answering these questions is difficult but not impossible. No matter how others behave and treat themselves, everyone should be able to observe the moral baseline and respect the basic rights and inner dignity of others. At the very least, no one should intentionally harm others through means such as violence, fraud, and abuse of public power.

To be sure, it is not easy for anyone to live with dignity under a regime that regularly tramples on dignity. A despotic regime not only enslaves its people, but also imprisons despots of all sizes as its slaves. Even the supreme ruler is a mere slave to his unchecked power, driven by the forces of ambition, lust, and the perpetual fear of being replaced by someone with similar aspirations. Anyone daring enough to challenge his superior risks immediate demotion. A conscientious official who desires to stay clean will be removed by the community of the corrupted, who see him as a stumbling block to their unrestricted rent-seeking. Judges' dependence on power means the fall of the last bulwark for protecting social justice. While outspoken intellectuals are systemically marginalized, countless academics "steer whither the wind blows" (见风使舵), and willingly render their services to the regime to which they are assimilated. Unable to vindicate their rights through institutional mechanisms, vulnerable groups such as farmers, street peddlers, and victims of city demolition find themselves with no choice but to resort to disgraceful petitioning or, in desperation, to violent and often indiscriminate retaliations. As a result, Chinese society is full of obedient slaves and violent mobs, with the conspicuous absence of citizens who are courageous enough to uphold their dignity through practicing democracy and defending the rule of law. As the government disrespects the people, nor do the people respect the government. Ultimately, regardless of power, status, fame, or wealth, everyone is reduced to a petty man, mired in a petty society replete with mutual defections, despises, harms, and insults.

However, the restoration of Chinese dignity has to start somewhere. In fact, as long as everyone cares a little more about their own dignity as a human being, it is not difficult to build a civil society with mutual respect. Bearing in mind that Confucianism is "a study for oneself" (为己之学), the whole essence of classical Confucian teachings can be distilled into one sentence: Focus on yourself and do what is worthy of you. Being a good person is obviously good for others, but first and foremost, it is good for yourself. The bad deeds of a bad person do hurt others and seemingly profit himself, but he is actually the biggest loser. Corrupt officials embezzle from the national treasury without being discovered, which fattens themselves at the expense of the taxpayers; producing and selling toxic food reduces the farmer's costs, while harming the health of countless consumers; academics who sell their soul and talent to tyranny by singing hymns to the tyrant may indeed be awarded with fame and wealth, while contributing to the corruption of national morals. In doing so, however, they pay the price of reducing themselves to "corrupt officials" (贪官), "dishonest profiteers" (奸商) and "court-hired literati."

Humans today are keen to take medicine when they catch colds, seek medical treatment when their little fingers get hurt, dye their hair and make up their faces for a youthful appearance, and even take good care of flowers and trees in their gardens. When their own souls have fallen into corruption, however, they not only show no interest in saving them, but even take secret delight and tirelessly indulge in aggravating the corruption. While one's body, appearance, and material possessions like power, wealth, houses, cars, and even flowers seem to belong to oneself, strangely enough, one's own soul decidedly does not. As Mencius said: "Why do you love yourself not as much as you love your plant? That is a failure of thinking taken to the extreme!"[45] Mencius posed to everyone a question worth contemplating: What is the self? What is truly "good" for "me"? What kind of life is worth pursuing? After all, life is lived only once, and a life without contemplation is not worth living.[46]

To take life seriously, one must first do justice to their profession which is, after all, the very basis of everyone's livelihood. The basic social contract in modern society implies the rough balance of giving and taking: Each person does his own job and contributes to others, while receiving commensurate rewards in return. A person who fails to fulfill the professional duty inevitably lives by deceit, which is in essence no different from the behavior of a thief. In China where the moral baseline has been collectively breached, it is not superfluous to reiterate some moral common sense. The duty of officials is to properly govern the country, rather than abusing public power for personal gain. The duty of soldiers is to safeguard all people from physical injuries, rather than defending the vested interest of the small ruling group, or squandering national wealth by colluding with the vested interests, much less peddling militarism to maintain their own status and interests. The duty of scholars is to explore truth and critically analyze the social problems, rather than collaborating with and assisting the tyrannical regime. The duty of businessmen is to offer safe and reliable products for consumers, rather than

[45] *Mengzi*, 6A: 13.

[46] Plato, *Five Dialogues*, trans. G. M. A. Grube (Indianapolis: Hackett, 1981), p. 41.

seeking profits through counterfeiting, producing shoddy goods, exploiting workers, or neglecting to control industrial pollution. The duty of farmers is to provide healthy and hygienic food for all, rather than jeopardizing the national health through various harmful, cost-cutting processes. Taking one's profession seriously means adhering to professional ethics and codes of conduct, doing one's best to fulfill one's own responsibilities, and making the appropriate contributions to society.

Only when all walks of life respect each other and perform their own duties can China return to a normal society and its people gain dignity. Everyone has an obligation to treat others as human beings, not merely as a means for profiteering. Officials should treat the people as human beings and be held accountable for their policies and decisions, rather than taking the public interest as their own property. Scholars should treat their students and the general public as humans, and refrain from misleading and corrupting the public with irresponsible remarks. Urban residents should treat peasants as humans and refrain from discrimination and deprivation, while peasants should treat the city residents as humans and ensure the quality of the food they produce.

In fact, when we treat others as mere means for profit, we have already given up our own dignity. By fully objectifying others, we have reduced ourselves to animals controlled by our own greed. Even if treated as a tool for profit by others, the legitimate response is not to reciprocate in kind, but to use laws to protect our dignity and rights from infringement and get beyond the zero-sum game of mutual debasement and reciprocal poisoning, in which Chinese society is currently trapped. If the government treats the people as objects of exploitation and oppression, laws alone may not suffice to protect their basic rights. The legitimate action is not colluding with it or harboring resentment towards the rich and powerful, which is commonly seen in Chinese society today, but actively engaging in the political process, reforming the government composition, and exerting control over public power. Only by making the constitutional and legal mechanisms work will the government be held accountable to the governed.

5.4.3 *The Transformation of Political Personality: From Subjects to Citizens*

Once positioned within a value system centered on human dignity, Confucianism and modern civic spirit are highly compatible. Under the authoritarian tradition and limited by the economic and educational conditions of the time, however, Confucians failed to envision the possibility of political democracy, taking for granted that only a small minority could become diligent, accomplished and upright "gentlemen," while the vast majority would regrettably remain "petty men" who had no choice but passively accept the rule of the "gentlemen." Yet, later generations are by no means destined to interpret Confucianism as a variant of moral dogmatism upholding political despotism. On the contrary, the technical progress of modern civilization has prepared the material conditions for universal education, providing everyone with the opportunity to receive basic education and become morally and intellectually mature "gentlemen." Therefore, Confucians no longer have reason to insist on an elitist ethics that defends political despotism. Since everyone has the inherent dignity that is capable of growing into a self-respecting, self-disciplined, self-reliant, and self-strengthening gentleman, everyone should have the right to actively participate in public affairs and political activities closely tied to their own interests, rather than passively accepting the rule of others. The state must not institutionally deprive the people of the right to political participation, as doing so would trample on their dignity and infringe on their basic rights to moral and political autonomy. In fact, under modern social conditions, Confucianism will neither uphold political despotism nor tolerate those passive and indolent "petty men," who have disregarded and given up their own political dignity. On the contrary, it will urge everyone to undertake the personal responsibility of political participation commensurate to their dignity, thereby simultaneously completing the personal transformation from subjects to citizens and the institutional transformation from despotism to constitutionalism.

The fundamental difference between modern citizens and subjects of a despotic regime lies in their political personality. While subjects lack political personality and thus are compelled to passively accept the rule by others, willingly reducing themselves to political slaves, citizens have a keen awareness of their intrinsic value and dignity. They insist on their personal independence and accept only governance according to general laws, in which they actively participate in forming. As a result of their active participation in the political process, citizens govern themselves by influencing the formation of institutions, laws, and policies. In the transition from despotism to constitutional democracy, the majority must first transform themselves from passive political subjects to active citizens.

Citizens not only have a sound moral personality, which is reflected in their respect for the intrinsic values of their own and others, but also cherish their rights and obligations to participate in public affairs. True citizens, never willing to passively accept the rule of others, actively exercise their right to vote, manage public affairs through elected representatives, establish laws that constrain their own behaviors and those of others, and supervise officials to faithfully enforce the law. Through free communication, citizens seek to understand the problems facing society, fellow citizens' opinions and various candidates' positions. To ensure free communication, they insist on complete freedom of speech, press, assembly and association, demanding that the government fully honors the right to know.

In summary, through a "creative transformation,"[47] Confucianism can become the foundation of modern civic morality, motivating and guiding ordinary people to complete the transformation from subjects to citizens. To live with dignity, people must first establish a sound moral and political personality and become self-reliant, self-respecting, and self-strengthening citizens. This transformation does not require shedding blood or causing harm to oneself and others for any "noble" revolutionary cause. Instead, it simply demands that everyone respects their own and others' life and dignity, recognizes their value as human beings in their daily lives, fulfills their moral responsibilities to their families and society, participates in local public affairs and safeguards their basic rights as citizens guaranteed by the constitution through actions. Every citizen has a responsibility to take their speech and actions seriously, cherish and maintain an environment friendly to freedom of speech and press, and actively participate in public discussions and periodic elections. Even if one cannot personally run for office, he should at least come out and vote on election day. Although the current system in China makes elections seem meaningless, they will never acquire meaning without active participation of citizens. Only when a majority of citizens begin to take their votes seriously can one find hope for China's constitutional democracy.

5.5 FROM CONSTITUTION TO CONSTITUTIONALISM

The Xinhai Revolution was originally aimed at enhancing China's national and personal dignity by overthrowing the imperial despotism and establishing a democratic republic. Unfortunately, the revolution not only failed to establish the political personality required by modern democracy, but also destroyed the traditional moral personality that could have facilitated China's political transition. The legacy of totalitarian barbarity is still a collective disgrace to all the Chinese people today and the root cause of global disdain for China. The totalitarian legacy continues to poison the Chinese personality, making everyone cower in fear under the mighty paws of the state. Popular apathy, myopia, and cowardice act as the very scaffold that maintains the

[47] For the transformative possibility of Confucian culture, see Tu Wei-Ming, *Confucian Thought: Selfhood as Creative Transformation* (Albany: SUNY Press, 1985).

totalitarian machine. To break free from this bondage, the support of conscientious forces within the regime is undoubtedly an important resource. However, to rely on the despotic regime as a whole, which benefits from its vested interest in maintaining despotism, is clearly seeking the impossible. In fact, it has been the greatest obstacle to China's path towards constitutionalism over the past century. As Lord Acton famously observed, "power corrupts, absolute power corrupts absolutely." The monopoly of political power has generated immense profits, corrupting the consciences of most power holders, who are most unlikely to change unless compelled to relinquish some power and interests under the pressure of an awakened citizenry. In the end, real change will emerge once the people themselves establish their own political personality based on the restoration of their moral dignity. Only when the people become capable citizens can they construct and sustain a true constitutional republic.

5.5.1 *Establishing the Social Contract*

The constitutional transformation begins with wide consensus and commitments among citizens concerning the mutual recognition and respect of human dignity inherent in every human being, giving rise to human rights and freedoms. Based on these mutual commitments, they establish a social contract for the reconstruction of their nation, determining the nature, form and powers of the state thus established, and formulating its constitution. Establishing a constitutional state entails that citizens place themselves under the law and are obliged to respect the dignity and rights of others. Only through the law can the state limit the freedom of citizens; any illegal act is void. Since fundamental rights touch the core of human dignity and are critical for maintaining constitutional democracy, they should not be restricted even by laws enacted through legitimate procedures.

In short, China's new social contract is characterized by four basic principles: liberty (自由), democracy (民主), the rule of law (法治), and federalism (联邦) or local autonomy. As the fundamental principles of modern constitutionalism, they are indispensable to any constitutional democracy and constitute the basic "pillars" (国体) of a modern constitutional state. The purpose of establishing a state is to protect the people's basic freedoms such as life, liberty, property, and the pursuit of happiness. While the nature of the state is a democratic republic, the governing scheme is the rule of law with checks and balances, with a reasonable division of powers between the central and local governments. The effective protection of local autonomy through the constitution means federalism for a sizable nation like China.

First, a constitutional state is a liberal state. Since the purpose of enacting a democratic constitution is to effectively safeguard the inherent dignity of every person, the state is obliged to respect the basic rights and freedoms of individuals, without which everyone would be reduced to a political slave under the tyranny of the despotic regime. Only in a liberal democracy can individuals live as independent, free, and rational citizens. Therefore, it is necessary for the constitution to protect the following basic rights and freedoms.

(1) Freedom of thought and expression (including speech, press, assembly, and association). The essence of democracy is that the national will is determined by the popular will, not the reverse. The majority's opinion should be formed in an open platform where the people can freely express, debate, accept or reject various views and ideas based on facts and information they freely receive. The state imposition of opinions is illegal and invalid. No party, organization or individual can legitimately claim a priori truth or force others to accept these self-proclaimed "truths." To ensure the free and peaceful formation of opinions, the state's legitimate violence is primarily limited to countering private violence, which usually occurs through action rather than speech. Only when a speech poses an imminent danger to society, leaving no time for meaningful discussion before material harm results, can the state suppress it through the law. Otherwise, debate is always the more effective way to explore truth and clarify errors.[48] Since the Chinese propaganda is fond of claiming that "the eyes of the masses are bright as snow," they should be allowed to decide for themselves. The ordinary people have the ability to choose among various claims what is most preferable to them, making it unjustified to suppress public debate and information disclosure. Whether a claim is deemed good or bad by the state or the majority, it can be freely spread unless it clearly vitiates public interest by means such as advocating violations of law or instigating violence. The harms hidden in a speech can only be exposed and countered by other speeches. Since the few elites in the government are no wiser than ordinary people, the latter is the final arbiter, capable of making informed judgments.

(2) The free practice of religion and belief. As the innermost human activity, religious and moral practices constitute the core of human dignity that is beyond the reach of the state. By cultivating virtues, purifying the soul, gathering moral courage, stimulating good deeds, and containing material desires, religious and moral beliefs play an indispensable role in uniting a

[48] See Justice Brandeis's concurring opinion in Whitney v. California, 274 US 357 (1927).

nation together and maintaining its solidarity, stability, and vitality. The decline of the Marxist orthodoxy in China illustrates that religions or beliefs can sustain their vitality only if they are kept separate from the state. Any collusion between a religion or belief and the state not only deprives equal freedom to other religions or beliefs, but also spoils its own strength and vitality. In the religious history, the Christian motto, "render unto Caesar the things that are Caesar's, and unto God the things that are God's,"[49] laid the first foundation for the separation of church and state. It also formed the earliest and foremost separation of "powers" in Western society: The earthly power cannot monopolize everything, at least not the religious or moral beliefs. In fact, one of their roles is precisely to provide criteria for evaluating the legitimacy of political power. The religious and moral realms simply have no room for the state to step in. The state cannot support or assist any particular sect, nor suppress or interfere with religious or moral practices. Endowed with moral and intellectual virtues, the vast majority of believers will not engage in harmful activities. Therefore, the government should trust their judgment and refrain from deciding on the rightness or wrongness of a particular belief. If a sect engages in criminal activities under the guise of "religion," the law can punish its activities without targeting the belief themselves.

(3) General freedoms. In a constitutional democracy where human dignity is respected and protected, the vast majority of citizens will abide by the law and refrain from misusing their freedoms to harm others. Therefore, protection of freedoms should be the governing principle of the state, and restriction the exception. All legal restrictions must be necessary in the sense that they serve the legitimate purpose of promoting the public interest, and the means adopted must be proportionate to that purpose. Only acts that seriously violate the rights of others or the public interest warrant criminal detention, the most severe restriction on personal freedom, and detained suspects must be promptly placed under judicial protection. Criminal trials must be conducted with procedural justice and, as a principle, through open trials. The right of criminal suspects to seek and meet with lawyers must be effectively guaranteed in order to prevent the use of torture to extract confessions, among other things, a common practice in China today.

(4) Property rights. As an institutional guarantee of personal independence, property rights are the external extension of human dignity. China's bitter lessons in the past decades have shown that the absence of private property

[49] *Mark*, 12:17; *Luke*, 20: 25.

rights is the root cause of social poverty and turmoil. To avoid the negative effects of "averagism" (平均主义) and the erosion of public property, state regulations should follow the wise advices of Aristotle and Mencius, allowing property to be private in principle, while its use can be regulated for the public interest.[50] As a key component of property rights, land ownership and its accompanying rights of use should, to the extent possible, be granted to individuals.[51] The state should implement Sun Yat-sen's policy that "the cultivator should own the land," and grant substantive ownership to land users. If the state needs land for important public interests, it is obliged to make every effort to first negotiate and reach agreement with the land users. Land expropriation should be a last resort to be pursued only if negotiations fail, in which case fair compensation at a market price should be provided.

(5) Equal protection of law. As a necessary component of human dignity, equal opportunity and treatment are indispensable for fair competition and social vitality. The law is obliged to treat similar people similarly, without discrimination based on extraneous factors such as gender, ethnicity, age, wealth, health status, or political affiliations. Education is critical for fostering awareness of dignity and civic morality. Equal access to education is particularly important for the youth, making them virtuous citizens in a democratic society. Under the influenced of the great Confucian idea advocating "education irrespective of classes" (有教无类), China's education system was once leading in the world, promoting social mobility through a relatively fair examination system (科举) in ancient times. Education in China today, however, is widely criticized for its severe discriminations of all forms. To provide minimally equal and healthy growth environment for all Chinese youth,[52] the state has an obligation to ensure regional equality of compulsory education through necessary financial appropriations, abolish all forms of educational discrimination and achieve at least complete formal equality in educational opportunity.

Second, a constitutional state is a democratic state, requiring periodic, universal, and direct elections based on "one-person, one-vote." To be sure, democracy is more than elections, but it cannot survive without them. The essence of

[50] For the ancient idea of the "well field system" (井田制), see *Mengzi*, 3A: 3.

[51] The flaws in the public land ownership system, as defined in Art. 10 of the 1982 Constitution, see Zhang Qianfan, *The Constitution of China: A Contextual Analysis* (Oxford: Hart Publishing, 2012), pp. 215–21.

[52] Serious educational discriminations in China have produced severe adverse social consequences. Ibid., pp. 203–5.

democracy is to allow the people to establish a government through elections that governs on their behalf. A true democratic state must permit all eligible voters to freely elect their leaders and representatives without interference from the government, or else it risks descending into an oppressive regime under the guise of "democracy." Political parties, as institutions that formulate and express the public will, should be free to form, organize, and operate within the bounds of the law, without state or any party suppression. Universal suffrage is vital for the state to represent the will and interests of all voters. With the exception of youth before maturity or those incapacitated by mental illness, citizens should not be deprived of the right to vote. Restrictions based on factors such as race, gender, property ownership status, or education level must be strictly prohibited. As the core of election, candidates must be freely generated according to specific conditions stipulated by law, free from arbitrary manipulation at the discretion of the government.[53] Free communication between candidates and voters must be guaranteed, and restrictions on campaign activities reduced to the necessary minimum. The election law should prohibit all fraudulent activities and illegal influences on voting, such as intimidation, coercion, and bribery. To avoid potential bribery and manipulation, representatives should generally be directly elected. Last but not least, all votes should be counted and recorded truthfully, with equal weight given to each vote (i.e., one-person, one-vote).

An important corollary of the democratic state is the rule of civilians (文官治国). Democracy implies that the state is governed by civilian authorities who are ultimately accountable to voters through periodic elections, rather than military forces imposing the will of a particular party or individual through force. The military must be under the command of the state, loyal to all citizens, and not aligned with any particular group or party. Decisions about war and peace should be made and declared by the parliament.

Third, a constitutional state is built upon the rule of law, requiring the proper separation of powers both vertically and horizontally. A legitimate government is based on general laws enacted by parliamentary representatives elected through proper procedures. Any public act without the authorization of the law is ultra vires and void. To prevent any single institution from enacting or implementing bad laws and to ensure compliance with good laws, legislative, executive and judicial powers must be vested in separate, independent institutions, ultimately accountable only to the voters.

[53] Electoral manipulations have been a particularly serious and widespread problem in China, reducing virtually every election of all levels of people's congresses to mere "rubber stamps." Ibid., pp. 143–7.

The rule of law requires the implementation of judicial independence. Independent and impartial judges embody the conscience of society and serve as the final safeguard for achieving social justice. The corruption of judges signifies the comprehensive corruption of society. To ensure fair trials, judicial institutions must be granted independent status. Judges must independently adjudicate cases, taking responsibility for their decisions based on their conscience, without interference from any personal, social or political forces, unless they are found through due process to have committed a crime or engaged in serious misconduct. To guarantee judicial independence, the remuneration of judges during their tenure must not be substantially reduced.

Finally, a constitutional state is a federal state characterized by local autonomy, a vital component for both democracy and the rule of law. Local governments, being closer to the voters, have a better understanding of local situations and needs. Therefore, all matters within the competence of local authorities should be reserved for local management. In large countries with significant regional disparities, imposing a uniform structure on local governments leads to "one size fits all" (一刀切), an inflexible approach that inhibits adaptation to local conditions and hinders beneficial local initiatives and experiments. As long as they adhere to the other three constitutional pillars – democracy, the rule of law, and the protection of human rights – local authorities should be empowered to manage local affairs through legislation and design local institutions best suited to their needs. The national government must avoid interfering in matters within the scope of local authority. In cases of power conflicts between the central and local governments, an impartial judicial body should be responsible for resolution. Local councils and executive officials should be freely elected by local voters, without interference from the central or superior governments. The central and provincial governments are obligated to safeguard the legality of local elections primarily through the judiciary.

5.5.2 *The Foundation of National Unification and Ethnic Harmony*

China has long been preoccupied with its history of "national humiliations" (丧权辱国) over the past century and considers national sovereignty and territorial integrity, especially the reunification of Taiwan, as its supreme goals and the primary criteria for measuring the legitimacy of its regime. Such a view of history reflects a despotic mentality, because only an absolute monarch is interested in expanding or maintaining *his* territory, population, and resources at the expense of his cannon fodder – the subjects who have no choice but to sacrifice their lives in wars. In contrast, democratic nations generally respect the wishes of local ethnicities and resolve any differences peacefully. National unity or division is never a fixed goal, but depends on the specific benefits that a particular sovereign arrangement will bring to the people. In a despotic regime, the subjects are treated as political slaves, regardless of whether they are ruled by their own or a foreign master. The concept of "nation" becomes nothing more than a grandiose symbol to appease their wounded ego, akin to a dwarf wearing a huge hat. Thorough brainwashing fosters delusional nationalism among the people, making them willingly serve the despots who enslave them.

Ironically, despite the relentless efforts of ambitious despots to expand their territories, despotism fails to achieve real unity. Although the Communist regime ended the wars, united most territories, and even recovered former colonies (Hong Kong and Macau) since 1949, China still faces the hidden danger of national secession. The superficial unity enforced by a despotic regime sows the very seed of secession, which will sprout and bear fruit as soon as the coercion eases. The rapid rise in economic and military power, combined with decades of distorted historical education and brainwashing, has led to an unbridled expansion of nationalist consciousness among the vast majority. Any peripheral conflicts in Xinjiang, Tibet, the Taiwan Strait, or the South China Sea could act as a catalyst for secession and civil war. Similar to China's constitutional democracy, its centennial project of peaceful reunification remains far from completion.

Indeed, without constitutional democracy, China cannot achieve genuine unity and stability. The "unity" built on totalitarian tyranny is merely a superficial peace that will ultimately lead to more violent secession and bloodshed. Like the domestic crisis in China, the "separatist crisis" in its peripheries is an inevitable result of poor governance and abuse of power brought about by the despotic regime.

Officials raised and nurtured in such a regime exhibit boundless greed and show no respect for the legitimate rights of local people, especially their freedom of belief and economic interests, inevitably provoking resentments and protests. By suppressing the free expression of public opinion, however, these local tyrants easily shift blame onto the independence movements in Tibet, Xinjiang, Taiwan and, more recently, Hong Kong. By exaggerating the danger of "separatist forces," they obtain more "stability maintenance" (维稳) funds from the central government, allowing vested interest groups such as local officials, security forces, and the military to hijack China's ethnic relations and policies. Under the current political system, no one can afford to be labeled as the culprit for destroying national unity; everyone relies on using force to temporarily quell institutionally caused divisions and maintain surface-level peace during their tenure, a strategy that guarantees short-term success but long-term failure. Such "peace" can only breed greater revolt, and such "unity" can only exacerbate the eventual secession. Economic and military strength can buy fear and silence only for a time, but cannot win the hearts and minds of the people. A violent outbreak is just a matter of time.

Only through constitutional democracy can China achieve true unity and gain genuine respect from the world. To become a globally recognized civilized nation rather than a war threat, China must fulfill its responsibility as a great power in a civilized manner. A despotic regime cannot accomplish this mission because despotism is inherently barbaric. Even if it pretends to be polite in front of foreign guests, it cannot hide in daily interactions the frivolity and cruelty ingrained in its very nature, and it never bothers to conceal its impudence towards its own citizens. For China to earn minimal respect, its people must first embrace their responsibility as modern citizens. Until they complete the reconstruction of moral and political character, China will not gain the world's respect. Its power and "sovereignty" will remain symbols of barbarity, instilling fear in the world, and its "unity" will be nothing more than a short-lived peace maintained through terror, inevitably mirroring the fate of the First Emperor (秦始皇), whose apparently invincible empire violently ended with his son.

To achieve domestic unity in China, its people must treat the separatist ethnic forces in places such as Xinjiang and Tibet with reason and moderation. No one is born a "terrorist" or "suicide bomber." The presence of separatist unrest indicates that the social contract, which serves as the foundation of a nation, ceases to be effective, as some ethnic groups no longer accept the basic premise of ethnic integration and coexistence within one nation. To truly achieve unity in China, then, the dominant Han ethnicity (汉族) must engage in calm and peaceful negotiations with ethnic minorities such as Tibetans and Uyghurs until all parties reach a basic agreement and establish a new contract. Genuine unity is premised on voluntary acceptance and emotional attachment; forced unity will only deepen divisions and foster more animosity. Suppressing free communication and debates on "sensitive" issues only conceals the truth, deepens misunderstandings, exacerbates estrangement, generates hatred and misses the opportunities for seeking peaceful reunion, allowing the separatist sentiment to grow stronger and mainland China to become susceptible to terrorist attacks fueled by ethnic hatred. Decades of distorted public opinion have led to misunderstandings and distrust among different ethnicities, which have reached an irreversible point. The street violence in Xinjiang and Tibet in 2008–09 showed that China's ethnic tensions have become dangerously heightened, and subsequent crackdowns and severe controls only delay inevitable outbreaks. The first step towards constitutional unity is to relax the control over speech and press, allowing the Han ethnicity to understand the root causes of the situation through free dialogue before effective solutions can be found.

To persuade ethnic minorities to support unity, the government must cease discriminatory and oppressive ethnic policies, uphold ethnic equality and religious freedom as mandated by the Constitution, implement local autonomy, fully respect local ownership and use of resources, and establish protective reserves for ethnic minority settlements if necessary. As the dominant population, the Han ethnicity must demonstrate Confucian generosity towards ethnic minorities and avoid arrogance, injustice, and greed. Otherwise, ethnic conflicts and grievances will continue to escalate. Ethnic minorities, as compatriots, should be respected and treated kindly. On the other hand, ethnic minorities should also understand that violence and unilateral separation are not the path to peace. As long as mainland China is not governed under constitutional democracy, achieving secession temporarily will only leave a powerful despotic regime as a time bomb ticking on the bedside. Genuine liberty and autonomy enabled by a constitutional regime are the only ultimate guarantee for peace, stability, and prosperity for all ethnicities in China. Through mutual respect, equal treatment, and free communication, China can undoubtedly achieve peaceful unity. A constitutional unity, voluntarily accepted and recognized by all ethnic groups, will surely be more stable and enduring than a military unity maintained only through despotic coercion.

Finally, the issue with Taiwan is indeed a historical legacy from the Chinese revolutions. The civil war between the two major revolutionary parties, each claiming sole authority and refusing to tolerate others, caused immense harm not only to themselves but also to the entire nation. In 1987, the Nationalist Party lifted the martial law that had been in place for thirty-eight years, allowing press freedom and the formation of political parties, thus initiating Taiwan's transition to democracy. The Nationalist transformation in Taiwan served as a positive example for its Communist counterpart in mainland China. The thorny relationship across the Taiwan Strait poses both challenges and opportunities for a better future, which should be jointly decided by the peoples on both sides through democratic processes, based on reciprocal respect. In the absence of a consensus on the sovereignty arrangement across the Strait, the governments on both sides should at least end the state of hostility, refrain from advocating military solutions, and avoid imposing unilateral decisions on each other. Unilateral promotion of unification by the mainland will only exacerbate the independence sentiment in

Taiwan, while pushing for independence on the island will simply fuel nationalist hawks on the mainland. Such unilateral impositions will be counterproductive, directly threatening the security of the Taiwan Strait.

The greatest obstacle to cross-strait security and unification lies in the cultural and institutional gaps between the two sides. A democratic Taiwan simply cannot accept the authoritarian mainland. This cultural gap is evident not only in interactions between political and business elites but also increasingly in exchanges among the general population. If the mainland fails to reform its existing system, the number of Taiwanese who identify with the mainland will keep dwindling, and the path towards peaceful unification will close. The key to achieving the goal of cross-strait unification, long desired by the mainland, lies in the hands of the mainland people themselves. Only by implementing constitutional democracy and gaining the support of the Taiwanese majority through institutional reforms can they realize the dream of cross-strait unification.

5.5.3 *Overcoming Impediments: Chinese Constitutionalism and Citizens' Moral Responsibility*

Over the past century since the Xinhai Revolution, the repeated failures of Chinese constitutional reform are largely attributed to the passivity of the people themselves. However, with the rapid spread of online information, the Chinese constitutional reform has gained new momentum since the Sun Zhigang tragedy in 2003. Indeed, incidents like this have given rise to a "model" under Sun's name, which is generally followed by China's civil rights movements.[54] For example, in 2007, the "collective walk" event in Xiamen opened up a more proactive model of civil rights activism, in which direct dialogue between residents and the city government successfully changed a decision of serious local environmental concern. Most recently, frustrated by the prolonged severe restriction of personal freedom during the Covid-19 outbreak, and sparked by the fire accident that caused heavy casualties in Urumqi, the university students and residents across the country initiated the "White Paper Movement" (白纸运动) on the eves of November 26–27, 2022, putting an abrupt end to the strict zero-Covid policy that had lasted for three years.[55] While these examples of civil rights activism

[54] Ibid., pp. 197–221.

[55] Only ten days after the movement, on December 7, the State Council issued a "new ten articles" (新十条), which essentially reversed its strict policy on pandemic control. See Kawashima Shin, "China: Exploiting the 'White Paper Protests' to revoke the zero-COVID

have brought vitality and hope to China's constitutional reform, their successes are limited due to adverse factors such as the high cost of activism, uncertain results, and lack of replicability.[56] In a country where normal channels for defending rights promised in the Constitution are clogged, civil rights activism remains rare, and popular constitutionalism lacks sufficient momentum. As abuses of public power go unchecked and the basic freedoms of ordinary people are severely restricted, the government–civilian relationship resembles that of fire and water, and Chinese society is steadily moving towards the brink of collapse.

The driving force for social and institutional progress ultimately comes from the people themselves, who must realize that only through constitutional democracy can they secure long-term felicity for themselves and future generations. Waiting until their own rights are violated is not a viable approach. It would be too late if they wait until their own land is expropriated, their own houses are demolished, or they themselves fall victims by miscarriages of justice before taking appropriate actions. Merely focusing on immediate interests or engaging in venting without addressing institutional causes cannot promote constitutional reform. Nor should they content themselves with selective punishment of a few corrupt officials as the scapegoats of the institutional evils, venting the anger and melancholy long suppressed under the despotic regime. Simple venting does nothing positive to promote constitutional reform, but aggravates the fear of losing power among the power holders and makes them even more resistant to reform. Only when the people recognize the institutional causes of corruption and take responsibility as citizens to promote institutional reforms can China's constitutionalism enter a virtuous cycle of government–civilian cooperation.

The immediate stumbling block to constitutional reforms in China lies in the interest groups maintained by the totalitarian regime. China's constitutionalism could have started with bold democratic reforms within the ruling party, creating and solidifying its legitimacy and popular support. However, party leaders fear that decentralizing reform might diminish their power and threaten their immediate interests. Zai Ze (载泽), one of the late Qing officials who traveled abroad to study constitutionalism, was apparently right when he observed that constitutionalism is beneficial to the people but detrimental to officials.[57] His plain point revealed the "secret" why China's

policy," *The Diplomat* (January 30, 2023), https://thediplomat.com/2023/01/china-exploiting-the-white-paper-protests-to-revoke-the-zero-covid-policy/.

56 Zhang, *The Constitution of China: A Contextual Analysis*, pp. 223–4.

57 Jing Zhiren, *Constitutional History of China* [in China] (Taipei: Taiwan Lianjing Press, 1984), p. 101.

constitutional reforms repeatedly failed ever since the Hundred Days' Reform in 1898.

However, plain as it is, the view is fallacious. Constitutionalism is not only beneficial to the people, but also to the officials themselves. By embracing constitutional reform, leaders can secure their place in history and leave a positive legacy for future generations. Ignoring for the moment the inherent dignity of the power holders, considering only their personal interests, constitutionalism is a "good deal," particularly to the top leaders, bringing them lasting fame and reputation. What can they stand to lose? Over two millennia ago, Mencius asked King Xuan of Qi (齐宣王) why he failed to implement benevolent politics (仁政) in his kingdom: "Is it not enough to satisfy your taste with fat and sweet, to comfort your body with soft warmth, to please your eyes with the colors of beauty or your ears with the sound of music? Or are there not enough courtiers to let them execute your orders?" The same questions are relevant to the leaders today. Why do they refuse to implement constitutionalism? Have they not gained enough wealth and power, and enjoyed enough prestige and luxury? What can more power, money, beauty, vanity, and pomp and ceremonies possibly add to their lives? If they stubbornly persist in monopolizing power and amassing wealth to the point of self-destruction, falling victims of power struggles and leading to condemnation and disdain by future generations, they can only blame their own stupidity, myopia, greed, and cowardice for their downfall.

Whether believing retribution in the afterlife, every leader will eventually face the judgment of history. After all, history is written by future generations rather than hired literati. Lies may be sustained for a time, but eventually, the truth will come to light. Chinese history textbooks may conceal certain truths for decades to come, but cannot deceive the people indefinitely. History will ultimately reveal the true nature of every historical figure, whether they were benevolent leaders or tyrants. This has been the Chinse tradition since the great historian, Sima Qian (司马迁), who suffered from the tyranny of Emperor Wu of Han (汉武帝). While benevolent kings such as Yao and Shun (尧舜) have been revered by later generations, tyrants such as Jie and Zhou (桀纣) have been cursed for thousands of years. If an enlightened leader can help China to achieve constitutional democracy and break the seemingly endless curse of absolute despotism, his or her achievement will far surpass those of revered historical figures like Yao and Shun. On the other hand, those who resist constitutional reform and cling to absolute power will be remembered in history as national criminals, akin to figures like Jie and Zhou. If someone refuses to be a great emperor, whose illustrious reputation would be remembered throughout history, and instead chooses to be a national criminal, thereby ensuring infamy for generations, such choice certainly defies reason.

The awakening of popular consciousness and the yearning for dignity will inevitably lead to the dawn of the constitutional era in China. No ruler, no matter how powerful while in position, can halt the progress towards constitutional democracy, nor can they permanently manipulate the judgment of history. What a ruling regime can do is to determine its own historical status through its actions. In the great historical drama where each actor plays with his own life, everyone is free to choose his own role and is solely responsible for his choices.

Those who positively contributed to the constitutional progress will be remembered and honored in the annals of Chinese history. Their names will be engraved on the monument of time.

Those who tirelessly labored to promote constitutional reforms, even if they do not witness the fruits of victory in their lifetime, will lead a fulfilling life without shame or regret.

Those who only complain and blame others, leading aimless lives without striving to make a contribution, will be forgotten like floating dust in the air.

Those who spend their lives obstructing progress, opposing reform, and resisting constitutionalism, however lofty the titles they may hold during their lifetime, will forever be condemned in the pillory of Chinese history!

When the light of justice dispels the haze of tyranny and shines on this troubled land with its eternal brilliance; when the rain of wisdom renourishes this long arid soil, purifying every soul tainted by dictatorship, this ancient nation, having experienced millennia of slumber and a century of incessant nightmares, will eventually awaken, bidding farewell to fear, cowardice, and madness, refusing to be enslaved and brainwashed any longer, bravely facing itself to become the master of its own destiny.

We dedicate this Manifesto to every Chinese, particularly to those spirited youth. If you desire to safeguard your natural rights and legitimate interests from the clutches of greedy dictators, to protect your inner dignity from the trampling of capricious tyranny, and to live without fear under a government that welcomes criticism and oversight; if you reject the prospect of dwelling in a home that could be seized and demolished without fair compensation, breathing air tainted by blind "development," and enduring institutionally caused meager salaries amidst high expenses, low social security, and extravagant government spending – in short, if you are no longer willing to passively accept the fate of exploited slaves heading towards collective destruction, or bear witness to the damage and disgrace inflicted daily by a despotic regime upon you and your country, then cease to be its stepping stone.

If you agree with the gist of this Manifesto, adopt it as your own and put it into practice. Spread and promote its principles until they gain widespread acceptance in your country. From this moment onward, let us treat each of our compatriots with equal dignity, recognizing them as more than mere instruments to further our own advantage. Officials must refrain from abusing their privileges, embezzling the national treasury, or treating the people as objects for exploitation. On the other hand, the people should discard cowardice, myopia, callousness, and distrust among themselves. These behaviors not only offend the dignity of others but, above all, erode our own dignity as human beings. As responsible citizens, we shall not tolerate the infringement of our legitimate rights, nor infringe upon the rights of others. In this highly interdependent society, each of us owes a minimum of respect and care to our fellow human beings.

Every respectable citizen, you may ask, of course, what your country can do for you, but even more, you should ask what you can do for your country – not only because you have a heart to dedicate yourself, but also because that is the only way to realize your personal value as a competent citizen. Please no longer pin your hopes for political reform on a Chiang Ching-kuo (蒋经国) or Gorbachev of mainland China.[58] The constitutional reform and the requisite personality transformation begin with each and every one of us!

Stand up, every Chinese citizen, and take your responsibility to defend your rights as a human being, for the sake of your own dignity, the happiness of your descendants, and the future of your nation. Embrace the dawn of constitutional civilization with your awakening conscience and courage, and establish a righteous nation with your knowledge and actions. What the people of Spain, South Korea, Taiwan, Eastern Europe, South Africa, Chile, Indonesia, Thailand, Nepal, Tunisia … have accomplished will equally be accomplished by the people of China!

[58] Chiang Ching-kuo, who virtually inherited presidency from his father Chiang Kai-shek in 1978, was widely admired by liberals in the mainland for lifting the Nationalist ban on opposition parties and newspapers in July 1987.

6

Towards the Future

Constitutional Design, Social Contract, and Human Dignity

During the Covid pandemic in 2020, liberal activist Yang Maodong (penname Guo Feixiong, 郭飞雄) drafted a survey entitled Chinese Liberal Intellectuals on Constitutional Democracy (中国良心知识分子谈宪政民主). I helped him to restructure and finalize the questionnaires, and prepared the first set of answers shown below, published on the 101st anniversary of the May Fourth Movement.[1]

6.1 SOCIAL CONTRACT

1. *What are the basic elements of constitutional democracy as you understand them? What is their core content?*

From a linguistic perspective, "constitutional democracy" refers to a democratic state established on a constitution. Democracy is the starting point but not the endpoint. In other words, democracy is a key element within the broader constitutional framework, but it does not encompass its entirety. Democracy, at its core, means the rule of the people. More precisely, it implies that those in charge of the daily operation of the government should be held accountable to the governed, at least to the majority, considering that individuals have differing interests and perspectives. Although ensuring that policies benefit the majority is not always easy, majority rule should not be an absolute principle. For instance, legislation passed by the parliament representing the majority should not deprive the basic rights of the minority.

[1] The answers of other Chinese liberal scholars can be viewed on www.chinese-future.org. For Mr. Guo's comment on my answer presented here, see www.chinese-future.org/articles/enr4pywjh3htjwajtmkdp7bac7s8zx?rq=执象.

Nor should the majority pass legislation and then disregard it during enforcement due to changes in public opinion. Even less should the majority representatives elected in one election manipulate legislation and distort election rules by gerrymandering, for example, to maintain a "permanent majority." All of these actions are clearly impermissible. Therefore, majoritarian democracy must be subject to the constraints of fundamental rights, the rule of law, and separation of powers. To paraphrase "bounded rationality," a concept coined by the economist Herbert Simon,[2] constitutional democracy can be seen as "bounded majoritarianism." While democracy undoubtedly serves as the cornerstone of all republican regimes, and an operational democracy must practice the rule of the majority produced through periodic elections, the majority rule must be constrained by other constitutional elements, such as the respect and protection of fundamental freedoms, the rule of law, and the separation of powers, to prevent it from degenerating into what Tocqueville referred to as the "tyranny of the majority."

A constitution should be based on the social contract, codifying the key elements of the social contract that all rational individuals can agree to and willingly uphold, making it tangible and concrete. Taking democracy as an example, the constitution needs to specify the type of democratic regime – federal or unitary, presidential or parliamentary, and the electoral system – proportional representation or winner-take-all in electoral districts. As all institutional designs have pros and cons, the optimal design for a specific nation is a much-debated matter. While these categories are broad and require further institutional specification, it is essential to understand that the principle of democracy is non-negotiable, with critical requirements defining a true democracy. As elaborated in Chapter 2, democracy, the rule of law and the protection of fundamental freedoms constitute the "political natural laws" (PNL) that any legitimate state must respect. As the core of constitutional democracy, adherence to the PNLs is the prerequisite for achieving sound governance. No nation can violate them and escape their painful sanctions in terms of violent conflicts and civil wars.

Of course, PNL is an "open list." Below is a rough overview of its core elements, without excluding the possibility of incorporating other elements, such as personal freedom and the core of private property.

First, the fundamental freedoms and rights of individuals must not be violated. This forms the foundation for constructing any rational state. As John Locke wisely observed, humans establish the state not to become its

[2] Herbert A. Simon, "Public Administration in Today's World of Organizations and Markets," Speech on Annual Conference of American Political Science, September 1, 2000.

slaves, but to better protect their rights and freedoms from being enslaved.[3] The PNLs encompass at least three categories of rights: freedom of speech (broadly understood to include freedom of the press, assembly and association), freedom of belief (including religious freedom and separation of church and state), and equality (anti-discrimination). The purpose of creating a state is to establish a civilized order, and these elements are essential for the order and peace of any country. For example, many deeply divided societies suffer from prolonged wars and violent conflicts precisely because they fail to treat different ethnic or religious groups equally.[4]

Second, individual freedoms need to be limited by law, and laws should be formulated by representative institutions, namely the parliament. The parliament must be elected through periodic elections, which should meet five specific requirements: The suffrage must be universal (all citizens meeting appropriate criteria, such as reaching eighteen years of age, have the right to participate as voters or candidates), the election must be direct (people's representatives should be directly elected by voters rather than indirectly elected by other representatives, as is the case for China's people's congresses above the county level) and free (communication between voters and candidates shall be unrestricted, the candidates shall be freely generated and the voting shall be voluntary), and the ballot shall be secret and carry equal weight ("one person, one vote"). Refer to Q11 for more details.

Last, once the parliament elected through universal suffrage determines the direction of the state through legislation, the laws should be administered faithfully by the government and adjudicated impartially by the courts, necessitating the maintenance of administrative neutrality and judicial independence. The administrative and judicial processes are meant to faithfully embody the legislative values, and shall be value-neutral in themselves, without being interfered with by any other powers. This implies that the judiciary and administrative bodies, such as civil servants, police, and the military, must be depoliticized. For deeply divided societies where social groups lack mutual trust among themselves, these institutions should be composed of a balanced representation of different ethnic or religious groups to foster social cohesion and mutual trust. Failing to address these issues often

3 John Locke, *Two Treatises of Government*, ed. Peter Laslett (Cambridge: Cambridge University Press, 1960), pp. 326–8.

4 Qianfan Zhang and Xiaoyang Wei, "Political natural law and human dignity: An empiricist perspective," *Journal of Chinese Philosophy* 50 (2023), 196–208.

results in conflicts and even civil wars, highlighting the indispensability of the PNLs, as the violation of any of these principles will disrupt national peace and stability.

2. *Do you consider constitutional democracy as the ideal form of government that all countries must strive for? What are your reasons for supporting or opposing it?*

Constitutional democracy, as defined above, is obviously indispensable for any country that seeks peace and good order. I want to emphasize that it is *not* a lofty concept, but rather the fundamental baseline of human civilization. The function of constitutional democracy is not to lead us to heaven but to keep us as far away from hell as possible. In constitutional democracies, there will still be conflicts, crimes, corruptions, etc. However, without constitutional democracy, the evils of public power abuses would continue unabated, eventually turning into the collective evils of society with no means of prevention or restraint. Imagine a country where speech is not free, and the government commits crimes but people are not even allowed to complain. Can such a country maintain peace? Establishing such a state would not be preventing evil, but rather perpetuating it, which is the very opposite end of a legitimate state. Only constitutional democracy can enable not only the government to restrain individual private evils, but also the people to restrain the public evils of the government.

Ultimately, human beings are rational and self-interested, as are those who wield state power. Of course, self-interest is not synonymous with evil. In fact, the wealth of civilized societies is largely created under self-interested motives. In that sense, it can even be considered the greatest good. However, if self-interest is allowed to expand without limits, it will inevitably harm others and ultimately oneself. Only to that extent has self-interest turned into an evil that must be controlled. To prevent the unlimited expansion of self-interest, we need government and laws. The government is a *necessary* evil precisely because the evil inherent in human nature requires external constraints. However, those who govern the state are not angels, but ordinary human beings with common flaws of human nature. To restrain their impulses to commit evils, namely to infringe upon the public interest for their private gain, it is not only necessary to make them mutually check against each other, but ultimately, to have the people hold them accountable through constitutional mechanisms. James Madison's profound statement in Federalist No. 51, expressed over two centuries ago, remains irrefutable truth today: "If men were angels, no government would be necessary. If angels were to govern men, neither external nor internal controls on government would be necessary."[5] Only constitutional democracy can provide such a mechanism of mutual restraint, preventing the government from placing the vested interests of a few above the interests of the many. A nation without constitutional democracy is a living hell where the government commits all sorts of evil, unless it encounters a rare and fleeting enlightened despot. However, even the latter only leads to a desperate dependence and illusion among the suffering people, who will suffer even more when they soon encounter a worse despot.

3. *Nationalism or populism has risen globally, posing major challenges to the constitutional democracies around the world. Do you still believe that constitutional democracy can withstand these tests and maintain strong vitality?*

Nationalism and populism have indeed presented severe challenges to constitutional democracy around the world. Despite these challenges, however, constitutional democracy can withstand the tests and maintain strong vitality for several reasons. First, throughout history, constitutional democracy has never been invulnerable or unshakable. It has faced various challenges and crises but has managed to grow and adapt. Like a healthy body that encounters various viruses, constitutional democracy can strengthen itself through overcoming challenges. If the body is weak, it may be consumed by powerful viruses, as was the case with the constitutional reforms during the late Qing dynasty in China. However, if a constitutional body has already withstood severe tests in the past, such as the Great Depression in the United States or the consolidation of constitutional democracy in Germany and Japan after the defeat of the Nazis and militarists during World War II, then it is better equipped to confront current populist reactions triggered by incidents like massive immigration or refugee crises. Therefore, it is unnecessary to panic at the slightest challenge, or question the vitality of constitutional democracy, or even take pride in failing to escape totalitarian dictatorship, the weakest regime in the world. The most robust regime is constitutional democracy, with effective mechanisms for preventing and rectifying errors.

Second, in its initial stages, populism is a form of democracy. However, it deviates from the constitutional framework when it violates one or more of the PNLs. For example, some American or European voters may turn a blind eye to politicians' attacks on press freedom or support ethnic discrimination for their own interests or prejudices. If unchecked, this tendency could lead to dictatorship and disaster. Fortunately, however, populist forces do not

[5] Alexander Hamilton, James Madison, and John Jay, *The Federalist Papers*, ed. Clinton Rossiter (New York: NAL Penguin, 1961), p. 322.

represent the mainstream in most European countries and the United States. Once the waves triggered by specific events like the election of Donald Trump or the refugee crisis subside, these countries will return to a stable constitutional democratic order.

Last, there is no better alternative for good governance than constitutional democracy. Embracing fascist dictatorships again would only lead to domestic disasters and global destruction. The path towards peace for any country is to firmly embrace constitutional democracy.

4. *Does the constitutional democracy meet the current realistic needs of China? Does it align with China's cultural tradition? The American political scientist, Samuel P. Huntington, once predicted the "clash of civilizations," particularly the conflict between Confucianism, Islam, and modern Western civilization. How do you view the relationship between Confucian and modern Western civilizations?*

Constitutional democracy is indeed a suitable model for meeting China's current needs, as it is for all countries. China's neighbor, North Korea, is an example that completely violates every PNL expected to be observed in constitutional democracy, inevitably leading to dire consequences for its people. In the past forty years of reform, China has made certain progress primarily because the elements of PNLs, as reflected in its Constitution, began to take limited effect, particularly in limited degrees of free speech and religious, personal and economic freedoms. Despite the failure of the state to protect these de facto freedoms, they have contributed to the social dynamism. Therefore, the desirability of constitutional democracy is indisputable; the controversy lies in its feasibility. China, like certain civilizations, may have deeply entrenched despotic culture due to its long history of absolute despotism, making it difficult for institutional change to take place or sustain constitutional democracy due to the inertia of despotic culture. This implies that constitutional democracy is more than an institution, requiring cultural support to be sustainable.

For example, in many Muslim-dominated countries, there is a fusion of church and state. Even during the Arab Spring, when there was an opportunity for a transition towards constitutional democracy, most of these countries experienced an exacerbation of the fusion between religion and politics, leading to a swift shift to an Arab Winter. This indicates that the majority of voters in these countries have not recognized the significance of separating religion from politics and have failed to exercise self-restraint in preventing their religious beliefs from interfering with politics. On the other hand, the wisdom of the American Framers was evidenced precisely in their self-discipline. Although the United States was a Christian-dominated nation in the eighteenth and nineteenth centuries, they refused to establish a Christian state and explicitly prohibited the Congress from establishing religion through the First Amendment. This constitutional requirement was later extended to the states through "selective incorporation" by the Supreme Court from the 1920s, preventing them from infringing upon the separation of church and state.[6]

To be sure, care should be taken to avoid cultural determinism. It is wrong to presume that certain religious traditions, such as Islam, can never break away from the fusion of church and state. Mustafa Kemal Atatürk, the founder of modern Turkey, was a great pioneer in promoting a secular state. Although Turkey is a Muslim-dominated nation, for almost a century since its founding, its mainstream political and military elites firmly upheld secularism.[7] However, the key to sustaining the separation of church and state lies in enabling the people themselves to recognize its necessity. While I do not have extensive knowledge of Islamic civilization, I believe that there is ample room for interpretation within any religious text. The Quran itself is not a talisman for the Islamic cultures to reject constitutional democracy. The crucial factor is whether believers' contemporary interpretation and practice of religious texts align with the principles of constitutional democracy, particularly the secular state.

My interpretation of Confucian culture can be roughly divided into two parts.[8] On the one hand, the Confucian political culture, having little worth to draw from today, is beyond rescue. Continuing to cling to outdated practices is not only foolish, but also a disgrace to the Confucian civilization. On the other hand, the Confucian ethics still hold rich nourishment and can make significant contributions to the contemporary world. My book, *Human Dignity in Classical Chinese Philosophy*, provides a comprehensive explanation of this view, in which Western scholars have shown keen interest.[9] In fact, the concept of dignity has gained popularity in the West in recent years, and I take pride in claiming that Confucianism offers one of the most systematic, persuasive and even scientific perspectives on human dignity

6 Everson v. Board of Education, 330 US 1 (1947).

7 Ergun Ozbudun and Omer F. Genckaya, *Democratization and the Politics of Constitution-Making in Turkey* (Budapest: Central European University Press, 2009), pp. 10–18.

8 For details, see Qianfan Zhang, *Human Dignity in Classical Chinese Philosophy: Confucianism, Mohism, and Daoism* (New York: Palgrave Macmillan, 2016).

9 For example, according to Professor Brett Scharffs of Brigham Young University, the book motivated him to organize an international conference on Asian Perspectives on Human Dignity (Laie/Hawaii: April 18, 2023).

among all civilizations. This statement may sound exaggerated, but it is not unfounded. It is our own myopia and lack of self-appreciation that prevent us from fully appreciating the shining elements inherited from our ancestors. Of course, moral and political cultures are not entirely separate. The traditional Confucian ethics had surely been negatively influenced by authoritarian politics. However, this alone is insufficient to deny the inherent vitality of the Confucian morality. The "third-generation" neo-Confucians such as Xu Fuguan and Zhang Junmai have already demonstrated that Confucian culture can coexist harmoniously with constitutional democracy,[10] which can easily be deduced from the Confucian notion of dignity. Not coincidentally, it was the Confucian gentry, who received traditional education, that most vigorously promoted constitutionalism during the late Qing dynasty and early Republic of China.

Returning to the previous argument, any culture can and needs to be reinterpreted. Why must we be so harsh on our own millennia-old tradition? Which ancient culture is impeccable from the contemporary perspective, free from any flaws or weaknesses? These flaws or weaknesses need to be continuously overcome by the inheritors of the civilization through practical application and interaction with other civilizations. "Civilization" is not a static concept but a manifestation shaped by the inheritance, reflection, and creative transformation of generations.[11] The quality of a civilization depends more on its course than its origin. Blaming all the past failures on tradition is, in fact, seeking an excuse to evade our own responsibilities.

5. *Is it necessary for China to formulate a new constitution? If so, how should a constituent power with representativeness be established? Should the draft constitution be subject to a popular referendum? Why?*

Considering the many shortcomings of China's current Constitution, there is every reason to formulate a new constitution in the future. Therefore, I am not absolutely opposed to drafting a new constitution. In fact, I encourage individual citizens, especially young students, to engage in constitution drafting as a good exercise, as it serves as excellent civic education. Over a century ago, during the provincial autonomy (联省自治) movement in southern China, voters in Zhejiang Province proposed more than a hundred constitutional drafts, demonstrating that the Chinese had the ability and enthusiasm for

[10] Mou Zongsan et al., *Manifesto on Behalf of Chinese Culture Respectfully Announced to the People of the World*, trans. Eirik Lang Harris (Indianapolis: Hackett, 2014).

[11] Tu Wei-Ming, *Confucian Thought: Selfhood as Creative Transformation* (Albany: SUNY Press, 1985).

constitution-making even when the education and social development were very backward. I have no doubt that this still holds true today.

However, I also believe that the key for China today lies not in constitution-making, but in constitutional implementation. A constitution is merely the materialization and codification of a social contract. In fact, it may not even matter whether there is a written constitution. The United Kingdom, for example, does not have a written constitution, yet it governs effectively because it possesses a "constitution engraved in the hearts of citizens,"[12] namely a social contract shared by those who constitute a "contract community." With a sufficiently large contract community, having a written constitution is surely convenient, but not absolutely necessary. On the other hand, without a strong contract community, even a beautifully written constitution is little more than a vase, good only for decoration. This is the root cause of why the constitutions of all generations in China have been mere decorations.

Therefore, although constitution-making is a process that might help form a social contract, it cannot be achieved overnight. The slow consolidation and expansion of the contract community rely on the daily practices through which the constitution is implemented. There are many beautiful constitutions in the world, but the ultimate test lies in their implementation. Obviously, rulers never want to implement the constitution; the more beautiful the constitution, the less they want to implement it since doing so would uphold the people's interest at the expense of their own. However, this is also why citizens should insist on implementing a seemingly ineffective constitution because a beautiful constitution generally embodies several PNL elements that rulers desire to evade, including freedom of speech, religious freedom, equal protection, electoral democracy, and judicial independence – all of which are stipulated in China's current Constitution. Insisting on implementing such a constitution not only helps uphold the people's rights, but also prepares them for contract-making and lays the foundation for drafting a new constitution in the future – this time an effective constitution, rather than another beautiful vase.

To formulate a constitution, the first step is to carefully design the constitution-making procedure. Generally speaking, it is necessary to balance various relationships, such as those between elites and the general public, and between secrecy and transparency. The process can take different forms, from completely confidential bargaining among elites, as seen in the Philadelphia Constitutional Convention in 1787, to active participation by representatives

[12] Jean-Jacques Rousseau, *On the Social Contract*, trans. Donald A. Cress (Indianapolis: Hackett, 1987), p. 48.

of the general public, as seen in the constitution-making process of the French Revolution. An open process allows the constitutional text to absorb and represent diverse social interests and serves as excellent civic education for the public. However, it can also lead to grandstanding to please the public or result in a fragmented constitutional text that amalgamates various interests. On the other hand, closed forms, such as roundtable discussions, enable major interest groups to reach compromises but may lack diverse representativeness in the constitution text. For instance, the US Constitution did not adequately represent the interests of women and minorities.

A better balance would be to entrust a committee of experts to draft the constitution, while the passage of the draft itself must be through a representative body, such as a parliament or an elected constituent assembly. The drafting process should also involve periodic solicitation of public opinion and engagement with society. Finally, the formal draft can be subject to a referendum to increase the democratic legitimacy of the constitution. However, this procedure is not mandatory and should not be burdened with excessively high expectations, as referenda can easily be manipulated by dictators and demagogues, as observed in countries like Venezuela.[13]

Returning to the topic of the social contract, the key point is that the constitution should serve as a codification of the social contract, which represents an agreement among rational individuals regarding the fundamental principles of the state. Although the "constitutional moment" is not literally a contractual process,[14] constitutional-making should strive to resemble a contract to the extent possible. This implies that constitutional-making differs fundamentally from an ordinary legislative process. General legislation is a simple majoritarian process, whereas constitutional-making requires not only a supermajority agreement but also high inclusivity of the constitution-making body. Therefore, the constitutional process must fully respect minority opinions and politically disadvantaged groups, and should not rely solely on simple majority rule.

While the fifty-five representatives who drafted the US Constitution were not highly representative, they still represented major interest groups from large and small states, as well as the North and the South. The constitutional text also gained approval through intense debates in all states, making it a contractual document at least among the mainstream interest groups. Despite

[13] Allan R. Brewer-Carias, *Dismantling Democracy in Venezuela: The Chávez Authoritarian Experiment* (Cambridge: Cambridge University Press, 2010), pp. 57–8.

[14] Bruce Ackerman, *We the People, Vol. 1: Foundations* (Boston: Harvard University Press, 1991), pp. 334–5.

its limited representativeness at the time, the US Constitution has upheld the long-term stability of American society, even amid the interruption of a bloody civil war. Had the Philadelphia Convention relied solely on a majority overpowering the minority, the small states and the South would have left the process early on, making it impossible to reach a national consensus. A constitution forcefully passed based on a majority vote, even through a referendum, might have led to the eruption of the American Civil War eighty years earlier.

6.2 CONSTITUTIONAL DESIGN

6. *Should China adopt a presidential or parliamentary system in the future? Why?*

Since Juan Linz proposed the "perils of presidentialism" in the 1990s, political scientists have been debating the merits and drawbacks of presidential and parliamentary systems.[15] In reality, both are broad categories, each with numerous variations, making generalizations difficult. Taking the standard examples of presidentialism in the United States and the Westminster parliamentary system in the United Kingdom, the fundamental difference between the two lies in the relationship between the legislature and the executive. As a classic democracy, the UK upholds parliamentary supremacy and the rule of law. The House of Commons, as the legislative body, enacts laws that are supreme in a state governed by law.

It is evident that the parliament must govern the executive, headed by the cabinet, which is in charge of law enforcement. The executive should be subordinate and responsible to the parliament through mechanisms such as votes of no confidence. If a major policy proposed by the cabinet fails to garner majority support in the parliament, indicating a loss of parliamentary confidence, the cabinet should collectively resign. This ensures a straightforward relationship between the parliament and the executive, where the cabinet, as the head of the executive, is elected by a parliamentary majority to which it is held accountable and aligned on major policy issues. This also ensures the unity of national sovereignty, namely unity under the parliament responsible for legislation.

The United States differs from the United Kingdom in that it does not recognize the absolute supremacy of the parliament and its laws. Instead,

[15] Juan Linz and Arturo Valenzuela, eds., *The Failure of Presidential Democracy (Vol. 1): Comparative Perspectives* (Baltimore: The Johns Hopkins University Press, 1994), pp. 14–15.

above the ordinary laws is a written constitution, which the United Kingdom lacks altogether. This raises a number of questions. What happens if the majority in parliament passes a law that violates basic human rights? Are the executive and judiciary obliged to apply it? The key to answer this question in the United States is the crucial concept of the "separation of powers," with checks and balances among the legislative, executive, and judicial branches, aimed at minimizing government infringement on people's liberties.[16]

One way to achieve this balance is to design a presidency directly elected by the voters, rather than by the parliament, and provide a fixed term that is *not* subject to a vote of no confidence by parliament. To prevent the president from acting unlawfully or abusing power, Congress can impeach the president, but impeachment cannot be initiated simply because the president disagrees with Congressional policies. In fact, the president has the power to veto bills passed by both houses of Congress. Disagreements between the president and Congress on major policy issues can produce legislative deadlocks: Bills favored by the president are rejected by Congress, while bills favored by Congress are unlikely to achieve the required two-thirds majority to override the presidential veto. In the United States, this phenomenon illustrates how checks and balances work. However, for less-developed countries in Latin America, Africa, and elsewhere, which lack a strong democratic and rule of law tradition like the United States, persistent legislative deadlocks may eventually lead to the collapse of the democratic regime. This is the main argument put forth by Linz and his allies. Worldwide, presidential systems indeed seem to have a shorter lifespan compared to parliamentary systems.[17]

Of course, the actual situation is more complex than what Linz et al. presented. First, the collapse of presidential systems in Latin America is not necessarily due to inherent defects in the system itself, but could be attributed to other issues in those specific countries, such as lack of economic development, low education levels and the lingering effects of past military dictatorships, from which many Latin American countries had suffered before democratic transition.[18] In such cases, adopting a parliamentary system may not resolve the instability problem.

Second, when controlling for factors outside the institutional framework, the performance of presidential systems is not necessarily poor, although it

[16] For Montesquieu's famous argument, see *The Spirit of the Laws*, trans. A. M. Cohler, B. C. Miller, and H. S. Stone (Cambridge: Cambridge University Press, 1988), p. 157.

[17] José Antonio Cheibub, *Presidentialism, Parliamentarism, and Democracy* (Cambridge: Cambridge University Press, 2007), p. 2.

[18] Ibid., pp. 2–5.

may not be as good as parliamentary systems overall.[19] Within the category of presidentialism, specific systems differ significantly in various institutional variables, such as the president's powers to dissolve the parliament, declare a state of emergency and enact decree laws. The absence of these powers in the US presidency might explain why its constitutional system remains stable, while Latin American or Russian presidents tend to become authoritarian due to excessive powers or long tenures granted by their constitutions.

Last, for many countries in Latin America, the choice between a presidential or parliamentary system is often not freely made, but heavily influenced by historical legacies and political traditions. The past institutional choices create inertia and path dependence, making it difficult to change the system easily. Instead of focusing solely on the debate over the overall system, it is more productive to engage in designing specific aspects, such as limiting presidential power, implementing an effective electoral and party system to prevent the abuse of presidential authority, and establishing reasonable term limits to ensure the stability of the presidential system.

Considering the different perspectives in the debate, it seems that supporters of the presidential system are generally in a defensive position. Faced with the challenges posed by the supporters of the parliamentary system, they often respond by highlighting that the presidential system is not as bad as claimed by Linz et al., or that under favorable conditions, it can roughly achieve what the parliamentary system does. Nevertheless, while the presidential system may not be as flawed as critics argue, its overall political stability and legislative efficiency seem to be inferior to the parliamentary system. Even in the United States, a nation with the oldest constitutional tradition, the election of Donald Trump as president in 2016 and the intense controversies around the 2020 presidential election have significantly polarized the nation. In less mature democracies, granting excessive power to the president is more likely to foster authoritarianism and personalized rule.

The rupture of the collaboration between Yuan Shikai and the Nationalist Party in the early days of the Republic of China serves as a cautionary lesson. The Provisional Constitution was, in fact, the earliest example of a "dual-heads" or "semi-presidential" system in the world, where the Nationalists sought to restrain the presidential power through a cabinet controlled by the Nationalist-dominated parliament. However, it quickly collapsed due to intense power struggles. Therefore, while liberal intellectuals in China tend to favor the separation-of-powers model due to American influence, they

[19] Matthew Soberg Shugart and John M. Carey, *Presidents and Assemblies: Constitutional Design and Electoral Dynamics* (Cambridge: Cambridge University Press, 2002), p. 44.

should also be aware of its inherent risks and remain vigilant against personal ambitions fueled by the presidential system. To be sure, American constitutional practices provide valuable experiences worth learning from for China, but it does not mean that the American model is flawless or that we must copy its every detail. Even if the presidential system functions reasonably well in the United States, it does not imply that it will operate smoothly in developing countries. The presidential system in developing countries often becomes a hotbed for dictators. From Chavez to Putin, the vast majority of dictators in countries such as Latin America, Africa, Russia, and Central and Eastern Europe bear the title of "president."

Overall, I support parliamentary systems like those in the United Kingdom, Canada, Australia, India, Germany, and the Nordic countries. While some of these countries, such as Germany, do have a ceremonial "president," their power is nominal. As a symbolic leader of the nation, such presidency may comfort the popular desire for a unified authority without exercising substantial power. Therefore, the ceremonial president should not be directly elected by the voters, but rather indirectly by the parliament. A directly elected president would possess democratic legitimacy independent of parliament and would inevitably exercise substantial power. On the contrary, in a parliamentary system, the actual administrative power should be exercised by the cabinet led by the prime minister, elected by and accountable to the parliament.

The people's congress system stipulated in China's current Constitution is akin to the Westminster model, where the President of State has little real power. Fixing China's future political system to be parliamentary, perhaps with a ceremonial presidency, will also contribute to a smooth and orderly transition.

7. *Should the parliament adopt a unicameral or bicameral system? Why?*

The debate over unicameral or bicameral systems has persisted since the establishment of the US Constitution in 1788 and Sieyès' publication of *What is the Third Estate?* during the French Revolution. Influenced by Rousseau's populist theory of the general will, Sieyès naturally insisted on unicameralism.[20] According to this view, bicameralism would lead to contradictory representation of the absolutely good "general will." If both houses always agree, the second house is redundant; if there are divisions between the houses, the "general will" becomes self-contradictory. On the other hand, during the same period, the United States adopted a bicameral system:

[20] See Emmanuel Joseph Sieyès, *Political Writings*, trans. Michael Sonenscher (Indianapolis: Hackett, 2003).

The House of Representatives represents the population, elected through "one person, one vote," with the number of representatives per state proportional to the size of its citizens, while the Senate represents the states, with each state having an equal number of seats. As a result of the Great Compromise at the Philadelphia Convention, the bicameral system was crucial for the unity of the United States, without which the Convention would have broken up because the delegates from the small states would have simply walked away. Therefore, bicameralism can be seen as a "social contract" of the United States, which is crucial for keeping the various states together. Indeed, it was entrenched in the sole "permanent clause" of the US Constitution, which can never be amended, permanently ensuring equal representation of the states in the Senate, regardless of their sizes. In fact, while bicameralism does not have to follow the American model, it is a necessary (though not sufficient) institution for federalism in general. Without an effective senate, a federal state cannot be genuine even if its constitution labels itself as "federal," as in Venezuela's constitution of 1999.

While Rousseau's holistic notion of "general will" is defective and cannot be used to refute bicameralism,[21] this does not imply that unicameralism is inherently undesirable. In small countries with a relatively homogeneous structure of social interests, a unicameral system can work well. In large nations with diverse interests, however, a single parliament elected solely through "one person, one vote" may not adequately represent all segments of society. In such cases, it may be necessary to establish a second house in order to represent other interests, such as peripheral regions and ethnic groups. The demand for bicameralism increases in proportion to the size and diversity of the nation. Indeed, since many small nations also have complex ethnic or religious structures, they may have good reason to adopt a bicameral or even federal system, as in the case of Nepal. Even though bicameralism requires more effort to pass legislation compared to unicameralism, it does offer a number of benefits, such as the improved quality of legislation and protection of minority groups from the "tyranny of majority." In conclusion, the added value of establishing a Senate as an independent institution should be weighed against considerations of legislative costs and efficiency, and the decision to adopt a unicameral or bicameral system should be based on the specific national circumstances and the need to represent diverse interests effectively.[22]

[21] Qianfan Zhang, "Against the holistic temptations: A critique of three related fictions in constitutional theory," *Peking University Law Journal*, 6 (2018), 371–91.

[22] Meg Russell, "What are second chambers for?," *Parliamentary Affairs* 54 (2001), 442–3.

A crucial question in the design of a bicameral system is whether the legislative power of the two houses shall be equal. In the United States, for example, every federal law must pass both the Senate and the House of Representatives, ensuring a strict parity in legislative power. However, many other bicameral systems operate differently, where the second house may only have the power to delay the legislative process in order to force the House to undertake a sober second thought on a particular legislation. For instance, the House of Lords in the United Kingdom, composed of appointed representatives, can only delay bills passed by the House of Commons. If the House of Lords disagrees with a bill passed by the House of Commons, its failure to pass it serves to make the House of Commons reconsider whether amendments are necessary. If the House of Commons passes it again without changes, the veto power of the House of Lords is effectively nullified.

Germany provides another example of an unsymmetrical bicameral system. Legislation that affects regional interests must pass both houses, but for bills that do not have such implications, the role of the Bundesrat (Federal Council) is similar to that of the House of Lords in the United Kingdom. Compared to Britain's essentially unicameralism and rigorously symmetric bicameralism in the United States, the German approach reflects a more nuanced balance between saving legislative costs and protecting regional interests.

8. *Does China need to adopt federalism in future? If so, how should the national power and local powers be divided? How many provinces or states should China be divided into? What are the reasons supporting your conclusions?*

As of today, all major countries in the world have implemented federalism, with China being the lonely exception. Countries of a much smaller scale, such as Germany, have adopted federalism. Indeed, even "micro-states" such as Nepal have implemented "ethnic federalism." The constitutional system of the former Soviet Union was actually a confederation, going even further than federalism in ethnic "self-determination," even though it became a highly centralized system due to one-party totalitarian dictatorship. Since the establishment of its first written constitution in 1908, China has adopted over ten constitutions, but the term "federalism" has never appeared in any of the constitutional texts. However, both the 1923 Constitution presided over by Cao Kun and the 1947 Constitution reflecting Sun Yat-sen's "principle of equal powers" (均权主义) contained detailed provisions on local powers, bearing federal characteristics. Given its large population, vast territory, complex ethnic composition, and great regional disparities, some form of federalism is clearly necessary for China.

In summary, federalism stands for the constitutionalization of local autonomy. This does not mean that only federalism can guarantee local autonomy. Unitary systems can also have a high degree of local autonomy, as seen in France where significant powers were devolved to local governments in 1982. However, local autonomy under a unitary system is based not on constitutional provisions, but on national legislation, which can grant and revoke local autonomy at any time. For example, Hong Kong is supposed to enjoy high degrees of autonomy in almost all aspects, but its Basic Law is actually a legislation enacted by the National People's Congress (NPC) in Beijing. Indeed, in 2020, the NPC Standing Committee enacted the Law of State Security (国家安全法) as an amendment to the Basic Law, effectively diminishing the Hong Kong autonomy and undermining the constitutional principle of "one-country, two-systems."

In comparison, changing the division of powers between the national and regional governments in a federal system requires a constitutional amendment, which is not solely the responsibility of the central government but also involves the regions. In the United States, for example, a constitutional amendment requires a proposal by a two-thirds majority of both houses in Congress and must be ratified by a three-fourths majority of the states. In Germany, amending the Basic Law only requires the approval of the Bundestag and Bundesrat, but the senators are appointed by the state governments, representing regional interests. Therefore, a federal constitutional system must possess at least two characteristics: (1) a clear constitutional delineation of powers between the national and sub-national governments, and (2) the power to decide the division of central–local powers must be at least partially in the hands of the regions through, for example, a senate representing local interests. Otherwise, a federal constitution may be enacted, but if the central government can change it at will, it can revert to a unitary system at any time.

The division of powers between the central and local governments should be based on the principle of equality, while the specific allocation of powers should be determined according to the scope of influence of particular powers. It is essential to establish the equality of status between the central and local governments, recognizing that, as a matter of principle, local governments are not inferior to the central government. Otherwise, if the central government is considered wiser and more important than local governments, it will perpetuate the vicious cycle of excessive centralization. Some matters must be handled by the central government not because it possesses superior qualities, but because they exceed the jurisdiction of local governments due to geographical limitations. For instance, air and water pollution often extend beyond the boundaries of individual regions, and can be effectively resolved only by the central government through the uniform implementation of strict environmental standards nationwide. On the other hand, if a matter can be managed by the local government, such as marriage registration, it is generally more effectively handled by the local government due to its familiarity with local conditions, proximity to voters, and lower enforcement costs. Therefore, the European Union has established a subsidiarity principle: So long as the matter falls within the jurisdiction of a member state, it should be managed locally, namely at the national level; the role of the Community should be *subsidiary*, reserved for matters beyond the national capabilities.

In general, the powers of the central government should be limited to issues that have a nationwide impact, such as national defense, foreign affairs, currency, weights and measures, environmental protection, and macroeconomic regulation. Local governments, on the other hand, should be responsible for matters limited to local impact, such as education, public security, healthcare, and poverty relief.[23] However, largely due to the continuous expansion of industrial economy, the national power has been expanding everywhere at the expense of local power. Even in the United States, the very first nation that created modern federalism, scholars have argued that its federal framework has seriously eroded since the New Deal of the 1930s, as the constantly expanding "interstate commerce" has been authorizing federal legislation to intervene in almost any matter, making it difficult to distinguish from a unitary constitution. On the other hand, the German Basic Law system features a federal framework legislation to be implemented by individual states, which bears some resemblance to China's compound unitary constitution, making it perhaps an easier model for China to emulate.

The estimation of the number of sub-federal units in China should be based on a comparative study of countries with similar population and geographical size, such as the United States or India, while respecting China's own history and cultural traditions. Each state or province should have a relatively homogeneous ethnic and cultural composition, preferably representing a historically continuous and integrated administrative unit. In principle, individual states or provinces should not have an excessively large population or extensive territory. Nor should provinces or states be too numerous, however, as it could result in excessively fragmented territory.

[23] Ronald L. Watts, *Comparing Federal Systems*, 3rd ed. (Montreal: McGill-Queen's University Press, 2008), pp. 41–3.

Based on the current population size, fifty to sixty sub-federal units may be optimal for China's federal framework.[24]

9. *On which level should local autonomy be implemented – provinces or counties? What are the most important elements of local autonomy?*

As mentioned above, local autonomy is divided into two levels: constitutional and legislative. While the former implies federalism, the latter represents a unitary framework in which local autonomy is granted by national legislation. Currently, China obviously lacks local autonomy in the constitutional sense, namely federalism. However, it is possible to implement local autonomy in a general sense, such as through the election of local people's congresses and self-governance of specific local affairs. These features are already stipulated in the current Constitution, which establishes a bottom-up framework for the election of people's congresses. Nevertheless, under a one-party system, it has, in practice, been turned into a system of top-down control. Despite practical difficulties, from the grassroots level of townships and counties to the National People's Congress at the very top, the current Constitution theoretically allows for primitive local autonomy in terms of personnel.

However, even primitive local autonomy encounters complex issues. For example, how should courts, procuratorates, civil servants and police at various levels be selected, and to whom should they be held accountable? The China's current Constitution stipulates uniformly a horizontal accountability mechanism, where the local people's congresses are responsible for the selection and supervision of administrative and judicial personnel at the same level. While this can be considered as a form of "local autonomy," local administrative and judicial organs are still subject to intervention from higher levels. On the other hand, local autonomy is not an absolute good. For example, the horizontal accountability system is likely to force local administration and judiciary to engage in local protectionism. Even in a country where personnel autonomy is truly implemented, it can only ensure the effective implementation of local legislation, rather than national legislation, by the local administration and judiciary. Indeed, local discrimination and protectionism may get even worse as the local autonomy is better implemented.

To solve such a problem, the American approach is relatively simple. As the federal and state governments are entirely separate, each forming a constitutional framework complete in itself, both the federal and state governments

[24] Zhang Qianfan, *National Sovereignty and Local Autonomy* [in Chinese] (Beijing: China Democracy Legal System Publishing House, 2012), 281–92.

have their own legislature, administration, and judiciary, with the latter primarily responsible for implementing their own legislation. The legislative conflicts between the federal and state governments are to be settled in court. In other words, the federal government primarily relies on its own administration and judiciary, rather than states and local governments, to implement federal laws, effectively preventing local protectionism, with the potential drawback of higher administrative and judicial costs.

The alternative model is represented by the German federal system, in which the federal and state governments share one set of institutions, similar to the situation in China. While the federal court is the highest court of the nation, the state courts serve as appellate courts, and the district courts are the trial courts. For a country with the size of Germany, local protectionism may not be a serious problem, especially since the major legislation is mainly the responsibility of the federal legislature. Since China is much larger in scale, however, it remains a question whether such a solution is feasible. In an effort to control local protectionism, the fourth phase of judicial reform implemented from 2014 to 2019 had the provinces partially take control of local judicial finances. Imitating the American system, the Supreme People's Court established several "regional circuit courts" (大区巡回法院), each overseeing the high courts of several provinces in a region.

Beyond the personnel autonomy, the second level of local autonomy is legislative autonomy at the local level. If such autonomy is entrenched in the constitution, implying that the central and local governments delineate their respective jurisdictions based on the scope of subject matters, the central government is prohibited from encroaching upon the legislative domain of local governments. Even without constitutionally granted powers, local governments may still enjoy legislative powers. For example, in China's current constitutional framework, local governments can formulate regulations or rules according to local needs.[25] In this case, however, the central legislative power is not subject to any constitutional restrictions, and is thus capable of repealing its devolutionary legislation at will.

Further, the implementation of constitutional local autonomy can be divided into the state and local levels. The US Constitution designates only states as sub-federal units, without mentioning local governments such as counties and municipalities, implying that local autonomy below the state level is not supported by the federal constitution. Some state constitutions allow for local units below the state level to exercise autonomy as a state constitutional power. In comparison, the German Basic Law explicitly

[25] Law on Legislations, Art. 72.

mentions local autonomy for counties and cities, while the Constitution of the Republic of China (1947), commonly regarded as a unitary constitution, specifically provides for county-level legislative powers. Given China's population and geographical size, it seems appropriate to implement legislative autonomy at both provincial and county levels. Compared to county-level legislative autonomy, however, the distribution of legislative powers between the national and provincial or state governments is of primary importance.

The third level of local autonomy is the so-called institutional autonomy, referring to the right of sub-national governments to design their own institutional framework. It is usually available only in a federal constitution, which allows the states or local governments to choose their governing structures through their own constitutions or basic laws. For instance, one state may adopt a parliamentary system, while the other can adopt a gubernatorial system akin to presidentialism at the federal level. In the United States, as each state has its own constitution, the role of the federal government, as defined in the Guarantee Clause, is limited to ensuring that each state has a republican form of government. In other words, as long as the political system of each state is republican rather than monarchical or dictatorial, the federal government has no authority to intervene in the institutional choice of a state. Of course, this does not mean that a state can make whatever constitution or laws it wants since they must not violate the US Constitution, such as its protection of the fundamental individual freedoms and prohibition of racial discrimination or slavery. Apart from these federal constitutional constraints, however, the state has considerable leeway in designing its constitutional structure. As observed by Justice Harlan, one great advantage of federalism is providing ample opportunity for local institutional innovation and competition, allowing each region to tailor and experiment with constitutional designs that best suit their own needs.[26]

Although China's current Constitution does not explicitly specify a centralized unitary system, it does impose a uniform framework of people's congresses on every local government. In the 1990s, some townships and even counties experimented with the direct elections of local leaders, who were supposed to be indirectly elected by the local people's congresses according to the Constitution. Although these local experiments turned out successful, they were later halted by the NPCSC, citing "unconstitutionality." Such restriction on institutional innovation severely limits the room for local experimentation. In fact, even under the "one country, two systems" principle, Hong Kong as a Special Administrative Region has no institutional autonomy.

[26] New State Ice Co. v. Liebmann, 285 US 262 (1932).

The Basic Law was tailored for Hong Kong by the NPC, rather than a constitution adopted by the Hong Kong people. As a result, universal suffrage in Hong Kong must be approved by the central government, whose refusal led to the massive protests and the ensuing crackdown in 2019.[27]

In summary, the lack of institutional autonomy was the root cause of the Hong Kong crisis. More specific, the crisis in Hong Kong stemmed from the conspicuous lack of coordination between the three levels of autonomy: While its legal autonomy far exceeds the federal system, its political autonomy is even weaker than a typical unitary system such as China, where local administrative leaders are supposed to be elected by the local people's congress rather than appointed by the central government, and the absence of institutional autonomy renders electoral reforms hopeless. It is unlikely that any breakthroughs in institutional autonomy will take place in the short term, or that the election method for the Chief Executive and the Legislative Council will be substantially improved. Indeed, the electoral change to the Legco constituted a wholesale retrogression, reducing the directly elected members from one half to barely over 20 percent.[28] However, such reform is not irreversible, and the directly elected members can still serve as the institutional basis for Hong Kong's future political reform. Despite the "executive-dominant" model adopted by the Basic Law, giving the Chief Executive significant power, which surpasses that of the US president under the separation of powers system, as long as part of the Legco is properly elected to represent the will of the Hong Kong people, the Chief Executive will find it difficult to govern alone for long. Dominated by the central government, the recent reform points to the opposite direction and must be reversed in the future.

10. *What kind of special status should Taiwan, Hong Kong, Macau, Xinjiang, and Tibet enjoy in the constitution? What suggestions do you have for Hong Kong's "dual universal suffrage" (双普选) in the future?*

Federalism is a flexible category that can take both symmetric and asymmetric forms. Symmetric federalism refers to a framework in which states or provinces are treated equally, such as in the United States. The German federalism is also largely a symmetric one, despite its fiscal equalization program through which financially disadvantaged states receive preferential treatment. On the

[27] For a review, see Amedeo Gasparini, "The Tale of Hong Kong: From Freedom to Crackdown," Policy Paper (Institute for Politics and Society, 2021), www.politikaspolecnost.cz/wp-content/uploads/2021/01/The-Tale-of-Hong-Kong-From-Freedom-To-Crackdown-IPPS.pdf.

[28] Basic Law, Annex II, www.basiclaw.gov.hk/en/basiclaw/annex2.html.

other hand, some federal states have adopted asymmetric federalism due to their unique circumstances, granting certain states or provinces special status in the federation. The predominantly French-speaking province of Quebec stands out as a prominent example in Canada, where the special status of the French language and culture has been the subject of constitutional disputes. In the 1990s, Quebec even held a referendum for independence.[29] Quebec's special constitutional status has helped appease French-speaking voters, making them more comfortable remaining within the federation. If a symmetric federalism were implemented, separatist referenda might have succeeded long ago, demonstrating how federalism, with its guarantee of local autonomy and flexible institutional design, may help maintain national unity. However, China's mainstream propaganda often resort to a smear tactic with ulterior motives by deliberately confusing federalism and local autonomy with separatism. In a diverse society, federalism clearly contributes to the maintenance of national unity, while a simplistic and rigid unitary system is more prone to disintegration.

As local autonomy at the first level, "dual universal suffrage" proposed by the liberals in Hong Kong does not require any special institutional arrangements, but shall be implemented as a fundamental democratic principle in any place, including mainland China. In fact, this is an explicit requirement in China's current Constitution. To maintain national unity, it is essential to grant local people the democratic right to elect their own representatives. "Hong Kong independence" (港独) forces emerged and developed in recent years precisely because extremes breed opposition. The central government's "comprehensive regulation" (全面管治) approach and the deprivation of universal suffrage greatly stimulated the independence demands. Such a turmoil would not have occurred had the central government responded properly to public opinion and granted Hong Kong people the autonomy and universal suffrage.

The same logic applies to Tibet, Xinjiang, Inner Mongolia, and other regions where ethnic minorities are concentrated. Some worry that democracy will encourage separatist forces in these regions, leading to "secession" from China. This confuses the cause with effect, as it is the excessive centralization and suppression that alienate the minorities and create centrifugal forces in these areas. When the central control is no longer effective, the separatist sentiments in these regions will rebound and redouble. Respecting the democratic autonomy and basic rights of these regions is in line with the

[29] Reference re Secession of Quebec, [1998] 2 S.C.R. 217.

will of their people, and will establish a solid foundation for national unity based on voluntary recognition.

China's uniqueness requires the establishment of an asymmetric federalism at different levels. However, this unique arrangement should be built upon universality. Regardless of special status, China needs to implement universal constitutional principles that respect fundamental freedoms, equality, rule of law, democracy, and local autonomy in all regions, which will address the vast majority of local issues and lay the institutional foundation for solid national unity. Of course, depending on specific circumstances, different institutional designs are needed for special regions such as Taiwan, Hong Kong, Macau, Tibet, Xinjiang, and Inner Mongolia. However, regardless of how local systems are designed, they must not violate the fundamental principles set by the national constitution, such as the prohibition of slavery or the separation of church and state.

At the moment, China grants certain legislative privileges to "ethnic minority regions" (少数民族区域) such as Tibet, Xinjiang, and Inner Mongolia, allowing them to enact legislation according to their customs and traditions and exempting them from certain national laws. In reality, the autonomy of ethnic minority areas is not substantially greater than that of ordinary mainland areas. In fact, they are subject to even stricter control for stability maintenance. Once the legislative relationship between the central and local authorities is clarified in the future, the legislative power of ethnic minorities will cease to be a problem because the central government has no authority to interfere in local legislation concerning religion or culture, which falls under the purview of local jurisdiction. It is also possible to emulate the "one country, two systems" model implemented in Hong Kong and Macau, granting a high degree of legislative autonomy to ethnic minority areas.

Hong Kong and Macau differ from the states in a typical federal state in that they do not apply the vast majority of national laws. In the future, they need to further advance "one country, two systems," implement genuine universal suffrage and achieve complete local autonomy. Finally, Taiwan and the mainland are currently in a state of divided sovereignty, requiring special institutional arrangements. In the future, Taiwan should not only exercise complete autonomy in legislation, administration, and judiciary, but also enjoy a high degree of autonomy in areas such as the military, defense, and foreign affairs.

In summary, China should implement a parliamentary federal system in the future. Vertically, the constitution should fully guarantee local autonomy and implement local democracy based on universal suffrage. Legislative powers between the central and local authorities should be defined based on the scope of impact, allowing local people to decide their policies and institutions within the scope of autonomy granted by the constitution. Special regions such as Taiwan, Hong Kong, Macau, Inner Mongolia, Xinjiang, and Tibet should have special right to autonomy.

Horizontally, local regions should determine their governing structure according to their needs, while the central government should adopt a parliamentary system or a ceremonial presidency based on models from countries like the United Kingdom and India. The parliament should consist of a bicameral system, with the cabinet elected by and held accountable to the lower house while being supervised by the upper house. The future constitution will share considerable continuity with the current Constitution, with significant similarities between parliamentarism and the existing people's congress system. While the new constitution is characterized by the direct election of all levels of parliament by voters, the current Constitution stipulates that the people's congresses at or above the county level are indirectly elected by the people's congress at the next lower level. Furthermore, the new constitution is characterized by the clear delineation of power between the central and local authorities, as well as the explicit constitutional guarantees for a high degree of autonomy in special regions, while the current Constitution lacks clear division of vertical powers and authorizes the NPC to formulate the Basic Laws for Hong Kong and Macau, limiting their autonomy to the legislative level.

The roadmap for constitutional reform aims to promote universal suffrage in all levels of people's congress elections in mainland China, achieve a high degree of autonomy for Hong Kong and Macau, and gradually advance the constitutionalization of local autonomy, particularly in ethnic minority areas. The continuous improvement of the constitutional framework will pave the way for a more democratic and inclusive governance system in China.

6.3 POLITICAL PARTY AND ELECTIONS

11. *How should a free and fair electoral system be designed? What are the basic requirements for an electoral system to be considered fair?*

A free and fair electoral system is crucial for democratic self-governance and for ensuring that governments are held accountable to the people. Whether an election is free and fair directly determines its authenticity and the nature of the political system. Without genuine elections, the regime is inevitably authoritarian. In general, a free and fair election must be characterized by the following five features: universal, direct, free, secret, and equal.[30]

First, universal suffrage. The right to vote must be universal, allowing all eligible citizens to participate as voters or candidates in the elections. The only restrictions should be based on citizenship and cognitive capacity. Voters must be adult citizens capable of understanding the relationship between their chosen candidates and the policies they represent, as well as the implications for their own interests and preferences. Therefore, most countries set age requirements for voting, usually eighteen years old. Some countries also require sanity and prohibit certain types of criminals from voting. Personally, I do not believe that these restrictions are necessary. Psychiatric patients are a small group in the population and are generally not involved in elections. Even if they participate, their influence on the election results is negligible since random choices cancel each other out. Similar rationale applies to criminals. China's Criminal Law even includes "deprivation of political rights" as an additional punishment that would apply to the criminal after serving the jail sentence. Such penalty constitutes unconstitutional deprivation of political rights and should be abolished.[31]

Second, direct election of legislators. Parliamentary representatives shall be elected directly by the voters rather than through indirect elections by other representatives, as in China's case where the people's congresses above the county level are elected by the people's congresses at one level below. Indirect elections conducted within small, closed circles are prone to fraud, manipulation, and bribery. Therefore, the indirect legislative elections in China should be abolished and replaced with direct elections by the voters.

Third, free electoral activities. If candidates cannot freely stand out to communicate with voters, or voters are forced to choose among "candidates" whom they do not choose and do not care to know the positions they represent and their relevance to their own interest, then what is to be elected? Candidates are not only the subject but also the essence of elections. Elections where candidates are manipulated are inevitably fake "elections."

Fourth, secret ballots. Free elections imply that ballots shall be cast secretly rather than publicly, as open voting can easily be influenced by bribery or intimidation. Australia introduced the first "Australian ballot" precisely to eliminate electoral corruption and protect the integrity of the voting process. When voting is conducted in secret, candidates or political parties cannot

30 Zhang Qianfan, *Introduction to the Study of Constitutional Law: Principles and Applications*, 3rd ed. [in Chinese] (Beijing: Law Press, 2014), pp. 403–6.

31 Ibid., pp. 460–1.

know how individual voters cast their votes, making bribery or intimidation useless.

Last but not the least, "one person, one vote," meaning that the weight of each vote must be equal. This is particularly important to countries that adopt the "single-member district" electoral system, where each district should roughly represent the same number of voters. Without equal representation, unfair outcomes that violate the democratic principle will arise. For instance, suppose that a nation composed of 100 districts elects a parliament with 100 seats, each district electing one representative. If 90 districts have 10,000 voters each while the other 10 districts have 100,000 voters each, then the 90 representatives actually represent only 900,000 voters, while the 10 representatives represent 1 million voters. In such a scenario, the ten representatives would hold only 10 percent of the seats, despite representing a larger number of voters. Such an unequal distribution of seats leads to extreme unfairness and an anti-majoritarian electoral result, where representatives of the majority become a minority in the legislature. To address this problem, the US Supreme Court established the principle of "one person, one vote" in a landmark decision in 1964.[32] Since the legislators are supposed to represent their people rather than acres, the weight of votes must be equal across various districts. Only then can representatives of the majority occupy a majority of seats in the legislature and legislate in the interests of the majority.

The people of Hong Kong protested in 2019 precisely because its electoral system based on functional groups seriously violates "one person, one vote." The combined votes of ordinary constituencies in the labor sector, making up the absolute majority in population, amount to only one-quarter of the total votes, while a small number of elites in other three sectors composed of finance, business, law, medicine, and the civil service constitute the vast majority of votes. This disparity is the very reason that the people of Hong Kong are striving for "genuine universal suffrage" (真普选) based on "one person, one vote."

12. *While the two-party system is predominant in the United States and the United Kingdom, multi-party systems are prevalent in the Continental Europe. Which model should China establish in the future? Why?*

First, it is essential to clarify that a two-party system is also a form of "multi-party system" and is fundamentally distinct from a one-party system. The crucial distinction is not the number of political parties, but whether the number is singular or plural. For the number of parties, the distinction

[32] Reynolds v. Sims, 377 US 533 (1964).

between 1 and 2 is far more significant than that between 2 and 100. Although the United States and United Kingdom have only one more party than China's one-party system, their difference is "qualitative," while the differences between the British and American two-party systems and the European multi-party systems are merely "quantitative."

While European countries usually have more than two major parties, two major parties in the United Kingdom and the United States encompass the vast majority of votes, although third parties do arise now and then. This distinction is explained by the Duverger's Law in electoral systems.[33] The parliamentary elections in the United Kingdom and the United States adopt a first-past-the-poll system, where the electoral landscape is divided into a certain number of electoral districts, each electing one representative. The candidate receiving the most votes is elected. For example, the US House of Representatives has 435 seats, elected from 435 single-member districts nationwide, with each state distributing seats in proportion to the number of voters within its jurisdiction. The consequence of this electoral system is "winner-takes-all": Since there is only one seat in each electoral district, a slight shortage in the number of votes will result in a complete loss for the other candidate. The winner-takes-all rule forces all parties to consolidate, leading to the emergence of a stable two-party scenario. Smaller parties have strong incentives to be absorbed by larger parties, as they would otherwise have no chance of winning. In contrast, European countries generally adopt proportional representation, where seats are allocated according to the percentage of votes each party receives nationwide in the elections. Even the smallest party can receive seats proportionally if the proportion reaches the threshold defined in the constitution or election law. As neither major nor minor parties face pressure for consolidation, a multi-party system naturally emerges.

Both two-party system and multi-party system have pros and cons. A multi-party system is fairer, as it allows seats to more proportionally reflect the preferences of the electorate. However, if political parties are too numerous, the parliamentary structure can become too fragmented, making it difficult to form a stable cabinet and prone to regime instability or even collapse. The Weimar Republic in 1919, which adopted an ideal proportional representation system, experienced frequent changes in government and ultimately handed power to Hitler within a decade. On the other hand, a two-party system can lead to the winner-takes-all scenario by major parties, eliminating

[33] See Maurice Duverger, *Political Parties: Their Organization and Activity in the Modern State* (London & New York: John Wiley & Sons, 1954).

smaller parties and distorting the parliamentary structure in representing the electoral preferences. In hypothetical extreme situations, a political party supported by 51 percent of voters nationwide can obtain 100 percent of the seats, while a party with 49 percent of the votes may end up with no seats at all. However, the advantage of a two-party system lies in its stability, usually with a majority party in parliament. As the majority and the minority parties take turns in governing, the political crisis caused by sheer number of political parties is effectively avoided.

Since both systems have their merits, many countries attempt to balance their strengths and weaknesses by adopting various forms of mixed systems. For example, under the post-war electoral system defined in the German Basic Law enacted in 1949, half of the seats in the Bundestag are elected through proportional representation, while the other half are elected through single-member districts, although it is almost purely proportional in effect. To avoid the parliamentary fragmentation, the election law established the 5 percent threshold, requiring political parties to receive over 5 percent of the votes nationwide to be eligible for proportional seat allocation. The purpose of the 5 percent rule is to prevent small, extreme parties from entering the parliament and to increase the stability of the parliament and the cabinet.

Since China has had a long history of one-party rule, the key is to open up elections while ensuring their order and stability. As multi-party competition is currently forbidden, proportional representation is not applicable. The existing electoral system is based on multi-member districts, which can produce certain effects of proportional representation if used properly. However, if proportional representation was implemented from the beginning, it would likely lead to numerous political parties and chaos. To ensure a smooth and stable transition, China should continue and reform its current electoral district system in the near future, with the hope of keeping the number of political parties under control and streamlining their structures. Once the party politics is stabilized and voters become familiar with democratic practices, they can decide whether to switch to proportional representation or incorporate its elements.

13. *What shall be the relationship between the ruling party and the state? What can be done to ensure administrative neutrality and depoliticization?*

While any state has a ruling party, the ruling party in a legitimate state is elected through periodic elections and holds the majority in parliament. Its role is to legislate and determine the major policies and value choices of the state during its term in office. The task of the administration is to faithfully implement the legislation enacted by the parliament, which has obtained the authorization of the majority of voters, rather than impose its own value judgments on the state. Essentially, the administration itself should be politically neutral, as political decisions have already been made by the elected parliament and reflected in the law. If the administration adds its own bias, it inevitably becomes authoritarian. Comparing the state to a person, the parliament is the brain, and the administration is the limbs. Just as the limbs of a normal person cannot act independently of the brain's commands, the state administration must not violate legislation or act at its own discretion. Therefore, in a state committed to democracy and the rule of law, the ruling party leads the state through legislation but should not interfere with administrative enforcement. Civil servants, police, military and other administrative forces must maintain political neutrality or, in other words, be "depoliticized."

This logic was clearly expressed in the report of General Secretary Zhao Ziyang at the thirteenth CCP Congress in 1987. In essence, it was summarized as the "separation of the Party and government" (党政分开). The role of the ruling party is to lead the NPC, the supreme legislature of the state, in legislation and at the same time supervise, but not interfere with, the administration and the judiciary. If the ruling party directly intervenes in the administration and the judiciary, it becomes both the player and the referee, violating the fundamental principle that "no one can be the judge in his own case." The prevalence of corruption in recent decades of reform is precisely due to the lack of implementation of the "separation of party and government." In fact, the merging of party and government has even intensified in recent years, inevitably exacerbating corruption and abuse of power in the long run.

14. *Do you think term limits for leaders should be established? How can term limits be implemented?*

Since the constitutional amendment in 2018, the issue of leadership term limits has been widely discussed both in and outside China. Under China's current system, the abolition of life tenure is undoubtedly a progress. It is a "politically correct" matter that needs no debate. However, life tenure touches only on a superficial issue rather than the essence. Especially, it can never be taken for granted that everything will be fine as long as life tenure is abolished. In fact, as long as leaders are not elected and their power is not effectively checked, it makes little difference whether their term is limited or not. It is entirely possible for a fresh group of "mosquitoes" to suck even harder. Moreover, as long as the state fails to practice constitutional democracy, there is nothing to prevent the resurgence of abolished life tenure. The constitutional amendment in 2018 has made this possibility a reality. Therefore, the key does not lie in term limits, but in constitutional democracy.

In a constitutional democracy, the desirability of implementing term limits depends on the nature of the position and cannot be generalized. First, if the position is elected by the people, and the re-election of an incumbent represents the will of the majority voters, implementing term limit actually contradicts majoritarian democracy. It is generally agreed that members of parliament can be re-elected indefinitely. Nor is the term of prime minister limited because it is a matter of right that the majority party in parliament becomes the ruling party through popular votes, and the leader of the ruling party leads the cabinet as the prime minister. Prime Ministers like Angela Merkel and Shinzo Abe were re-elected for many terms, and can continue to be re-elected indefinitely as long as they are the choice of voters. To be sure, they can be too old to perform their functions properly,[34] but the decision to remove them ultimately lies with the voters.

Second, if a position is vested with substantial power, it is necessary to limit its term to prevent incumbents from monopolizing and abusing power, even if they are capable of being re-elected through elections. Term limits commonly apply to strong presidencies in presidential systems. It is well known that George Washington set a great precedent by serving only two terms. Some African, Latin American, and Central Asian countries have long or even unlimited presidential terms, a sign of autocracy. In Russia, President Putin exchanged positions with the prime minister to bypass the two-term limit.

Finally, since ceremonial heads of state hold no substantive power and are generally not directly elected, it is usually unnecessary to limit their terms. Extreme examples are the constitutional monarchs such as the Japanese Tenno and the British King. For example, Queen Elizabeth II held her throne for as long as seven decades, while the United Kingdom is universally recognized as a constitutional democracy. These hereditary lineages can be permanent without arousing fear precisely because they are almost purely symbolic.

In summary, in a constitutional democracy where the public power is effectively checked and balanced, term limits are a minor issue. Without

[34] This has become a serious and common problem in contemporary American politics, where certain Congressional incumbents appear to remain in office indefinitely. For instance, Senate Minority Leader Mitch McConnell, now eighty-one years old, has been serving as a senator since 1985. This tenure exceeds that of most dictators around the world. Rebecca Shabad et al., "Mitch McConnell escorted away from cameras after freezing during a news conference," NBC News (July 27, 2023), www.nbcnews.com/politics/congress/watch-mitch-mcconnell-freeze-press-conference-rcna96486.

constitutional democracy, term limit becomes a major issue, but it is futile to focus on it since it can be resolved only through constitutional democracy. Therefore, it is necessary to shift the focus to the fundamental issues away from superficial ones such as term limits. Breaking life tenure was a small step taken by Deng Xiaoping in the direction of political reform – an expedient stopgap allowed by the political situation at the time. However, it should not be seen as a substitute for more fundamental political reforms, without which term limits are not only of little significance but also unsustainable. Benjamin Franklin put it well: "Those who would give up essential liberty to purchase a little temporary safety deserve neither liberty nor safety." Term limits provide a false sense of security without genuine safeguards. Only through comprehensive democratic reforms, coupled with the decentralization and separation of powers, can term limits be meaningful and institutionally durable.

15. *How do you evaluate the current situation of China's judiciary? How can China realize judicial independence in future?*

The current situation of China's judiciary can be evaluated on two levels. On the one hand, academic research and education have made significant progress over the past three to four decades. Despite many "sensitive words" in the field of constitutional study, legal scholars have gained a largely accurate understanding of Western legal systems, which has positively influenced the knowledge structure of China's judiciary. Large numbers of law graduates who enter the courts, procuratorates, and civil service each year contribute to a generally sound knowledge structure.

On the other hand, neither the moral caliber of judicial personnel nor the judicial power structure have experienced significant improvement. In contrast to the considerable presence of "healthy forces" (健康力量) within the system in the 1980s, the intensified political control over the past four decades has led to a complete "reverse selection" within the system, through which the "healthy forces" have effectively been eliminated. Although the current Constitution stipulates the "independence of trial" (审判独立) in Article 41, the ruling party explicitly rejects "judicial independence," while the implementation of the "president responsibility system" (院长负责制) within the courts means that individual judges are subject to the political and administrative control. The judicial reform that began in 1999 made a "loud thunder with little rain," failing to touch upon the internal power structure of the courts. In 2008, Wang Shengjun (王胜俊), nicknamed the "law-blind" (法盲) President of the Supreme Court, reversed the trend of the previous reforms, abandoning the principle of judicial professionalization and returning to the populist "mass line" (群众路线) approach. The most recent judicial reform attempted to return to the path of professionalization, aiming to grant judges greater individual autonomy, but insiders suggest that the overall environment of increasing politicization has limited its effectiveness in enabling judges to resist superior pressure and instruction. Heading for the west but driving to the east, the ruling party has consistently paid lip service to judicial fairness while repeatedly rejecting judicial independence.

Judicial independence is clearly a necessary condition for judicial fairness. Achieving judicial independence can follow two paths: an easy one and a hard one. The easy path relies on the awakening of the powerholders to implement top-down judicial reform without altering the political system. This path has been attempted since 1999 but has proven to be ineffective. Once the vested interests realize that judicial reforms under the same political system will still affect their interests, this path will quickly come to a standstill, as China's judicial reform has experienced since 2008. To be sure, if the leaders are enlightened and understand the significance of judicial independence for the legitimacy of governance, thus implementing enlightened authoritarianism similar to that in Singapore, judicial reform may have a chance. However, China never seems to be so fortunate. If top-down reforms cannot sustain, then substantial progress in judicial reform can only be achieved through the hard path of political democratization.

6.4 SEPARATION OF POWERS

16. *The essence of democracy is the rule of majority. How can the basic rights of minorities be protected in democratic China?*

Under methodological individualism, the "people" are not a sacred, lofty, singular whole, but rather composed of self-interested individuals. Democracy cannot possibly make everyone happy with every decision. Facing disagreements and conflicting interests, the only option is to vote, and policies endorsed by the majority usually only satisfy the majority. However, the majority is also composed of individuals who can make mistakes. As early as 399 BC, the Athenian juries twice condemned Socrates to death. At one point in history, considerable portions of both the population of the Soviet Union and Nazi Germany supported totalitarian regimes, voting them into power. These are typical examples of the "tyranny of the majority." Of course, the possibility of such tyranny does not negate the essential merit of democracy. After all, the vast majority of tyrannies throughout history across the world have been rule by a minority rather than the majority. It means simply that democracy is not an unqualified good and also needs to be constrained, especially to prevent the majority from violating the basic rights of minorities as protected in the constitution. This is the very reason why we advocate for "constitutional democracy": Democracy as the rule of the majority can neither be abandoned nor unconditionally accepted; rather, it should be subject to the constraints of other constitutional elements.

The main mechanism for protecting the rights of minorities is judicial review, both at the constitutional and legal levels. First, the principle of the rule of law requires that only laws enacted by a popularly elected legislature can affect individual rights. Second, restriction of personal freedom must be done through judicial proceedings. To prevent arbitrary rule by man, the will of the majority cannot surpass the law and the judiciary. Finally, individuals can resort to judicial review to challenge and invalidate legislation that violates the rights protected by the constitution. For example, the courts can refuse to apply certain criminal punishments that are excessively cruel and unusual, protecting individuals from potential abuse of the majoritarian power.[35]

17. *Constitutionalism means governing the country according to the constitution. How do you think the lofty status of the Constitution should be guaranteed in future China? How should the mechanism for constitutional review be designed? Does the court have the power to interpret the constitution?*

The supreme status of the constitution, as the supreme law of the land, can be guaranteed only by an effective system of judicial review. In other words, it is necessary to establish a court with the authority to review the constitutionality of ordinary legislation. First and foremost, it is important to understand that litigation is the necessary means to enforce any law. Where there is a law, there will be litigations, which must be adjudicated by an impartial court. While China has civil courts for civil law, criminal courts for criminal law, and even administrative courts for administrative law, it has neither a constitutional court nor constitutional litigations. It is no wonder that China has "a constitution without constitutionalism."[36] To govern according to the constitution, it is essential to establish a mechanism for constitutional review, and it is the role of the court to interpret, apply, and enforce the constitution.

Why should it be the court and not the legislature, the executive, or other institutions that are entrusted to interpret the constitution? This is because the constitution is also a law, and the interpretation of the constitution or any law

[35] The US Constitution, 8th Amendment.

[36] Qianfan Zhang, "A constitution without constitutionalism? The paths of constitutional developments in China," *International Journal of Constitutional Law* 8 (2010): 950–76.

is inherently a judicial function. The legislature is responsible for making laws, the executive for enforcing laws, and both legislative and executive activities involve understanding, interpreting, and applying the law. But the ultimate power of interpreting laws belongs specifically to the judiciary. Clearly, criminal proceedings cannot be decided by the police according to its interpretation of criminal law. In that case, why even bother having a court? Without a court, is there still anything that can be called a "litigation"? The police can simply incarcerate the suspect and put him in prison. The purpose of litigation is precisely to control the police and administrative power by law, which the court must have the power to independently interpret, and the judicial interpretation must supersede administrative interpretation of the same law.

Just as administrative litigation aims to assess whether an administrative act complies with the law, constitutional litigation aims to assess whether the law itself complies with the constitution. However, if the constitutionality of legislation is decided by the legislature itself, how is that different from allowing the police to decide the legality of their own arrest? Both cases violate the basic logic of the rule of law, which dictates that no one should be the judge of their own case. China's current Constitution stipulates in Article 61 that the NPC Standing Committee (NPCSC) interprets and implements the Constitution, while the vast majority of national legislations are formulated by the Standing Committee itself. How can any legislature be expected to declare its own laws unconstitutional? This is one of the root causes why China has "a constitution without constitutionalism," leaving its Constitution unenforced.

It is thus evident that the court has not only the power but also the obligation to interpret and enforce the constitution. China today is plagued by a widespread misunderstanding that Article 61 of the 1982 Constitution, authorizing the NPCSC to interpret and implement the Constitution, means the NPCSC is the only one authorized to interpret the Constitution. This misunderstanding has led to a long-standing inaction by the courts in constitutional interpretation and application, rendering the Constitution merely a beautiful castle in the air. The truth is that the Constitution itself does not prohibit any institution from interpreting the Constitution. Indeed, it cannot, since any institution created by the Constitution must interpret and apply the Constitution in order to act constitutionally. Thus, Article 61 can only be understood as the Standing Committee being the highest but not the sole institution for interpreting the Constitution. Therefore, the court is certainly authorized to interpret the Constitution. In 2001, the Supreme People's Court cited the Constitution for the first time in the Qi Yuling case, setting a precedent for "constitutional adjudication."[37] Like the anticlimactic judicial reform, however, the precedent was abolished in 2008. It is necessary to first abolish the absurd misunderstanding that only the Standing Committee but not the court is authorized to interpret the Constitution before China's constitutional review can take root.

There are primarily two models of judicial review. One is the decentralized review represented by the United States, where the courts have general jurisdiction without subdivision into special disciplines of law. As a result, almost any ordinary court, federal or state, can handle constitutional issues in litigation. The other is the centralized review represented by Germany which, under the French influence, traditionally adopted specialized courts for civil, criminal, administrative, and other jurisdictions. In 1949, the Basic Law adds constitutional law as a new jurisdiction handled specifically by the constitutional court.

Although China's current legal system is closer to the continental system, it is difficult to establish a constitutional court in the short term. A possible approach is to emulate Taiwan's Grand Conference of Justices (大法官会议), allowing constitutional issues from different areas of law to be handled by a specialized committee established within the Supreme People's Court. In the future, China may be more suitable to adopt the centralized review similar to Germany. Overall, the German model is more contemporary, carefully designed, and consistent with China's long-standing legal practice.[38]

18. *What roles can human rights lawyers and the legal profession as a whole play in advocating judicial independence, the rule of law, and constitutional transformation in Chinese society?*

Lawyers are individuals who have passed the national judicial examination, obtained legal qualifications recognized by the state, and specialize in legal affairs. Upholding the rule of law relies not only on judges, but also on lawyers who are more numerous and enjoy a relatively independent status. In the era of planned economy, China had no rule of law, resulting in a spectacle where judges and prosecutors were many times more than lawyers. Indeed, the very profession of "lawyer" was unknown to many in society, having only witnessed "public trials" (公审) conducted by majestic judges. Since the start of the reform in 1978–79, the number of lawyers has steadily increased and now exceeds that of judges. In 2005, a unified judicial examination was implemented for judges, prosecutors, and lawyers, leading to the proposal that

[37] Ibid., 960–3.

[38] See Zhang Qianfan et al., *Comparative Study on the Systems of Judicial Review* [in Chinese] (Nanjing: Yilin Press, 2011), pp. 103–22.

China has formed a common "legal community," working together towards the common goal of upholding the rule of law. After more than a decade, however, the "community" proved to be illusory since, after all, the judges and prosecutors belong to the vested interest within the system. Some lawyers began to take a different path, refusing to collude with the system. Some "die-hard lawyers" (死磕律师) even had intense clashes with the judiciary.

To be sure, there are still "healthy forces" within the system, but I am pessimistic about their capacity and motivation to uphold the rule of law in the absence of an independent status. In fact, lawyers can be considered as individuals who are partly within the system since those who engage in legal work shall at least accept the constitutional and legal system. In China, however, the Constitution and laws are often for show rather than practical use. It is precisely the lawyers who insist on using the Constitution and laws that are often violated by the state power. As a result, some human rights lawyers have faced severe suppression, such as in the July 9 Incident in 2015. However, compared to those within the system, lawyers as a whole face less control and therefore possess a stronger capacity and motivation to uphold the rule of law. They have become a cornerstone in promoting the rule of law and rectifying miscarriages of justice.

Historically, lawyers have been the indispensable driving force of constitutional transition. Lawyers involved in the Beautiful Island Incident (美丽岛事件) in 1979, such as Chen Shui-bian (陈水扁), Hsieh Chang-ting (谢长廷), and Su Tseng-chang (苏贞昌), have made positive contributions to Taiwan's transition, which were recognized by the fact that they were later elected as major leaders during the process of democratic consolidation. President Ma Ying-jeou, elected in 2008, has received systematic legal training as a Harvard law graduate. Social transformation needs the participation of numerous independent and liberal legal professionals, who advocate societal change without going to extremes. Similarly, individuals within the system who have received legal education and think like lawyers generally have a professional baseline, without being blindly conservative. By combining legal professionals from both within and outside the system, it is possible to facilitate a successful constitutional transition.

19. *The institutional arrangements of decentralization, checks and balances, and the rule of law are designed to maximize the protection of freedom. In your opinion, how should China expand and enhance individual rights and freedoms in the future? How can social autonomy be expanded and enhanced? How should China handle the relationship between ensuring government efficiency and national capacity, on the one hand, and safeguarding individual rights and freedoms on the other?*

State capacity, government efficiency, individual rights, and freedom are not contradictory terms. In most situations, they are consistent with each other because the "state" is composed of individuals, and the strength and stability of a nation depend on the foundation of individual freedoms. Only by protecting individual freedom can the government truly achieve "efficiency" rather than simply pursuing the speedy growth of GDP figures. Paradoxically, to enhance national capacity, it is necessary to limit state power and prevent the government from doing whatever the government officials want. Instead, it is important to safeguard individual freedoms to the greatest extent and encourage individual initiative. Many things can be accomplished effectively by civil society without excessive reliance on the government. If everything relies on the government, it will inevitably lead to excessive concentration of power and the dependence of the people. In such a scenario, the "state capacity" and "government efficiency" will not be reflected in the benefits that the people receive, but in the deprivation of the people's interests. On the other hand, individual freedom is not unlimited; the state has the authority and obligation to govern the externalities of individual actions, including crime control, addressing market failures, providing compulsory education, and ensuring basic welfare.

Ultimately, constitutional democracy aims to establish a reasonable boundary between individuals and the state. First, the fundamental rights and freedoms embodied in the constitution must not be violated by the state. Second, the direction of national development and major policies should ultimately be determined by the people through free speech and elections, rather than imposed on them by the government. The people should have the opportunity to periodically evaluate the government's performance in an environment where free speech and press are guaranteed, and decide by votes who will better represent their interests. Third, the government must govern according to the law made by an elected parliament, limiting itself to undertakings authorized by the law. Finally, if the laws themselves exceed the scope of power granted by the constitution or infringe upon individual constitutional rights, they should be reviewed and revoked by the constitutional court. Only in this way can the government be ensured to do what it should do within constitutional boundaries and refrain from doing what is prohibited by the constitution.

6.5 RESPECT AND PROTECTION OF INDIVIDUAL RIGHTS

20. *What is the standing of free speech and press in constitutional democracies? How should China protect freedom of speech from state intervention*

or manipulation? What is the relationship between tolerance and freedom of speech?

As one of the two foundational freedoms in the First Amendment of the US Constitution, freedoms of speech and press are often referred to as the "cornerstone" of all constitutional rights. Speech is a distinguishing characteristic of human beings and the foundation upon which human civilization is built. Without freedom of speech and press, thoughts cannot be disseminated to benefit the populace, nor can information be exchanged to facilitate individual choices in practical life. If the population is subjected to ideological indoctrination and manipulation, and lacks accurate information about the reality of the world and one's own situation, how can such an ignorant nation be governed rationally? If even the intangible freedoms of thought and speech are absent, how can the government be expected to respect tangible rights such as personal liberty and property?

More important, freedom of speech and press are clearly indispensable for constitutional democracy. If voters and candidates cannot freely communicate with each other, how can such an "election" have any meaning? Therefore, China categorizes freedom of speech and press and the right to vote collectively as "political rights" (政治权利). However, I would rather refer to them as "institutional rights," which are not only crucial for individuals but also the very foundation of constitutional democracy. One of my books opens with freedom of speech as the first chapter precisely because it holds foundational significance for constitutional democracy.[39]

In a country with an effective constitution, the government naturally refrains from rashly infringing upon people's free speech, as it would immediately face the risk of being ousted by voters. Officials also tend to be more aware of constitutional principles and usually do not commit blatant constitutional mistakes. Even if constitutional violations occur, there are effective mechanisms such as judicial review to correct them. If the government suppresses freedom of speech and press, citizens can simply take the matter to court. However, in countries where the constitution is not effectively enforced, the protection of freedom of speech has to rely on citizens themselves. Obviously, there is no free lunch. The government will not voluntarily choose to respect constitutional rights. It takes the effort of citizens for the constitution to take effect and for free speech to be respected. All rights and freedoms, from freedom of speech, press, assembly and association to religious freedom and the right to vote, are realized only through citizens practicing

39 Zhang Qianfan, *Principles of Constitutional Law* [in Chinese] (Beijing: Law Press, 2011).

them. Although the government maintains strict control over speech and the media are predominantly state-owned, leaving little room for press freedom, the development of the Internet has provided great convenience for free expression. Despite the government's continuous upgrading of surveillance technology and active deletion of sensitive information on a daily basis, China will maintain a degree of de facto free speech so long as citizens do not give up on spreading truth and common sense.

As a part of the social contract, freedom of speech not only binds the government, but also applies to citizens as a mutual moral commitment among themselves. True citizens not only actively exercise their freedom of speech, but also respect the free speech of others, especially those who disagree with their own opinions, refusing the temptation to use public power to suppress different viewpoints. When the government suppresses dissenting opinions, regardless of left or right, all citizens should unite in saying "no!" If such agreement, whether tacit or explicit, is lacking, the government will be happy to suppress either the left or the right, and still enjoy considerable social support since the people themselves are hopelessly divided among themselves, so that suppressing either side will be cheerfully welcomed by the other. In such a scenario, the government will never be obliged to respect freedom of speech, which is reduced to a "toothless" right lying idly on a piece of paper on which it is printed with other constitutional rights.

Therefore, freedom of speech also requires a tolerant civic character. The government is not always right like a god, nor should citizens put themselves in the position of a god, pretending that they are always right. Instead, to be true liberals, they should always maintain an open mind, respect the equal dignity of others, and leave some free space for different opinions. Only when tolerance becomes a widely accepted social norm and a significant portion of people consider free speech as a principle in their conduct, can they establish a social contract and resist the government's encroachment on freedom of speech.

21. *What position do freedoms of assembly and association hold in a constitutional democracy? How can they be realized in China?*

As the extension of ordinary free speech, freedoms of assembly and association share the same rationale. In countries with a constitution but without constitutionalism, these freedoms can be realized only by citizens in the process of exercising them. Large-scale assemblies often serve as catalysts for political transformations, while associations serve as trials and rehearsals for party politics. This is why authorities are so apprehensive and fearful of the freedoms of assembly and association, and the risks associated with exercising these freedoms are much higher than that of ordinary free speech. In particular, assemblies are considered as an absolute "red line" that cannot be tolerated. Even gatherings such as "dining and drinking in the same city" (同城饭醉) face severe intimidation and interference. In April 2023, Xu Zhiyong (许志永) and Ding Jiaxi (丁家喜) were sentenced to fourteen and twelve years in prison, respectively, for allegedly committing "subversion of the state power," while the primary substantiating evidence was their organization of such a gathering of a dozen activists in Xiamen.[40]

Therefore, at present, assemblies are not a feasible option for citizens to practice their constitutional rights. In comparison, the risks associated with the freedom of association are slightly lower, making various forms of informal associations and social networks a more viable option. In a sense, WeChat groups can be considered a form of virtual association. Although WeChat groups lack privacy and are often subject to interference, they still serve as a virtual community for citizens to jointly exercise their deliberative capacities.

22. *What is the position of religious freedoms in a constitutional democracy? How can China protect religious freedom against encroachment?*

Similar to freedom of speech and press in the First Amendment of the US Constitution, religious freedom is also a constitutive part of the social contract. It consists of two components: free exercise of religion and the separation of church and state. Religion was significant not only for America in the eighteenth century, but also for the entire world in the long run. Although the world has been experiencing secularization in the past century, religion remains a major concern, particularly for atheist countries like China. After decades of Marxist atheist indoctrination, China's structure of belief is the very opposite of the global trend. According to the statistics of Pew Research Center, approximately 63 percent of the world's population is identified as religious, while the figure is only around 10 percent in China as 90 percent of the Chinese population is identified as non-religious, with a staggering 54 percent being "firm atheists."[41] Over the past forty years, however, while religious freedom has never been institutionally protected, the substantial relaxation in religious regulations has led to significant increase in the number of religious believers. On the other hand, the lack of institutionalized protection continues to hinder the development of religious communities in China and

[40] Nectar Gan, "'A democratic China must be realized in our time': Beijing jails two prominent legal activists for subversion," CNN (April, 11, 2023), https://edition.cnn.com/2023/04/10/china/china-lawyers-xu-zhiyong-ding-jiaxi-sentences-intl-hnk/index.html.

[41] Gallup International, "Religion prevails in the world," www.gallup-international.bg/en/36009/religion-prevails-in-the-world/.

greatly lowers the moral standards of Chinese society. Stemming ultimately from the absence of religious freedom, widespread moral indifference and mutually defective behaviors within Chinese society pose major obstacles to the establishment of social contract and constitutional democracy.

From a consequentialist perspective, religious beliefs play an invisible but essential role in any society. It is evident that no civilized society can exist without moral beliefs. As long as the "selfish gene" of humankind remains unchanged, and the primary (though not the only) motive for individual behavior is self-interest, a society lacking mutual trust will be trapped in the ubiquitous Prisoner's Dilemma, making it impossible to cooperate and form a civilized order. In other words, civilized life cannot exist without moral beliefs.[42] Although religion constitutes only a part of moral belief, it is a crucial and core component. While beliefs can be secular, they are often not as deep and steadfast compared to religious beliefs, and thus are often insufficient to help a self-interested society overcome the Prisoner's Dilemma. The instinct to seek benefits and avoid harm is inherent in human nature. When conflicts arise between worldly interests and moral principles, secular believers tend to compromise and dilute their faith, rendering it a self-deceptive slogan. The secular function of religion extends the calculation of worldly benefits to the afterlife and compels believers to unconditionally abide by moral rules through the divine authority. This is probably why many steadfast rights activists in China today are Christians, as it is incredibly challenging to uphold faith in adversity.

Since religion is so important, does it mean that religion needs to be "administered" or supported by the state? Absolutely not. State intervention is the kiss of death to any religion or moral belief. Wherever government intervenes, it inevitably leaves behind a barren desert of faith. Look at those corrupt officials in China today, who eloquently speak from the podium of lofty ideals but are taken away by disciplinary committees as soon as they step down. Such spectacles are most destructive of faith in the official ideology. True faith cannot be born out of regulation; religious regulations can only create hypocrisy and deceit. On the contrary, true faith can only result from the free dissemination and voluntary acceptance. A faith becomes genuine only when it can be freely turned down.

On the other hand, faith resides in the deepest sanctuary of human mind, and will remain hidden if not expressed. Therefore, the state control over faith is futile unless it reaches the totalitarian extreme like North Korea. But is that any good for the nation when the entire population seemingly believes in one

[42] Zhang, *Principles of Constitutional Law*, pp. 374–5.

"Juche idea"? Without religious freedom, a country will either lack true faith or, like many Islamic states, be trapped in the tight control of a theocratic regime where the people have no choice but to adopt the orthodoxy, ultimately descending into ignorance, fanaticism, and paranoia. Therefore, freedom of religion and belief must be absolutely protected, and the separation of church and state must be strictly maintained. In fact, religious freedom even precedes freedom of speech in the First Amendment because the constitutional protection of religious freedom is even more absolute.

After examining democracy in America, Tocqueville incisively observed that a highly oppressive authoritarian society may not need religion because people there are controlled by the state like animals, while a free society cannot survive without religious beliefs. A good test of Tocqueville's observation is China, which gained limited freedom during the past four decades of reform, while material desires seem to exceed every moral bound. What it needs most is freedom of religion and belief, through which the free dissemination of beliefs will make more true believers whose behaviors observe a minimal moral baseline. How can religious freedom be achieved? Like freedom of speech, religious freedom is gained through the fights of citizens themselves because it is their faith and freedom. If they are not willing to believe or fight for their own beliefs, what is the use of the constitution granting religious freedom? Although most Chinese are agnostics or even atheists after decades of Marxist education, they should at least understand the importance of supporting religious freedom and prohibiting the government from interfering with religion and belief. Otherwise, they will have to pay the price for their own blind prejudice and myopic ignorance.

23. *What is the position of university autonomy in a constitutional democratic system? How can China achieve university autonomy (大学自治) in the current context?*

As a university faculty member, I do not want to unduly emphasize the importance of universities. In fact, I believe that primary and secondary education is more critical since it directly contributes to forming the character of citizens. By the time students reach undergraduate and graduate levels, their malleability is already limited. However, it cannot be denied that universities are places where ideas converge, and influential scholars gather. It is not an exaggeration to say that universities are the soul of a nation. If universities are filled with unscrupulous opportunists driven solely by profit or mediocre individuals who simply nod and obey, then the soul of the nation has died. Pursuing "innovation" and "excellence" in a nation without its soul and universities without ideas would truly be an empty China *dream*.

Like beliefs, ideas perish whenever controlled. It is the ideas that rule the government, not the reverse. Genuine ideas cannot possibly be born out of government control but only in an environment where freedom of thought, belief, and expression are effectively guaranteed. Whether in the era of Spring and Autumn (春秋战国) before the first Qin dynasty (220 BC) or in the era of the Republic (1911) after the last Qing dynasty, China's golden ages of thought were almost always the product of political disorder and government incompetence. If government control could produce thoughts and if officials know more than scholars, then why not let the ministries directly run universities? For example, the Ministry of Finance can run universities of finance and economics, the Ministry of Transportation can run transportation universities, and the Ministry of Justice can run universities of politics and law. If officials could directly take on the podium, all the faculties should be laid off!

Therefore, universities cannot be controlled, nor do they need to be controlled. They are simply about teaching, writing, and publishing. At most, some coordination is needed regarding the courses to be offered, much like how cases are allocated among judges. None of these requires government intervention. If the dean can write better papers for all faculties, then let him write every paper; if the party secretary can give better lectures in all areas, then let him deliver all the lectures. How much more efficient and cost-effective would a university be if each college needed only a dean and a party secretary, while all others can be laid off simply because they have nothing to do!

That is why I always believe that universities and courts are two places where least regulation is required. The concept of university autonomy means that universities manage their own matters according to the principles of education, through which professors and students govern themselves separately, achieving "rule by faculty" (教授治校) rather than by bureaucrats. Of course, this requires some time and effort from the faculty, as they may need to spend half a day in monthly meetings discussing academic and administrative matters, but the freedom of universities and faculties is thus preserved. Its achievement ultimately depends on the faculties' consciousness of self-governance.

To be honest, however, I am not optimistic about the current condition of university faculty in China. It is to be noted that all prominent universities in China are publicly owned, with their leadership appointed by the Ministry of Education or other government entities. Since the faculties have to survive within the system, few dare to speak up, let alone actively demand self-governance. This situation is more serious with young generations since they face practical pressure for publication and promotion, leading to even less independence. Indeed, the outspoken young scholars are significantly fewer compared to those born in 1950s and 1960s. On the other hand, a considerable proportion of scholars seem to be conscious of the basic principles of right and wrong, making it difficult to initiate another Anti-Rightist Movement or Cultural Revolution, which engage them in mutual criticism and incrimination. At the present stage, the prospects for active university autonomy seem bleak, but it is still possible for society to exert pressure on university leadership and demand minimal respect of intellectual freedom.

24. *What is the position of civil society in a constitutional democracy? How can the concept of "popular sovereignty" be formalized and put to daily practice within a constitutional democracy?*

Civil society refers to a social condition in which a significant portion of citizens actively exercises their constitutional rights, engaging in discussions and participating in public affairs. In a civil society, a considerable portion of citizens understands and accepts the basic elements of the social contract and regards political natural law as the guiding principle for their action. Clearly, civil society forms the social foundation of constitutional democracy. It is inconceivable for a constitutional democracy to function in a passive and apathetic society of subjects. Without a civil society, citizens would be isolated and divided, unable to achieve private autonomy or counterbalance the abuse of state power. Dependence on the state in every matter leads to an excessive public power, which neither respects its own limits nor the constitutional freedoms of the people. Therefore, for constitutional democracy to function smoothly, it requires the collective actions of many citizens to share and uphold common values within a civil society.

Civil society enables citizens to determine the composition of state power through the exercise of various constitutional rights, thereby holding it accountable to the people. However, the term "popular sovereignty," like "general will" should be used cautiously as it carries holistic connotation.[43] In practical terms, popular sovereignty means that the government is ultimately accountable to the people through liberal democratic mechanisms such as periodic elections. Achieving this requires a comprehensive set of constitutional mechanisms, including freedom of speech, press, assembly and association, the right to vote and be elected, as well as judicial independence and checks and balances within the government. Only through practicing

[43] Zhang, "Against the holistic temptations," 371–91.

constitutional democracy is popular sovereignty formalized and put to routine practice.

25. *What is the situation of China's civil society today? Does the distinction of active and passive citizens have any practical significance for China today?*

With forty years of economic and legal reform, China's civil society has experienced remarkable growth. A group of conscientious responsible citizens with constitutional awareness have grown up, particularly within the communities of lawyers and journalists. However, the power of civil society is far from sufficiently strong to directly counteract the suppression of state power. In past years, as the state control was relaxed, civil society had developed smoothly; as the state tightened its control in recent years, the space for civil society has been severely squeezed. Strict control over news and publication, as well as various forms of speech restrictions, have exacerbated government control and brainwashing over society, intensifying social divisions. The people are prevented from freely discussing major historical events such as the Great Famine, the Cultural Revolution, and the Tiananmen Square crackdown, as well as the current issues within the existing system and the potential advantages of constitutional democracy, leading to a stifling of the formation of social evaluation and consensus. While a return to the isolated state of the 1950s and 1960s is no longer possible, the driving force for breaking through forbidden areas is limited. The development of civil society in China is currently in a state of stagnation, making steadfast resilience of the liberal community a top priority.

If "active" citizens are distinguished from the "passive" ones based on their awareness and actions, I believe that only active citizens can be considered qualified citizens. A qualified citizen not only understands the principles of constitutional democracy, but also take actions to actively put them into practice, at the very least by participating openly or engaging in discussions related to constitutional democracy. To be sure, cautions should be taken to weigh the risks and gains of their actions for the purpose of self-protection. However, an individual who never takes action cannot truly be considered a citizen.

26. *While the "first-generation" rights primarily refer to negative civil and political rights, the "second-generation" rights encompass positive economic, social, and cultural rights. What is their respective significance in a constitutional democracy? Is it feasible to promote both sets of rights simultaneously in China's process towards constitutional democracy?*

Negative rights are considered innate and inalienable rights that individuals possess by virtue of their birth, such as freedoms of thought, speech, religion, personal freedom, and private property. On the other hand, positive rights are not inherently endowed, but are considered essential interests that the state is obligated to provide, such as shelter, healthcare, food, and compulsory education. The term "first-generation" rights emerged because, prior to the Great Depression in 1929, the Western world was committed to market capitalism, believing that individuals could achieve a prosperous life through their own efforts. The role of the state, acting as a "night watchman," was limited to matters such as national defense and public order. However, the economic crises exposed the limitations of laissez-faire. The idea of "self-regulatory" market proved to be an unattainable myth, necessitating macroeconomic regulation by the state. Additionally, market economies inevitably result in wealth disparities, with a certain proportion of the population unable to secure a decent standard of living and provide adequate education for their children. Addressing these issues through progressive taxation, reducing wealth inequality and ensuring basic survival for all became a public interest that the state was obliged to fulfill.

The two generations of human rights are interdependent and mutually reinforcing. Without negative freedoms, basic individual rights would not be protected, since the government would have unchecked power, inevitably resulting in a situation where the government does only harm and fails to do good. It is no more than wishful thinking to expect a government that does not respect negative rights to provide positive rights. On the other hand, without minimum "safety net" provision, impoverished individuals would be unable to meet their basic needs, let alone have access to decent education. In such a scenario, negative rights such as freedom of thought and speech is rendered meaningless. When discussing positive rights, however, caution is necessary since negative rights merely prevents the government from doing evil, while positive rights demand the government to do good – a demand that the government may not have the capacity to fulfill. Excessive demands on government action may result in an unconstrained concentration of power, through which the government may ultimately not only fail to provide positive good to the people, but also infringe upon negative rights such as private property. This is why negative rights emerged earlier in history as the "first-generation" rights, and serve as the foundation for positive rights and have historically preceded them. Authoritarian regimes constantly boast of rights to "survival" and "development," but they have inverted the relationship between positive and negative rights, reducing their promises to mere deception.

While I am not opposed to promoting positive rights, I do insist that it is crucial to first establish a proper understanding of the relationship between the two generations of rights. Negative rights serve as the litmus test for the integrity of a state that promises human rights because they do not require the state to possess any specific capacities for positive actions as a prerequisite. All they require is that the state do nothing to actively infringe upon individual rights, a negative requirement that any legitimate state is able to fulfill. If a state fails to fulfill the negative requirement, it is due not to its inability but unwillingness. When a state possesses excessive power, it is unable to restrain the impulse to infringe upon people's rights. If it is unwilling to respect negative rights, how can it be expected to respect positive rights? Therefore, it is essential to prioritize the implementation of negative rights as the primary task. Only under this premise can the pursuit of positive rights be promoted, given that the state has such capacity.

27. *What social roles do equality or anti-discrimination play? How can equality and the prohibition of discrimination be effectively implemented?*

First, it is important to clarify that equality in the context of anti-discrimination is a negative right rather than a positive right. Anti-discrimination simply requires the government to provide equal opportunities to all individuals, rather than demanding it to achieve equal outcomes or promoting substantive egalitarianism (平均主义). For example, needs-based distribution (按需分配) achieves equal outcomes where everyone receives benefits regardless of their efforts. On the other hand, merit-based distribution (按劳分配) ensures equal opportunities where individuals are rewarded based on their labor and contributions, with greater contributions resulting in higher rewards. Equal opportunities only require similar treatment for similarly situated individuals and prohibit differential treatment based on extralegal factors such as race, gender, age, and religious or political affiliations. To be sure, if someone is too old to perform a certain job, then age becomes a relevant factor justifying differential treatment. For example, can the law ban citizens above the age of thirty-five from taking civil service exams? The answer depends on whether such a restriction has socially acceptable justifications, without which it constitutes age discrimination.

Therefore, as a part of the social contract, equal opportunity is a principle that rational societies must uphold. Without equal opportunities, a society will inevitably be filled with absurd and irrational discrimination. While carriers of non-communicable viruses such as hepatitis B were unable to find employment or pursue education, banks would require specific height standards for male and female employees, and insurance companies would prioritize hiring

Communist Party members.[44] An irrational society will be filled with hostility and violence. For example, in Zhejiang Province, a carrier of the hepatitis B virus who was excluded from the civil service stabbed and injured a government employee responsible for the recruitment process, while killing another who had no involvement in his case.[45]

The myriads of discrimination rampant in China are largely due to its conspicuous lack of mechanisms to address and combat discrimination. Constitutional democracies typically employ three approaches to prohibit discrimination: legislative, administrative, and judicial. First, it is necessary to enact comprehensive anti-discrimination legislation, at least addressing employment discrimination since it is particularly widespread. Second, such legislation shall establish an administrative body dedicated to implementing anti-discrimination measures. Last but not least, an independent judiciary is crucial to apply constitutional principles and anti-discrimination laws, effectively safeguarding equal rights.

In China, the courts are unable to interpret and apply the Constitution, reducing the equality principle in Article 33 to an empty promise. Nor is there a generic anti-discrimination legislation, apart from the Employment Promotion Law, which merely mentions equality without substantiating remedy, or establishing a dedicated anti-discrimination institution. As a result, discriminatory practices are prevalent, even within the government itself, particularly evident in the recruitment of civil servants, making it virtually impossible to combat discrimination effectively across society.

In the future, China's efforts to combat discrimination must achieve breakthroughs at all three levels, including enacting comprehensive anti-discrimination legislation, establishing a dedicated administrative body to address discrimination, and ensuring an independent judiciary that upholds the principles of equality as defined in the constitution and laws. Only through such comprehensive measures can China fulfill its promise of equality as articulated in Article 33 of the Constitution.

28. *What role do the women's rights movement and the labor movement play in a constitutional democracy? Are there any pitfalls they should avoid?*

Both the women and the laborers are two large and vulnerable social groups, making movements advocating for their rights of obvious social significance. To successfully advocate for their rights, both movements need to operate

[44] Zhang Qianfan, *The Constitution of China: A Contextual Analysis*, (Oxford: Hart Publishing, 2012), p. 205.

[45] Ibid., pp. 206–7.

within a constitutional framework. Without freedom of speech and press, how can society hear their demands? Without freedom of association, how can they efficiently organize collective actions? It is important to note that the absence of freedom of association not only affects women and manual laborers but any groups or classes, such as taxi drivers, police officers, schoolteachers and students, and even officials. Without freedom of association, they all become "vulnerable groups" (弱势群体). Even powerful and influential officials like Bo Xilai, when subjected to disciplinary measures, are stripped of all rights to due process, and incidents of "being suicided" (被自杀) are not uncommon.[46] Are they not vulnerable groups as well? Vulnerable groups are the special product of authoritarian regimes. To shed the label of "vulnerable groups," women and laborers must support the movement for constitutional democracy.

Indeed, this is a potential "pitfall" of these movements. Vulnerable groups arise from unbalanced social power structures. It is common to see women oppressed by men and laborers exploited by employers. Understandably, these vulnerable groups direct their grievances towards the powerful social groups. While it is legitimate to protect their rights through proper means, such as promoting anti-discrimination legislation, they must resist the temptation of the government and refuse to assist in suppressing other forces within civil society. A despotic regime often portrays itself as the savior and protector of vulnerable groups, selectively extending olive branches to some of them. However, its objective is to weaken society as a whole through divide and conquer, rendering all social groups completely vulnerable and defenseless against its tyranny. Therefore, the advocacy of vulnerable groups must follow the right path – the path of constitutional democracy where the freedoms of all are respected.

29. *How should China protect the language, culture, right to education, and fair opportunities for ethnic minorities? How can ethnic harmony be maintained during the process of democratic transition in China?*

Similar to vulnerable groups such as women and laborers, the rights of ethnic minorities can be realized only within the overall framework of constitutional democracy. To protect the equal rights of ethnic minorities, the first step is to implement the Constitution and uphold the principle of equality, prohibiting all forms of discrimination against ethnic minorities. Only upon this

[46] This is a sarcastic term to describe those officials who died during investigation, while the causes of death appeared suspicious. Some might have committed suicide because they could no longer stand the torture and pressure, and others might have been killed to silence them.

foundation can the issue of special treatment for ethnic minorities be meaningfully discussed. The special protection for ethnic minorities cannot be separated from the general framework of equal protection. In fact, most special issues regarding the language, culture and local customs of ethnic minorities can effectively be resolved through strengthened local autonomy in a standard framework of constitutional democracy, without deviating from the principles of democracy and the rule of law. To be sure, ethnic minorities usually reside in disadvantaged areas where the economy and education are underdeveloped, requiring special treatments such as affirmative actions to address the imbalances. For example, the central government should increase investment in education in these regions. In the context of national college entrance examinations and admissions, it is also necessary to ensure a proportional quota for regions with significant minority ethnic populations such as Tibet, Xinjiang, Inner Mongolia, Qinghai, and Gansu.[47]

During the transitional process, it is crucial to uphold the principle of prohibiting any measure that would further disadvantage ethnic minorities. All the rights to which they are entitled within the constitutional framework should be restored to them in exchange for their support for the constitutional transition. In addition to general constitutional rights and freedoms, particular emphasis should be placed on ensuring equal protection, electoral democracy, and local autonomy for ethnic minorities. Local autonomy includes the autonomy over public property within their jurisdiction, which is particularly important for regions rich in natural resources such as Xinjiang and Inner Mongolia. Under China's centralized unitary system, the nationalization of natural resources has deprived these regions of their wealth, sowing the seeds of ethnic conflicts and even secession. The greatest guarantee for ethnic harmony and unity lies in ensuring the fundamental rights and interests of ethnic minorities through constitutional democracy.

6.6 THE PATH OF CONSTITUTIONAL TRANSFORMATION

30. *Will implementing federalism and local autonomy lead to political fragmentation or military conflicts in China's border regions? How can these problems be avoided?*

The notion that democratization leads to secession or civil war has long been a propaganda narrative. In reality, the unity in China today is a result of centralized coercion; once the coercion can no longer be sustained, the

[47] Zhang, "Against the holistic temptations," 381–7.

country will surely disintegrate. Thus, the centralized coercion is the very catalyst for ethnic hatred, conflicts and, ultimately, civil war and secession. The grievances and alienation of ethnic minorities are the consequences of long-term disregard and serious violations of their basic human rights. True unity can only be built on the foundation of respecting fundamental rights and guaranteeing local autonomy through constitutional democracy. Only constitutional democracy can prevent the risk of secession and create a genuinely unified nation, where all ethnic groups can live peacefully in freedom, equality, democracy, autonomy, and the rule of law.

However, since the centralized coercion has already planted pervasive seeds of division, the transition process inevitably carries the risk of division and even violent conflicts. There is no panacea to prevent such conflicts and guarantee peace. Simply avoiding transition and relying on coercion is obviously futile because centralized coercion cannot be sustained indefinitely. Although the transition carries risks, with the right strategies, it is still possible to avoid the realization of these risks. The key lies in the political elites from all groups during the transition period, who should have foresight, tolerance, and a sense of responsibility. Through mutual respect and compromise to resolve differences, the transition can proceed smoothly, minimizing the occurrence of unforeseen events that help bring extreme forces to power. It is crucial to swiftly reach a social contract, on which basis a constitutional framework is established. The majority ethnic group should no longer condescend and bully others, but fully respect the legitimate demands of minority ethnic groups. Ethnic minorities should also recognize that their past misfortunes were caused by the centralized despotism, through which the ethnic majority is also victimized and enslaved. For both the majority and minority ethnic groups, neither absolute unity nor national independence is a feasible option for peace. Instead of embarking on the path of violent conflict, it is better to jointly build a constitutional democracy with other ethnic groups and safeguard their rights through a high degree of autonomy.

31. *Does China currently have political opposition? What should a "loyal opposition" be loyal to and oppose?*

The concept of loyal opposition originated from the nineteenth-century English term "loyal opposition to His Majesty," referring to the parliamentary minority that remained loyal to the monarchy but opposed the majority in Parliament. After the Glorious Revolution in 1688–89, the British monarchy became a constitutional monarchy, assuming an increasingly symbolic role in divisive politics. As the ministers and members of the parliament had less reason to be "disloyal" to the crown, the term now refers to the constitutional monarchy rather than a particular monarch in Britain. Today, the loyalty is extended to the British constitutional system, while opposition is limited to specific legislation and policies passed by the parliamentary majority. In practice, the loyal opposition today may even challenge certain aspects or interpretations of the constitutional system itself. For example, some may not accept the existing parliamentary system and advocate for a presidential system instead, or vice versa. However, since the majority has chosen the current constitution and its governing mechanisms through a fair democratic procedure rather than coercive imposition, the loyal opposition is still obliged to honor that constitution and may seek to change it only through peaceful, democratic means. More accurately, both the opposition and the ruling parties uphold their social contract, and both are loyal to the constitutional system that expresses the social contract, differing only in specific legislation and policies enacted in that constitutional system.

The notion of a "loyal opposition" is essential because it embodies the essence of constitutional democracy. Democracy is about voters choosing the ruling party, and the ballot is impartial. As Chiang Ching-kuo (蒋经国) well said on the eve of the transition in Taiwan, "there is no permanent ruling party."[48] The essence of democracy is the periodic rotation of power, implying that viable alternatives must be available. Therefore, the opposition should not be fragmented and disorganized, but rather be prepared to take over at any time, requiring it to be highly organized like the ruling party, with a complete set of governing principles and policy agendas. Indeed, the opposition party in the British parliamentary system forms a "shadow cabinet," ready to govern once the cabinet loses the confidence of the majority in parliament. In many Commonwealth countries, the constitution explicitly stipulates the position of the opposition leaders, granting them a high constitutional status.

As China has long suppressed organized political opposition, its political dissent is limited to the realm of thought and speech. The lack of organization and opportunities for political participation has made political oppositions fragmented and disconnected from social reality. China today resembles France during the period of the Revolution, where the ruling authorities were autocratic and oppressive, prohibiting criticism and dissenting opinions while denying any avenues for political participation.[49] On the other hand, public intellectuals engage in satirical writings and hyperbolic criticisms, while

[48] Chen Zufen, "There is no permanent ruling party in this world,"《民權時報》(January 14, 2022), https://new.crtnews.com.tw/2022/01/14/20220114-03/.

[49] Alexis de Tocqueville, *The Old Regime and the French Revolution*, trans. Stuart Gilbert (New York: Doubleday, 1955), p. 64.

lacking practical experience in running the daily routine of the country, thus reinforcing the myth that the ruling party is irreplaceable. An effective opposition does not need to be politically high-pitched, but it does need to establish grassroots connections, a deep understanding of societal needs, and a solid grasp of governing strategies. In the extremely limited political space, China's political oppositions today have a large gap to bridge before they are ready to participate in governance.

32. *What role does moral courage play in an era of striving for freedom? Is the prevalent silence among Chinese intellectuals a forgivable human weakness or a relinquishment of their moral responsibility?*

As mentioned earlier, the majority of people in China are non-religious. In a predominantly atheist nation, moral courage plays a crucial role in establishing constitutional democracy. A criterion for evaluating the quality of a political institution is the extent to which it requires heroes to make it work: In a good institution, ordinary citizens have various ways to safeguard their rights without fear; in a flawed institution, only heroes dare to speak up and stand out. Not surprisingly, heroes are few in any society, and thus are unable to push for social reforms alone. The goal of institutional reform is to reduce the social reliance on heroes, but the process itself cannot proceed without conscientious and courageous pioneers.

In a sense, the prevalent silence among Chinese intellectuals is understandable. No one has any right to demand others to be heroes or martyrs, nor should anyone have excessively high expectations of any class or group. On the other hand, intellectuals are supposed to be "knowers," who should know what has happened to China in recent decades, the pressing problems of the present age, the path to be taken in the future and the models to emulate. If they make blatant lies with their eyes wide open, collude with tyranny, or contribute to brainwashing for personal gain, they have reduced themselves to unforgivable criminals.

I believe, however, that moral condemnation is useless and is not the Confucian attitude, which never points finger to others. Instead of criticizing others for their cowardice, it is better to focus on improving ourselves, setting an example for society through actions, learning from the experiences and lessons of the past, spreading truth and common sense, striving to improve the social mores, seeking support both within and outside the system, and encouraging more people to join the cause of constitutional democracy.

33. *Is it possible for China in the future to achieve peaceful constitutional transition through comprehensive political compromise and a multi-party roundtable?*

34. *Some propose that moderate center-right and center-left factions ally to form a major social coalition. In practical operation, what is the feasibility of such a proposal for China in the future?*

While I am not proficient at making predictions about the future, I can discuss these two questions together. The political spectrum for transformative change in society generally consists of four forces: hardline conservatives and moderate reformers within the system, as well as moderate reformists and radical revolutionaries outside the system. Hardliners reject any substantial political reform, while moderates gradually push for political and legal reforms within the existing framework. Outside the system, moderate reformists are willing to form an alliance with moderate forces within the system, while radical revolutionaries insist on a complete overhaul of the existing system to achieve genuine institutional change.

I believe the most crucial alliance lies between the reformers within the system and the moderate reformists outside the system. While alliances between different spectrums in society are also important, they cannot be easily formed through persuasion alone. Once a moderate axis is established between the moderate forces within and outside the system, the number of radical forces outside the system will decrease, naturally gravitating towards the moderate axis. While the external moderate forces can utilize existing social resources to exert pressure on the government, the internal moderate forces can actively respond and implement political and even institutional reforms. The effective interaction between the internal and external forces and their positive social effects not only leave hardliners with no options but also facilitate the transformation of radical forces, leading them to join the moderate axis.

Political scientist Samuel Huntington clearly described the dynamics of political transformation.[50] He argued persuasively that a successful political reform results from a strong alliance between moderate forces within and outside the system, marginalizing hardliners within and radical forces outside the system. On the other hand, failed reforms inevitably lead to the situation where either the hardliners suffocate any possibility of reform or the radicals overthrow the existing system, with the consequence of either establishing a new authoritarian regime or being trapped in unceasing internal strife.

Since the Hundred Days' Reform in 1898, China has never succeeded in establishing a stable moderate axis. The repeated failures of reform have

[50] Samuel P. Huntington, *The Third Wave: Democratization in the Late Twentieth Century* (Norman: University of Oklahoma Press, 1993), pp. 141–63.

fueled the unceasing growth of revolutionary forces, constantly pushing China further away from constitutional democracy. The same pattern repeated itself in 1989 when the "healthy forces" within the system were largely purged. Decades of constant reverse elimination seem to have silenced all enlightened individuals with conscience. Apart from rare exceptions like former Premier Wen Jiabao (温家宝), no one dares to openly discuss political reform in the past thirty years. The greatest challenge for peaceful transformation in China today lies in its conspicuous lack of forces within the system that can openly form an alliance with the moderate forces outside the system. To be sure, in an extremely closed political system the actual situation remains unclear beneath the deceptive surface.

On the other hand, it is important to recognize that the past four decades of opening to the external world have weakened the intensity of the totalitarian system. Half a century ago, during the Cultural Revolution in the 1960s, Yu Luoke (遇罗克) and Wang Peiying (王佩英) were sentenced to death for exercising freedom of speech, such as criticizing the class birth theory (出身论) and the illegal persecution of Liu Shaoqi (刘少奇), then the President of the State.[51] While dissenting opinions are still suppressed today, the severity has reduced significantly. The decline in totalitarianism has not only reduced the social cost of fighting for rights, but also fostered the growth of conscientious forces and a greater awareness of the rule of law both within and outside the system. As a result of their joint efforts, the death of Sun Zhigang in 2003 led to the abolition of the age-old "custody and repatriation" (收容遣送) system, marking the beginning of the "Sun Zhigang model" in the era of rights defense. While the Sun Zhigang model has been fragile, costly, and unpredictable, it at least indicated that the system had some healthy forces left, making institutional reforms possible in the future. Despite the comprehensive reversal of reform in the most recent decade, the irreversible presence of the liberal forces, whether moderate or radical, and the general awakening of society after four decades of reform make it impossible to return to the pre-reform state. When the momentum of regression wanes, a new wave of reform will inevitably rebound.

Currently, in the adversity of fighting alone, the moderate forces both within and outside the system must firmly uphold the bottom line of constitutional democracy. Instead of passively waiting for the magic dawning of a "constitutional moment," they should actively and cautiously promote the ideas of constitutional democracy, make full use of the limited freedom to promote the formation of social contract, and encourage as many citizens as

[51] For a description of the red terror at the time, see Xi Lian, *Blood Letters: The Untold Story of Lin Zhao, a Martyr in Mao's China* (New York: Basic Books, 2018).

possible to embrace and practice the principles of political natural law. The social contract is the foundation of all forms of constitutional democracy, as demonstrated by China's own lessons. Without a social contract, even the best constitutional texts remain empty promises. Constitutional democracy *is* a set of institutions, but the functioning of these institutions requires a matching civic culture centered on the social contract. Without a citizenry that truly understands, believes in, and commits themselves to personally practice political natural laws, what use is a constitution even if it embodies the complete set of these laws? In the late Qing dynasty, the renowned jurist Shen Jiaben (沈家本) expressed his hope: "A law is established, and all under heaven uphold it."[52] But if the people are unwilling to uphold their social contract, how can a constitution be truly established? To be sure, in a country where constitutional democracy has not yet been established, constructing a social contract is fraught with difficulties, but there is no viable alternative.

35. *In your opinion, which positive factors from the past 70 years, 100 years, and 2,000 years of history should the future constitutional democracy in China inherit and preserve?*

The past seventy years witnessed more negative lessons than positive experiences, especially in the first thirty years, lessons were learned through great calamities amid constant political movements. In the subsequent thirty years of the Reform and Opening, it became evident that a society thrives only with freedom – not only in terms of material wealth, but also intellectually, spiritually, artistically, and scientifically. The last decade has shown that true progress requires more than just fleeting moments of freedom, but necessitates a foundation built on constitutional democracy to ensure lasting growth and prosperity.

Looking back at the past century, China's journey towards constitutional democracy experienced both successes and failures. Unfortunately, due to a weak foundation and unfavorable circumstances, the imperial reforms and the republican experiment with democracy ultimately ended up with failure. As discussed in Part 4, the main lesson for this period is the importance of having a substantial portion of the population, especially political elites, who embrace the fundamental principles of a social contract to successfully establish and maintain a constitutional democracy.

Regarding China's ancient tradition, orthodox Confucianism has proven inadequate in contributing positively to modern constitutional democracy.

[52] Shen Jiaben, "On the vicissitudes of legal studies," www.lawview.net/Item/Show.asp?m=1&d=1998.

If "neo-Confucians" today continue to cling to those outdated and defective aspects, they are simply heading towards a dead end. Even the Qing official Zhang Zhidong's proposal of "Chinese essence, Western applications" (中体西用) advocated reforming political and legal systems, while preserving the core of Confucian ethics. Clinging to remnants and deficiencies also means turning a blind eye to the valuable moral teachings within Confucian and other traditional schools, thus abandoning the true values of Chinese cultural tradition.

As previously mentioned, the transition to constitutional democracy requires a significant number of morally courageous citizens, drawing inspiration from religious or secular cultural beliefs. While fully respecting religious freedom, a "complete Westernization" (全盘西化) in culture may not be a wise solution. It is also doubtful that foreign religions can dominate China's vast "marketplace of beliefs" – to paraphrase Justice Holmes.[53] Even in regions such as South Korea and Taiwan, where religious freedom was granted after lifting martial law, the proportion of the population adhering to foreign religions like Christianity remains limited. I point this out as a simple fact, without making value judgments between indigenous and foreign beliefs.

Throughout history, Confucian ethics have played a limited role in curbing the abuse of state power. However, despite slurs and attacks from totalitarian propaganda in the first three decades since 1949, Confucianism continues to resonate with generations of Chinese people. Since it is neither entirely negative nor purely positive, it should neither be wholly embraced nor completely rejected. The neo-Confucian task today is to carefully sift through traditional Confucianism, identifying and promoting the valuable essence while discarding the less beneficial aspects.

In my research, I have discovered and highlighted the concept of "human dignity," which I believe accurately encapsulates the essence of traditional Chinese thought. This concept can serve as a bridge for cultural exchange between China and the rest of the world. There has been an increasing focus on the concept of dignity in Western nations in recent years, leading to the publication of numerous comparative studies. Through a comprehensive review of these comparative studies, I have developed a firm belief that the original Confucian teachings of Confucius and Mencius on the concept of dignity are not only profoundly insightful but also highly compatible with modern values. Integrating the Confucian understanding of dignity can

[53] For the notion of "marketplace of ideas," see his dissent opinion in Abrams v. United States, 250 US 616 (1919).

significantly benefit the construction of constitutional democracy in China and also make unique contributions to promoting global peace today.

In my research, I have discovered and highlighted the concept of "human dignity," which I believe accurately encapsulates the essence of traditional Chinese thought and serves as a bridge for cultural exchange between China and the rest of the world.[54] Western nations have traditionally emphasized human rights, but have been focusing increasingly on human dignity in recent years, leading to the publication of numerous comparative studies.[55] Through a comprehensive review of these studies, I have developed a firm belief that the original Confucian teachings of Confucius and Mencius on this concept are profoundly insightful and highly compatible with modern values. Integrating the Confucian understanding of dignity can not only benefit the construction of constitutional democracy in China, but also make unique contributions to promoting global peace.

36. *In your opinion, how should China handle its relationship with democratic nations in Europe and America? How can China more effectively promote peace, civilization, and freedom for humanity?*

From the perspective of respecting and protecting human dignity, does China have any reason to decline good relations with democratic nations anywhere in the world, which represent the mainstream of global civilization, and maintain close ties with totalitarian and theocratic regimes like North Korea, Russia, and Iran, which constantly trample upon dignity? Of course not. In this aspect, China's practice has lagged far behind its theory. Although traditional Chinese culture contains rich ideas of dignity, they have not been effectively reflected in institutional safeguards. Especially in the past seventy years, China has fallen far behind civilized nations in this regard. Today, it must follow the example of Japan's Meiji Restoration, setting aside its ego, learning humbly, and borrowing actively from the experiences of other nations.

With one-fifth of the world's population, China holds the responsibility of civilizing its own people, which is the greatest driving force for human civilization. The Covid-19 pandemic and the resulting global public health emergency have demonstrated that, if China fails to properly take care of its own affairs, the world will suffer with it. To earn the respect of the world, China must embark on the path of constitutional civilization. How can a

[54] Zhang, *Human Dignity in Classical Chinese Philosophy*, pp. 2–3.

[55] See, e.g., Marcus Düwell et al. eds., *The Cambridge Handbook of Human Dignity: Interdisciplinary Perspectives* (Cambridge: Cambridge University, 2014).

closed, ignorant, vulgar, and barbaric nation expect respect from others? To gain true respect, the Chinese people must first become civilized humans by accepting political natural laws, establishing social contract among themselves, and aligning with the global trend of constitutional democracy.

As the United Nations stated in the Universal Declaration of Human Rights (1948) in its very opening article: "All human beings are born free and equal in dignity and rights. They are endowed with reason and conscience and should act towards one another in a spirit of brotherhood."[56] The world should be a civilized community in which free individuals treat each other with equal dignity. Each nation must first respect and protect the dignity of its own citizens to gain entry into the global civilized community. The goal of constitutional democracy is precisely to ensure that the dignity of every citizen is respected by the state and to enable civilized individuals to live together in a civilized nation. Consistent with Confucian teachings, the key to entering the gate of global civilization lies in our own hands. Particularly, in a hospitable global environment where constitutional civilization has become the mainstream, the Chinese people today have no reason to resign themselves to self-destruction and abandonment, clinging to an abhorrent autocratic system and isolating themselves from the civilized community. As long as they maintain self-respect and treat others with equal dignity, their long march towards constitutional civilization cannot be stopped by any force.

[56] It is to be noted that the deputy sent by the Republic of China, one of the postwar major powers that participated in the drafting of the Universal Declaration, made a positive contribution to the opening article. Hans Ingvar Roth, *P. C. Chang and the Universal Declaration of Human Rights* (Philadelphia: University of Pennsylvania Press, 2016).

Bibliography

BOOKS, JOURNALS, NEWSPAPERS, AND WEBSITES

"709 Crackdown," (n.d.), https://en.wikipedia.org/wiki/709_crackdown.

Acemoglu, Daron and James A. Robinson, *Economic Origins of Dictatorship and Democracy* (Cambridge: Cambridge University Press, 2006).

Ackerman, Bruce, *We the People, Vol. 1: Foundations* (Boston: Harvard University Press, 1991).

We the People, Vol. 2: Transformations (Boston: Harvard University Press, 1998).

Allardt, Erik and Stein Rokkan eds., *Mass Politics: Studies in Political Sociology* (New York: New Press, 1970).

Angell, Alan, *Democracy after Pinochet: Politics, Parties and Elections in Chile* (London: Institute for the Study of the Americas, 2007).

ARD, "温州的十字架之战 [The fight for the holy cross in Wenzhou]," *DW*. (September 5, 2014), www.dw.com/zh/温州的十字架之战/a-18141254.

Arendt, Hannah, *The Origins of Totalitarianism* (San Diego: Harcourt Brace Jovanovich, 1979).

Barany, Zoltan, "Democratic consolidation and military: The East European experience," *Comparative Politics* 30 (1997): 21–43.

Brewer-Carias, Allan R., *Dismantling Democracy in Venezuela: The Chávez Authoritarian Experiment* (Cambridge: Cambridge University Press, 2010).

Buchta, Wilfried, *Who Rules Iran: The Structure of Power in the Islamic Republic* (Washington, DC: Washington Institute for Near East Policy, 2002).

Cai Chongguo, "温家宝的挫败 [The failure of Wen Jiabao]," BBC Chinese (November 9, 2005), http://news.bbc.co.uk/chinese/simp/hi/newsid_4420000/newsid_4420900/4420946.stm.

Cai Shankang, "饥饿年代的个人体验与记忆标本 [Personal experience and memory specimen in the age of hunger]," 新三届 [*New Three Classes*] (March 27, 2018), https://posts.careerengine.us/p/5e607ed716582d20f74923a5.

CCPCC, 中共中央关于完善社会主义市场经济体制若干问题的决定 [Decision of the CCPCC on Certain Issues Concerning the Establishment of a Socialist Market Economic System] (November 14, 1993), www.gov.cn/test/2008-08/13/content_1071062.htm.

CCPCC, 中共中央关于完善社会主义市场经济体制若干问题的决定 [The CCPCC Decision on Improving the Socialist Market Economy System] (October 14, 2003), www.gov.cn/gongbao/content/2003/content_62494.htm.

CCPCC and State Council, 中共中央、国务院关于进一步加强土地管理切实保护耕地的通知 [Notice of the CCPCC and the State Council on Further Strengthening Land Management and Effectively Protecting Cultivated Land] (April 15, 1997), www.mohurd.gov.cn/gongkai/fdzdgknr/zgzygwywj/200106/20010614_155380.html.

CCPCC Department of Organization, 关于实行干部考核制度的意见 [Notice regarding Opinion on Implementing the Cadre Assessment System] (November 21, 1979), www.pkulaw.com/chl/a43b6e34befa663ebdfb.html?keyword=关于实行干部考核制度的意见&way=listView.

CCPCC Department of Organization, 关于试行地方党政领导干部年度工作考核制度的通知 [Annual Work Assessment Plan for Leading Cadres in Local Government Departments (Trial Implementation)] (June 6, 1988), www.pkulaw.com/chl/3eb44a1812bf5cc5bdfb.html?keyword=地方政府工作部门领导干部年度工作考核方案&way=listView.

Chang Jiang, "论政府阻挠国会之非 [On the government's fault in obstructing the congress]," 《国风报》 [*National Morale Daily*], no. 17 (1910).

Cheibub, José Antonio, *Presidentialism, Parliamentarism, and Democracy* (Cambridge: Cambridge University Press, 2007).

Chen Ruxuan, 《中国宪法史》 [*Constitutional History of China*] (Taipei: Wenhai Press, 1985).

Chen Zufen, "世上沒有永遠的執政黨 [There is no permanent ruling party in this world]," 《民權時報》 [*Civil Rights Times*] (January 14, 2022), https://new.crtnews.com.tw/2022/01/14/20220114-03/.

Cheng Wei, "新文化运动与五四运动: 两种"精神"的缠斗 [The New Culture Movement and May Fourth Movement: The entangled struggle between two 'spirits']," 《中华读书报》 (July 13, 2011), https://culture.ifeng.com/sixiang/detail_2014_01/13/32963795_0.shtml.

Chow Tse-tung, *The May Fourth Movement: Intellectual Revolution in Modern China* (Boston: Harvard University Press, 1960).

Chu Heng, ed., "官员为何热衷读博士? [Why are officials keen on doctoral degrees?]," 《瞭望中国》 [*Outlook China*] (December 10, 2010), www.outlookchina.net/html/news/201012/2032.html.

Commentary, "七农民工讨薪失败一起自杀 [Seven peasant workers committed suicide after failing to get paid]," 《新京报》 [*New Capital Daily*] (October 27, 2004), http://news.sina.com.cn/c/2004-10-27/04164046097s.shtml.

Conquest, Robert, *Reflections on a Ravaged Century* (New York: W. W. Norton & Co., 1999).

Dahrendorf, Ralf, *Society and Democracy in Germany* (New York: W. W. Norton & Co., 1967).

Dalu zhimin, "最近之世纪大事变迁史 [History of recent great changes in the century]," 《浙江潮》 [*Zhejiang Tide*], no. 6 (1903).

Dawo, "新社会之理论 [A theory of a new society]," 《浙江潮》 [*Zhejiang Tide*], no. 8 (1903).

Deng Ke, "杨集试验: 选举镇长书记候选人 [The Yangji experiment: Electing candidates for town chief and party secretary]," 《南方周末》 [*Southern Weekend*] (September 19, 2002).

Deng Xiaoping, "1992年邓小平南巡讲话 [Deng Xiaoping's Southern Tour Speech in 1992]," 求是理论网 (January 29, 2018), www.71.cn/2018/0129/984317_3.shtml.

Dicey, A. V., *Introduction to the Study of the Law of the Constitution*, 8th ed. (London: Macmillan, 1915).

Du Yaquan, "迷乱之现代人心 [The confused modern mind]," 《东方杂志》 [*Eastern Journal*], 15, no. 4 (1918), 2–3.

Duverger, Maurice, *Political Parties: Their Organization and Activity in the Modern State* (New York & London: John Wiley & Sons, 1954).

Düwell, Marcus et al. eds., *The Cambridge Handbook of Human Dignity: Interdisciplinary Perspectives* (Cambridge: Cambridge University, 2014).

Editorial, "少数'死磕派'律师栽跟头是必然的 [It is inevitable that the minority die-hard lawyers will stumble]," 《环球时报》 [*Global Times*] (May 12, 2015), http://opinion.people.com.cn/n/2015/0712/c1003–27291548.html

Editorial "社论, "国民之新灵魂 [New soul of nationals]," 《江苏》 [*Jiangsu*], no. 5 (1903).

Editorial, "对于政府之民心 [Public opinion for the government]," 《民心》 [*Public Opinion*], no. 5 (1911).

Fang Hanqi, 《中国近代报刊史》 [*The History of the Modern Chinese Press*] (Taiyuan: Shanxi Education Press, 1981).

Fitzpatrick, Sheila, *The Russian Revolution: 1917–1932* (Oxford: Oxford University Press, 1982).

Friedrich, Carl J. ed., *The Philosophy of Hegel* (New York: Random House, 1953).

Friedrich, Carl and Z. K. Brzezinski, *Totalitarian Dictatorship and Autocracy*, 2nd ed. (New York: Praeger, 1967).

Fung Yu-lan, "An outline of the historical development of Chinese philosophy," in ed. Yu-lan Fung, *A Collection of Papers on the History of Chinese Philosophy* (Macao: Xinfeng Books, 1962).

Gallup International, "Religion prevails in the world," (April 10, 2017), www.gallup-international.bg/en/36009/religion-prevails-in-the-world/.

Gan, Nectar, "'A democratic China must be realized in our time': Beijing jails two prominent legal activists for subversion," CNN (April, 11, 2023), https://edition.cnn.com/2023/04/10/china/china-lawyers-xu-zhiyong-ding-jiaxi-sentences-intl-hnk/index.html.

Gao Gao and Yan Jiaqi, 《文化大革命十年史: 1966–1976》 [*A Decade's History of the Cultural Revolution, 1966–76*] (Tianjin: Tianjin People's Publishing House, 1986).

Gao Hua, *How the Red Sun Rose: The Origin and Development of the Yan'an Rectification Movement, 1930–1945*, trans. Stacey Mosher and Guo Jian (Hong Kong: The Chinese University of Hong Kong Press, 2019).

Gao Quanxi,《中国宪制史》[*The Constitutional History of China*] vol. 1 (Hong Kong: City University of Hong Kong Press, 2022).

Gasparini, Amedeo, "The Tale of Hong Kong: From Freedom to Crackdown," Policy Paper (Institute for Politics and Society, 2021), www.politikaspolecnost.cz/wp-content/uploads/2021/01/The-Tale-of-Hong-Kong-From-Freedom-To-Crackdown-IPPS.pdf.

Ge Gongzhen,《中国报学史》[*The History of Study on Chinese Press*] (Shanghai: The Commercial Press, 1927).

Ginsburg, Tom, *Judicial Review in New Democracies: Constitutional Courts in Asian Cases* (Cambridge: Cambridge University Press, 2003).

Ginsburg, Tom and Tamir Moustafa eds., *Rule by Law: The Politics of Courts in Authoritarian Regimes* (Cambridge: Cambridge University Press, 2008).

Gough, J. W., *The Social Contract* (Oxford: Clarendon Press, 1957).

Gregor, A. James, *Totalitarianism and Political Religion: An Intellectual History* (Stanford: Stanford University Press, 2012).

Guangdong Provincial Research Committee on Cultural and Historical Materials ed.,《广东辛亥革命史料》[*Historical Materials on Xinhai Revolution in Guangdong*] (Guangzhou: Xinhua Book Store, 1962).

Guo Feixiong, "'宪政工程学'的雏形和深度–评张千帆的《中国良心知识分子谈宪政民主》答卷" (May 4, 2020), www.chinese-future.org/articles/enr4pywjh3htjwajtmkdp7bac7s8zx.

Guo Shaomin, "大变局: 帝制，共和与近代中国国家转型 [The great transformation: Imperial system, republic and the national transition of modern China],"《中外法学》[*Peking University Law Journal*], no. 5 (2011), 903–26.

Haffner, Sebastian,《从俾斯麦到希特勒》[*Von Bismarck zu Hitler*], trans. Zhou Quan (Nanjing: Yilin Press, 2016).

Hamilton, Alexander, James Madison and John Jay, *The Federalist Papers*, ed. Clinton Rossiter (New York: Penguin, 1961).

He Haiming, "亡中国者和平也 [It is the peace that will destroy China],"《大江报》[*Great River Daily*] (July 11, 1911).

《天意报》[*Heavenly Justice*], Combined Collection of no. 15 (January 15, 1908) and nos. 16–19 (March 15, 1908).

Hu Gongxian, "民约说及其批评 [Social contract theory and its critics],"《社会科学论丛》[*Social Science Series*], 1, no. 3 (1929), 11–27.

"民约说伦理的谬误 [The logical fallacy of social contract theory],"《社会科学论丛》[*Social Science Series*], 1, no. 6 (1929), 67–78.

"民约说及其批评: 民约说内容之分析 [Social contract theory and its critics: An analysis of the content of social contract theory],"《社会科学论丛》[*Social Science Series*], 1, no. 4 (1929), 64–78.

"民约说及其批评: 民约说价值之批评 [Social contract theory and its critics: A critique of the value of social contract theory],"《社会科学论丛》[*Social Science Series*], 1, no. 5 (1929), 54–61.

Hu Shih,《容忍与自由》[*Toleration and Freedom*] (Beijing: Law Press, 2011).

"The natural law in the Chinese tradition," in ed. E. F. Barrett, *Natural Law Institute Proceeding* 5 (1953): 142–4.

Hu Yaobang, 胡耀邦在中国共产党第十二次全国代表大会上的报告 [Hu Yaobang's Report on the Twelfth CCP National Congress] (September 1, 1982), http://cpc.people.com.cn/GB/64162/64168/64565/65448/4526430.html.

Huang Kan, "大乱者, 救中国之妙药也 [Great chaos is the magic medicine to save China]," 《大江报》 [*Great River Daily*] (July 26, 1911).

Huntington, Samuel P., *The Third Wave: Democratization in the Late Twentieth Century* (Norman: University of Oklahoma Press, 1991).

Jiang Xue, "家中看黄碟, 丈夫被刑拘 [Husband was put under criminal detention for watching obscene video at home]," 《华商报》 [*China Business News*] (October 25, 2002).

Jiang Zemin, 江泽民在中国共产党第十四次全国代表大会上的报告 [Jiang Zemin's Report on the Fourtennth CCP National Congress] (October 12, 1992), http://cpc.people.com.cn/GB/64162/64168/64567/65446/4526308.html.

Jin Chongji and Hu Shengwu, 《辛亥革命史稿, 第四卷: 革命的成功与失败》 [*Manuscript on the History of the Xinhai Revolution, Vol. 4: Success and Failure of Revolution*] (Shanghai: Shanghai People's Publishing House, 1991).

Jin Guantao and Liu Qingfeng, 《观念史研究: 中国现代重要政治术语的形成》 [*Study on the History of Concepts: The Formation of Important Political Terms in Modern China*] (Beijing: Law Press, 2009).

Jing Zhiren, 《中国立宪史》 [*Constitutional History of China*] (Taipei: Taiwan Lianjing Press, 1984).

Kawashima Shin, "China: Exploiting the 'White Paper Protests' to revoke the zero-COVID policy," *The Diplomat* (January 30, 2023), https://thediplomat.com/2023/01/china-exploiting-the-white-paper-protests-to-revoke-the-zero-covid-policy/.

Lau, Mimi, "China orders clergy to toe Communist Party and socialist line," *South China Morning Post* (February 19, 2021), www.scmp.com/news/china/politics/article/3122253/china-orders-clergy-toe-communist-party-and-socialist-line.

Li Fan, 《温岭试验与中国地方政府公共预算改革》 [*The Wenling Experiment and the Public Budgetary Reform of Chinese Local Government*] (Beijing: Intellectual Property Publishing House, 2009).

Li Oufan, 《铁屋中的呐喊: 鲁迅研究》 [*Shouting in the Iron House: A Study of Lu Xun*], trans. Yin Huimin (Hong Kong: Sanlian Bookstore, 1991).

Li Peng, 1993年国务院政府工作报告 [Government Work Report of the State Council in 1993] (March 15, 1993), www.gov.cn/test/2006-02/16/content_200926.htm.

1995年政府工作报告 [Government Work Report of the State Council in 1995] (March 5, 1995), www.gov.cn/test/2006-02/16/content_201109.htm.

Li Qingxia, 中国特色财政; 联邦制: 争议及反思 [Fiscal federalism with Chinese characters: Debates and reflections]," 《财政研究》 [*Fiscal Studies*], 25–27, no. 3 (2011).

Li Yan, "最牛钉子户坚守孤屋 [The strongest holdout sticks to the isolated house]," 《新京报》 [*New Capital Daily*] (23 March 2007).

Li Zehou and Liu Zaifu, 《告别革命》 [*Farewell to Revolution*] (Hong Kong: Cosmos Books, 1995).

Liang Jingqiu, "广州三月二十九日革命经过 [The Story of Guangzhou Revolution on March 29]," in ed. Guangdong Provincial Research Committee on Cultural and Historical Materials,《广东辛亥革命史料》[*Historical Materials on Xinhai Revolution in Guangdong*] (Guangzhou: Xinhua Bookstore, 1962).

Liang Qichao, "开明专制论 [On enlightened despotism],"《新民丛报》[*New People's Gazette*], no. 76 (January 1911).

"民约论聚自卢梭之学说 [The theory of Rousseau, a great social contract scholar],"《新民丛报》[*New People's Gazette*], 2, no. 3 (1900), 39–71.

"历史上的中华民族之观察 [Observations on the 'Chinese nation' in history],"《新民丛报》[*New People's Gazette*], no. 17 (1905).

"吾今后所以报国者 [What I have for serving my country from now on],"《饮冰室合集, 文集之三十》[*Collection of Ice Chamber Papers, Set 30*] (Beijing: Chung Hwa Book Co., 1936).

《欧游心影录》[*Reflections on the Trip to Europe*] (Beijing: The Commercial Press, 2014).

《新民说》[*On New People*] (Beijing: Chinese Literature and History Press, 2013).

Linz, Juan J., "An authoritarian regime: Spain," in eds. Erik Allardt and Stein Rokkan, *Mass Politics: Studies in Political Sociology* (New York: New Press, 1970).

Linz, Juan and Arturo Valenzuela eds., *The Failure of Presidential Democracy (vol. 1): Comparative Perspectives* (Baltimore: The Johns Hopkins University Press, 1994).

Locke, John, *Two Treatises of Government*, ed. Peter Laslett (Cambridge: Cambridge University Press, 1960).

"洛克之主权论 [Locke's theory on sovereignty],"《新民丛报》[*New People's Gazette*], 42–3 (1903), 28–31.

Lu Yuegang, "虚构国度里的非虚构写作 [Non-fiction writing in a fictional state]," www.chinesepen.org/blog/archives/151626.

Ma Jianbiao, "暧昧的联合: 五四运动时期北京大学与'研究系' [Euphemistic alliance: Peking University and the Study Society during the period of the May Fourth Movement]," *Fudan University Journal*, no. 5 (2018) 61–70.

Ma Yong,《叠变: 鸦片，枪炮与文明进程中的中国 (1840–1915)》[*Convoluted Changes: Opium, Guns and Canons, and China in the Progress of Civilization (1840–1915)*] (Beijing: Encyclopedia of China Publishing House, 2022).

MacFarquhar, Roderick, *The Origins of the Cultural Revolution, Vol. 1: Contradictions among the People, 1956–1957* (New York: Columbia University Press, 1974).

The Origins of the Cultural Revolution, Vol. 3: The Coming of the Cataclysm, 1961–1966 (New York: Columbia University Press, 1987).

Malden, Henry Elliot ed., *Magna Carta: Commemoration Essays* (London: Royal Historical Society, 1917).

Mao Zedong, 湖南农民运动考察报告 [Hunan Peasant Movement Investigation Report] (March 1927), www.marxists.org/chinese/maozedong/marxist.org-chinese-mao-192703.htm.

中国人民解放军宣言 [Declaration of the Chinese People's Liberation Army] (October 10, 1947), www.marxists.org/chinese/maozedong/marxist.org-chinese-mao-19471010.htm.

将革命进行到底 [Carry on the Revolution to the End] (December 30, 1948), www.marxists.org/chinese/maozedong/marxist.org-chinese-mao-19481230.htm.

介绍一个合作社 [Introducing a Cooperative] (April 15, 1958), www.yhcw.net/famine/Documents/mzdwg/d070076.html.

ed., *Magna Carta: Commemoration Essays* (London: Royal Historical Society, 1917).

Marx, Karl and Friedrich Engels, *The Communist Manifesto* (New York: International Publishers, 1948).

McDonell, Stephen, "China's protest village of Wukan crushed," BBC News (September 13, 2016), www.bbc.com/news/blogs-china-blog-37351737.

McKechnie, William Sharp, *Magna Carta: A Commentary on the Great Charter of King John*, 2nd ed. (New York: Burt Franklin, 1960).

Medushevsky, Andrey N., *Russian Constitutionalism: Historical and Contemporary Development* (London: Routledge, 2006).

Miles, James, "China tries to stop academics from taking its constitution literally," *The Economist* (February 16, 2019), www.economist.com/china/2019/02/16/china-tries-to-stop-academics-from-taking-its-constitution-literally.

Miller, John, "The Glorious Revolution: 'Contract' and 'abdication' reconsidered," *The Historical Journal* 25 (1982): 544–55.

Montesquieu, *The Spirit of the Laws*, trans. A. M. Cohler, B. C. Miller, and H. S. Stone (Cambridge: Cambridge University Press, 1988).

Moore, Barrington, Jr., *Social Origins of Dictatorship and Democracy: Lord and Peasant in the Making of the Modern World* (Boston: Beacon Press, 1966).

Mou Zongsan et al., *Manifesto on Behalf of Chinese Culture Respectfully Announced to the People of the World*, trans. Eirik Lang Harris (Indianapolis: Hackett, 2014).

Murong Xuecun, "China's 'zero Covid' policy was a mass imprisonment campaign," *The Guardian* (April 18, 2023), www.theguardian.com/commentisfree/2023/apr/18/china-zero-covid-policy-xi-jinping.

Nathan, Andrew J., "China's changing of the guard: Authoritarian resilience," *Journal of Democracy* 14 (2003): 6–17.

News of the Communist Party of China, 中国共产党大事记·1966年, http://cpc.people.com.cn/GB/64162/64164/4416081.html.

No Name, "预备立宪之满洲 [Manchuria preparing for constitutionalism]," 《民报》 [*People*], no. 19 (1908).

Orr, Bernard, "Nearly 2 million excess deaths followed China's sudden end of COVID curbs, study says," Reuters (August 25, 2023), www.reuters.com/world/china/nearly-2-million-excess-deaths-followed-chinas-sudden-end-covid-curbs-study-2023-08-25/.

Ozbudun, Ergun and Omer F. Genckaya, *Democratization and the Politics of Constitution-Making in Turkey* (Budapest: Central European University Press, 2009).

Patience, Martin, "China's Wukan village stands up for land rights," BBC News (December 15, 2011), www.bbc.co.uk/news/world-asia-china-16205654.

Payne, Stanley G., *Fascism: Comparison and Definition* (Madison: University of Wisconsin Press, 1980).

Plato, *Five Dialogues*, trans. G. M. A. Grube (Indianapolis: Hackett, 1981).

Popper, Karl R., *Open Society and Its Enemies* (Princeton: Princeton University Press, 2013).

Powers, Michael R., "'Middle-income trap'? Perhaps a false proposition for China," *China Daily* (February 16, 2022), https://cn.chinadaily.com.cn/a/202202/16/WS620cec67a3107be497a0691f.html.

"Prominent Chinese scholars push for consensus in hope of mild political reform, not revolution," Associated Press (December 26, 2012), www.foxnews.com/world/prominent-chinese-scholars-push-for-consensus-in-hope-of-mild-political-reform-not-revolution.

Qian Liqun, "大学里绝对精致的利己主义者 [The absolutely delicate egoists in universities]," www.rfa.org/mandarin/zhuanlan/fuyouluntan/women-01062017144854.html.

Qin Hui, "中国经济发展的低人权优势 [The human rights deficiency advantage of China's economic development]," 爱思想 (April 14, 2008), www.aisixiang.com/data/16401.html.

《走出帝制》[*Out of the Monarchy*] (Beijing: Qunyan Press, 2015).

Ran Ran, "中国左翼青年的崛起和官方的打压 [The rise of Chinese leftist youth and the official suppression]," BBC Chinese News (December 28, 2018), www.bbc.com/zhongwen/simp/chinese-news-46616052.

Ren Ze, "汪精卫驳梁启超论卢梭 [Wang Jingwei's refutation of Liang Qichao's view on Rousseau]," 《经济观察报》[*Economic Observer*] (July 8, 2018).

Rosenfeld, Michel, "Contract and justice: The relation between classical contract law and social contract theory," *Iowa Law Review* 70 (1985): 769.

Roth, Hans Ingvar, *P. C. Chang and the Universal Declaration of Human Rights* (Philadelphia: University of Pennsylvania Press, 2016).

Rousseau, Jean-Jacques, *Discourse on Origin and Foundations of Inequality among Men*, trans. Maurice Cranston (New York: Penguin Books, 1984).

On the Social Contract, trans. Donald A. Cress (Indianapolis: Hackett, 1987).

Russell, Meg, "What are second chambers for?" *Parliamentary Affairs* 54 (2001), 442–3.

Schmitt, Carl, *The Concept of the Political* (Chicago: University of Chicago Press, 1996).

Shabad, Rebecca et al., "Mitch McConnell escorted away from cameras after freezing during a news conference," NBC News (July 27, 2023), www.nbcnews.com/politics/congress/watch-mitch-mcconnell-freeze-press-conference-rcna96486.

Shen Jiaben, "法学盛衰说 [On the vicissitudes of legal studies]," (December 22, 2020), www.lawview.net/Item/Show.asp?m=1&d=1998.

Shugart, Matthew Soberg and John M. Carey, *Presidents and Assemblies: Constitutional Design and Electoral Dynamics* (Cambridge: Cambridge University Press, 2002).

Sieyès, Emmanuel Joseph, *Political Writings*, trans. Michael Sonenscher (Indianapolis: Hackett, 2003).

Sima Changfeng,《文革始末》[*The Beginning and End of the Cultural Revolution*] (Hong Kong: Baiye Book Store, 1976).

Simon, Herbert A., "Public Administration in Today's World of Organizations and Markets," Speech at the Annual Meeting of the American Political Science Association (September 1, 2000).

Special Commentator, "实践是检验真理的唯一标准 [Practice is the sole standard for testing truth]," 共产党员网 [Communist Party Network] (May 11, 2021), www.12371.cn/2021/05/11/VIDE1620688440356938.shtml.

State Council, 全民所有制工业企业转换经营机制条例 [Regulation on the Transformation of Operational Mechanism of the Industrial Enterprises Owned by the Whole People] (July 23, 1992), www.pkulaw.com/en_law/4f987c00d4b595e7bdfb.html.

关于实行分税制财政管理体制的决定 (December 15, 1993), http://fgcx.bjcourt.gov.cn:4601/law?fn=chl044s002.txt.

国务院关于深化城镇住房制度改革的决定 (July 18, 1994), www.gov.cn/zhuanti/2015-06/13/content_2878960.htm.

城市房屋拆迁管理条例 (June 13, 2001), www.gov.cn/gongbao/content/2001/content_60912.htm.

Sun Hongyun, "1905–1907年汪精卫, 梁启超关于种族革命的论战与Bluntschli国家学之关系 [Wang Jingwei and Liang Qichao's debate on racial revolution and its relation to J. K. Bluntschli's theory of the state]," 《学术研究》 [*Academic Study*], no. 6 (2002).

Sun Liping, "中国社会正在加速走向溃败 [The Chinese society is accelerating towards a rout]," 人民网 [*People's Net*] (February 16, 2011), https://cmcn.org/archives/22568.

Talmon, J. L., *The Origins of Totalitarian Democracy* (New York: Praeger, 1960).

Tan Jingxiang, "任志強判刑18年來龍去脈 [The reasons why Ren Zhiqiang was sentenced to 18 years in prison]," 《亚洲周刊》 [*Asia Weekly*], no. 39 (2020), www.yzzk.com/article/details/特別報道/2020-39/1600917266288/任志強判刑18年來龍去脈.

Tao Ke, "当事人还原真实的雷锋 [Insider recovers a true Lei Feng]," 新华网 (March 6, 2014), https://gongyi.ifeng.com/news/detail_2014_03/05/34441619_0.shtml.

Tocqueville, Alexis de, *Democracy in America*, trans. George Lawrence (New York: Harper & Row, 1969).

The Old Regime and the French Revolution, trans. Stuart Gilbert (New York: Doubleday, 1955).

Tu Wei-Ming, *Confucian Thought: Selfhood as Creative Transformation* (Albany: SUNY Press, 1985).

Tucker, Robert ed., *The Marx-Engels Reader*, 2nd ed. (New York: W. W. Norton & Co., 1978).

Tushnet, Mark, "Authoritarian constitutionalism," *Cornell Law Review* 100 (2015): 391.

"Veteran Chinese journalist Gao Yu jailed for seven years for leaking state secrets," *South China Morning Post* (April 15, 2015), www.scmp.com/news/china/society/article/1768290/veteran-chinese-journalist-gao-yu-jailed-seven-years-revealing.

Wang Jia'an, "孙中山'世界潮流'题词考 [An examination of Sun Yat-sen's inscription on 'Global Trend']," 《团结报》 [*Solidarity Daily*] (October 14, 2021), www.tuanjiewang.cn/2021-10/14/content_8918448.htm.

Wang Lefei, "'第三次国共合作'流产的台前幕后 [The Third Cooperation before the stage and behind the scene]," 人民网 (April 17, 2019), http://zhouenlai.people.cn/n1/2019/0417/c409117–31035474.html

Watts, Ronald L., *Comparing Federal Systems*, 3rd ed. (Montreal: McGill-Queen's University Press, 2008).

Weingast, Barry, "The political foundations of democracy and the rule of law," *American Political Science Review* 91 (1997): 245–63.

Wu Guoguang, "试论改革与'二次改革'[On reform and 'second reform']," 爱思想 (August 4, 2004), www.aisixiang.com/data/3821.html.

Xi Lian, *Blood Letters: The Untold Story of Lin Zhao, a Martyr in Mao's China* (New York: Basic Books, 2018).

Xiao Shan, "传习近平严批官员装病或磨洋工逃避政治风险 [It is rumored that Xi Jinping harshly criticized officials for faking illness or lying down on job to evade political risk]," RFI (May 22, 2016), www.rfi.fr/cn/中国/20160522-传习近平严批官员装病或磨洋工逃避政治风险.

"孙立军19大后组建的'政治团伙'? 都是些什么人? [Who are those in the political group constructed by Sun Lijun after the 19th Party Congress?]," RFI (September 26, 2022), www.rfi.fr/cn/中国/20220926-孙立军19大后组建的-政治团伙-都是些什么人.

Xu Kaiwen, "患有'空心病'的汉子多半有着七个迹象 [The majority of those suffering from hollow heart disease have these seven symptoms]," www.163.com/dy/article/H494269O0552IA4A.html.

Xu Qingquan, "摸着石头过河," DW Chinese (August 19, 2020), www.dw.com/zh/摸着石头过河漫话中共党史术语系列之三/a-54594439.

Xu Sir, "郑州大学曝丑闻 [Zhengzhou University scandal]," www.163.com/dy/article/I4FACT4C0544QVMF.html.

Xu Xin, "民国北京政府时期顾维钧外交成就初议 [Preliminary discussion on Gu Weijun's diplomatic achievements during the Beijing government of the Republic of China]," 《西部学刊》 [*Western Academic Journal*], 119 (July 2020), 123–5.

Yan Deru and Han Liqun, "被逐渐放逐的卢梭: 议梁启超的认知为中心 [The gradually banished Rousseau: Focusing on Liang Qichao's understanding]," 《北京科技大学学报(社会科学报)》 [*Beijing Science and Technology University Journal (Social Science Edition)*], no. 2 (2011).

Yan Zenghua, "孙中山最后的日子 [The Last Days of Sun Yat-sen]," 《人民文摘》 [*People's Digest*], no. 9 (2013), http://paper.people.com.cn/rmwz/html/2013-09/01/content_1307470.htm.

Yang Jisheng, 《墓碑: 中国六十年代大饥荒纪实》 [*Tombstone: A Documentary Report on China's Great Famine in 1960s*] (Hong Kong: Cosmos Books, 2009).

Yu Zhi, "2020美国大选是否存在大规模舞弊? [Did massive fraud exist in the 2020 American Election?]," 《联合早报》 [*Lianhe Zaobao*] (January 11, 2021).

Yuan Sun, "露西亚虚无党 [The Lucia Nihilist Party]," 《江苏》 [*Jiangsu*], no. 4 (1903).

Zhang Guofu, 《民国立宪史》 [*The Constitutional History of the Republic of China*] (Beijing: Sino-Culture Press, 1991).

Zhang Kaiyuan and Chen Huisheng, 《中国近代史普及读本》 [*Popular Reader of Modern Chinese History*] (Wuhan: Hubei People's Publishing House, 1983).

Zhang Lun, "中国良心知识分子谈宪政民主" [Chinese Liberal Intellectuals on Constitutional Democracy] (May 4, 2020), 中国：历史与未来网 [China: History and Future], www.chinese-future.org/articles/l2ssnll7h7hte5sgcbh8tzyt8fbpnd.

Zhang Qianfan, "宪法变通与地方试验 [Constitutional flexibility and local experimentation]," 《法学研究》 [*Chinese Journal of Law*], no. 1 (2007), 63–73.

"A constitution without constitutionalism? The paths of constitutional developments in China," *International Journal of Constitutional Law* 8 (2010): 950–76.

"为什么改革会越改越糟? [Why will the reform keep getting worse?]," *China Digital Times* (September 15, 2010), https://chinadigitaltimes.net/chinese/104972.html.

《宪政原理》[*Principles of Constitutional Law*] (Beijing: Law Press, 2011).

《国家主权与地方自治》[*National Sovereignty and Local Autonomy*] (Beijing: China Democracy Legal System Publishing House, 2012).

The Constitution of China: A Contextual Analysis (Oxford: Hart Publishing, 2012).

《宪法学导论：原理与应用》[*Introduction to Constitutional Law: Principles and Applications*], 3rd ed. (Beijing: Law Press, 2014).

"刑法适用应遵循宪法的基本精神：以'寻衅滋事'司法解释为例 [The application of criminal law shall adhere to the spirit of the constitution: Taking the judicial interpretation of picking quarrel as an example]," 《法学》[*Legal Science Monthly*], no. 4 (2015), 3–9.

Human Dignity in Classical Chinese Philosophy: Confucianism, Mohism, and Daoism (New York: Palgrave Macmillan, 2016).

"Against the holistic temptations: A critique of three related fictions in constitutional theory," *Peking University Law Journal* 6, no. 2 (2018): 371–91.

Zhang Qianfan and Xiaoyang Wei, "Political natural law and human dignity: An empiricist perspective," *Journal of Chinese Philosophy* 50 (2023): 196–208.

《司法审查制度比较研究》[*Comparative Study on the Systems of Judicial Review*] (Nanjing: Yilin Press, 2011).

《城市化进程中的农民土地权利保障》[*The Protection of Peasants' Land Rights in the Process of Urbanization*] (Beijing: China Democracy Legal System Publishing House, 2012).

Zhao Ziyang, 1981年政府工作报告 [Government Work Report in 1981] (November 30, 1981), www.gov.cn/govweb/test/2006-02/16/content_200802.htm.

1982年国务院政府工作报告 [Government Work Report of the State Council in 1982] (November 30, 1982), www.gov.cn/govweb/test/2006-02/23/content_208652.htm.

1983年国务院政府工作报告 [Government Work Report of the State Council in 1983] (June 6, 1983), www.gov.cn/test/2006-02/16/content_200823.htm.

1985年政府工作报告 [Government Work Report in 1985] (March 27, 1985), www.gov.cn/test/2006-02/16/content_200841.htm

1987年政府工作报告 [Government Work Report in 1987] (March 25, 1987), www.gov.cn/test/2006-02/16/content_200857.htm.

On the Separation of the Party and Government, Speech on the Preparatory Meeting for the Seventh Plenary Session of the 12th CCPCC (October 14, 1987), www.china.com.cn/ch-80years/lici/12/12-7/1.htm.

赵紫阳在中国共产党第十三次全国代表大会上的报告 [Zhao Ziyang's Report on the Thirteenth CCP National Congress] (October 25, 1987), http://cpc.people.com.cn/GB/64162/64168/64566/65447/4526368.html.

March along the Socialist Road with Chinese Characters, Report on the 13th National Congress of the CCP (October 25, 1987), http://cpc.people.com.cn/GB/64162/64168/64566/65447/4441804.html.

Zheng Hanliang, "薄熙来闻判后怒喊裁决不公不义 [Bo Xilai angrily yelled that the judgment was unjust and unfair after hearing the sentencing]," RFI (September 23, 2013), www.rfi.fr/cn/中国/20130923-薄熙来闻判后怒喊裁决不公不义.

Zhu Rongji, *Zhu Rongji on the Record: The Road to Reform, 1991–1997*, trans. June Y. Mei (Washington, DC: Brookings Institution Press, 2013).

Zhuo Yuan, "唐福珍自焚凸显中国内在难题 [Tang Fuzhen's self-immolation reflects China's inherent dilemma]," FT Chinese (December 11, 2009), www.ftchinese.com/tag/唐福珍.

LEGAL CASES AND STATUTES

Abrams v. United States, 250 U.S. 616 (1919).
Everson v. Board of Education, 330 U.S. 1 (1947).
New State Ice Co. v. Liebmann,, 285 U.S. 262 (1932).
Reynolds v. Sims, 377 U.S. 533 (1964).
Secession of Quebec, [1998] 2 S.C.R. 217.
United States v. Nixon, 418 U.S. 683 (1974).
Whitney v. California, 274 U.S. 357 (1927).
The U.S. Constitution, 8th Amendment.
Basic Law, Annex II, www.basiclaw.gov.hk/en/basiclaw/annex2.html.

CONFUCIAN TEXTS

《论语》*Analects*, 7: 22.
《论语》*Analects*, 8: 13.
《论语》*Analects*, 12: 2.
《论语》*Analects*, 12: 11.
《论语》*Analects*, 13: 3.
《论语》*Analects*, 13: 20.
《论语》*Analects*, 14: 30.
《论语》*Analects*, 15: 19.
《论语》*Analects*, 15: 24.
《论语》*Analects*, 17: 23.
《礼记》*Book of Rites*, Chapter 9.
《孟子》*Mengzi*, 1B: 8.
《孟子》*Mengzi*, 2A: 2.
《孟子》*Mengzi*, 2A: 7.
《孟子》*Mengzi*, 3A: 3.
《孟子》*Mengzi*, 3A: 4.
《孟子》*Mengzi*, 3B: 2.
《孟子》*Mengzi*, 4A: 8.
《孟子》*Mengzi*, 4B: 8.
《孟子》*Mengzi*, 6A: 13.
《孟子》*Mengzi*, 6B: 17.

《孟子》*Mengzi*, 7A: 6.
《孟子》*Mengzi*, 7A: 4.
《中庸》*Principle of the Mean*, Sections 10, 14.
《荀子》*Xunzi*, Chapter 31.

BIBLE VERSES

Gospel of Luke, 20:25.
Gospel of Mark, 12:17.

Index

For EU product safety concerns, contact us at Calle de José Abascal, 56–1°, 28003 Madrid, Spain or eugpsr@cambridge.org.

www.ingramcontent.com/pod-product-compliance
Lightning Source LLC
Chambersburg PA
CBHW050250231225
37194CB00004B/167

* 9 7 8 1 0 0 9 5 0 4 1 1 9 *